POPULAR MUSIC CULTURE

Now in an updated third edition this popular A–Z student handbook provides a comprehensive survey of key ideas and concepts in popular music culture. With new and expanded entries on genres and subgenres, the text comprehensively examines the social and cultural aspects of popular music, taking into account the digital music revolution and changes in the way that music is manufactured, marketed and delivered. New and updated entries include:

- Social networking
- Peer to peer
- American Idol
- Video gaming
- Music retail

- Formats
- Goth rock
- Emo
- Electronic dance music
- Sexuality

With further reading and listening included throughout, *Popular Music Culture: The Key Concepts* is an essential reference text for all students studying the social and cultural dimensions of popular music.

Roy Shuker is Associate Professor in Media Studies at Victoria University of Wellington, New Zealand. His previous publications include *Understanding Popular Music Culture* (3rd Edition, 2008).

ALSO AVAILABLE FROM ROUTLEDGE

Musicology: The Key Concepts
David Beard and Kenneth Gloag

**Communication, Cultural and Media Studies:
The Key Concepts (Fourth Edition)**
John Hartley

Understanding Popular Music Culture (Third Edition)
Roy Shuker

POPULAR MUSIC CULTURE

The Key Concepts

Third Edition

Roy Shuker

Routledge
Taylor & Francis Group

LONDON AND NEW YORK

First published as *Key Concepts in Popular Music*, 1998
by Routledge

Second edition published as *Popular Music Culture: The Key Concepts*, 2005
by Routledge

This edition published 2012
by Routledge
2 Park Square, Milton Park, Abingdon, Oxon OX14 4RN

Simultaneously published in the USA and Canada
by Routledge
711 Third Avenue, New York, NY 10017

Routledge is an imprint of the Taylor & Francis Group, an informa business

British Library Cataloguing in Publication Data
A catalogue record for this book is available from the British Library

Library of Congress Cataloging in Publication Data
Shuker, Roy.
  Popular music culture: the key concepts/Roy Shuker. — 3rd ed.
  p. cm. — (Routledge key guides)
  Revision of: 2nd ed. Popular music: the key concepts, 2005.
  Includes bibliographical references and index.
  1. Popular music—Encyclopedias. I. Shuker, Roy. Popular music. II. Title.
  ML102.P66S58 2011
  781.6403—dc23   2011025026

ISBN: 978-0-415-59865-1 (hbk)
ISBN: 978-0-415-59866-8 (pbk)
ISBN: 978-0-203-15430-4 (ebk)

Typeset in Bembo
by Book Now Ltd, London

Printed and bound in Great Britain by
TJ International Ltd, Padstow, Cornwall

CONTENTS

ACKNOWLEDGEMENTS

The preparation of this book owed a great deal to the detailed comments on the second edition provided by Michael Hannan, Peter Mills and several anonymous reviewers arranged by Routledge. Although I have not been able to incorporate all their suggestions, the scope and structure of the book benefited greatly. A number of people provided useful ideas, materials or feedback on the general scope of the project and on specific draft entries: Lauren Anderson, Nick Anderson, Shelley Brunt, Rowan Mansfield, Lawrence Macdonald and Mary Jane Shuker. Unpublished research papers or theses by graduate students, and discussions on these with them, helped shape the entries on alt. country (Tonya Cooper), authenticity and pop (Amanda Mills), indie rock (Amanda Creiglow), and punk and new folk (John Encarnacao). Students in my popular music courses over recent years have provided useful insights and suggestions, especially on the impact of digital music, and the contemporary status of genres such as heavy metal, indie, emo and hip hop.

I have relied extensively throughout on the insights of numerous writers on popular music culture; to name them all risks leaving out someone, a check of the text references provides a roll call of sorts, and I thank you all. Many of the 'best' ideas here are theirs, responsibility for the errors of fact and argument – the bum notes – must remain mine. I have also benefited enormously from my membership of IASPM, the International Association for the Study of Popular Music, and its conferences, publications and e-mail lists.

I owe a huge thanks to Sophie Thomson at Routledge who not only provided very useful comments at various points in the development of the manuscript, but graciously accepted my delays in completion of it.

LIST OF KEY CONCEPTS

INTRODUCTION

Although it is based on *Popular Music: The Key Concepts* (2nd edition), which was published in 2005, this is essentially a new book. Drawing on feedback on that earlier edition, from students, colleagues in popular music studies and reviewers (including several commissioned by Routledge), and my own extensive annotations and additions to the entries over the past 5 years, I have been in the fortunate position of being able to recast the volume. I believe that the resultant changes provide fuller, more current coverage and guidance on the study of popular music culture.

The title has been changed to *Popular Music Culture: The Key Concepts*, to more clearly signal the book's orientation towards social and cultural aspects of popular music, rather than musicology (although there continues to be reference to this). As such, it sits alongside my general text: *Understanding Popular Music Culture* (Third Edition, Routledge, 2008). In some cases, more detailed discussion of particular concepts, along with examples of them, can be found there.

In terms of the text itself, there have been a number of major changes and the book is 20,000 words longer. I have been able to give more sustained attention to a number of topics which were only briefly treated in the earlier edition. In particular, I have completely reorganized the treatment of genre, utilizing the concept of metagenres: historically, socially and geographically situated overarching, umbrella categories, each embracing a range of associated genres. The metagenres of rock and pop were at the heart of the second edition, with a range of associated (sub) genres within them also considered. Twelve metagenres are now included: in addition to pop and rock, these are blues (including R&B), country, EDM (Electronic Dance Music), folk, heavy metal, hip hop, jazz, reggae, soul and world. The complex issues associated with defining and bounding these is taken up in their respective entries. Each metagenre is given its own general entry, while there are separate entries on selected constituent genres included within it. The latter are obviously chosen from a much wider range of genres subsumed within the metagenre; they have been chosen for their influence on commercial, 'mainstream' popular music, and to illustrate particular themes in the study of popular music culture (such as crossover, musical hybridity, authorship and the use of technology). For example, in addition to a general entry on the blues, there are now separate entries on blues rock, Chicago blues, classic blues, Delta blues and R&B. In the case of country, there are also entries on traditional ('old-time' country), bluegrass; country rock; new country; and alt. country. For the awkward metagenre of world music, I include examples which have had a greater impact on 'Western' musical culture, such as bhangra and salsa; their visibility is in part due to the diasporic spread of people and their music from their original geographic locations. With rock and pop, the previous entries have been revised, updated and expanded.

Given their enormous scope, the general entry on each metagenre can clearly only be very introductory, acting as a prompt and guide to further investigation. The emphasis is on how each has been regarded by critics, musicians and fans/consumers. I am especially interested in how various narrative genre histories and general studies (with their associated canons of styles, performers and recordings) have been constructed and contested. More extensive coverage of the genres, and their artists and recordings, can be found in the studies suggested in the 'further reading', in volumes such as the various *Rough Guides* and *All Music Guides*, and in the music press.

There has also been a reorganization and, in some cases, expansion of many of the concepts previously included. The continued impact of the internet and digital music on the production, distribution and consumption of music is emphasized, along with new entries on the nature and impact of social network sites; mobile music (the iPod); P2P and downloading. Film continues to have a general entry, but is also linked to separate discussions of popular/rock musicals, soundtracks, biopics and documentary. Recording formats, previously considered individually, are now combined into a general entry. These changes are, in part, a consequence of feedback on where most readers logically (or automatically) 'look for' topics. An instance is performance, which was previously subsumed into entries on live music, concerts, touring and making music (and these are still included), and is now accorded separate consideration.

I have retained and updated the groups of related entries that were part of the earlier edition of the guide: the music industry; scenes and subcultures; history and related entries such as heritage; consumption; the music press; radio and television (now giving American Idol its own entry); musicians and the process of creating music; and general social concepts (class, ethnicity, gender and identity).

As far as possible given the constraints of length, I have indicated important contributions to the critical academic literature on popular music *and* 'popular' accounts: it is worth remembering that some of the best writing in the field comes from music journalism and the efforts of fans. A major innovation, to make the book more 'user friendly', is the inclusion of the 'further reading' references in full with each specific entry. Given the continued growth of studies of popular music culture, this represents a selection; the emphasis is on suggesting useful and accessible resources (written, aural and visual) upon which further inquiry can be based. In some cases, I have drawn on material in the major music magazines, and indicated where recent (and presumably more accessible) issues of these provide useful treatments of genres and performers. More general references, frequently referred to across a number of concepts, are located in the Selected References section, placed at the end of the book).

A new appendix provides a comprehensive timeline, summing the key changes/events in popular music culture since the advent of sound recording.

POPULAR MUSIC CULTURE

The Key Concepts

A CAPPELLA

'a cappella', a term borrowed from early European church music, is group or choral singing without instrumental accompaniment. Religious orders, blues field hollers and some traditional folk music all exemplify early forms of the style, which is sometimes regarded as a 'purer' and more authentic musical form, since it is not mediated by technology, a view connected to the notion of the human voice as the instrument par excellence. In addition to a cappella groups as such, some contemporary popular songs and genres (e.g. doo-wop) include close vocal harmony sections without instrumental accompaniment, a form of a cappella. Gospel quartets and choirs frequently sing a cappella, while there are prestigious US college a cappella competitions (Rapkin, 2008). A common practice in popular a cappella is making vocal noises to simulate instrumental sounds, as in Bobby McFerrin's a cappella hit song 'Don't Worry Be Happy'.

Interestingly, given their relative absence as performers from many genres, it has been claimed that women dominate membership of a cappella groups. This may be a reflection of a style not requiring technical resources (instruments), and able to be undertaken, initially at least, in domestic social settings. For example, Sweet Honey on the Rock are an all-woman, African-American a cappella group, active since the mid-1970s; heavily gospel influenced, their work comments on contemporary political, social and personal concerns.

See: **doo-wop**; **voice**

Further reading:
Potter, J. ed. (2000) *The Cambridge Companion to Singing*, Cambridge, UK: CUP.
Rapkin, M. (2008) *Pitch Perfect: The Quest for Collegiate a Cappella Glory*, New York: Gotham Books.

Listening: 'All Around My Hat', on Steel Eye Span, *Portfolio*, Chrysalis, 1988; Sweet Honey on the Rock, *Live at Carnegie Hall*, Flying Fish, 1988; Bobby McFerrin, 'Don't Worry Be Happy', recorded by McFerrin overdubbing his vocal; *Ben Folds Presents University a cappella*, Sony, 2009

ADVERTISING

Popular music has historically used advertising to promote itself as a commodity form for leisure consumption, using posters, street advertising (through handbills, stickers and posters), and the press (especially the Music Press). Popular music has also become a central part of advertising through the broadcast media (radio, television, cinema and the Internet). It frequently provides a 'soundtrack' to product advertising, usually by associating products and brands with particular lifestyles and values (e.g. the use of classic rock songs by Levis to promote their jeans as symbolic of youthful 'cool'). Contemporary hip hop has been closely associated with product placement and has abetted a shift from ghetto fashion to street fashion.

Such advertising has proven very effective, with some artists receiving huge sums to license their music to marketing campaigns (e.g. The Rolling Stones in 1995 for the use of 'Start Me Up' in Microsoft's Windows 95 promotional campaign). Artists can raise their public profile and achieve celebrity status with such associations; for example, Madonna's 'Like a Prayer' and Pepsi Coke in 1989, Fat Boy Slim's 'Right Here Right Now' (1999) and Moby's 'Porcelain' (2002) to a range of products. Artists can also lend their own persona to advertisements, as in the United Kingdom with Iggy Pop's recent endorsement of car insurance, and John Lydon's plugging of Country Life butter. These can be considered part of the incorporation of music into commerce, especially when the music involved has initially fallen under the 'alternative' rubric. Performers licensing their work for advertisements are often accused of 'selling out', sacrificing credibility and authenticity with their fans and critics.

The use of popular music in advertising represents one of the fullest examples of the merger of cultural and commercial objectives (see Klein, 2010, for an extended discussion).

See: **commodification**; **marketing**

Further reading:
Ewen, S. (1988) *All Consuming Images: The Politics of Style in Contemporary Culture*, New York: Basic Books.
Fowles, J. (1996) *Advertising and Popular Culture*, Thousand Oaks, CA: Sage.
Klein, B. (2010) *As Heard on TV: Popular Music in Advertising*, Aldershot: Ashgate.
Tagg, P. and Clarida, B. (2003) *Ten Little Title Tunes: Towards a Musicology of the Mass Media*, New York: The Mass Media Musicologists' Press (the musical structuring and effectiveness of music used in advertisements).

AESTHETICS

In a general sense, aesthetics is the philosophical study of art, with particular emphasis on the evaluative criteria applied to particular styles/texts in order to distinguish the identifying characteristics of those of value. In its traditional form, aesthetics concentrates on the study of the work of art in and of itself (cf. an emphasis on the context of artistic production), and developed out of idealist philosophy. This approach included the notion that there existed universal and timeless criteria to determine beauty, 'good' taste, and (aesthetic) value in art works: 'transcendent values'. This has been challenged by more recent work, including Marxist and feminist aesthetics, and 'postmodern' aesthetics.

As Beard and Gloag observe (2005: 4): 'An aesthetics of music asks some fundamental questions about the subject, such as what is its nature? What does music mean?' They provide a succinct history of the philosophy of music, which has arguably been dominated by the views of Kant, Hegel and later German philosophers. The debates their views engendered about the nature and significance of music have continued into the twentieth century and have been given a contemporary dimension by Kramer (2002). An underpinning issue in musical aesthetics is whether it is possible to construct interpretive strategies that apply across a range of musical genres and context or do different types of music require different approaches?

An aesthetic approach can be seen in several aspects of popular music studies. Firstly, in a negative fashion, it underpins the frequent criticism of popular culture forms, including popular music, as debased, commercialized, devalued and lacking in artistic value. The best-known example of this is the high/**mass culture** critique, primarily associated with the Frankfurt School and the writings of Adorno. Secondly, and more significantly, although in a rather amorphous and general sense, aesthetic criteria are routinely applied to various forms of popular music. This occurs in everyday discourse around music, amongst fans and musicians, and in the judgements of music critics (see **music press**). The evaluative criteria employed are often unacknowledged, but are frequently underpinned by notions of authenticity, and perceptions about the relative value of musical genres associated with particular gender and ethnic groups (e.g. the denigration of dance pop and its female audience, compared with the validation of various styles of rock and black music). Third, and more specifically, there is the aesthetic analysis of popular music through the application of musicology. This varies in the degree to which such analysis simply takes as a given the concepts/tools of traditional musicology, which is largely oriented towards classical music, or modifies these in relation to popular music. Indeed, there is argument as to whether popular music even merits such a 'serious' analysis.

All this raises questions as to how we make musical value judgments, and how these articulate with different listening experiences (Frith, 1996; Gracyk, 1996; von Appen, 2007).

The notion of a trash aesthetic is sometimes used in relation to popular media culture, including particular styles of music. An example of this is the glorification of recordings and genres regarded as lacking in aesthetic value, or simply 'bad'. Instructive and entertaining examples are Marsh's extended discussion of the 'primitive but compelling' proto punk classic song 'Louie, Louie' (Marsh, 1993), and the essays collected in Washburne and Derno (2002).

See: **canon**; **taste**

Further reading:

Beard, D. and Gloag, K. (2005) *Musicology: The Key Concepts*, London: Routledge.

Frith, S. (1996) *Performing Rites: On the Value of Popular Music*, Cambridge, MA: Harvard University Press.

Grayck, T. (1996) *Rhythm and Noise: An Aesthetics of Rock*, Durham, NC: Duke University Press.

Kramer, L. (2002) *Musical Meaning: Towards a Critical History*, Berkeley, CA: University of California Press.

Marsh, D. (1993) *Louie, Louie: The History and Mythology of the World's Most Famous Rock Song*, New York: Hyperion.

von Appen, R. (2007) 'On the aesthetics of popular music', *Music Therapy Today*, 8, 1, April: 5–25.

Washburne, D. and Derno, M. eds, (2004) *Bad Music: The Music We Love to Hate*, New York: Routledge.

AFRICAN-AMERICAN; BLACK MUSIC

The concept of black music is sometimes equated with African-American music (which replaced the earlier term Afro-American), or the two terms are used interchangeably. Both concepts are linked to emotive arguments over essentialism, authenticity and the historical incorporation and marginalization of the music of black performers. The existence of black music is predicated on a notion of musical coherence and an identifiable constituency. According to George (1988: Introduction), 'black music is that which is recognized and accepted as such by its creators, performers and hearers ... encompassing the music of those who see themselves as black, and whose musics have unifying characteristics which justify their recognition as specific genres'. In such formulations, particular genres are considered 'black', most notably the blues, soul and rap. This has led to questions and debate over how this 'blackness' can be musically identified, how 'black' performers can be defined or recognized, and how do we situate a song by a white composer being performed by a black artist?

In the development of popular music it has generally been agreed that the interaction between black and white styles, genres and performers has been crucial. Black slaves shipped from Africa to the Americas brought with them their own kinds of music, which eventually mixed with the European music of white Americans to produce a fusion of styles. Early African-American music had had three characteristics: a melodic line; a strong rhythmic accent and songs which alternate improvised lines, shouts and cries, with repeated choruses. These were incorporated into ragtime, the blues and R&B. These characteristics aside, it has been argued that it is difficult to identify common factors that characterize black music, rejecting the idea that there is an 'essence' to black music (Tagg, 1989; Gilroy, 1993).

Nonetheless, some writers consider black music to be a useful and important term. Brackett (1995), for example, uses 'the presence or absence of musical elements that many writers have identified with African-American musical styles, elements derived in particular from gospel music and African-American preaching', to consider the relative success of a number of songs which crossed over from Billboard's R&B to the Hot 100 charts in 1965. The concept of diaspora has been applied to the notion of black music to signal a community of musical expression transcending nationalism, but which avoids musical essentialism.

See: **crossover**; **diaspora**; **history**; also the entries on **blues**, **rap** and **soul**, which engage with the issue of their relationship to 'black music'

Further reading:

Brackett, D. (1995) 'The Politics and Musical Practice of Crossover', in Straw, W. *et al.* (eds) *Popular Music: Style and Identity*, Montreal: The Centre for Research on Canadian Cultural Industries and Institutions.

George, N. (1989) *The Death of Rhythm and Blues*, New York: Pantheon.

Gilroy, P. (1993) *The Black Atlantic: Modernity and Double Consciousness*, Cambridge, MA: Harvard University Press.

Longhurst, B. (2007) *Popular Music and Society*, 2nd edition, Cambridge: Polity, Chapter 4: Black Music.

Neal, M. (1999) *What the Music Said: Black Popular Music and Black Popular Culture*, New York: Routledge.

Oliver, P. ed. (1990) *Black Popular Music in Britain*, Buckingham: Open University Press.

Tagg, P. (1989) 'Black Music', 'African-American Music', and 'European Music', *Popular Music*, 8, 3: 285–98.

ALBUM

An album is a musical work of extended duration, a collection of recordings, usually at least thirty minutes in length. These have been released
across a range of record formats, but became largely associated with the
twelve-inch, 33-and-a-third revolutions per minute disc, primarily
between 1955 and 1985. The album became prominent as a format in
the 1960s, but its vinyl form was largely displaced by CDs in the 1980s.
As Keightley observes, the meaning of albums may be structured in
opposition to the single; singles are expensive, transient and commercial;
albums, on the other hand, are artistic, have greater longevity and cultural
value. Albums 'foreground the authorial intentions of performers, thereby
contributing to their legitimation as serious artists' (Keightley, 2003:
612). Most discussions of the popular music canon are based on albums.

Several special types of album can be identified: concept albums, tribute and benefit albums. Concept albums, which include rock operas, are
unified by a theme, which can be instrumental, compositional, narrative
or lyrical. In this form, the album changed from a collection of heterogeneous songs into a narrative work with a single theme, in which individual songs segue into one another. Tribute albums are compilations of
covers of a performers' songs, put together ostensibly in celebration or
homage of the original work. The form has become increasingly popular,
though there is some cynicism about the economic motives behind their
release. Artistically well-received examples include albums on the music
of Neil Young, The Carpenters, Gram Parsons and Van Morrison. The
critical and commercial status of tribute albums is indicated by their
increasingly being included as separate 'best of' lists in genre music
guides, as with Popov's 'The Top 15 [Heavy Metal] Tribute Albums of
All Time', in *The Collector's Guide to Heavy Metal*, Toronto: Collector's
Press, 1997: Appendix 6).

Benefit albums are collections of songs by artists who have donated
their concert performances, and the subsequent recordings of these, to a
particular political or humanitarian cause. Among early examples is The
Concert for Bangladesh (1971), organized by George Harrison and Ravi
Shankar. Probably the best known is Live Aid (1985). Later examples
include Red Hot & Blue (1989), supporting Aids awareness and research,
the various Concerts for Tibet during the 1990s; concerts in New York
following 9/11, expressing American solidarity and raising funds for
police and fire officers killed in the attacks and, in 2011, concerts held
internationally following the Japanese earthquake and tsunami disaster.

Albums can now be brought online as MP3s, with the option of buying individual tracks enabling purchasers to customize rather than obtain the entire recording.

Further reading:

Keightley, K. (2003) 'Album; Album Cover; Concept Album; Cover Version', in Shepherd *et al.* (eds) *The Continuum Encyclopedia of Popular Music, Volume One: Media, Industry and Society*, London: Continuum, pp. 612–17.

ALBUM COVER ART

Cover art, especially on vinyl LPs (albums), has become considered as an art form, with the publication of anthologies of album covers (Ochs, 1996) and collected volumes of the work of artists such as Roger Dean. Part of the appeal of albums during the 1960s was the development of their covers as an art form, with some creative packaging, and the inclusion of supplementary material, in releases such as The Small Faces, *Ogden's Nut Gone Flake* (Sony, 1968) and The Who, *Live at Leeds* (MCA, 1970).

The album covers of the Beatles recordings were especially notable: 'groundbreaking in their visual and aesthetic properties (and) their innovative and imaginative designs' (Inglis, 2001: 83). They forged a link with the expanding British graphic design industry and the art world, while making explicit the connections between art and pop in the 1960s. The prestigious Grammy's began including an award for best album cover, won by the Beatles in 1966 for *Revolver* and again in 1967 for *Sgt. Pepper's Lonely Hearts Club Band*, designed by Peter Blake, undoubtedly the most celebrated album cover.

Particular record companies are associated with a 'house' style of covers, for example, the jazz label Blue Note from the mid-1950s employed a talented graphic artist, Reid Miles, who designed most of its album sleeves (nearly 400 of these are reproduced in Marsh and Callingham, 2003). Art work on vinyl singles, as well as albums, was part of the aesthetics of indie releases from labels such as Factory Records in the 1980s. Despite their smaller format, CDs have managed to feature some innovative packaging and artwork (Rivers, 2003).

Album covers perform several important functions: they are a form of advertising, alerting consumers to the artist(s) responsible, and thereby sustaining and drawing on an auteur/star image; and they make an artistic statement in relation to the style of music by association with particular iconography, for example, the use of apocalyptic imagery in **heavy metal**, and the fantasy imagery of **progressive rock**. Album cover liner notes function as a literary and advertising form, while the practice of printing song lyrics on covers often signals a 'serious' genre and artist.

See: **rock opera**

Further reading:
Inglis, I. (2001) '"Nothing You Can See That Isn't Shown": The Album Covers of the Beatles', *Popular Music*, 20, 1: 83–98.
Machin, D. (2010) *Analysing Popular Music. Image, Sound, Text*, Los Angeles, CA: Sage. Chapter 2: Album Iconography: Postures, Objects, Settings.
Marsh, G. and Callingham, G. (eds) (2003) *Blue Note Album Cover Art: The Ultimate Collection*, San Francisco, CA: Chronicle Books.
Ochs, M. (1996) *1000 Rock Covers*, Cologne: Taschen.
Rivers, C. (2003) *CD-art: Innovation in CD Packaging Design*, Crans-Pres-Mies, Switzerland; Hove: RotoVision.

ALT. COUNTRY; AMERICANA

Along with 'No Depression' and 'Roots Rock', Americana and alt. country began being used in the 1990s for performers who positioned themselves as producing 'something heartfelt and worthwhile outside the foul and cancerous dreck which typifies country music in the last 15 years' (Tom Russell, *UNCUT* May 2004: 98). Russell's comment typifies the discourse surrounding alt. country, with authenticity a central referent. The music evokes 'traditional', often threatened, American cultures and peoples, and rural landscapes, and the universality of these themes is integral to its broader international appeal. The difficulty of more precisely defining alt. country can also be considered an inherent part of its appeal. Alt. country is sonically ambiguous, with many disparate artists seen as falling under the alt. country umbrella, from Gillian Welch and Lucinda Williams to Wilco, Ryan Adams and Justin Townes Earle. The loose style was picked up and marketed by record labels such as Hightown, and championed and popularized by the magazine *No Depression* (which took its name from the Carter Family song, later covered by Uncle Tupelo). Other music magazines began devoting considerable coverage to alt. country, notably *UNCUT* in the United Kingdom, helping internationalize interest in the style and its performers. An understanding of the relationship between cultural capital, authenticity and the audience acts as the theoretical basis for understanding the enjoyment fans find in the genre.

On the surface, the aesthetic characteristics of alt. country appear obvious. As the name suggests, it is a genre that mixes, combines or juxtaposes alternative rock and country tendencies to create a new musical style. Critics, musicians and the audience construct the genre in relation to the perceived authenticity of particular artists. *No Depression*, alt. country's major magazine, has a tagline: 'A magazine about alt. country (whatever that is.)'. Remaining vague on the aesthetic markers of alt. country artists, *No Depression* instead prefers to discuss them in relation to their perceived authenticity and sincerity. The magazine's editors, Grant Alden and Peter Blackstock, write, 'We are not biologists. It is not our purpose to identify, quantify, and codify a subgenus called alt. country, or to limit ourselves to its study ... It is our purpose to write and assign articles about artists whose work is of enduring merit' (Alden and Blackstock, 2005: viii). This indicates the way in which the magazine attempts to represent itself as acting outside the music industry to align itself with alt. country's perceived anti-commercial and anti-modernist stances (Peterson and Beal, 2001: 237). The genre is partially defined by its audience, along with the music press, producers, record executives and the musicians. Collectively, this community constructs the genre's trajectory, acting as gatekeepers, and working to define what music is and (perhaps more importantly) is not indicative of the genre.

Fluidity and a lack of aesthetic boundaries are frequently celebrated by commentators as being an integral part of the genre. Others suggest that paradoxical aspects such as the tension between commerce and authenticity, further add to the genre's appeal (Fox and Ching 2008: 1–27). Peterson and Beal discuss how alt. country itself is an empty term, which was an advantage when the genre emerged and was discovering its parameters (2001: 234). Goodman offers a more precise definition. 'The "No Depression" sound is the alternation or a joining of grinding punk, country rock and acoustic country; a focus on the darker side of small town life; and a heightened social/political consciousness' (cited in Peterson and Beal, 2001: 235). Fans of the genre commonly refer to the idea of a mixture of styles or the ways in which alt. country represents a complication of country music.

Richard Peterson (1997) highlighted the importance of Bourdieu's concept of cultural capital in underpinning the (perceived) authenticity of the genre of country more generally, and his work with Bruce Beal (Peterson and Beal, 2001) extended this approach to include alt. country. Their work demonstrated the tension between the commercial imperatives of country and the assertion of its fans that the music is more heartfelt and sincere than other, more commercially explicit genres. Notions of authenticity are cultivated and reaffirmed by alt. country artists and the genre's gatekeepers not only to give the genre cohesion in light of its sonic disparities, but also for commercial reasons: the financial reward that can be gained by musicians cultivating a persona of authenticity that appears natural. (On the commercial advantage of authenticity and the contradictory nature of this, see Fox and Ching, 2008: 1–28.) The persona of the alt. country artist is integral to cultivating an authentic musical style: musicians must know the lineage of the genre, dress as their fans dress and epitomise the Do-It-Yourself aesthetic of the music, which is utilised to compose songs that are autobiographical, revelatory and deemed to be heartfelt by the audience. These notions of authenticity are adopted and interpreted by alt. country's audience/fans. Peterson and Beal claim that, 'life seen through the lens of an alt. country lyric is a series of failed relationships and late night rebellions' (2001: 239). Lyrics also serve a seemingly autobiographic function, as they are frequently regarded as reflecting the lived experience of the artists.

As both a musical genre and an ideological construct, alt. country has cultivated a relationship with an imagined American ideal of the past, a relationship that raises issues of nostalgia and authenticity. Alt. country appears to be a search for identity, a response to the modern malaise, with lyrical preoccupations of lost love, alcoholism and searching for home. When combined with the use of traditional instruments, this offers a sense of escapism to its largely city-dwelling audience.

See also: **authenticity**; **country**

Further reading:
Alden, G. and Blackstock, P. (2005) *The Best of No Depression: Writing About American Music.* Austin, TX: University of Texas Press.
Ching, B. and Creed, G.W. (1997) 'Recognising Rusticity: Identity and the Power of Place', in Ching, Barbara and Creed, Gerald W. (eds) *Knowing Your Place: Rural Identity and Cultural Hierarchy*, London: Routledge, pp. 1–38.
Fox, P. and Ching, B. eds (2008) *Old Roots, New Routes: The Cultural Politics of Alt. Country.* Michigan, MA: University of Michigan Press.
No Depression, now published on line.
Peterson, R.A. (1997) *Creating Country: Fabricating Authenticity.* Chicago, IL: University of Chicago Press.
Peterson, R.A. and Beal, B. (2001) 'Alternative Country: Origins, Music, Worldview, Fans and Taste in Genre Formation', *Popular Music and Society*, 25,1: 233–49.

Listening: Ryan Adams, *Gold*, Lost Highway, 2001; The Duke and the King, *Long Live The Duke and the King*, Loose/Silver Oak, 2010; Justin Townes Earle, *Harken River Blues*, Bloodshot, 2010; *No Depression: What it Sounds Like. Vol. 1*, Dualtone, 2004 (A compilation by the editors of *No Depression*); Whiskeytown, *Strangers Almanac*, Outpost Records, 1997; Wilco. A.M., *Yankee Hotel Foxtrot*, Nonesuch, 2002; Lucinda Williams, *Car Wheels on a Gravel Road*, Mercury, 1998

ALTERNATIVE ROCK

A broad label, and (arguably) a loose genre/style, alternative rock (sometimes shortened to alt. rock) became used in the late 1960s for popular music which was seen as less commercial and mainstream, and more authentic and 'uncompromising'. At the historical heart of alternative music was an aesthetic rejecting the commercial music industry, and placing as emphasis on rock music as art or expression rather than as a product for sale for economic profit. Sonically, though hard to pin down, alternative music embraces 'a twisting of musical conventions, and so listening expectations' (Felder, 1993: 3).

The use of the label 'alternative' emerged in response to the co-option of rock music by the record industry in the late 1960s and through the 1970s; for example, in the late 1960s the slogan 'The Revolution is on CBS' was used by the record company to market psychedelic rock. The term was originally used in the late 1960s to refer to UK and US underground or counter-culture performers. The broad genre was closely associated with independent record labels, and was accordingly sometimes referred to as indie music. Like rock, however, alternative soon became a marketing category: 'a corporate demographic and a new set of industry practices', as the indie labels effectively served as A&R wings for the majors (Weld, 2002: 212). By the 1990s, major record retail outlets usually featured an 'alternative' section.

Nonetheless, elements of the alternative constituency sought to maintain its original aesthetic of anti-commercialism (at least at a rhetorical level) and authenticity. Punk in the late 1970s was clearly alternative, and the subsequent styles identified as alternative (e.g. American hardcore and 1980s indie rock) built on punk. The alternative label was applied to the grunge bands of the late 1980s and 1990s, remnants of the underground/counter-culture and various local scenes (e.g. Takasugi, 2003; Tucker, 1992). Such was its considerable commercial success during the 1990s, in part due to its association with the influential US college radio scene, that observers began referring to alternative as the new 'hip-mainstream'. Part of this process of incorporation was the move of leading performers from independent labels to major companies; e.g. U2, REM and Nirvana.

By the mid-1990s, alternative was an extremely broad constituency, including indie rock, rap and various styles of heavy metal and post-punk. While such breadth makes alternative a ridiculously vague term, the rubric performs a useful function for the music industry, indicating an *attitude*. This is commonly accompanied by an attention to internal personal demons rather than public sphere political concerns, addressed to youth very much in terms which they can relate to. Another common thread to the patchwork of alternative music was the appearance of many of the performers in the high-profile Lollapalooza tours of 1991 onward, and documentaries such as *Hype!* (1996).

In the 2000s, the term 'indie' (or indie rock) largely displaced 'alternative' in the music press, fan discourse and the recording industry and music retail.

See: **authenticity**; **counter-culture**; **indie**; **scenes**

Further reading: (see also the contemporary references in **indie**)
Felder, R. (1993) *Manic Pop Thrill*, Hopewell, NJ: Eco press.
Takasugi, F. (2003) 'The Development of Underground Musicians in a Honolulu Scene, 1995–1997', *Popular Music*, 26, 1: 73–94.
Tucker, K. (1992) 'Alternative Scenes: America, Britain', in De Curtis, A. and Henke, J. (eds) *The Rolling Stone Illustrated History of Rock and Roll*, 3rd edition, New York: Random House (includes useful discographies).

Listening: Pere Ubu, *Terminal Tower: An Archival Collection*, Twin/Tone, 1985; X, *See How We Are*, Elektra, 1987; Pearl Jam, *Vs*, Epic/Sony, 1993; Hole, *Live Through This*, DGC, 1994; Pixies, *Surfa Rosa*, 4AD, 1988; *Left of the dial: dispatches from the 80s underground*, Rhino, 2004 (A 4 CD box set; includes an excellent 62 pp. booklet)

AMBIENT

A loosely bordered genre, ambient and its variants (ambient dance, ambient house, ambient trance, hard trance) developed out of, and alongside, techno and electronic dance music more generally. Broadly, ambient music is designed to lull your mind through more soothing rhythms, with the addition of samples in the case of ambient dance. Brian Eno's recordings of the early 1970s are usually seen to have practically invented the form. Eno chose the term ambient to refer to a group of his instrumental pieces which favoured 'minimal musical syntactical content and presented in a slowly unfolding soundscape' (Zak, 2001: 208). Other central figures are Dr Alex Paterson, who formed The Orb and Richard James, the Aphex Twin. Ambient was also an element of new age music and is part of the musical palette of musicians working in a range of styles, including Goth, psychedelic and Celtic.

See: **new age**; **EDM**

Further reading:

Prendergast, M.J. (2003) *The Ambient Century: From Mahler to Moby – The Evolution of Sound in the Electronic Age*, London: Bloomsbury.

Zak, III, A.J. (2001) *The Poetics of Rock: Cutting Tracks, Making Records*, Berkeley, CA: University of California Press.

Listening: Brian Eno, *Another Green World*, EG Records, 1975; U.F.Orb. *Big Life*, 1992; Aphex Twin, *Selected Ambient Recordings 85–92*; R&S, 1993; Mazzy Star, *So Tonight That I Might See*, Capitol, 1993

AMERICAN IDOL; POP IDOL

Pop Idol is a televised reality TV show, first screened in the United Kingdom in 2001, then in the United States (as *American Idol*). The show went on to become a global phenomenon, being produced and aired in more than 35 countries. American Idol has been enormously successful, especially the earlier series, with all the winners and some finalists going on to recording and touring careers. American/Pop Idol is essentially a talent competition, with contestants initially selected (from auditions) by a panel of expert judges, followed by a series of elimination rounds, culminating in a final. Audience voting plays a major determining role in the outcome of each programme. Although primarily about musical talent, however, that is defined by the judges and the viewers, the appeal of *Idol* is arguably its focus on the character development of an ever-dwindling pool of contestants, as they handle the increasing pressure.

The antecedents of Pop Idol lay in the high rating *Popstars* television series held in New Zealand and Australia, in 1999 and 2000, respectively. The first part of this was a talent quest, auditioning singers to make up a band; the second part followed the band touring, making a record, and gelling (or not) as a group. The New Zealand winners, True Bliss, attracted a good deal of media attention and had some chart success, although this was fairly short lived. The concept and the format were then picked up in the United Kingdom, and developed and screened (as *Popstars*) by LWT. After one season, it was rebranded and reshaped as *Pop Idol* by Simon Cowell and Simon Fuller, both of whom previously had considerable success as pop producers, along with Alan Boyd from Granada Television (Cowell, 2003: 97–114). The first series was aired on the ITV channel in 2001 and demonstrated enormous audience appeal, with the consequent attractiveness of such high ratings to advertisers. The 2002 final of *Pop Idol* (UK) was watched by 15 million viewers and received some 8.7 million phone votes (though it is important to note that there was no limit on the number of votes an individual viewer could cast). Initially one of the judges in both series, Cowell's realistic/ruthless treatment of some contestants created considerable publicity.

Cowell then helped create the US show *American Idol*, which he also judged on. *American Idol* enjoyed even greater success than its UK predecessor, and it is currently (2011) in its tenth consecutive year. Although its popularity has declined since the early series, in its ninth season it remained the most watched television show in the United States, and has been a 'cash cow' for the Fox network. The winner of the first series, Kelly Clarkson, has had a number of high charting records; according to *Billboard* she has been the most commercially successful of the series contestants.

Academic analysis of the idol phenomenon has focused on the construction of the contestants as 'ordinary', enabling closer audience identification with them; the associated role of viewer interactivity, through the voting system; the industry tie-in and the adaptation of the format internationally. With the judges having a background in production or performance, the winner is usually guaranteed a recording contract, with a 'massive body of deeply invested fans' (Stahl, 2004: 212) ensuring at least initial commercial success.

Further reading:
Cowell, S. (2003) *I Don't Mean To Be Rude, BUT. . .*, London: Ebury Press.
Fairchild, C. (2008) *Pop Idols and Pirates*, Aldershot: Ashgate, Chapter 6.
Rautianen-Keskustalo, T. (2009) 'Pop Idol: Global Economy – Local Meanings', in Scott, D. (ed.) *The Ashgate Research Companion to Popular Musicology*, Farnham; Burlington, VT: Ashgate.
Stahl, M. (2004) 'A Moment Like This. *American Idol* and Narratives of Meritocracy', in Washburne and Derno (eds) *Bad Music*.

Stratton, J. (2008) 'The *Idol* Audience: Judging, *Interactivity and Entertainment*', in Bloustein, Peters and Luckman, S. (eds) *Sonic Energies: Music, Technology, Community, Identity*, Aldershot: Ashgate.

APPROPRIATION

Appropriation can be considered an umbrella term, a synonym for 'use', which includes related concepts such as transculturation, hybridization and indigenization. Collectively, these refer broadly to the process of borrowing, reworking and combining from other sources to form new cultural forms and spaces, in a process that Lull (1995) terms 'cultural reterritorialization'. In relation to popular music, appropriation has been applied primarily to musical re-workings, ranging from borrowings by individual performers of musical sounds, accents and styles (adoptions, copies, reworking).

A major issue in discussions of appropriation has been its moral status, especially in regard to musical borrowings from marginalized genres and relatively disempowered social groups (see the introduction to Born and Hesmondhalgh, 2000). The debate here is strongly present in discussions of United States popular music culture, primarily around white appropriations of black music (see **African-American**). Accordingly, the concept of appropriation is a contested one, with difficulties associated with determining when musical homage and acknowledged borrowings become musical 'ripoff'; exemplified in the debate around Paul Simon's *Graceland* album (1986), and later similar excursions into world music, notably the Deep Forest albums. Simon won a Grammy Award for album of the year, but his critics accused him of exploiting the South African music and musicians featured on *Graceland* (see the discussion of the album and its reception in Keil and Feld, 1994, Chapter 8).

Appropriation is often seen as exploitative of weaker social and ethnic group's music by more dominant cultures, but it is often part of a process of symbolic struggle, through which disenfranchised or marginal social groups reformulate dominant musical styles as a means of renegotiating their social situation. This is evident, for example, in the global adoption of rap by many immigrant communities and its re-articulation to the new context, and the adoption of US country music by Australian aboriginal performers. (For a positive view of appropriation, and some instructive examples of it, see Gracyk, 2001: Chapter 5.)

Appropriation has also been applied to whole genres/works being based on earlier ones, as when 1990s Britpop bands used sixties bands such as the Beatles and the Kinks as reference points for much of their music. The creative adaptations of subcultural style can also be considered a form of appropriation (see **bricolage**). This can include adoption of preferred musical styles, as in white youth's appropriation of black musical styles, such as reggae. This can involve considerable contradictions, as with skinheads' adoption of **ska**, a musical genre popular among the West Indian immigrants targeted by the racist skins.

See: **rap**; **syncretism**; **world music**

Further reading:
Born, G. and Hesmondhalgh, D. eds (2000) *Western Music and its Others: Difference, Representation and Appropriation in Music*, Berkeley, CA: University of Berkeley Press.
Gracyk, T. (2001) *I Wanna Be Me: Rock Music and the Politics of Identity*, Philadelphia, PA: Temple University Press.
Keil, C. and Feld, S. (1994) *Music Grooves*, Chicago, IL: University of Chicago Press.

Listening: Paul Simon, Graceland, *WB*, 1986

AUDIENCES; CONSUMERS

The study of media audiences is broadly concerned with the who, what, where, how and why of the consumption of individuals and social groups (see Albertazzi and Cobley, 2008). Historically we can identify a range of competing media study approaches to the investigation of audiences. At the heart of theoretical debates has been the relative emphasis to be placed on the audience as an active determinant of cultural production and social meanings. Music is a form of communication, and popular music, as its very name suggests, always has an audience.

Social theorists critical of the emergence of mass culture in the later nineteenth and early twentieth centuries first used the term 'mass audience', alarmed at the attraction of new media for millions of people. Their fears were based on a conception of the audience as a passive, mindless mass, directly influenced by the images, messages and values of the new media such as film and radio (and, later, television). This view emphasized the audience as a manipulated market; in relation to popular music, it is best seen in the work of Adorno (see **Frankfurt School**). Later analyses placed progressively greater emphasis on the uses **consumers** (the term represents a significant change of focus) made of media:

uses and gratifications, which emerged in the 1960s, largely within American media sociology; reception analysis and subcultural analysis stressed the active role of the audience. Most recently there has been an emphasis on the domestic sphere of much media consumption, and the interrelationship of the use of various media forms. The opposition between passive and active views of audiences must not be overstated. What needs highlighting is the tension between musical audiences as collective social groups and, at the same time, as individual consumers. (For an overview of the development of audience theory, see Ross and Nightingale, 2003.)

Studies of the audience(s) and consumer(s) of popular music reflect these broad shifts in the field of audience studies. Historically, such studies have drawn on the sociology of youth, the sociology of leisure and cultural consumption to explore the role of music in the lives of 'youth' as a general social category, and as a central component of the 'style' of youth subcultures and the social identity of fans. The previously neglected adult audience for popular music is also now being examined. The main methodologies used are (i) empirical surveys of consumption patterns, relating these to sociological variables such as gender and class, and sometimes supplemented by more qualitative data from interviews and participant observation and (ii) work primarily in a qualitative vein, especially studies of music and youth subcultures.

Two factors are seen to underpin the consumption of popular music: the role of popular music as a form of cultural capital, with records as media products around which cultural capital can be displayed and shaped, and music as a source of audience pleasure. To emphasize these is to privilege the personal and social uses people make of music in their lives, an emphasis which is within the now dominant paradigm of audience studies. This stresses the *active* nature of media audiences, while also recognizing that such consumption is, at the same time, shaped by social conditions.

The emerging information age is seeing a reorganization of everyday life: 'people are integrating both old and new technologies into their lives in more complex ways', and within an increasingly cluttered media environment, this means 'being an audience is even more complicated' (Ross and Nightingale, 2003: 1).

See: **consumption, demography, Frankfurt School, culture**

Further reading:

Albertazzi, D. and Cobley, P. (2008) *The Media. An Introduction*, 3rd edition, Harlow: Pearson. Part 4: Audiences, influences and effects.
Ross, K. and Nightingale, V. (2003) *Media and Audiences*, Buckingham: Open University Press.

AUTEUR; AUTEURSHIP

Auteur theory attributes meaning in a cultural text to the intentions of an individual creative source. The auteur concept is historically linked to writing and literary studies, where it has been applied to 'significant' works deemed to have value, which accordingly are considered part of high culture. An ideological construct, it is underpinned by notions of creativity and aesthetic value. The concept of auteur has been especially important in relation to film, emerging as a core part of fresh critical studies in the 1950s, with the auteur usually regarded as the director. The concept has since been applied to other forms of popular culture and their texts, in part in an attempt to legitimate their study vis-à-vis 'literature' and 'art'.

Applying auteurship to popular music means distinguishing it from mass or popular culture, with their connotations of mass taste and escapist entertainment, and instead relating the field to notions of individual sensibility and enrichment. The concept underpins critical analyses of popular music which emphasize the intentions of the creator of the music (usually musicians) and attempt to provide authoritative meanings of texts, and has largely been reserved for the figures seen as outstanding creative talents. It is central to the work of some musicologists, who identify popular music auteurs as producers of 'art', extending the cultural form and, in the process, challenging their listeners. Auteurship has been attributed primarily to the individual performer(s), particularly singer songwriters, but has also been attributed to producers, music video directors, songwriters and DJ's.

In the late 1960s, rock criticism began to discuss musicians in auteurist terms. John Cawelti, for example, claimed that 'one can see the differences between pop groups which simply perform without creating that personal statement which marks the auteur, and highly creative groups like the Beatles who make of their performance a complex work of art' (Cawelti, 1971: 267). American critic Jon Landau argued that 'the criterion of art in rock is the capacity of the musician to create a personal, almost private, universe and to express it fully' (cited in Frith, 1983: 53). By the early 1970s 'self-consciousness became the measure of a record's artistic status; frankness, musical wit, the use of irony and paradox were musicians' artistic insigna – it was such self commentary that revealed the auteur within the machine. The skilled listener was the one who could recognize the artist despite the commercial trappings' (Frith, 1983: 53). The discourse surrounding sixties rock established a paradigm aesthetic which has, until recently, dominated the application of the concept of authorship in popular music (see **ideology**).

At a common sense level, auteurship would appear to be applicable to popular music, since while they are working within an industrial system, individual performer(s) are, at least primarily, responsible for their recorded product. There are 'artists' – the term itself is culturally significant – who, while working within the commercial medium and institutions of popular music, are seen to utilize the medium to create their own unique visions (Toynbee, 2000). Such figures are frequently accorded autuer status (and will frequently be stars as well). The concept of auteur stands at the pinnacle of a pantheon of performers and their work, an hierarchical approach used by fans, critics and musicians to organize their view of the historical development of popular music and the contemporary status of its performers. Auteurs enjoy respect for their professional performance, especially for their ability to transcend the traditional aesthetic forms in which they work.

To take **rock** music as a genre example, musicians that are accorded the status of auteur include The Beatles, The Rolling Stones, Bob Dylan, James Brown, Jimi Hendrix, David Bowie, Prince, Michael Jackson, Bruce Springsteen and Radiohead, who have achieved commercial as well as critical recognition. (The absence of women from this list should be noted: see **canon, gender**.) The status of several may have diminished, with later work largely being found wanting when placed against their earlier output, as with Bob Dylan and The Rolling Stones. However, such figures retain auteur status on the basis of their historical contribution, as do those careers were cut short, for example, Jimi Hendrix and Kurt Cobain. There are also performers whose work has had not only limited commercial impact but are regarded as having a distinctive style and oeuvre which has taken rock music in new and innovative directions, such as Frank Zappa, Eno and Captain Beefheart.

Since all music texts are social products, performers working within popular genres are under constant pressure to provide their audience with more of the music which attracted that same audience in the first place. This explains why shifts in musical direction often lose established audiences while, hopefully for the performer, creating new adherents. This is to emphasize the contradiction between being an 'artist' and responding to the pressures of the market and to claim particular performers as auteurs despite their location within a profit-driven commercial industry (a process similar to that applied in film studies in the 1950s to Hollywood cinema's studio system). This leads to judgements of musical value and hierarchies of performers which are problematic, since all musical texts 'arrive on the turntable as the result of the same commercial processes' (Frith, 1983: 54). Furthermore, as in any area of 'creative' endeavour, there is a constant process of reworking the 'common stock' or traditions of generic popular forms, as continuity is self-consciously combined with change (see **appropriation**).

As in literary studies, auteurship in popular music is open to criticism: only some musicians are accorded such status, while achieving auteurship is regarded as possible in some musical genres but not in others. Further, as with contemporary film-making, the creative process in popular music is a 'team game' with various contributions melding together, even if the particular artist is providing the overall vision (see **cultural intermediaries**). The concept of auteur represents a form of cultural hegemony, based on a Romantic conception of 'art', used to validate certain performers and styles of work.

See: **biography**; **stars**

Further reading:
Cawelti, J. (1971) 'Notes Towards an Aesthetic of Popular Culture', *Journal of Popular Culture*, 5, 1(Fall): 255–68.
Frith, S. (1983) *Sound Effects*, London: Constable.
Straw, W. (1999) 'Authorship', in Horner, B. and Swiss, T. (eds) *Key Terms in Popular Music and Culture*, Oxford: Blackwell, pp. 199–208.
Toynbee, J. (2000) *Making Popular Music: Musicians, Creativity and Institutions*, London: Arnold.

AUTHENTICITY

A central concept in the discourses surrounding popular music, authenticity is imbued with considerable symbolic value. In its common sense usage, authenticity assumes that the producers of music texts undertook the 'creative' work themselves; that there is an element of originality or creativity present, along with connotations of seriousness, sincerity and uniqueness and that while the input of others is recognized, it is the musicians' role which is regarded as pivotal. Important in identifying and situating authenticity are the commercial settings in which a recording is produced, with a tendency to dichotomise the music industry into (more authentic, less commercial) independent labels and the majors (more commercial, less authentic). Perceptions of authenticity (or non-authenticity) are also present in the degree to which performers and records are assimilated and legitimized by particular subcultures or communities. Authenticity is traditionally associated with live performance, a view undermined by the rise of disco and club cultures. Thornton suggests the existence of two distinct kinds of authenticity here, one involving issues of originality and aura, and another, natural to the community and organic to the subculture (see **club culture**).

The use of authenticity as a central evaluative criterion is best seen in the discussions of the relative nature and merits of particular performers and genres within popular music culture; for example, vernacular community based styles of folk, country blues and roots music are frequently perceived as more authentic than their commercialized forms. In a similar fashion, commerce and artistic integrity are frequently utilized to demarcate rock from pop music. This romantic view has its origins in the 1960s, when leading American critics – Landau, Marsh and Christagau – elaborated a view of rock music as correlated with authenticity, creativity and a particular political moment: the sixties' protest movement and the counter-culture. Closely associated with this leftist political ideology of a rock authenticity was *Rolling Stone* magazine, founded in 1967. This view saw authenticity as underpinned by a series of oppositions: mainstream versus independent; pop versus rock and commercialism versus creativity, or art versus commerce.

Inherent in this polarization is a cyclical theory of musical innovation as a form of street creativity, versus business and market domination and the co-option of rock into the 'mainstream'. It assumes commerce dilutes, frustrates and negates artistic aspects of the music. This uneasy alliance between art and commerce is frequently placed at the heart of the history of popular music and is widely alluded to by musicians, fans and critics. Counter to this is the view that popular culture is never simply imposed from above, but reflects the complex interrelationship of corporate interests, the intentions of those who create the music and the audience perceptions and use of musical texts.

Moore (2002) usefully moves the discussion of the concept beyond simple polarities (authentic versus unauthentic), by postulating a tripartite typology dependent on asking who, rather then what, is being authenticated. As he suggests, authenticity is most usefully conceived of as 'a construction made in the act of listening' (Moore, 2001: 210). Accordingly, we should be asking not if particular stylistic characteristics can be considered 'authentic', or non-authentic, but rather how authenticity is constructed in particular music genres and performers, and the strategies involved (see the examples in Butler, 2003; Regev, 1994; Weisethaunet and Lindberg, 2007).

Authenticity continues to serve an important ideological function, helping differentiate particular forms of musical cultural capital. It is also central to debates around the use of studio musicians (in genres such as bubblegum), sampling, turntablism and other innovative recording and performing techniques (see **rap**), and practices such as lip synching.

See: **auteurship**; **sampling**

Further reading:
Barker, H. and Taylor, Y. (2007) *Faking It. The Quest for Authenticity in Popular Music*, New York: Norton.
Butler, M. (2003) 'Taking it Seriously: Intertextuality and Authenticity in Two Covers by the Pet Shop Boys', *Popular Music*, 22, 1: 1–20.
Dettmer, K. and Richey, W. eds (1999) *Reading Rock and Roll: Authenticity Appropriation, Aesthetics*, New York: Columbia University Press.
Moore, A. (2002) 'Authenticity as Authentication', *Popular Music*, 21, 2: 225–36.
Regev, M. (1994) 'Producing Artistic Value: The Case of Rock Music', *Sociological Quarterly*, 35: 85–102.
Weisethaunet., H. and Lindberg, U. (2010) 'Authenticity Revisited: The Rock Critic and the Changing Real', *Popular Music and Society*, 33, 4: 465–485.

AVANT GARDE; EXPERIMENTAL

Terms applied to innovative new movements in art; usually associated to breaks with established traditions, styles and convention. The recordings of a number of performers working within genres such as jazz and rock have been considered to be avant garde, or experimental; although their commercial success has usually been limited, they often have something of a cult following (see Martin, 2002; Young, 2002). Performers working at the interface between various musical genres, or in the vanguard of new styles (e.g. bebop in jazz), are more likely to be considered avant garde, with their work claimed as in some sense more authentic.

In the late 1960s, musical experiment was part of the work of The Velvet Underground, associated with Andy Warhol and the New York avant garde art scene and Frank Zappa and the Mothers of Invention. Alex Ross (2009) considers the interactions between minimalist composers and rock bands in the 1960s and 1970s. In his ambitious volume *Lipstick Traces*, Greil Marcus argues for a clear connection between the avant garde European Bauhaus movement and punk rock in the late 1970s. In the 1980s, alternative bands such as The Fall, Sonic Youth and My Bloody Valentine experimented with unusual tuning systems, dissonant sounds and song structures, and performers such as Mary Margaret O'Hara utilized unique **vocal** styles. Progressive rock bands also frequently experiment with sound and song structures.

Such performers and their work are sometimes referred to as avant rock (Martin, 2002; Young, 2009).

See: **progressive rock**

Further reading:

Martin, B. (2002) *Avant Rock: Experimental Music from the Beatles to Björk*, Chicago, IL: Open Court.

Marcus, G. (1989) *Lipstick Traces. A Secret History of the Twentieth Century*, Cambridge, MA: Harvard University Press.

Ross, A. (2009) *The Rest is Noise*, New York: HarperCollins.

Young, R. ed. (2002) *Undercurrents. The Hidden Wiring of Modern Music*, London: Continuum.

Young, R. ed. (2009) *The WIRE Primers. A Guide to Modern Music*, London: Verso. A selection of articles from a series 'The Primer', 'conceived as potted guides to the work and, by extension, to the lives of significant individual artists, groups or umbrella genres' (Introduction: 7).

The WIRE: magazine.

Listening: Sonic Youth, *Daydream Nation*, DGC, 1988; Frank Zappa and the Mothers of Invention, *Freak Out*, 1966; Laurie Anderson, 'O'Superman', 1981, on *Big Science*, WB, 1982; My Bloody Valentine, *Isn't Anything*, Creation/Sire, 1988

BACK CATALOGUE

The back catalogues are the recordings available to record companies for reissue, which they still hold copyright on. These are often of commercial value given the introduction of new formats, especially the CD, and new technology enabling the remastering of the original recordings, combined with the lack of development capital required since the early versions already exist. Both box sets and 'Greatest Hits' recordings can be considered part of the back catalogue. These various forms of reissue are a very significant revenue stream for the music industry (indicated by the recent success of such releases by The Beatles (including through iTunes) and The Rolling Stones in 2010–11).

The exploitation of their back catalogue by the recording companies was given a major boost in the 1980s, as they realized the sales potential of listeners, especially the affluent baby boomer generation, upgrading their vinyl collections by replacing them with CDs. There was also the appeal of adding bonus/rarity/alternative takes to the longer space available on the CD format, as for instance with the 1996–97 reissue of The Byrd's original 1960s albums. In some cases, the majors licenced rights, or created subsidiary labels for the purpose of releasing such 'new' recordings.

The 1970s saw the first companies dedicated to reissues, producing intelligent compilations of vintage genres such as early rock'n'roll and doo-wop. Sire in the United States (along with its contemporary artists), and Charlie in the United Kingdom, were joined in the 1980s by Ace, Demon/Edsel and Rhino (the United States), the leading contemporary reissue company, with an extensive catalogue. Leading reggae and dub company Trojan became primarily a reissue label. These companies exploited the market niche created by the major labels reluctance to release obscure, vintage material for small specialized audiences and the collector market.

The back catalogue in general, and reissues in particular, represent a form of canonization, elevating performers, styles and historical periods to 'classic' status. The remastering and other practices involved raise questions of what constitutes the definitive music text; see, for example, Ford's discussion (2004) of the various best of James Brown recordings now available. Many such issues are targeting the affluent record collecting market.

See also: **box set**

Further reading:
Ford, C. (2002) 'The Very Best of James Brown?' *Popular Music*, 21, 1: 127–31.
Music magazines routinely have a 'reissues' category in their review sections.

BEAT MUSIC (BRITISH BEAT)

A music style, and loose genre, characterized by a simple, strong beat. The term beat music was applied to the music of the Beatles and other English groups in the early 1960s: Gerry and the Pacemakers, the Dave Clark Five, the Searchers and the Hollies. Accordingly, the form is sometimes referred to as 'British Beat'. These performers had a repertoire grounded in rock'n'roll and rhythm'n'blues. Initially encouraged by the simplicity of skiffle, beat groups characteristically had a line up of drums, lead guitar, bass and rhythm guitars, and a lead vocalist (sometimes, as with the Beatles, this would be one of the instrumentalists). Strong regional versions were present, with Liverpool (Merseybeat) the major focus. The beat bands were central to the **British invasion** of the American charts in the early 1960s.

See: **British invasion; Merseybeat; skiffle**

Further reading:
The music and its performers are a 'standard' part of music histories of the period, and are frequently covered in magazines such as *Record Collector* (the United Kingdom); see also:
Clayson, A. (1995) *Beat Merchants*, London: Blandford.
McAleer, D. (1994) *BEATBOOM! Pop Goes the Sixties*, London: Hamlyn.
Thompson, G. (2008) *Please Please Me: Sixties British Pop, Inside Out*, Oxford: Oxford University Press.

Listening: The Searchers, *The Most of the Searchers*, EMI, 1994 CD; The Beatles, *Live at the BBC* (1962–1965), Apple/Capitol, 1994

BHANGRA

An Anglo-Indian musical genre, bhangra is traditional Punjabi folk dance music played on percussion instruments, which has been combined with elements of Western pop styles by Asian musicians in the United Kingdom since the 1970s. The genre exemplifies the complex cultural relationship between a European metropolis and its former colony, and the role of diasporic communities in musical hybridization.

Bhangra developed in three waves in Britain: as dance pop music played on synthesizers, guitars and drum kits in migrant Indian communities in the late 1970s; incorporating house and dance music and drum machines in the 1980s and combining with rap, sampling and Jamaican ragga or dancehall rhythms in the early 1990s to become bhangramuffin (Mitchell, 1996). The last was commercially successful throughout Asia, and in the United Kingdom with artists such as Sheila Chandra and Apache Indian. Bhangra was then hybridized with emergent styles of electronic dance music, in the work of performers such as Asia Dub Foundation and Cornershop.

Bhangra illustrates the role played by music in processes of relocation and cultural assimilation. For young Asians, bhangra is part of an assertion of cultural identity, creating a cultural space distinct from that of the establishment and their parents. At the same time, it has helped preserve the Punjabi language in the English-dominated environment.

Further reading:
Bennett, A. (2000) *Popular Music and Youth Culture: Music, Identity and Place*, London: Macmillan; Chapter 5.
Mitchell, T. (1996) *Popular Music and Local Identity*, London: Leicester University Press.

Poole, A. (2004, March) 'South Asian Music Education in Essex: An Ethnography of Bhangra', *British Journal of Music Education*, 21: 7–24.

Listening: Sheila Chandra, *The Struggle*, Caroline Records/Indipop, 1995; Apache Indian, *Make Way for the Indian*, Island, 1995; East 2 West. *Bhangra for the Masses*, Music Collection International, 1993; Cornershop, *When I Was Born for the 7th Time*, Wiija Records, 1997; Asia Dub Foundation, *Community Music*, FFRR, 2000

BIOGRAPHY; AUTOBIOGRAPHY

A biography is a life history, usually a literary form, though it can also be visual (see **biopic**; **documentary**). An autobiography is where such a history is written by the subject; often, in the case of popular culture figures, with the help of a professional journalist. Here, I use the term biography as shorthand for both types of work, which includes the lives of artists and groups and key figures in the music industry. Label histories, usually of independent recording companies, can also be considered a form of institutional biography (for instance, Bowman, 1997, a history of Stax Records).

Popular music biography plays an important role in popular music. In relation to individuals they 'create, reinforce and also challenge the dominant representations of popular musicians' (Strachan, 2003: 13). The biography interpolates and reflects on fandom, stardom, marketing and promotion. In spite of the proliferation of general academic writing in the past 20 years, the journalistic biography has historically been a staple of the music press, and remains so; it is essential to the construction and maintenance of fandom. A number of journalists are strongly identified with the biographical form, including Dave Marsh, Barney Hoskyns, Victor Brockis and Peter Guralnick, while biographical profiles are an integral part of edited collections (see **music press**). Most autobiographies are written with the aid of professional music journalists (see the examples below).

Musical biographies include a wide range of musical performers, and vary widely in quality. There is a constant turnover of 'quickie' publications on the latest pop sensations. These remain interesting as they trace 'how star appeal has been defined at different historical moments' (Frith, 1983: 272). There are serious historical approaches that imbue particular performers, their musical styles and their recordings with meaning and value, situating them as part of a critical tradition and the musical canon (e.g. Marcus, 1991). In some instances, such biographies seek to undermine the general perception of stars figures, highlighting the scandalous aspects of their lives; these are biographical exposes, as with Albert Goldman's studies of Elvis Presley and John Lennon. A new style of biography emerged in the United Kingdom and the United States in the 1990s, the 'confessional memoir', in which fans describing their encounters with music, and, at times, their own unsuccessful attempt as musicians to 'break into' the music industry, with these often represented as 'celebrations of failure' (Strachan, 2003: 13; e.g. Giles Smith, *Lost in Music*).

As with literary biography, writers of popular music biographies grapple with issues of sources materials and objectivity; the links between the subject's life and the social context within which it occurred and questions of musical production, creativity and authenticity. (For an insightful discussion of this process, from the author's perspective, see the introduction to Guralnick, 2002.) An instructive specific example is provided by Perchard, who, with reference to several biographies of the saxophonist John Coltrane, considers 'the ways that biographical narratives are constituted from disparate source materials and the ideological agendas and political problems that attend this creative act' (2007: 119). With reference to several detailed examples, Swiss (2007) considers 'what constitutes a "good" rock autobiography?'

Several recent **rock** biographies exemplify the insights the form can offer into the music industry, musical creativity and particular musical genres, sounds and scenes, along with their 'readability' and entertainment value (Letts, 2007; Benatar, 2010; Richards, 2010; Smith, 2010).

See: **music press**

Further reading:

Examples:

I have also included useful biographies in specific genre entries.

Benatar, Pat, with Patsi Bale Cox (2010) *Between a Heart and a Rock Place. A Memoir*, New York: HarperCollins. A woman rock star in a male dominated industry.

Letts, Don, with David Nobakht (2007) *CULTURE CLASH. Dread Meets Punk Rockers*, London: SAF. Punk and reggae in 70s London.

Richard, Keith, with James Fox (2010) *Life*, London: Weidenfeld & Nicholson. Rock Culture and the Rolling Stones.

Smith, Patti (2010) *Just Kids*, London; Bloomsbury. Bohemia, art and punk in 60s New York.

General:

Guralnick, P. (2002) *Lost Highway: Journeys and Arrivals of American Musicians*, Edinburgh: Canongate.

Perchard, T. (2007) 'Writing Jazz Biography: Race, Research and Narrative Representation', *Popular Music History* 2,2: 119–45.

Strachan, R. (2003) 'Music Journalism', in Shepherd *et al. The Continuum Encyclopedia.*

Swiss, T. (2005) 'That's Me in the Spotlight: Rock Autobiographies', *Popular Music* 24, 2: 287–94.

BIOPIC

A biopic is a biography presented as a film or television feature, but differing from a **documentary** in that it is aimed at a popular audience and will balance reliability and accuracy against commercial considerations and the need to entertain. A popular music biopic is 'a film which purports to tell, in part or in full, the biography of a musical performer (living or dead), and which contains a significant part of his or her music'. (Inglis, 2007: 77; he was referring to rock/pop biopics, but his definition can stand for the genre). The subjects for music biopics can be found in a range of genres, including blues, rap, jazz, soul and country, and rock and pop (Inglis, 2007).

As Leigh (2009: 348) observes, reviewing the biopic *Nowhere Boy*, to some degree makers of such films are, of necessity, 'playing fast and loose with the truth', as they are constrained by the limited time to tell a story that covers several years, and may include considerable musical content. In *Nowhere Boy*, the record that brings together John and his aunt Julia, who raised him, is Screaming Jay Hawkins 'I Put A Spell On You', released in 1958. Leigh notes that: 'There is no evidence that John was turned on by this wonderfully garish record although it is reasonable to assume that he was' (349). The original source material, where there are widely varying popular biographies/memoirs and so forth of a figure like Lennon, can also become problematic.

Using illustrations from a range of historical examples, Inglis explores

> the relationship between music, film and history; the inevitability of interpretation, imagination and invention in the films' portrayal of history; the inevitable tensions between historical accuracy and commercial considerations; the options open to film-makers in their reconstruction of musical performances; and the attraction of the genre for producers and consumers of film and popular music.

Viewing: *Bird*, Clint Eastwood, 1988; about Charlie Parker; *Ray*, Taylor Hackford, 2004; about Ray Charles; *Walk The Line*, James Mangold, 2005, about Johnny Cash; *Nowhere Boy*, Sam Taylor wood, 2009, on the early life of John Lennon

Further reading:

Inglis, I. (2007) 'Popular Music History on Screen: The Pop/Rock Biopic', *Popular Music History*, 2, 1: 77–93.

Leigh, S. (2009) Review of *Nowhere Boy*, *Popular Music History*, 4, 3: 348–50.

BLACK MUSIC

see **African–American**

BLUEGRASS

A style of American country music with regional origins in Kentucky in the mid-1940s, though with antecedents in 'hillbilly' music and minstrel styles. The style became recognizably formalized and widely popular through the work of Bill Monroe and his original Bluegrass Boys (who gave the music its name) during the years 1945–48. Prominent features of traditional bluegrass were a melodic, three-finger style of banjo picking (popularized by Earl Scruggs), the use of the mandolin as a lead instrument, often soloing against a rhythmic background, and close harmony singing. Bluegrass influenced rockabilly, notably in Elvis Presley's version of Monroe's 'Blue Moon of Kentucky' on his Sun debut.

In the late 1960s, encouraged by **folk rock**, several bluegrass performers shifted from playing purely traditional bluegrass and expanded their appeal by incorporating a more accessible electric sound (The career of the Dillards exemplifies this transition).

The style was maintained and is evident in the work of 'mainstream' artists such as Emmylou Harris. Bluegrass gained wider attention in the 1990s with the crossover success of Alison Krause, and the soundtrack of the movie *O'Brother, Where Art Thou?* showcasing a range of traditional bluegrass songs covered by contemporary artists. Subsequently, bluegrass was an element in the music of the highly commercial Dixie Chicks. The continued appeal of bluegrass can be partly attributed to its connotations of authenticity, as a form of roots music.

See: **roots**

Further reading:
Escott, C. (2003) *The Story of Country Music*, London: BBC. Chapter 6.
Weissman, D. (2005) *Which Side Are You On? An Inside History of the Folk Music Revival in America*, New York: Continuum. (Weissman sees bluegrass as a form of folk music).

Listening: *Best of Bill Monroe*, MCA, 1975; Emmylou Harris, 'If I Could Only Win Your Love' (1975). A cover of the Louvin Brothers original bluegrass recording, which gave their music greater exposure; Alison Krause + Union Station, *New Favorite*, Rounder, 2001; *O'Brother, Where Art Thou?* Soundtrack, Mercury, 2000; The Dillards, *Wheatshaw Suite*, double CD reissue of their first three albums, 1965, 1968 and 1970; Various artists, 40 *Years of Rounder Records*, Box Set, Rounder, 2010

Viewing: *Lost Highway*, documentary series (2003): episode 2

BLUES

A musical metagenre, the blues have been hugely influential on the whole corpus of popular music. The blues are usually linked back to Africa and slavery in the United States, where they were initially a fundamental part of black secular music (Barlow, 1989). Muir notes that, in the United States during the period of 1850–1920, before the coalescence of the blues into a coherent genre, there was a substantial body of popular songs referencing the music: 'as blues was moved into the mainstream, it absorbed some of the features of popular music, thereby producing a style that contained a varying mixture of popular and folk elements' (2009).

Beginning roughly around the 1920s, drawing on these earlier antecedents, the blues developed as a number of identifiable subgenres, which can be historically and geographically located (for introductory overviews, see Evans, 2002; Weisman, 2005; and the essays in Bogdanov *et al.* 2003). A number of the more prominent of these, listed below, are accorded separate treatment; note that the periods they are most associated with are approximate.

- Classic blues (1920s)
- Delta (country) blues (1920s, 1930s)
- R&B (1930s–50s; includes jump blues)

- Chicago (electric) blues (1950s)
- Blues rock

In the late 1950s and into the 1960s, the blues lost their appeal for many of its original black listeners, who associated the form with oppression and hard times, and turned more towards **soul** music. Established performers such as B.B. King and Howling Wolf struggled. Strong blues scenes were maintained though, in cities such as Chicago, in the United States, while the genre became prominent in hybrid styles internationally.

Interest from white musicians and audiences, attracted by the authenticity and mythology of performers such as Robert Johnson (who died in 1938) contributed to something of a blues revival in the 1960s. Earlier recordings of classic and delta blues musicians were repackaged and rereleased; leading Black American bluesmen toured Britain and the continent, sometimes recording with white rock musicians and in some cases rescued from obscurity by blues fans, several performed at leading American festivals, notably Newport. In the early 1960s, British groups such as the Rolling Stones, The Animals and The Who covered blues and R&B songs, and exported the form back to the United States through their recordings and tours.

Blues has been maintained as an identifiable and viable genre, through a network of blues oriented record labels (Alligator), magazines and venues. Major black bluesmen still performing include B.B. King, Buddy Guy and Robert Cray; white musicians such as Eric Clapton continue to work within the genre The earlier recordings of labels such as Chess, and the work of key historical figures such as Robert Johnson and Charlie Patton, have been compiled in reissues, including substantial box sets. In the United States, 2003 was the Year of the Blues, with a range of documentaries (notably Martin Scorsese, 2003), celebratory concerts, presentations and even postage stamp issues featuring major blues musicians.

There is a considerable body of scholarship on the blues, one which continues to expand. Recent studies include reissues of classic general histories (e.g. Davis, 2003), fuller investigations of the origins of the blues (Muir, 2009) and studies of particular styles (see related entries).

See: **blues rock; Chicago blues; classic blues; Delta blues; R&B**

Further reading:
Barlow, W. (1989) *Looking Up At Down: The Emergence of Blues Culture*, Philadelphia, PA: Temple University Press. An in-depth history.
Bogdanov, V., Woodstra, C., Erlewine, S. eds (2003) *All Music Guide to the Blues*, 3rd edition, San Franciso AMG: Backbeat Books. This is a compendious guide

to performers, with useful essays on genres and key-related aspects (such as independent labels). Now updated on the AMG website.

Davis, F. (2003; first published 1995) *History of the Blues*, Cambridge: Da Capo Press.

Eder, B. (2003) 'Beginners Guide and History – How to Listen to the Blues', in Bogdanov, V., Woodstra, C. and Erlewine, S. (eds) *All Music Guide to the Blues*, 3rd edition, pp. 711–16.

Evans, D. (2002) The Development of the Blues, in Moore, A. (ed.) *The Cambridge Companion to Blues and Gospel*, Cambridge: Cambridge University Press. Chapter 3.

Moore, A. (ed.) (2002) *The Cambridge Companion to Blues and Gospel*, Cambridge: Cambridge University Press, pp. 194–201. An excellent collection of essays, with extensive notes, a substantial bibliography and a selected discography and videography.

Muir, P.C. (2009) *Long Lost Blues: Popular Blues in America, 1850-1920*, Urbana: University of Illinois Press.

Weisman, D. (2005) *Blues The Basics*, New York: Routledge.
A concise introduction, with a quite comprehensive bibliography and discography, usefully arranged by genres and topics

Magazines:

Living Blues. The Magazine of the Afro-American Blues Tradition.

The Blues Collection, (1993–94) London: Orbis Publishing. Editorial Consultant: Tony Russell.
A 26-part collection, published serially, with binders subsequently available. Each issue is accompanied by a cassette tape. Includes well-written and informative performer profiles, with discographies and listening notes, along with a regular feature 'The Story of the Blues'. The series was then extended, but the major performers and styles are primarily in the initial issues. Copies/sets/the tapes all still appear on web trading sites.

Listening: Historical overviews: *The History of Rhythm and Blues*. Three box sets, each with four CDs and an excellent booklet. Part One: The Pre-War Years, 1925–42; *The Blues, vols 1–6*, MCA 1986–89; originally released by Chess in the mid-1960s as a sampler of the labels extensive blues catalogue; Contemporary Blues; Eric Clapton, *From the Cradle*, Reprise, 1994; ZZ Top, *Deguello*, WB, 1979; Buddy Guy, *Damn Right I Got The Blues*, Silvertone, 1991; Robert Cray, *Strong Persuader*, Mercury, 1986

Viewing: *Martin Scorsese Presents the Blues: A Musical Journey* (2003), Vulcan Productions, MADMAN Cinema. A seven part series, individually available and as a box set. Not a narrative history as such, but 'a series of personal and impressionistic films viewed through the lens of seven world-famous directors who share a passion for the music' (box set). The films vary in their scope and effectiveness (see the discussion in Weisman, 2005: 143–55), with a general strength being the inclusion of hard to locate/new footage of some key historical figures

BLUES ROCK

American and English white musicians popularized the electric blues in the early 1960s. Mining earlier blues for inspiration and material, they brought the style to white **rock** audiences, and the British and American charts, through the mid-1960s and early 1970s.

In the United Kingdom, performers such Alexis Korner's Blues Incorporated, The Rolling Stones, The Yardbirds, John Mayall's Bluesbreakers, Cream, Led Zeppelin and the Pretty Things produced what is sometimes referred to as British R&B (Neill, 2004), and subsequently labelled 'blues rock' in the later 1960s. The concerts and recordings of super group Cream, provide examples of the adaptation and reworking of songs such as Crossroads (originally performed by Robert Johnson), I'm So Glad (Skip James) and Rolling and Tumbling (Muddy Waters) (see Headlam).

In the United States, performers such as The Paul Butterfield Blues Band and Electric Flag in the 1960s.

Further reading:

Headlam, D. (1997) 'Blues Transformation in the Music of Cream', in Covach, J. and Boone, G.M. (eds) *Understanding Rock: Essays in Musical Analysis*, New York: Oxford University Press, pp. 59–89.

Neill, A. (2004, February 2004) 'Hoochie Coochie Men. The British R&B Explosion, 1962–1966', *Record Collector*, Issue 294: 68–88 (includes a good discography).

Listening: Paul Butterfield Blues Band; Cream, *The Very Best of Cream*, Polygram, 2001

BOOGIE-WOOGIE

A percussive, rhythmic style of black piano-playing boogie-woogie began in the mid- to late 1920s and flourished during the 1930s. It is sometimes referred to as 'the left hand of god' because of the left hand playing repeated bass patterns, while the right hand plays short melodic figures (riffs). The style was based on the **blues** progression, but was freely improvised. Boogie is derived from bogey, meaning spirit, woogie was the name of pieces of wood tying railway tracks together; many of the black piano players associated with the style travelled on the railroad from town to town, playing for 'rent' parties (held by people to raise the rent money). Boogie-woogie strongly influenced the development of rockabilly and early rock'n'roll in the 1950s.

See: **rockabilly**; **rock'n'roll**

Listening: *Blues Piano Orgy*, Delmark, 1972; Jerry Lee Lewis, 'Whole Lotta Shakin' Goin' On', 1957; *On 18 Original Sun Greatest Hits*, Rhino, 1984; *My Blue Heaven: Best of Fats Domino*, EMI, 1990; *Little Richard, His Biggest Hits*, 1959; Speciality, 1991

BOOTLEGS

Bootlegs are illegally produced and distributed recordings, which enjoy a rather ambivalent status. Bootleg recordings have been prolific and have warranted a substantial history (Heylin, 1995) and a major study (Marshall, 2005).

Frequently associated with a mystique and cultural cachet for avid consumers and completist fans, they are anathema to record companies, and criticized by many artists. There are several kinds: (1) unauthorized **reissues**, usually of rare or out-of-print material; (2) counterfeits, which simply duplicate official, authorized releases (see **piracy**) and (3) unreleased live performances. At times these are semi-condoned: *ICE* magazine refers to them as 'gray area, live recordings'; although containing a regular column on bootleg releases, the magazine notes that while bootlegs are readily available in Europe, they 'cannot definitely advise as to their legality in the US'. Bootleggers can claim to be fulfilling an important cultural preservation role.

In some cases, bootlegs attain legendary status, occasionally prompting record companies to release an official/original recording; for example, Prince's *Black Album*, WB, 1995, originally recorded in 1987 but not commercially released; Bob Dylan, *The Basement Tapes*, Columbia, 1995; and Bruce Springsteen, *Live 1975–85*, Columbia, 1986, the last two a reaction against the flood of bootlegs of the artists' concert performances. In some instances, artists have condoned concert recordings – most notably the Grateful Dead (the deadheads). Authenticity is central to the nature and appeal of bootlegs, and the majority of bootlegs are of rock artists who are regarded as exemplars of it: Dylan; The Rolling Stones; Springsteen; Led Zeppelin.

A growing trend in the music industry is the increasing number of official bootleg recordings being released, best exemplified by the extensive SONY series of Bob Dylan bootleg recordings and Tori Amos's *Original Bootlegs*. This trend has can be attributed to the pervasiveness of digital downloading, and has undermined the traditional cultural capital bootleg recordings embodied (Farrugia and Gobatto, 2010).

See: **copyright**; **piracy**

Further reading:
ICE. *The CD News Authority*: 'Going Underground' section; Marshall, L. (2005) *Bootlegging: Romanticism and Copyright in the Music Industry*. London: SAGE.
Farrugia, R., and Gobatto, N. (2010) 'Shopping for Legs and Boots: Tori Amos's *Original Bootlegs*, Fandom, and Cultural Capital', *Popular Music and Society*, 33, 3: 357–75.

BOSSA NOVA

Bossa nova is a Brazilian popular music which combines samba, Brazil's most popular traditional form, and 'cool jazz', a smooth, light and relaxed style of the 1950s. Bossa nova is the Brazilian genre most familiar internationally.

It emerged in the 1950s with the work of a group of musicians who 'smitten with American cool jazz, began applying complex, bebop-derived harmonies, a light, almost detached style, and sparse instrumentation (often just Spanish guitar and voice) to samba' (Meeder, 2008: 173). Bossa nova reflected the lifestyle of the leisured Brazilian upper class, with lyrics about beautiful beaches, blue skies and attractive girls, and was criticized from the political left for its light pop style.

Leading musicians included Carlos (Tom) Jobim (d. 1994), Carlos Lyra and Joao Gilbert, who is considered the 'original voice of the bossa nova, the one most credited with inventing the style' (Nidel, 2005: 328. For fuller discussion of bossa nova and its leading practitioners, see McGowan and Pessanha, 2009). The music Jobim wrote for the play *Orfeo Negro*, produced in Paris in 1956, was included in the subsequent classic film *Black Orpheus* (1959, along with Luis Bonfa's 'Manha de Carnival', and brought Brazilian music to a European audience.

In 1961, American jazz guitarist Charlie Byrd toured Brazil, and brought the style back to play for tenor saxophonist Stan Getz. The two recorded an album together, *Jazz Samba*, which, despite its title, showcased bossa nova. It included a version of Jobim's 'Desafinado', which was a huge chart success and won a Grammy (Best Instrumental Jazz Performance). The style was adopted by other jazz musicians, attracted by the samba rhythms. Getz himself continued to record entire bossa nova albums, or include bossa tracks on his albums. As a highly accessible hybrid style, with its exotic origins outside of the Anglo-American music world, bossa nova and its leading performers became internationally popular in the 1960s. 'The Girl From Ipanema', written by Tom Jobim and sung by Astrud Gilberto, epitomized the appeal of the genre. The song launched a Brazilian music boom in the United States in the early 1960s and won the Grammy for Record of the Year in 1964.

Gilberto Gill 'moved bossa nova forward, internationalized it and rocked it, while combating the snobbish left who rejected bossa as commercial and too pop' (Nidel, 2005: 329). A political activist, who achieved widespread popularity in the late 1960s, he was forced to leave Brazil and move to England in 1970, but later returned to his home country.

Bossa nova, and later variants of it, continued to be successful, but without reaching the peak of the golden period, 1958–64. The genre 'became a permanent subset of jazz, and countless jazz and pop composers would incorporate bossa melodies harmonies, rhythms, and textures into their songs in succeeding decades' (McGowan and Pessanha, 2009: 78).

Marketed as part of the metagenre of **world music**.

Further reading: (see also world music, and the general references with that entry) McGowan, C., and Pessanha, R. (2009) *The Brazilian Sound. Samba, Bossa Nova, and the Popular Music of Brazil*, Philadelphia: Temple University Press, Chapter 3. Includes a select discography and resources, (including documentary DVDs, music labels and Internet sites).

Listening: Gilberto Gill, *Louvacao*, Philips, 1967; *Samba Bossa Nova*, Putumayo, 2002; *Bossa Nova*, Verve, 2006

BOX SET

In its most extreme form, the exploitation of the back catalogue is represented by the boxed set: the extensive repackaging of performer's work to present a career overview. While sometimes criticized as exploiting consumers, such releases also preserve popular music history, making it more accessible, especially to younger listeners. A case in point is the phenomenal successful of the Robert Johnson's boxed set, *The Complete Recordings*. (Columbia, 1990) bringing the blues legend to the attention of a new audience. Other types of boxed sets have been multi-album releases by a performer (e.g. George Harrison, *All Things Must Pass*, 1970), concert packages (e.g. *Woodstock*, 1970) and, a recent trend, collections of singles (e.g. The Smashing Pumpkins; Alanis Morissette). The last include creative repackaging of 1960s artists (The Who, The Rolling Stones), primarily for the collector market.

BOY BANDS

A term widely used in the 1990s and since for bands regarded as manufactured pop, in the sense of being deliberate industry constructions aimed primarily at teenage audiences, though there were significant examples from the 1960s onward (notably, The Monkees in the 1960s: see Stahl, 2002; and 1970s British **New Pop**). Several boy bands enjoyed huge commercial success, while a few members went on to establish solo careers. Key examples are the Backstreet Boys, Take That (Robbie Williams), N'Sync and New Kids on the Block. One response was the creation and success of female equivalents of the boy bands (The Spice Girls), utilizing a similar marketing approach. The late 1990s phenomenon of using reality television shows to produce such groups has continued, although their membership may be more of a gender mix; as with S Club 7 (see **television**). The use of music video, the coverage in the music press, the album covers and posters and distinctive performance styles (especially the highly choreographed use of dance), the emphasis on vocals, the 'masking' of instrumental accompaniment: (see the N'Sync concert DVD) all contribute to the construction of a distinct image for boy bands: essentially they are teens marketed for teens, especially girls.

The discourse surrounding boy bands mirrors that of teen- and chart-oriented pop more generally, especially their perceived lack of authenticity, seen as reflecting the power of the music industry to commodify such performers and their audiences. More complex analyses move past simple condemnation to consider the dynamics of the processes of creation and presentation of the boy bands and their music, and the nature of their appeal, especially their representations of masculinity (Marshall, 1997; Jarman-Ivens, 2007).

There has been a recent resurgence of boy bands in the United Kingdom, with several (Take That) reforming as 'man bands'.

See: **commodification**; **girl groups**; **pop**

Further reading:
Jarman-Ivens, F. ed. (2007) *Oh Boy! Masculinities and Popular Music*, New York: Routledge.
Marshall, P.D. (1997) *Celebrity and Power*, London: University of Minnesota Press; Chapter 6 includes a case study of New Kids on the Block.

Listening: Backstreet Boys, *Backstreet's Back*, Zomba/Mushroom records, 1997

Viewing: N'Sync, *Pop Odessey*, DVD, Zomba, 2002

BRICOLAGE

The concept of bricolage was initially developed by anthropologist Levi-Strauss, who observed that primitive people's modes of magic – superstition, sorcery, myth – while superficially bewildering, can be regarded as implicitly coherent, connecting things which enable their users to satisfactorily explain and make sense of their own world.

Bricolage has been applied in popular music studies primarily in considerations of the nature and cultural significance of cultural style, especially in youth subcultures and in relation to musical appropriations.

The Birmingham cultural studies writers, most notable Hebdige and the contributors to Hall and Jefferson (1976) applied and developed the structured improvisations of bricolage to explain the spectacular youth subcultures which emerged in the United Kingdom in the 1950s and 1960s. These subcultures appropriated a range of goods from the dominant culture, assigning new meanings to them. Symbolic objects – music, language, dress, appearance – formed a unified signifying system in which borrowed materials reflected and expressed aspects of the subcultural group (see the essays in Hall and Jefferson, 1976). Punk best emphasized such stylistic bricolage.

'Normal' youth can also operate as bricoleurs. Clarke suggests that an examination of male working-class youth in the United Kingdom reveals that 'normal' dressing means using elements drawn from government surplus stores, sportswear, subcultural clothing appropriated from different historical eras via the second-hand clothing markets (in Hall and Jefferson, 1976). McRobbie (1988; 1991) demonstrated that this was not a process confined to boys, with fashion conscious young girls also putting together ensembles. Mass market fashion itself contains forms of recontextualized meaning, as with ski jumpers, track suits and work overalls.

A number of studies have utilized bricolage in a more general sense to examine the social role of particular musical styles. Grossberg (1997: 481) argues that rock'n'roll is a particular capitalist and postmodernist form of bricolage:

> It functions in a constant play of incorporation and excorporation (both always occurring simultaneously), a contradictory cultural practice, in which youth celebrates the very conditions of its leisure – boredom, meaningless and dehumanization – through technology, commodity fetishism, repetition, fragmentation and superficiality.

In more precise terms, various musical styles have been credited with bringing a sense of play to the arts of bricolage, utilizing different musical sounds, conventions and instrumentation. Lipsitz, for example, documents how Los Angeles's Chicano rock'n'roll musicians drew upon street slang, car customizing, clothing styles and wall murals for inspiration and ideas, in addition to more traditional cultural creations such as literature, plays and poems: 'Their work is intertextual, constantly in dialogue with other forms of cultural expression, and most fully appreciated when located in context' (Lipsitz, 1997: 358). All this is to see a process of semiotic guerrilla warfare at work in and through popular music, operating in sites such as the home, school and the workplace.

See: **subculture** (and the readings listed there)

BRITISH INVASION

A term used by the popular press, and subsequently by historians of popular music, for the impact of British groups on the US popular music scene and their dominance of the American charts from early 1960 to 1964–65. A strong British grassroots popular music scene emerged in the late 1950s, encouraged by skiffle, and drawing on American rock'n'roll and R&B for inspiration (**beat music**). The beat boom bands inflected these sounds with their own styles and increasingly produced their own material. The main centres were Liverpool (Merseybeat) and London's R&B based scene.

The Beatles were the crucial performers. Their success opening the way for the Dave Clark Five, Gerry and the Pacemakers, the Rolling

Stones, etc. Prior to this, few British recording artists had found sustained popularity in America. Indeed, Capitol Records, the US subsidiary of EMI, initially declined to release Beatles records in the United States, licencing them to smaller labels; for example, Vee Jay Records released 'Please Please Me' in February 1963, and a modified version of the group's first album (*Please Please Me*) as *Introducing the Beatles* in July 1963. With little accompanying promotion, these releases failed to do well on the charts, despite their UK success. This all changed with the bands first US tour in 1964, and the accompanying Beatlemania and chart domination (see Starr and Waterman, 2003). The British invasion withered in the mid-1960s, as the Beatles stopped touring in 1966, and the United States produced a number of successful bands who drew heavily on the British groups and their music (notably The Byrds).

Lester Bangs (1992) is critical of much of the music as 'by and large junk: perfect expressions of the pop aesthetic of a disposable culture' and 'innocuous but raucous'. The British invasion was nonetheless important in reshaping American popular music in early 1960s, while validating the emerging youth culture. Although it stifled the emergent black R&B and the girl groups, it prompted the emergence of garage bands and American power pop. The success of the Beatles, followed by the other British groups, created a standard rock group line up, usually consisting of four, or possibly five players, with drum kit; lead, rhythm and bass guitars, plus vocals delivered by one (on lead) and all (chorus). The Beatles also established the importance of the singer songwriter, and the cultural significance of groups performing their own material.

See: **beat music**; **garage bands**; **girl groups**; **power pop**

Further reading:
Bangs, L (1992) 'The British Invasion' in DeCurtis and Henke (eds) *The Rolling Stone Illustrated History of Rock and Roll*, 3rd edition.
The 'standard' histories of rock include coverage of the period (see **history**; **rock**)

Viewing: *Dancing in the Street*, episode 3: 'So You Wanna Be a Rock'n'Roll Star?'

BRITPOP

The general label applied to the British guitar-based pop/rock bands of the 1990s, initially by the UK music press, with a distinctively British musical aesthetic. Britpop was a loose constituency of several distinct music styles. Performers looked for inspiration to 1960s British pop/rock bands such as the Beatles, the Who, and the Kinks; post-punk British rock of the 1980s (The Smiths, The Jam), elements of glam rock (T. Rex was an acknowledged influence), and British 'new pop' of the 1980s (see **New Romantics**). From an American perspective, Britpop has been described, not unfairly, as a 'defiantly nationalistic anti-grunge movement'. Whereas grunge had idealized an anti-star approach, Britpop was regarded as 'firmly cemented in snotty arrogance and aspirations to stardom' ('The Empire Gobs Back', *Rolling Stone, Yearbook* 1995: 32–4). Major Britpop bands included Blur, Suede, Pulp and, above all, Oasis; with the label also applied to Ash, Echobelly and Ride, among others. Along with electronic dance music, Britpop dominated the British charts through the 1990s, with Oasis's debut one of the biggest selling records in UK history. Oasis also succeeded in the American market, where *Morning Glory* sold 3.26 million copies during 1995–96, supported by extensive touring there, but otherwise Britpop had only limited impact in the United States. Through its leader Tony Blair, the (then in) opposition New Labour Party cultivated connections to Britpop, which it invoked as symbolic of the need to reinvigorate British culture and the economy.

In a major study of Britpop, Harris (2003) argues that the groups who defined it ended up shifting British indie rock from its ideological and aesthetic traditions into the commercial mainstream of UK music. His account traces its rise, success and dilution into a celebration of Britishness for its own sake, and a decline from artistic endeavour into drug-fuelled indulgence (notably in the case of Oasis).

While several Britpop bands remain active (Blur, Oasis), Britpop as a generic label is now generally regarded as a historical curiosity. There continues to be considerable popular and academic interest in it, focusing on questions of its antecedents, its constitution in terms of class and gender and its legacy.

See: **indie**

Further reading:

Baxter-Moore, N. (2006) 'This is Where I Belong: Identity, Social Class, and the Nostalgic Englishness of Ray Davies and The Kinks'. *Popular Music and Society*. 29, 2: 145–65.
Bennett, A., and Stratton, J. eds (2010) *Britpop and the English Music Tradition*. Farnham: Ashgate.
Britpop. (2009) London: Mojo.
Cloonan, M. (1997) 'State of the Nation: "Englishness" Pop, and Politics in the Mid-1990s'. *Popular Music and Society*. 21, 2: 47–70.

Harris, J. (2003) *The Last Party: Britpop, Blair and the Demise of English Rock*. London: Fourth Estate.

Wiseman-Trowse, N. (2008) *Performing Class in British Popular Music*. Basingstoke: Palgrave Macmillan.

Listening: Blur, *Parklife*, Capitol, 1994; Oasis's *Whats The Story) Morning Glory?* Creation, 1995; *Suede*, self-titled debut, Columbia, 1993

Viewing: *Live Forever. The Rise and Fall of Britpop*, DVD, 2003

BUBBLEGUM

A derogatory label initially applied to a genre of highly commercial and rather cynically manufactured **pop** of the late 1960s, usually aimed at pre-teenage listeners and reflecting their emerging purchasing power. The term came from the rock-based jingles that were produced for bubblegum adverts in the United States. It was largely an American phenomenon, associated with the Buddah label and performers like the Lemon Pipers, the Archies (whose 'Sugar Sugar' single was the best selling single of 1969), and the Ohio Express ('Yummy Yummy Yummy'). Bubblegum recordings often made extensive use of session musicians. Although frequently critically denigrated, bubblegum was at the core of commercially very successful performers such as the Monkees, Tommy Roe and Tommy James and the Shondells. Subsequently, bubblegum became the general term for popular music regarded as 'lightweight' and chart oriented. Musically, it is associated with strong melodies and rhythms: insidious, catchy hooks. Although frequently denigrated, bubblegum has exercised a continued fascination, with ongoing reissues and compilations and coverage in the music press.

See: **power pop**

Further reading:
Bangs, L. (1992) (includes discography) 'Bubblegum' in DeCurtis, A., and Henke, J. (eds) *The Rolling Stone Illustrated History of Rock and Roll*, 3rd edition, New York: Random House: 452–4.

Cooper, K., and Samy, D. eds (2001) *Bubblegum: Music Is the Naked Truth*. Los Angeles: Feral House. An exhaustive fan coverage of the music, its performers, the fans and the labels.

Listening: *Very Best of the Ohio Express*, Buddah, 1970; Tommy James and the Shondells, *Anthology*, Rhino, 1980; *The Ultimate Bubblegum Pop Collection*, Rajon Music (double CD compilation), 2005

CANON

A canon is usually a list, or a group of cultural works, which are regarded as exemplary ('the best') in their field, in terms of aesthetics, complexity and depth of expression (Regev, 2006). The canon embraces value, exemplification, authority and a sense of temporal continuity (timelessness). Critics of the concept point to the general social relativism and value judgements embedded in it, and the often associated privileging of Western, white, male, and middle-class cultural work. Issues related to the construction and nature of such canons have long been at the centre of literary scholarship, and underpin several major public literary disagreements, most notably the 'Great Books' debate.

Notions of a canon are frequently present in popular music discourse, implicitly in everyday conversations among fans, and more directly in critical discourse. Music critics and the music press are major contributors to the construction of a musical canon, with the use of ratings systems for reviews, annual 'best of' listings and various 'guidebooks' (e.g. see Shuker, 2008: Chapter 9; also **music press**). A number of academic studies of popular music have focused on the historical construction of particular genre canons; instructive examples here include analyses of the Western classical tradition (Tagg and Clarida, 2003: Chapter 1), and jazz (Gabbard, 1995).

An example of this process at work is provided by Dougan, in his insightful discussion of canonization and blues record collectors in the United States. He describes these collectors as 'musical archaeologists, culture brokers, creators, keepers, and, though their entrepreneurial efforts (influenced by the release of Harry Smith's 1952 compilation *Anthology of American Folk Music*) disseminators of a blues canon'. He sees this role as playing a vital part in the taxonomy of the genre:

> At its core, canon formation among blues record collectors involves organizing and defending a set of selections made from several possible sets of selections. The resulting 'canon' represents the essence of the tradition, and the connection between the texts and the canon reveals the veiled logic and internal rationale of that tradition.
>
> (*Dougan, 2005: 42, 45*)

The nature of the canon and the difficulties surrounding it are evident in the recurring presentation of a 'mainstream' canon of rock and pop recordings in 'Best Of/Greatest Albums of All Time' lists. Von Appen and Doehring (2006) provide a meta-analysis of such lists, drawing on 38 rankings made between 1985–89 and 2000–4. This 'top thirty' is domi-nated by artists' rock albums of the 1960s and 1970s, notably the Beatles, and there is an absence of women and black artists. The list represents the staple musical repertoire for 'classic rock' radio, which both reflects and reinforces the visibility and value accorded to such performers and albums. They suggest that two criteria underpin this pattern: aesthetic and socio-logical. The aesthetic places a premium on artistic authenticity, and there is at times a limited relationship between such rankings and sales and chart success. The exclusion of compilation and greatest hits albums from most of the lists included reflected the view that the album must represent a showcase of the work of an artist at a particular point in time. Von Appen and Doehring's discussion of the sociological factors at work here shows the role of the music press and industry discourse in shaping taste, and the cultural capital and social identities of those who voted on the lists.

The gendered nature of the musical canon and its dominance by Anglo-American performers and recording has been strongly critiqued. Citron (1993) examines the question: 'Why is music composed by women so marginal to the standard "classical" repertoire?' Her study looks at the practices and attitudes that have led to the exclusion of women composers from the received 'canon' of performed musical works, impor-tant elements of canon formation: creativity, professionalism, music as gendered discourse and reception. The marginalization of women in pop-ular music histories, along with the privileging of male performers and male-dominated or -oriented musical genres, is reflected in the conse-quent domination of popular music canons by male performers.

The concept of the canon, and the question of its nature and continued utility, continue to receive attention in popular music studies (see the arti-cles in a forum in the *Journal of Popular Music Studies*, 22, 1, 2010).

Further reading:
Citron, M. (1993) *Gender and the Musical Canon*, Cambridge: Cambridge University Press.
Dougan, J. (2006) 'Objects of Desire: Canon Formation and Blues Record Collecting', *Journal of Popular Music*, 18, 1: 40–65.
Gabbard, K. (1995) *Jazz Among the Discourses*, Durham, NC: Duke University Press.
Kärjä, A.-V. (2006) 'A Prescribed Alternative Mainstream: Popular Music and Canon Formation', *Popular Music*, 25, 1(January): 3–20.
Regev, M. (2006) 'Introduction' to Theme (Canon), *Popular Music*, 25, 1.
Von Appen, R. and Doehring, A. (2006) 'Nevermind The Beatles, Here's Exile 61 and Nico: "The Top 100 Records of All Time" - A Canon of Pop and Rock Albums From a Sociological and an Aesthetic Perspective', *Popular Music*, 25, 1(January): 21–40.

CASSETTE CULTURE

Compact cassette audio tape and cassette tape players, developed in the mid-1960s, appealed because of their small size and associated portability. Initially a low-fidelity medium, steady improvement of the sound, through modifications to magnetic tape and the introduction of the Dolby noise reduction system, enhanced the appeal of cassettes. The transistor radio and the cassette had become associated technologies by the 1970s, with widely popular cheap radio cassette players, and the cassette player incorporated into high-fidelity home stereos.

Tape cassettes posed considerable problems of illegal copying and the violation of copyright. Fuelled by home taping, sales of blank cassette audio tapes peaked during the 1980s. Conversely, the advent of the CD, led to a sharp and ongoing decline in the market share of prerecorded audio cassettes, which dropped below 20 per cent in 2002. In Western countries, many music retailers no longer stock the format.

An efficient format for the expansion into remote markets, tape cassettes became the main sound carriers in 'developing' countries, and by the end of the 1980s, cassettes were outselling other formats three to one. As a portable recording technology, the tape cassette has been used in the production, duplication and dissemination of local musics (Manuel, 1993) and the creation of new musical styles, most notably punk and rap, thus tending to decentralize control over production and consumption. Individuals (home tapers) creating mix tapes, were re-sequencing music to create new configurations and links across diverse recordings and genres. The term **cassette culture** was applied to the 'do it yourself' ethic that underlies such practices, and the network of musicians and listeners it embraces.

Making copies of recordings is a significant aspect of people's engagement with popular music. During the 1970s and 1980s, this was primarily through audio tape. Aside from the convenience of ensuring access to preferred texts, selected (particularly with albums) to avoid any 'dross' or material not liked sufficiently to warrant inclusion, there was an economic aspect to such home taping. Willis saw it as a strategy directly tailored to recession conditions: 'The tape cassette has proved to be a practical, flexible and cheap way of consuming and distributing music' (1990: 62). Home taping was primarily from the radio, but 'Young people frequently rely on friends, with larger record collections to make tapes for them. There is something of an informal hierarchy of taste operating here' (ibid.: 63). Home taping was significant as an aspect of consumption largely beyond the ability of the music industry to influence tastes.

The same practices continue with digital music, through downloading and the use of i-Tunes, and sound carriers such as the iPod, with a proliferation of guidebooks and suggested playlists.

See also: **formats**; **iPod**

Further reading:
Manuel, P. (1993) *Cassette Culture – Popular Music and Technology in Northern India*, Chicago: University of Chicago Press.
Moore, T. (2005) *Mix Tape: The Art of Cassette Culture*, New York: Universe.
Willis, P. *et al.* (1990) *Common Culture*, Milton Keynes: Open University Press.

CCM (CONTEMPORARY CHRISTIAN MUSIC)

A rather loose musical genre, sometimes labelled 'Christian Rock', applied initially to those artists associated with the emergence of a Christian music industry established by American evangelicals (in the 1970s) as an alternative to the mainstream 'secular' entertainment business. *Billboard* has a Top Contemporary Christian Music (CCM) category. A magazine, *Contemporary Christian Music* (later *CCM*) began in 1978. CCM has become a widely used term for artists whose work 'melds faith and culture. It is called Christian because of the messages in the lyrics, or at least because of the faith backgrounds of the artists' (Thompson, 2000: 11). While the beat and melody are indistinguishable from other mainstream music forms, differences are noted in the lyric content, where themes frequently used are personal salvation, the witnessing of one's faith, living by example, human frailties, rebellion, sin, forgiveness, God's love and mercy.

There is a debate over whether Christian music is primarily 'ministry' or 'entertainment' or whether particular artists' work is 'sacred' or 'secular'. The considerable commercial success of some artists have fuelled this debate; for example, Amy Grant (Romanowski, 1993). Christian themes are an element in the work of commercially successful performers who are located within general musical genres, including pop-metal (Stryper in the late 1980s), rock (Jars of Clay; POD) and pop (DC Talk, Sixpence None the Richer). Thompson's study of the 'birth, evolution, and growing popularity of Christian Rock Music' (2000; back jacket) shows a rich diversity of performers and musical styles.

The work of some 'mainstream' performers has, at times, been influenced by their Christian beliefs, usually in terms of a more mystic

Christian spirituality; examples include Bob Dylan (*Slow Train Coming*, Columbia, 1979), Van Morrison ('When Will I Learn to Live in God?' on *Avalon Sunset*, Polydor, 1989) and U2 (*The Joshua Tree*, Island, 1987).

See: **gospel**

Further reading:
Romanowski, W. (1993) 'Move Over Madonna: The Crossover Career of Gospel Artist Amy Grant'. *Popular Music and Society*, 17, 2: 47–68.
Thompson, J. (2000) *Raised by Wolves. The Story of Christian Rock & Roll*, Toronto: ECW Press.

Listening: Amy Grant, *Heart in Motion*, A&M, 1991; Jars of Clay, 'Flood' (draws on the imagery of baptism and Noah's Ark), on the album *Frail*, Silvertone, 1995. The most successful Christian **crossover** single ever; DC Talk, *Jesus Freak*, Virgin, 1995

CELEBRITY

see **stars**

CELTIC MUSIC

Irish in origin but more widely influential, contemporary Celtic popular music is an example of a hybrid genre, variants of which have crossed over into the mainstream of popular music. Descriptions of it tend to be vague and lack specificity: 'The element that the music of the Celtic lands most commonly shares is a feeling or quality that evokes emotions of sadness or joy, sorrow or delight' (Sawyers, 2000: 5).

The influence of Celtic music is evident in the 'mainstream', commercially and critically successful music of Van Morrison, Clannad, the Chieftains, Enya (Celtic New Age), and the Corrs. Celtic music frequently involves a blending of traditional and modern forms, for example, the Celtic-punk of the Pogues; the ambient music of Enya and Canada's Coreena McKennitt; the Celtic-grunge of Cape Breton fiddle-player Ashley MacIsaac; the Celtic-rock of Rawlins Cross and Horslips. In much of this work, traditional Irish melodies are given a pop/rock dimension, with the lyrics sometimes in Gaelic.

The emergence of various hybrids of Celtic and popular music forms is part of a broader awakening of interest in Celtic traditional music and Gaelic culture and language. This appeal is attributed to the 'realness' and 'honesty' of the music, in other words, its authenticity as music of the people.

Celtic music is frequently considered part of world music.

See: **diaspora**; **world music**

Further reading:
McLaughlin, N. and McLoone, M. (2000) 'Hybridity and National Musics: The Case of Irish Rock Music', *Popular Music*, 19, 2: 181–99.
Sawyers, J. (2000) *The Complete Guide to Celtic Music*, London: Arum Press.

Listening: Horslips, *Dance Hall Sweethearts*, RCA, 1974; Sarah McLachlan, *Solace*, Arista, 1991; The Pogues, *Rum, Sodomy & the Lash*, MCA, 1995; Enya, *Watermark*, Reprise, 1988

CENSORSHIP

Censorship occurs whenever particular words, images, sounds, and ideas are suppressed or muted. This usually occurs through legislation at the national or local level, but can also take place through self-regulation and codes of practice within the media and communication industries. In a major study of the operation of popular music censorship in Britain, Cloonan (1996: 75) initially defines it as 'an attempt to interfere, either pre- or post-publication with the artistic expressions of popular music artists with a view to stifling, or significantly altering, that expression. This puts the emphasis on censorship as a *deliberate* act'.

Censorship operates at a number of levels in popular music. There is a long history of record companies refusing to distribute potentially contro- versial records or videos, of recordings subject to bans by radio, and recordings being subject to court action. Much of the associated debate is between supporters of the basic right of free speech, and those calling for the regulation of obscenity. A further dimension is a more covert one, where the market effectively acts as a censor. This includes record compa- nies' decisions not to sign artists, or to fully support releases, because of their perceived lack of commercial potential; decisions by large retail out- lets not to stock less commercial or controversial artists/genres; and deci- sions by radio stations not to play records which do not fit their general format. While these decisions are based on commercial rather than moral considerations, their net effect may be censorial. The licencing and regulation of live venues by local authorities also operates as a form of censorship (see **policy**).

In Britain and the United States, calls for stricter censorship of popular media culture have been strongly associated with the political activism and influence of the New Right, a loose amalgam of religious and conservative groups. Cloonan (1996) details a number of themes in the censorship of popular music in the United Kingdom: the ebb and flow of censorship in relation to contemporary events, with often high-profile crimes causally linked to viewing violent media; the tendency of proponents of censorship to portray the popular music audience as passive dupes of the industry, accompanied by an aesthetic critique of pop; a concern for the welfare of children and adolescents; and xenophobia, as with the early British attacks on rock'n'roll which emphasized its American roots. Variants of these are present internationally, particularly in the views of the Parent's Music Resource Center (PMRC) in the United States, formed in 1985.

A historical succession of moral panics/censorship episodes around particular genres and performers have been identified and examined (see Shuker, 2008: Chapter 13).

See: **gangsta rap**; **moral panic**

Further reading:

Cloonan, M. and Garofalo, R. eds (2003) *Policing Pop*, Philadelphia, PA: Temple University Press.

Cloonan, M. (1996) *Banned! Censorship of Popular Music in Britain: 1967–92*, Aldershot: Arena.

Winfield, B.H. and Davidson, S. eds (1999) *Bleep! Censoring Rock and Rap Music*, Westport, CT: Greenwood Press.

CHARTS

The popular music chart is a numerical ranking of current releases based on sales and airplay, usually over a 1-week period of time; the top ranked album/single is No. 1 and the rest are ranked correspondingly. The first UK chart appeared in 1928 (*Melody Maker's* 'Honours List'); in the US, *Billboard*, the major trade paper, began a 'Network Song Census' in 1934. Such charts quickly became the basis for radio 'Hit Parade' programmes.

Chart listings remain a feature of magazines such as *Billboard*; more general music magazines, such as *Rolling Stone*; and genre-oriented publications, such as *F-Roots*, with its various world music, folk and roots charts.

The precise nature of how contemporary charts are compiled, and their basis, varies between the various publications, and national approaches differ. In the United States, singles charts are based on airplay, while the album charts are based on sales. Current releases are generally defined for the singles charts as 26 weeks after the release. In the United Kingdom, the charts are produced by market research organizations sponsored by various branches of the media. In both countries, data collection is now substantially computerized and based on comprehensive sample data. Airplay information is compiled from selected radio stations, sales information from wholesalers and retailers, assisted by bar coding. This represents a form of circular logic, in that the charts are based on a combination of radio play and sales, but airplay influences sales, and retail promotion and sales impacts on radio exposure.

Changes in the presentation of the charts can have important repercussions for the relative profile of particular genres/performers. The charts are broken down into genre categories; these can change over time, acting as a barometer of taste, as with the change of 'race' records to R&B. The decline of the single has influenced the way the charts are constructed: In the United Kingdom, in 1989, the music industry reduced the number of sales required to qualify for a platinum award (from 1 million to 600,000) to assist the promotional system, and ensure charts continued to fuel excitement and sales. In 2006, the inclusion of online sales downloads of singles reflected their increasing market share (Shuker, 2008: 40), while also making it possible to 'hijack' the chart. In Christmas 2009, a campaign on Facebook encouraged people to download Rage Against The Machine's 'Killing in the Name' (originally released back in 1992, when it made the United Kingdom top 30), to get it to the prestigious Christmas number 1 slot ahead of the X Factor winner. The success of this campaign highlighted the power of the public to influence the chart. In addition, album tracks not released a singles, but popular with downloaders, have made the charts.

The popular music charts represent a level of industry and consumer obsession with sales figures almost unique to the record industry. The charts are part of the various trade magazines (e.g. *Billboard*, *Variety*, *Music Week*), providing a key reference point for those working in sales and promotion. The record charts play a major role: 'to the fan of popular music, the charts are not merely quantifications of commodities but rather a major reference point around which their music displays itself in distinction and in relation to other forms' (Parker, 1991: 205).

The charts both reflect and shape popular music, especially through their influence on radio playlists. Historically, there has been frequent controversy over attempts to influence the charts (see **payola**), and debate still occurs over perceived attempts to manipulate them. Charts provide the music industry with valuable feedback and promotion, and help set the agenda for consumer choice. They have been an influential source of data for analyses of trends in the music industry (see **market cycles**), and the historical impact, commercially at least, of genres/performers. In addition to music magazines and the trade press, there is a market for chart listings. Only rarely, however, has the operation and significance of the charts received sustained academic attention.

See: **discography**; **payola**

Further reading:
Parker, M. (1991) 'Reading the Charts: Making Sense of the Hit Parade', *Popular Music*, 10, 2: 205–17.

CHICAGO BLUES

A very influential part of electric blues, Chicago blues developed from the late 1950s, when blacks from the south moved to urban centres such as Chicago, Memphis and New Orleans, looking for work and better lifestyle opportunities. Larger audiences in the clubs necessitated the use of greater amplification and saw the popularization of the electric guitar (Waksman, 1996) and the use of drums. Major performers included Muddy Waters, B.B. King, John Lee Hooker and Willie Dixon, who was also a prolific and successful songwriter (Dixon, 1989). Chicago Blues flourished into the 1960s, when it was influential on white rock performers, who began covering songs by the black performers.

See: **blues**; **blues rock**

Further reading: (see also the general references in the blues entry)
Cohodas, N. (2001) *Spinning Blues Into Gold. The Chess Brothers and the Legendary Chess Records*, New York: St Martins.
Dixon, W. (1989) *I Am the Blues: The Willie Dixon Story*, London: Quartet Books.
Waksman, S. (1996) *Instruments of Desire: The Electric Guitar and the Shaping of Musical Experience*, Cambridge, MA: Harvard University Press, Chapter 4.
Whiteis, D. (2006) *Chicago Blues. Portraits and Stories*, Urbana: University of Illinois Press.

Listening: Muddy Waters, *The Chess Box*, MCA Chess, 1989; B.B. King, *Live at the Regal*, MCA, 1971; John Lee Hooker, *The Healer*, Chameleon, 1989; *Chicago the Blues Today*

CLASS

Class is one of the fundamental types of social classification. The main theoretical tradition within sociology derives from the work of Marx and Weber, with an emphasis on defining classes primarily in economic terms. Subsequent theoretical debates have centred around the primacy of economic determinations of classes, compared with cultural indicators. Most contemporary classifications of class rely on employment categories, with class formation and identity variously related to educational attainment and life chances, and to patterns of cultural consumption. It is the last that has been a significant part of popular music studies.

Bourdieu observes that 'nothing more clearly affirms one's class, nothing more infallibly classifies, than tastes in music' (1986: 18). The class nature of popular music preferences is international, with class-linked taste cultures seemingly fairly fixed over time (compare Riesman, 1950, with more recent studies). The internationally evident class nature of music preferences in relation to pop and rock was documented consistently in studies through into the 1990s, with class-linked taste cultures seemingly fairly fixed over time. The relative and sometimes greater influence of gender, ethnicity, age and location as influences shaping musical tastes has also been acknowledged (Shuker, 2008: Chapter 10).

Genre studies include consideration of the class location of audiences and fans, linking this to the nature and the appeal of the genre. Wiseman-Trowse (2008: 2), for example, extensively considers the role historically played by class in popular music in the United Kingdom, through case studies of folk music, punk and hardcore, dream pop and 'Madchester', with an emphasis on 'the ways in which representations of class in British popular music are used to articulate authenticity'. He considers class to be 'a mythological concept, constructed through the musical text' in order to assure the listener of the authenticity of their tastes. More specifically, McDonald explores the ways in which Canadian progressive rock band Rush have been the voice of the suburban middle class: 'Rush's critique of suburban life – and its strategies for escape – reflected middle-class aspirations and anxieties, while its performances manifested the dialectic in prog rock between discipline and austerity, and the desire for spectacle and excess'.

See: **consumption**; **taste cultures**

Further reading:
McDonald, C. (2010) *Rush, Rock Music and the Middle Class. Dreaming in Middletown*, Bloomington, IL: Indiana University Press.
Riesman, D. (1950) 'Listening to Popular Music', *American Quarterly*, 2; republished in Frith, S. and Goodwin, A. (eds) *On Record: Rock, Pop, and the Written Word*, New York: Pantheon Books.
Wiseman-Trowse, N. (2008) *Performing Class in British Popular Music*, Basingstoke: Palgrave Macmillan.

CLASSIC BLUES

Classic blues was the first blues styles that came to the attention of a wider, white, listening public in the United States. It evolved in the 1920s, usually featuring a woman vocalist, with jazz group or piano backing, sometimes as part of a minstrel show.

The first vocal blues recording, 'Crazy Blues' by Mamie Smith, was released in 1920 by Okeh. Its huge success encouraged other record companies to sign up blues talent, and

> established something of a formula that would be used for the next few years: a female star drawn from the northern vaudeville or cabaret scene or working in a current stage show, performing a song by a male professional songwriter (who might also be her pianist, band leader, manager, or husband), accompanied by a five-to-eight piece jazz band.
>
> (*Evans, 2002: 27*)

In addition to Mamie Smith, other important figures included Alberta Hunter, Ethel Walters, and Ethel Waters. In 1923, a new wave of female singers from the southern vaudeville circuit began to record. Leading performers included Bessie Smith, Ida Cox and Ma Rainey, who gave her music the name 'blues'.

The early blues recordings by black artists were initially released in their regular popular series by labels such as Okeh, Columbia and Paramount, and the black-owned Black Swan. Although they were usually available to white buyers, the majority of purchasers were black. To better target this main market the companies by the mid-1920s established series of 'race records': blues, gospel and jazz music to be marketed almost exclusively in black communities (Evans, 2002: 27–8).

Male self-accompanied solo blues singers also began to record, most notably Blind Lemon Jefferson, in Chicago in 1926, and Lonnie Johnson in St Louis. Contributing to their success, and that of similar artists in later years, was the invention of electrical recording: 'The use of a microphone enabled records to convey a wider frequency range of sound, reducing surface noise and allowing regional accents (as well a light voices and instruments such as guitars and pianos) to be heard better' (Evans, 2002: 29).

See: **blues**

Further reading: (see also the general references in the general blues entry)

Evans, D. (2002) 'The Development of the Blues', in Moore, A. (ed.) *The Cambridge Companion to Blues and Gospel*.

Harrison, D. (1988) *Black Pearls. Blues Queens of the 1920s*, New Brunswick: Rutgers University Press.

Keil, C. (1966) *Urban Blues*, Chicago, IL: University of Chicago Press.

Mellers, W. (1986) *Angels of the Night. Popular Female Singers of Our Time*, Oxford: Blackwell.

Listening: Bessie Smith, *The Complete Recordings, vols 1 & 2*, Columbia/Legacy, 1991 (includes her first major success, 'Downhearted Blues', 1923)

CLASSIC ROCK

Classic rock refers to a canon of albums and singles, usually produced from the mid-1960s through to the late 1970s. These provided the playlist for a radio format, became a loosely defined genre, and, more recently, a general marketing category.

As a **radio** format, classic rock has its origins in progressive rock radio in the mid-1960s. DJs began playing tracks from albums such as The Beatles *Sergeant Pepper's Lonely Hearts Club Band* (1967) which had not had any singles released from them. A subsequent variant of this practice was album-oriented rock (AOR), which emerged in the mid-1970s, and which evolved into 'classic rock' on many of the new FM radio stations, a format that included singles along with album tracks (Barnes, 1988). The first station to call itself 'classic rock' was WYSP in Philadelphia, in January 1981, and the format became firmly established over the next few years. Some radio stations used the related term 'classic hits', mixing the classic rock playlist with hits from pop and R&B, and drawing on both historical and contemporary material. Classic rock radio became prominent in part because of the consumer power of the ageing post-war 'baby boomers', and the appeal of this group to radio advertisers. The format continues to concentrate on playing 'tried and proven' past chart hits which will have high listener recognition and identification. Its play-lists are largely drawn from the Beatles to the end of the 1970s, and emphasize white male rock performers (see Thompson, 2008).

Ideologically, 'classic rock' serves to confirm the dominant status of a particular period of music history – the emergence of rock in the mid-1960s – with its associated values and set of practices: live performance, self-expression, and authenticity; the group as the creative unit, with the charismatic lead singer playing a key role, and the lead guitar as the primary instrument. This was a version of Romanticism, with its origins in art and aesthetics. It incorporated particular notions of authenticity, valourized by first-generation rock critics such as Robert Christgau, Dave Marsh and Lester Bangs (see **music press**). Dave Thompson celebrates the affective qualities of the loosely defined genre, which he sees as rooted in the period 1968–76:

> A classic rock classic needs substance and soul before it can attain that standing. It could be a bluesy belter, a progressive charmer, a metal monster, a hard rock cruncher. It can be anything it wants to be. But, from the instant the first downstroke richochets into earshot, to the second when the final notes echo of your brainspan, the song must stand not only as a magic carpet ride for the listener's soul, but also a sonic record of a singular moment, firmly cemented in time and place.
>
> (2008: 11)

Classic rock depends heavily on British hard rock and progressive rock bands; notably, The Rolling Stones, The Who, Pink Floyd, Led Zeppelin and Cream. American artists who are staples of classic rock include Jimi Hendrix, The Doors, Creedence Clearwater Revival, Lynyrd Skynrd and Fleetword Mac. However, these artists represent only a selection of the music of the 1960s and 1970s. Some commercially successful rock acts, such as Kiss and Grand Funk Railroad, receive only limited airplay on classic rock radio. There are also examples of commercially successful styles that coexisted with rock during the period, such as soul, funk and Motown, and performers such as Sly and the Family Stone and James Brown are noticeably absent. The reasons for such absences warrant further investigation.

In addition to its presence on radio, classic rock continues to be celebrated and consolidated through the music press, documentary (the *Classic Albums* series) and feature film, re-releases, and its prominence in 'rock museums' (see **heritage**). A dedicated magazine, *Classic Rock*, began in the United Kingdom in late 1998, with the first issue featuring rock band Guns N'Roses. Recent issues of the now well-established magazine illustrate its commitment to the tradition, with covers of Keith Richards, Lynyrd Skynrd, Metallica, AC/DC and Rush. Other UK- and US-based music magazines also show a strong commitment to classic rock, notably *MOJO*, *UNCUT* and *Rolling Stone*. A 2004 MOJO Special Limited Edition, *The Greatest Classic Rock Albums Ever!* Maintaining the selective tradition of music by white male groups, it features largely post-1980 albums, from AC/DC; Queen; Led Zeppelin; Van Halen, Metallica, Aerosmith, Guns N'Roses and Ozzy Osbourne. Illustrating the music's perceived timelessness, and essential appeal to post-war baby boomers, the issue is subtitled: 'The Music That *Still* Rocks Your World'.

See: **canon**; **rock**

Further reading:
Barnes, K. (1988) 'Top 40 Radio: A Fragment of the Imagination', in Frith, S. (ed.) *Facing the Music*, New York: Pantheon Books.
Classic Rock Magazine, Future Publishing, Bath, UK. www.classicrockmagazine.com
MOJO (2004) Special Limited Edition, *The Greatest Classic Rock Albums Ever!*
Thompson, D. (2008) *I Hate New Music. The Classic Rock Manifesto*, New York: Backbeat Books. Includes appendix: 'The Top 100 Classic Rock Songs, 1968–1976'.

CLUBS; CLUB CULTURE

Clubs emerged historically as venues where people met regularly to pursue shared interests, usually paying a membership fee. During the early 1900s, clubs became major venues for live music on a regular and continuing basis, often associated with particular genres (e.g. jazz, blues). They have continued to serve as training grounds for aspiring performers operating at the local level, and provide a 'bread and butter' living for more established artists, often through being part of an organized circuit of venues (as with British folk clubs in the 1960s). They are also social spaces: 'At their best, clubs are places where the marginalized can feel at home, where we can experiment with new identities, new ways of being. They are places where cultures collide' (Garrett, 1998: 321).

Clubs have historically assumed mythic importance for breaking new acts, and can also establish and popularize trends. English punk at London's 100 Club and the Roxy in the late 1970s. A community network of clubs or pub venues can help create a local club **scene**, at times based around a particular sound. Several historical examples of this have been the subject of various biographical recollections, journalistic accounts and academic studies. These include **Merseybeat** in Liverpool in the 1960s; Greenwich Village (New York) and **folk** music in the early 1960s; and **folk rock singer songwriters** in LA in the period 1967–83 (on each, see their related entries). While the cohesion of their 'common' musical signatures is frequently exaggerated, such localized developments provide marketing possibilities by providing a 'brand name' which the local clubbers, and fans more widely, can identify with.

In the 1970s, club venues were important for popularizing disco, and for subsequently establishing the various forms of **electronic dance music**. The cult of the **DJ** became a central part of these club scenes, a star figure whose skill is to judge the mood on the dance floor, both reflecting and leading it, all the while blending tracks into a seamless whole.

Dance clubs have historically been important to growing up, especially in Britain, where young people have traditionally not been as mobile than their American counterparts. **Club culture** is

> the colloquial expression given to youth cultures for whom dance clubs and their eighties offshoots, raves, are the symbolic axis and working social hub. The sense of place afforded by these events is such that regular attendees take on the name of the spaces they frequent, becoming 'clubers' and 'ravers'.
>
> (*Thornton, 1996: 3*)

Club cultures are associated with specific locations which continually present and modify sounds and styles,

> regularly bearing witness to the apogees and excesses of youth subcultures. Club cultures are **taste cultures**. Club crowds generally congregate on the basis of their shared taste in music, their consumption of common media, and, most importantly, their preference for people with similar tastes to themselves. Crucially, club cultures embrace their own hierarchies of what is authentic and legitimate in popular culture.
>
> (*Ibid.*)

The explosion of dance music in the 1990s saw a number of academic and popular studies of the new phenomenon and its associated club culture (see **dance music**). These often drew on their authors' status as participants in such scenes, mixing ethnographic method and social theory.

See: **DJ**; **EDM**; **rave**

Further reading: (see also the references in **rave** culture)
Garrett, S. (1998) *Adventures in Wonderland: A Decade of Club Culture*, London: Headline.
Thornton, S. (1996) *Club Culture: Media, Music and Subcultural Capital*, London: Polity Press.

COLLECTING; RECORD COLLECTING

As Clifford observes, 'collecting has long been the strategy for the deployment of a possessive self, culture, and authenticity' (Clifford, 1988: 218). Historical studies show the development of a collecting sensibility, linked to possessive individualism, historically present since the Greeks, but more fully realized under contemporary capitalism. Today, 'the gathering together of chosen objects for purposes regarded as special is of great importance, as a social phenomenon, as a focus of personal emotion, and as an economic force' (Pearce, 1995: Preface). The now extensive literature on collecting embraces a now fairly standard set of motifs and an associated vocabulary. Collectors and the collecting process are variously associated with longing, desire and pleasure; ritualistic, near-sacred and repetitive acquisition; passionate and selective consumption; stewardship and cultural preservation and obsession and linked pathologies such as completism, accumulation and a preoccupation with collection size. Collectibles can be of almost infinite type, but are usually regarded as 'things removed from ordinary use and perceived as part of a set of non-identical objects or experiences' (Belk, 2001: 67), thereby placing a premium on their intrinsic value. The collection exhibits a series of attributes: it is a source of pleasure, an economic investment; an exhibition of logic, unity and control; an indicator of cultural and social capital and a socially sanctioned form of materialist and competitive consumption, consumer culture taken to excess.

Collecting in relation to music includes the collection of musical instruments and printed scores, both prominent since the seventeenth century. Material was largely acquired through dealers and at auction, and historical studies have used their lists and catalogues to reconstruct particular collectors and their collections (see King, 1963; Coover, 1988; Song collecting, especially in the nineteenth century, with its emphasis on cultural preservation, was a major part of studies of various forms of folk music, and has been considered separately. Here, I focus on two more contemporary dimensions of collecting in relation to popular music: song collecting, especially in the late nineteenth century; 'record collecting' evident since the 1900s; and the collecting of memorabilia, which has become increasingly prominent since the 1980s.

In each of these various types of music collecting, individual collectors have historically been linked to institutional collections: they have frequently provided the basis for these through donations (including bequests), through lending material for display, and, at times, have been directly involved in the development of exhibitions and the acquisition of material for them (Blecha, 2005).

Record collecting: 'Record collecting' can be considered shorthand for a variety of distinct but related practices. Foremost is the collection of sound recordings, in various formats, by individuals. Such recordings include various official releases, in a variety of **formats**; bootleg recordings (largely of concerts); radio broadcasts, and sound with visuals – the music video or DVD. Individual collecting also frequently includes the collection of related literature (music books and magazines) and music memorabilia (e.g. concert tickets and programmes, tour posters). There is also the record collecting undertaken by institutions, which frequently includes sheet music and other printed music literature, in addition to recordings, musical instruments and popular music ephemera (see **heritage**).

There is a central distinction between (simply) liking the music – in the sense of a fan or music lover – and methodically seeking out and acquiring it. Consequently, possessing an abundance of records is a necessary but not sufficient condition for the self-recognition of a 'collector'. The central factor is the systematic approach to acquiring new material for the collection, a characteristic commonly seen as distinguishing collecting: 'In the collecting form of consumption, acquisition is a key process. Someone who possesses a collection is not necessarily a collector unless they continue to acquire additional things for the collection' (Belk, 1996: 66). While fans will collect records, record collectors are more often characterized by what can be termed 'secondary involvement' in music, activities beyond 'simply' listening to the music: the seeking out of rare releases, such as the picture discs and bootlegs; the reading of fanzines and specialized discographies in addition to the commercial music press; and an interest in record labels and producers as well as performers.

Pearce distinguishes three coexisting modes of the relationship of collectors to the collected object: souvenir, fetishistic and systematic. In souvenir collecting, 'the individual creates a romantic life-history by selecting and arranging personal memorial material to create what ... might be called an object autobiography, where the objects are at the service of the autobiographer'. In contrast, in fetishistic collecting 'the objects are dominant and ... are allowed to create the self of the collector, who responds by obsessively collecting as many items as possible'. Third, systematic collecting is characterized by an 'intellectual rationale', with the emphasis placed on the completeness of the collection (Pearce, 1995: 32). She stresses that the three approaches are not exclusive, and can coexist in each collection. Each of these collecting modes are represented among record collectors, broadly corresponding to varying emphases: on recordings as part of identity formation and life history (souvenir collecting); accumulation and completism (fetishistic collecting) and discrimination and connoisseurship (systematic collecting).

During the mid- to late nineteenth century, a mix of capitalism and consumerism, increased leisure time and disposable income, and nostalgia, made collecting a significant aspect of the social identity for the new middle classes of Europe, Britain and its colonies and the United States. Record collecting as a social practice was a logical extension of such activities.

Sound became 'a thing', a material product for sale in the market, at the end of the nineteenth century (see **sound**). Its subsequent reproduction as a cultural and economic artefact produced the 'sound recording' in its various historical formats, along with related technology, memorabilia and literature.

Record collectors through to the advent of vinyl in the 1950s, collected 78s and, in some cases, early cylinders as well. This group established 'record collecting' with a distinctive set of practices and a related literature. These early collectors were associated with the emergence of what can be termed a **gramophone culture**, which embraced a number of *sites*: physical and social spaces, and institutions that facilitated and shaped the production and consumption of recorded music. These included the early recording companies; record clubs and appreciation societies; music retail and the second-hand market and the music press. By the introduction of vinyl records in the 1950s, record collecting was already a well-established 'hobby'.

The history of record collecting since the 1960s is one of the steady expansion of the overarching infrastructure within which the hobby was already embedded: the rise of record fairs, specialist record shops, increased major label interest in reissues and their back catalogue, specialist reissue labels, and a collector press. This has been well-documented in the United Kingdom and the United States, while such developments are also evident internationally. Today, record collecting is a major form of collecting, with its own set of collecting practices. It includes an associated literature (the music press generally, but especially the specialist collector magazines, fanzines, discographies and general guidebooks); the recording industry targeting of collectors (reissue labels; promotional releases, remixes, boxed sets) and dedicated sites of acquisition (record fairs, second-hand and specialist shops, eBay and high-profile auctions).

There are a number of studies of record collectors and record collecting (see Shuker, 2010). In addition to the academic literature and popular journalism, the representation of record collectors and collecting in various popular culture texts has been important in establishing a stereotypical view. Popular discourse around record collectors and collecting, in common with discussions of collecting generally, construct a dominant representation of record collectors as obsessive males, whose passion for collecting is often a substitute for 'real' social relationships, and who exhibit a 'train spotting' mentality toward popular music, a concern with the details of recordings. This is very much the case in the best-known representation of record collectors, the novel *High Fidelity* (Hornby, 1995), and the subsequent film of the same name released in 2000. Both book and film portray record collectors as obsessive males, whose passion for collecting is often a substitute for 'real' social relationships, and who exhibit a 'train spotting' mentality towards popular music. This image of the record collector as anti- or asocial has been reinforced by the manner in which the phenomenon is treated in other popular texts, including the film *Ghost World*, and the cartoons by Robert Crumb and Harvey Pekar featuring record collectors.

While this image has much in common with some academic discussions of collectors and collecting, it represents only a partial account of record collectors. A detailed study of self-identified record collectors (Shuker, 2010) showed them to have considerable awareness of the 'High Fidelity' stereotype, along with a concern to distance personal practice from this. They displayed a range of characteristics associated with the label 'record collector', while demonstrating that the concept is far from a unitary one. This complex mix included a love of music; obsessive–compulsive behaviour, accumulation and completism, selectivity and discrimination and self-education and scholarship. In sum, as a social practice, record collecting presents itself as a core component of individual social identity and a central part of the life cycle.

See: **memorabilia**; **song collecting**

Further reading:
Goldmine magazine (US).
Record Collector magazine (UK).
Coover, J., compiler (1988) *Antiquarian Catalogues of Musical Interest*, London: Mansell Publishing.
King, A.L. (1963) *Some British Collectors of Music*, c. *1600–1960*, Cambridge: CUP.
Shuker, R. (2010) *Wax Trash and Vinyl Treasure: Record Collecting as Social Practice*, Aldershot: Ashgate.

Viewing: High Fidelity (2000) Feature film; director Stephen Frears; *Vinyl* (2000) Documentary; director Alan Zweig

COMMERCIALISM; COMMODIFICATION

Commercialism is the general influence of business principles and practices upon social life, including leisure activities. A central part of the process of commercialization is the commodification of cultural commodities and symbolic goods; that is, their production as material commodities for a market, consumer economy. The **Frankfurt School** theorists stressed the commodification of popular cultural forms under the conditions of capitalist production and the constant quest for profit.

While historically always present, both processes were given increased prominence with urbanization, industrialization and the rise of consumer society in the nineteenth century; along with the creation of global markets. With increased and more differentiated consumer demand, individual social identity became more closely identified with the consumption (and display) of goods. Associated with these developments, was the rise of advertising as part of increasingly sophisticated marketing techniques and the significance of brand names (Fowles, 1996: Chapter 1). These concepts have been at the heart of the ongoing debate over the nature and influence of mass culture.

There are aspects of popular music as a commodity form which distinguish it from other cultural texts, notably its reproducibility, its ubiquity of formats and its multiple modes of dissemination. While creating and promoting new music (the industry term is 'product') is usually expensive, actually reproducing it is not. Popular music has been increasingly commodified, recorded and reproduced in various formats – vinyl, audio tape, CD, DAT and video – and variations within these: the dance mix, the cassette single, the limited collector's edition and so on. These are disseminated in a variety of ways – through radio airplay, discos and dance clubs, television music video shows and MTV-style channels and live performances. In addition, there is the memorabilia available to the fan, especially the posters and the T-shirts; the use of popular music within film soundtracks and television advertising; and the ubiquity of 'muzak'. The range of these commodities enables a multi-media approach to the marketing of the music, and a maximization of sales potential, as exposure in each of the various forms strengthens the appeal of the others.

The capitalist music industry historically has been central to the process of making and marketing recorded music, and remains a major part of it, despite the impact of digital music culture. There is a spectrum of aesthetic experience and material practices that ranges across the artistic to the commercial in all musical genres, including the classical. Early practices, such as the eighteenth-century patronage of composers, the commissioning of work and the advent of public (but paying) concerts, show that Western classical music was hardly immune from commercial influences and constraints. In the nineteenth century, the sale of home pianos, sheet music and the phonograph further demonstrated the considerable commercial potential of popular music. Commodification was accelerated with the advent of recorded sound in the late nineteenth century, and the subsequent rise of record companies, licencing and copyright legislation and the establishment of associations of composers and musicians (Chanan, 1995). An instructive historical example of how the means of sound reproduction are a significant part of the commodification of music is Farrell's account of the early days of the gramophone in India (Farrell, 1998).

Commodification has been used in recent popular music studies to critically analyse the relationship between the music industry, the market, and music making. The term became largely used in a negative sense, in critiques of the aggressive and calculated marketing of popular music trends, as with the British 'New Pop' performers of the early 1980s, associated with the rise of music video and MTV (see **New Romantics**). New musical genres are frequently seen to begin with Romantic overtones (essentially valuing creative over commercial considerations), but are soon commodified. There is a familiar historical litany here, moving through rock'n'roll in the 1950s, soul in the 1960s, reggae and punk in the 1970s, rap in the 1980s and alternative in the 1990s, with a considerable discourse around the extent and cultural significance of episodes (see **political economy**).

See: **gramophone culture**

Further reading:
Farrell, G. (1998) 'The Early Days of the Gramophone Industry in India', in Leyshon, A., Matless, D. and Revill, G. (eds) *The Place of Music*, New York: The Guildford Press, pp. 57–82.

Fowles, J. (1996) *Advertising and Popular Culture*, Thousand Oaks, CA: Sage.
Hesmondhalgh, D. (2007) *The Cultural Industries*, 2nd edition, London: Sage.

COMMUNICATION

Communication is (i) the conveying of information from A to B, with effect (Lasswell's classic flow model); and (ii) the negotiation and exchange of meaning. Music is a fundamental form of human communication, along with many other animal species, humans use organized sound to communicate. We are musically 'wired' at birth; infants respond to intonation and at 6 months of age are able to recognize musical structures and identify 'wrong' notes. There has been a good deal of experimental, laboratory research on the manner in which the brain handles such processes (see **psychology**).

'Music is a passionate sequencing of thoughts and feelings that expresses meaning in a manner that has no parallel in human life' (Lull, 1992: 1). That music produces 'sense' and conveys meanings is clear and unquestionable. What needs to be considered are 'the attributes of the processes governing *musical* meaning' (Middleton, 1990: 172), and how these operate in particular contexts. This requires an examination of: (1) the communicative role of musicians, who communicate – 'speak' – directly to individual listeners and to particular audience constituencies, often through particular genres; in addition to doing this through recordings, musicians interact with their audiences through live performances, with practices such as the 'banter' between songs. (2) The communicative role of the music; for example, the conveying of implicit political messages ('protest song') and, often at a more implicit level, ideologies of romance, personal and social identity and so forth. (3) The communicative role of the means by which the music is transferred to its audiences, and the influence of these 'communicative vehicles' (Negus, 1996: 169), which are far from neutral (see **technology**). (4) The ways in which music is received, listened to, interpreted and used by listeners in a wide variety of contexts.

This last dimension has been the subject of considerable analytical discussion. People and groups interact with popular music in a physical way (e.g. singing along, clapping, foot tapping, dancing, 'air guitar'); emotionally (e.g. romanticizing, letting the music 'wash over you', becoming 'lost in music'); and cognitively (e.g. stimulating thought, framing perceptions, processing information). These different modes of engagement can be in a very personal manner, through individual listening to relax or escape or distance oneself from other commitments and people, but it is the social experience of music which is more frequent. Music provides a soundtrack for daily experience; for example, studying, doing domestic chores, shopping (see **muzak**); and the stimulus to physical activities, notably dancing, but also aerobics, driving and sex. Music can operate as a companion, something to 'unwind' and relax with; its use contributes to the context and meaning of many other activities, for example, as film soundtrack, weddings and sporting events.

Music as organized sound is traditionally defined in terms of beat, harmony and melody, and, in much popular music, song lyrics. Particular popular music texts shape audience consciousness through sheer thematic repetition (hooks), and by repeated exposure via radio and music video channel playlists.

See: **listening**; **musicology**; **psychology**

Further reading:
Lull, J. ed. (1992) *Popular Music and Communication*, 2nd edition, Newbury Park, CA: Sage.

Viewing: *Music and the Mind*, documentary series, BBC, 1996

COMPILATIONS

A compilation is an album of recordings grouped together by genre, performers, period, location (scenes/sounds), chart status or recording label. The more ambitious or comprehensive will be marketed as box sets.

The function of compilations is usually to create publicity and create revenue, but they can become important historical documents and collectibles. Compilations have been important for documenting the initial emergence of scenes and sounds, as with those featuring live punk recordings from CBGB's in New York (*c.* 1974), Max's in Kansas City and The Roxy in London (January–April 1977).

Record companies have used compilations, usually termed 'samplers', to showcase new styles/artists and profile their catalogue. This has been a marketing strategy used by major labels to popularize new sounds (an early example is CBS, 'The Rock Machine Turns You On', 1968, and, more commonly by independents seeking to establish a market presence (for instance, Island Records, 'You Can All Join In', 1979).

Tribute albums can also be considered a form of compilation, as can benefit albums, and 'greatest hits'. The last present an important revenue stream for record labels, as they reposition and repackage established (sometimes dead) performers without significant recording costs. Adding additional 'rare' or previously unreleased tracks, and the remastering of the material, adds cachet to such recordings. The best-known compilations are those series packaging chart hits, notably 'NOW' and 'That's What I Call Music'.

See: **back catalogue**; **box set**

CONCERT

Popular music concerts are complex social phenomena, involving a mix of music and economics, ritual and pleasure, for both performers and audiences. Concerts assert and celebrate the values of the music, endorse performers and provide solidarity in a community of companionship (see Sardiello, on the Grateful Dead's concerts and their fans). There is a tension between concerts as exemplifying a sense of community, albeit a transient one, and their economic and promotional importance.

Concerts are a ritual for both performers and their audience. Symphony orchestra concerts celebrating 'the power holding class in our society' (Small, 1987); popular music concerts frequently celebrate youth, not purely as a demographic group, but the *idea of* youth. The behaviour of concert goers depends on the performer(s) and their associated musical style(s); for example, audiences at rock and heavy metal concerts are considerably more outgoing and demonstrative, consistent with the essential physicality of the music. Musicians themselves conform to ritual forms of behaviour in performance, with particular performance styles and images associated with specific genres. For example, the typical 'rock' stage performance is heavily theatrical and physically energetic, especially in the case of the lead singer and lead guitarist.

See: **live (music)**; **performance**; **tour**

Further reading:
Small, C. (1987) 'Performance as Ritual', in White, A. (ed.) *Lost in Music. Culture, Style and the Musical Event*, London: Routledge.
Sardiello, R. (1994) 'Secular Rituals in Popular Culture: A Case for Grateful Dead Concerts and Dead Head Identity', in Epstein, J.S. (ed.) *Adolescents and Their Music: If It's Too Loud, You're Too Old*, New York: Garland Publishing.

CONSUMER SOVEREIGNTY

The view that consumers/audiences exercise of their 'free' choice in the market place is a major determinant of the nature and availability of particular cultural and (economic) commodities. Consumer sovereignty emphasizes the operation of human agency: while the elements of romance and imagination that have informed individual personal histories and the history of popular musical genres are frequently marginalized in the commodification process, they remain essential to the narratives people construct to help create a sense of identity. In some early approaches to cultural studies, consumer sovereignty was tied to the notion of the active audience, to produce a debated view of semiotic democracy (see Fiske, 1989; Hesmondhalgh, 2002).

An emphasis on consumer sovereignty as the primary factor whereby social meaning is created in music is in contrast to the view that the process of consumption is constrained by the processes of production: production determines consumption (see **political economy**). Yet production and consumption are not to be regarded as fixed immutable processes, and are engaged in a dialectic. While economic power does have a residual base in institutional structures and practices; in this case, the record companies and their drive for market stability, predictability and profit, this power is mediated and never absolute.

See: **audiences**; **fans**

Further reading:
Fiske, J. (1989) *Understanding Popular Culture*, Boston: Unwin Hyman.

CONSUMPTION

The study of the consumption of economic and cultural goods has paid particular attention to the patterns and of such consumption and the processes whereby it occurs. Popular music consumption embraces a wide variety of social practices (the more significant are treated separately); these include record collecting; attending live performances; clubbing, watching music videos/YouTube; listening to the radio, making tape compilations (home taping) and downloading from the Internet. The discussion here briefly covers patterns and processes evident in the consumption of popular music (for a detailed overview, see Shuker, 2008: Chapter 10; for a general discussion of the concept of consumers, and its relationship to audience studies, see **audience**).

Patterns of consumption

Profiles of music consumption show a clear pattern of age and gender-based genre preferences (see, e.g., the annual data provided on the RIAA website). Ethnicity is more important in relation to genres such as rap and reggae, which serve as carriers of ideology, creating symbols for listeners to identify with. Historically, the main consumers of popular music, especially post-1950 genres of rock and pop music, have been young people, between 12–25. At the same time, adult tastes are very significant, with the ageing of rock's original audience underpinning the market for classic rock and reissues. Older listeners also tend to be more invested in genres such as world music, blues and jazz (see **demography**). The tastes of the older consumer are now being paid more attention by researchers.

Modes of consumption

Studies of the process and nature of music consumption have used qualitative methodologies to examine the consumption practices of individual record buyers, those downloading, concert goers, radio listeners and music video and YouTube viewers. These reveal a complex set of influences upon the construction of individual popular music consumption. Even younger adolescent consumers, who are often regarded as relatively undiscriminating and easily swayed by the influence of market forces (see **teenyboppers**), see their preferences as far from straightforward, with the views of their friends' paramount.

Both patterns and modes have consumption have been a major part of a trend towards studies of music in 'everyday life' (DeNora, 2000).

See: **cassette culture**; **P2P**; **record collecting**

Further reading:
Crafts, S.D., Cavicchi, D., Keil, C. and the Music in Daily Life Project (1993) *My Music*, Hanover: Wesleyan University Press.
DeNora, T. (2000) *Music in Everyday Life*, Cambridge: Cambridge University Press.

COPYRIGHT

Copyright is central to the music industry. The basic principle of copyright law is the exclusive right to copy and publish one's own work. That is, the copyright owner has the right to duplicate or authorize the duplication of their property, and to distribute it. The full legal nature of copyright is beyond our scope here, its significance for popular music studies lies in its cultural importance. Copyright is closely linked to the historical evolution of property rights, and arguments about scarcity, value and intellectual effort. The development of new technologies of sound recording and reproduction raise issues of intellectual property rights, copyright and the control of sounds.

In addition to deriving income from unit sales of records, record companies, performers, songwriters and music publishers derive income from the sale of rights. Ownership of rights is determined by copyright in the master tape, the original tape embodying the recorded performance from which subsequent records are manufactured. This rights income includes: (i) mechanical income: payable by record companies (to the owner of the copyright) for permission to reproduce a song on record; this is a fixed percentage of the recommended retail price; (ii) performance income: a licence fee paid by venues, TV and radio stations for the right to publicly perform or broadcast songs and (iii) miscellaneous income: payment for the use of songs in films, adverts and so on (see Hull, Hutchinson, and Strasser, 2010, Chapters 3–5). Rights income is collected by various local and regional agencies, such as the Australasian Mechanical Copyright Owners Society (AMCOS) and the Australasian Performing Rights Association (APRA).

The first US copyright statute was enacted in 1909, and protected the owners of musical compositions from unauthorized copying (**piracy**), while making a song into a commodity product that could be brought and sold in the market place. With copyright protection, sheet-music writer-publishers could afford to spend a great deal of money promoting a new song because other printers could not pirate the valuable properties thus created. Their activity fostered musical innovation, most notably in ragtime and jazz. Similar legislation was enacted in Britain in 1911. The development of recording raised the question of whether the publishers of recorded and sheet music could claim the same rights as literary publishers. British and American legislation differed on this, with the former being more restrictive in its approach.

Copyright laws provided no mechanism for collecting the royalties from the public performance of music. In 1914, the American Society of Composers, Authors and Publishers (ASCAP) was formed, to issue licences and to collect all due royalties from three sources: the performance of songs, with recording artists receiving income based on the revenue made from the sale of their records; the sale of original music to publishers, and subsequent performance royalties and money paid to the publishers for their share of the sales and performances, usually split

50–50 between composers and publishers. ASCAP's role was confirmed by a Supreme Court decision in 1917 validating the organization's right to issue membership licences and collect performance royalties. However, broadcasters resisted all ASCAP's attempts to collect royalties for music played on the radio, and went so far as to create their own organization to break what they claimed were ASCAP's monopolistic tactics, establishing Broadcast Music Inc. (BMI) in 1939.

The Rome Convention and the Berne Convention are the major international agreements on copyright. The International Federation of the Phonographic Industries (IFPI) globally regulates the application and enforcement of copyright (not always successfully – see **piracy**). However, attempts to ensure international uniformity in copyright laws have met only with partial success; even within the European community conventions and practices vary considerably. Attitudes towards copyright diverge depending whose interests are involved. The 1990s saw an emerging hostility towards copyright among many music consumers and even some musicians, due to its regulatory use by international corporations to protect their interests. On the other hand, the companies themselves are actively seeking to harmonize arrangements and curb piracy, while the record industry associations (especially the IFPI), which are almost exclusively concerned with copyright issues, largely support the industry line. Ultimately, it is market control which is at stake. There is a basic tension between protecting the rights and income of the original artists, and the restriction of musical output.

Different State governments have demonstrated a range of responses to the development of copyright, depending on the nature of interest groups that make up the local performing rights societies, and national concerns about the potential exploitation of local music, the outflow of funds to overseas copyright holders, and the stifling of local performers' ability to utilize international material (see the national examples in Frith, 1993; Frith and Marshall, 2004).

During the 1990s, the advent of new technologies of sound recording and reproduction have coincided with the globalization of culture, and the desire of the entertainment conglomerates to maximize their revenues from 'rights' as well as continuing income from the actual sale of records. What counts as 'music' was changing from a fixed, authored 'thing' which existed as property, to something more difficult to identify. The legal and moral arguments surrounding the **sampling** used in records by the JAMS, M/A/R/R/S, De La Soul and others showed the issues involved to be extremely complex. They coalesced around the questions of what is actually 'copyrightable' in music? Who has the right to control the use of a song, a record or a sound? And what is the nature of the public domain?

The music industry's historical concern with threats to copyright has been exacerbated in the past decade, notably in the debate surrounding sampling and practices such as Internet downloading. Articles and exchanges have proliferated around the impact of new technologies and the Internet upon the nature and operation of copyright in an era of new technologies (see **Internet**).

See: **bootlegs**; **MP3**; **piracy**; **sampling**

Further reading:

Frith, S. ed. (1993) *Music and Copyright*, Edinburgh: Edinburgh University Press.
Frith, S. and Marshall, L. eds (2004) *Music and Copyright*, 2nd edition, Edinburgh: Edinburgh University Press.
Strasser, R. (2010) *Music Business. The Key Concepts*, London: Routledge (copyright and related entries on agencies involved).

COUNTER-CULTURE

Indicating a loose, expressive social movement, the term 'counter-culture' was initially applied to groups such as the beats in the 1950s, and subsequently to the largely middle-class **subcultures** of the mid- to late 1960s. The 1960s counter-culture was most evident in North American communal and anti-conformist lifestyles, but it quickly became an international phenomenon. It was strongly present in the United Kingdom, where it was more commonly referred to as the underground (for an entertaining insiders account, see Farren, 2002). Both terms continue to be applied to various groups/subcultures outside of, and at times in opposition to, the social and economic mainstream (see **scenes**).

The counter-culture had its origins in the beats (or beatniks) of the 1950s. The beats developed in post-war Paris, on the student area the Left Bank, influenced by the French bohemian artistic intelligentsia. Strongly centred around existentialist values: the futility of action and a nihilism about social change, the beats also took on board Eastern mysticism, jazz, poetry, drugs (primarily marijuana) and literature. Popularized by writers such as Kerouac and Ginsburg, the movement spread across America in the early 1960s, centred initially on Greenwich Village in New York. The beats had a romantic, anarchic vision, with individualism a major theme, and were highly antagonistic to middle-class lifestyles and careers. They were influential on the values of the later counter–culture and Generation X, and helped bring jazz, especially its more modern forms such as bebop, to wider attention.

In the 1960s, the term counter-culture was used by social theorists, such as Roszak and Marcuse, as an integrative label for the various groups and ideologies present in the American movement. The counter-culture was seen as a generational unit, the 'youth culture' challenging traditional concepts of career, education and morality, and seeking an identity outside of occupational role or family. The 1960s counter-culture/underground embraced a range of groups and lifestyles, who broadly shared values of drug use, freedom and a broadly anti-middle-class stance. In the United States, elements of the counter-culture were sympathetic to New Left politics (Students for a Democratic Society), and embraced some political concerns, especially community activism in relation to health, education, and the environment. While this led some observers to see youth as a generationally political progressive group, at heart the movement represented a form of symbolic, cultural politics (exemplified by the hippies). The counter-culture embodied a series of contradictions; for example, it developed at a time of relative economic prosperity, enabling the economy to carry substantial numbers of voluntarily unemployed people living on subsistence incomes, who were antagonistic to the 'mainstream' economy and society.

A significant part of the counter-culture, the hippies, initially centred on San Franciso's Haight Ashbury district, came into international prominence during 1966–67. 'Soft' drug use (cannabis, LSD), long hair, communes, peace, love-ins/free love, flowers and psychedelic/acid rock were all aspects picked up on by the press. Hippies represented a form of cultural politics, ostensibly rejecting 'mainstream' society and values, but with clear contradictions present. They were generally from comfortable middle-class backgrounds, but the material affluence of the Western economies during the 1960s made their opting out possible; they were anti-technology but often possessed impressive sound systems; and their espoused 'freedom' at times sat uneasily alongside sexism and gender stereotyping.

Musically, the counter-culture was linked to the genres of progressive and psychedelic rock. The hippies' preference for psychedelic rock was consistent with the other values of the subculture, especially its 'laid back' orientation and drug use. Counter-culture 'radical' youth, mainly college/university students, were part of the US Civil Rights movement, with its use of political folk songs and negro spirituals, and supported the Campaign for Nuclear Disarmament in the United Kingdom, which drew on similar sources, along with trad. jazz during its marches in the late 1950s. These genres were soon subject to **commodification**, with sincerity becoming highly marketable during the mid-1960s.

The counter-culture persisted into the 1980s and onwards, though arguably more in terms of the encapsulation of its values in the private lives of the baby boomer generation. Along with the notion of an underground, it remains evident in various alternative scenes and subcultures, notably those associated with indie rock.

See: **progressive rock**; **psychedelic rock**

Further reading:
Dogget, P. (2010) *There's a Riot Going On. Revolutionaries, Rock Stars & the Rise & Fall of 60s Counter Culture*, London: Canongate.
Farren, M. (2002) *Give the Antichrist a Cigarette*, London: Pimlico.
Reich, C.A. (1970) *The Greening of America*, New York: Penguin.

COUNTRY

Country music is an American metagenre now internationally popular; it has been variously known in the past as folk music, old-time music, hillbilly, C&W/country & Western. According to its most prominent historian, Bill Malone (1985: 1), 'it defies precise definition, and no term (not even "country") has ever successfully encapsulated its essence'. Country evolved into primarily an American form, with a number of identifiable styles and international versions of these.

As an identifiable genre, country can be traced back to the American rural south in the 1920s; and the independent label Okey issued the first 'country' catalogue in 1924. Prior to 1939, the music was variously termed hillbilly, country or old-time; it was, according to Lange, 'essentially a folk art form' and 'country music performers directed their product at a predominantly rural regional audience of working class southerners' (2004: 3). Histories of country music stress its subsequent shift from a narrow base (Southern, rural, white, working class) to a broader appeal, a struggle for respectability within mainstream popular music markets in the United States. A key moment/turning point occurred in 1939, when the Grand Ole Opry received network status, going on to become country music's most prominent radio show. Later, the role of the Country Music Association, the industries primary trade body, was crucial in consolidating a respectable identity for country, moving it away from traditional 'hillbilly' associations (Pecknold, 2007).

Following Lang (2004), several major developments can be identified in country music from 1939 through to the mid-1950s: (1) Reflecting modifications in audience tastes and changes in Southern society brought about by the Second World War, country music became more sophisticated; musical styles altered with the expansion of the audience in urban and non-southern areas. (2) Country music styles combined with one another and with American popular music, and, subsequently, alternative subgenres emphasizing country music's southernness emerged; and (3) Nashville was established as the hub of country music. 'The sum of these developments was the modernization of country music: a reflection of sociocultural changes in southern society and of the genre's transformation from regional particularity to national acceptance' (Lange, 2004: 4).

Since the mid-1950s, country music has consolidated its market; it has maintained established, more traditional genres, along with the emergence of new genres. Through their ability to **crossover** into the mainstream pop/rock market, country artists such as Garth Brooks and Shania Twain have been among the highest selling performers of the past 20 years.

As a metagenre, country music contains a number of identifiable subgenres and related styles, although these often overlap and performers may move between and across them. These include traditional old-time country (sometimes referred to as 'hillbilly' music), Western Swing, bluegrass, Outlaw country and new country. This is hardly an exclusive list (see *All Music Guide* and Escott, for a fuller consideration of the many genres and styles included under 'country'). Country is also a significant part of genres such as rockabilly, cajun and country blues. I have included separate entries on three key country genres: **old-time country**, **bluegrass**, and **new country**; along with two hybrid styles which have had a considerable impact on commercial popular music: **country rock**, and **alt. country**.

Further reading:
The literature on country music is huge, and the following are simply some suggested starting points, along with several recent detailed academic histories.
Erlewhine, M., Bogdanov, V., Woodstra, C. and Erlewhine, S. eds (2003) *All Music Guide to Country*, 2nd edition, San Franciso: Miller Freeman.
Escott, C. (2003) *The Story of Country Music*, London: BBC.
    This concise but comprehensive and well-illustrated history accompanies the TV series, *Lost Highway* (see below), which it can be read in conjunction with. Escott includes a section, 'Lifelines', which provides brief performer biographies, and offers suggestions for further reading and listening.
Lange, J. (2004) *Smile When You Call Me a Hillbilly. Country Music's Struggle for Respectability, 1939-1954*, Athens and London: The University of Georgia Press.
Malone, B. (1985) *Country Music USA*, Austin, TX: University of Texas Press.

Pecknold, D. (2007) *The Selling Sound: The Rise of the Country Music Industry*, Durham, NC and London: Duke University Press. Pecknold subdivides the 1920s through to the 1970s into six periods or key transitional moments, underpinned by the gradual commercialization of the genre.

Peterson, R.A. (1997) *Creating Country Music: Fabricating Authenticity*, Chicago: University of Chicago Press.

Viewing: *Lost Highway*, documentary series (four episodes), BBC, 2003

COUNTRY ROCK

Representing an amalgam of country and rock styles, the term 'country rock' was first applied in the mid-1960s to American rock performers who looked to country music for inspiration, including the Byrds, The Flying Burrito Brothers and Gram Parsons (a short, but influential career; see Meyer, 2009). Country rock was carried into the 1970s with the Eagles, Poco, Ozark Mountain Daredevils and the Amazing Rhythm Aces, all of whom mixed country with other rock genres, and enjoyed some commercial success. Country rock combined traditional country harmonies and phrasing with a rock beat, adding instruments such as the pedal steel guitar, the dobro and mandolin to the electric guitar and bass of rock music. The most commercially successful performers were The Eagles, though their (blander?) FM radio friendly music drew criticism from more traditionally oriented country rock critics and fans.

In the 1980s and 1990s, country has been drawn on by various artists as part of a hybridization of musical styles; for example, Jason and the Scorchers, The Blasters. While primarily a male-dominated genre, some women performers enjoyed critical and commercial success with 'soft' country rock; for example, Emmylou Harris. In the 1990s, country rock became indistinguishable from much contemporary country music. The audience for country rock is under researched, but appears to be a mix of those favouring either, or both, of the parent genres. Urban listeners were arguably drawn to country rock's rural aesthetic and associated authenticity.

Further reading:

Doggett, P. (2000) *Are You Ready for the Country? Elvis, Dylan, Parsons and the Roots of Country Rock*, London: Viking/Penguin Group.

Einarson, J. (2001) *Desperados: The Roots of Country Music*, New York: Cooper Square Press.

Meyer, D.N. (2009) *Twenty Thousand Roads. The Ballad of Gram Parsons and His Cosmic American Music*, London: Bloomsbury.

Q Magazine Special (2004) *Johnny Cash & the Story of Country Rock* (includes '30 country rock albums you must own').

Listening: Gram Parsons, *GP/Grievous Angel*, Reprise, 1990 (rerelease, both albums on single CD); The Byrds, *Sweetheart of the Rodeo*, Edsel, 1997; Bob Dylan, *Nashville Skyline*, Columbia, 1969; Emmylou Harris, *Luxury Liner*, WB, 1977

COVERS

Cover versions are performances/recordings by musicians not responsible for the original recording. Historically, these were often 'standards' which were the staples of singers for most of the 1940s and 1950s, with record companies releasing their artists cover versions of hits from their competitors. In the 1950s, white singers covered the original rock'n'roll recordings by black artists (e.g. Pat Boone's cover of Little Richard's 'Tutti Frutti'), in an effort by record companies to capitalize on the ethnic divide in American radio. Criticism of this frequently exploitative practice led to covers being equated with a lack of originality, and regarded as not as creative, or authentic, as the original recording. This view was reinforced by the aesthetics and ideology of 1960s rock culture, valuing individual creativity and the use of one's own compositions.

However, the negative image of covers is undeserved: they often serve as a way for artists to authenticate themselves with their audience, by identifying with respected original artists, and some cover versions provide distinctive and influential versions of the original compositions (see *The Wire*, 2005).

A particular form of covers are represented by 'Song families', a term developed primarily by Hatch and Millward (1987), to describe particular songs which are revived and reworked. Constructed out of existing lyrical, melodies and rhythmic structures, they are adapted to new musical developments by successive generations of musicians, reshaping generic conventions in the process. Willie Dixon's 'Spoonful', recorded by a number of artists, illustrates this process, both musically and in terms of the social meanings ascribed to various renditions of the song (Shuker, 2008: 101).

See: **authenticity**

Further reading:
Keightley, K. (2003) 'Covers', in Shepherd, J., Horn, D., Laing, D., Oliver, P. and Wicke, P. (eds) *The Encyclopedia of Popular Music of the World*, Volume 1. London: Cassell.

Plasketes, G., Guest Editor (2005) 'Special Issue: Like a Version – Cover Songs in Popular Music'. *Popular Music and Society*, 28, 2.

Solis G. ed. (2010) *Play It Again: Cover Songs in Popular Music*, Ashgate.

Weinstein, D. (1998) 'The History of Rock's Past Through Rock Covers', in Swiss, T., Herman, A. and Sloop, J.M. (eds) *Mapping the Beat: Popular Music and Contemporary Theory*, Malden, MA: Blackwell Publishers, pp. 137–51.

The Wire, 'The singer not the song', Issue 261, November 2005: 44–51. Profiles of '69 covers that rattle the state of the song, plus Alan Licht investigates the motives for covering other artists work.

Listening: Cowboy Junkies, 'Me and The Devil' (original: Robert Johnson); and 'Sweet Jane' (original: Lou Reed; Velvet Underground), on *2,000 More Miles. Live Performances 1985-1994*, BMG Canada, 1995; Joan Jett, *The Hit List*, Epic, 1990 (an album of cover versions); The Chimes, 'I Still Haven't Found What I'm Looking For', CBS, 1990; first recorded by U2; Metallica, *Garage Inc.* Vertigo, 1998

CROSSOVER

Crossover describes the move of a record/performer from success in one genre/chart area to another, usually one with a more mainstream audience. The term is usually associated with black music achieving more mainstream chart success. Less commonly, crossover has also been applied to the early 1990s success of 'new country', and to gay musicians 'coming out'.

R&B in the 1960s provides several examples of crossover. With the exception of a brief period (November 1963–January 1965), *Billboard* had a separate R&B chart, with some R&B records 'crossing over' to the pop chart, as with The Four Tops, 'I Can't Help Myself', Motown, 1965. Music classified as R&B was neither promoted as heavily as 'pop' nor did R&B recordings have access to the extensive distribution network of pop records, so Berry Gordy at Motown successfully pursued a policy of making black music attractive to a white audience, especially with the records of The Supremes. Brackett (1995) provides an interesting case study of five R&B songs that achieved varying degrees of crossover success in 1965. He demonstrates a clear connections between their musical style and the degree to which they crossed over, and argues that the country and R&B charts served as 'testing grounds' to identify potential crossover records to the mainstream pop chart. In the 1980s, with the success of performers such as Michael Jackson and Prince, *Billboard* in 1987 inaugurated a Hot Crossover 30 chart, codifying the pacesetting nature of black music.

Crossover is predicated on the existence of discrete boundaries, and a hierarchy of racially distinct genres and audiences. At times this sits awkwardly with the bi-racial composition of those working within particular genres; for example, 1950s rock'n'roll.

Crossover music has been criticized by some (notably Nelson George) as a sell-out of the tougher styles of black music, and as a threat to the livelihoods of independent black entrepreneurs, linked to the notion of compromising the authenticity of black music. Other commentators (e.g. Perry, 1988) view crossover as a metaphor for integration and the upward social mobility of the black community. Crossover is not such an issue in music markets outside the United States. In the United Kingdom, the term is rarely used, and then usually to refer to successful dance and indie music doing well in the main pop charts (see *Music Week*).

The popularization of American indie music via grunge in the early 1990s; Britpop's moving UK indie into the mainstream; and 'country' star Shania Twain's success in the pop charts, provide recent examples of crossover.

See: **Motown; R&B; soul**

Further reading:
Brackett, D. (1995) *Interpreting Popular Music*, Cambridge: Cambridge University Press.
Perry, S. (1988) 'The Politics of Crossover' in Frith, S. (ed.) *Facing the Music*, New York: Pantheon Books, pp. 51–87.

Viewing: *Dancing in the Street*, episode 3; how Motown shaped its music and performers to appeal to the white mainstream pop market in the United States

CULTURAL CAPITAL

see **taste**

CULTURAL IMPERIALISM

Cultural imperialism developed as a concept analogous to the historical, political and economic subjugation of the Third World by the colonizing powers in the nineteenth century, with consequent deleterious effects for the societies of the colonized. This gave rise to global relations of dominance, subordination and dependency between the affluence and power of the advanced capitalist nations, most notably the United States and Western Europe, and the relatively powerless underdeveloped countries. This economic and political imperialism was seen to have a cultural aspect, with local cultures becoming variously challenged, dominated and displaced by imported cultural values, products and practices (Hesmondhalgh, 2007: Chapter 6; Lewis, 2008).

Evidence of cultural imperialism was provided by the predominantly one way international media flow, from a few international dominant sources of media production, notably the United States, to media systems in other national cultural contexts. This involved the market penetration and dominance of Anglo-American popular culture, and, more importantly, established certain forms as the accepted ones, scarcely recognizing that there are alternatives (Garofalo, 1993). The international dominance of the media conglomerates and the associated major record companies, suggested that the cultural imperialism thesis was applicable to popular music. The extent to which this situation be seen in terms of cultural invasion and the subjugation of local cultural identity has been debated (Wallis and Malm, 1984).

The cultural imperialism thesis gained general currency in debates in the 1960s and 1970s about the significance of imported popular culture. Such debates were evident not only in the Third World, but in 'developed' countries such as France, Canada, Australia, and New Zealand, which were also subject to high market penetration by American popular culture. Adherents of the thesis tended to dichotomize local culture and its imported counterpart, regarding local culture as somehow more authentic, traditional and supportive of a conception of a distinctive national cultural identity. Set against this identity, and threatening its continual existence and vitality, was the influx of large quantities of commercial media products, mainly from the United States. Upholders of the cultural imperialism view generally saw the solution to this situation as some combination of restrictions upon media imports and the deliberate fostering of the local cultural industries, including music.

Although the existence of cultural imperialism became widely accepted at both a 'common-sense' level and in left academia, its validity at both a descriptive level and as an explanatory analytical concept came under increasing critical scrutiny into the 1980s. It was argued that it concealed a number of conceptual weaknesses and problematic assumptions about national culture and the nature of cultural homogenization and consumerism. In the 1980s, the active audience paradigm in media and **cultural studies**, with its emphases on resistance and polysemy, challenged the value of cultural imperialism as a concept.

While specific national case studies demonstrated the immense influence of the transnational music industry on musical production and distribution everywhere, they 'just as clearly indicate that world musical homgenization is not occurring' (Robinson *et al.*, 1991: 4). A complex relationship, often more symbiotic than exploitative, exists between the majors and local record companies in marginalized national contexts such as Canada and New Zealand (Shuker, 2008: Chapter 12). Local musicians are immersed in overlapping and frequently reciprocal contexts of production, with a cross-fertilization of local and international sounds. Attempts at the national level to foster local popular music production are primarily interventions at the level of the distribution and reception of the music. They attempt to secure greater access to the market, particularly for local products in the face of overseas music, notably from England and the United States (Wallis and Malm, 1992).

The **globalization** of Western capitalism, particularly evident in its media conglomerates, and the increasing *inter*-national nature of Western popular music undermined the applicability of cultural imperialism, at least in any straightforward fashion. However, it remains a useful concept in popular music studies, provided that it is seen as a contested process rather than an inflexible and deterministic one.

See: **globalization**

Further reading:

Garofalo, R. (1993) 'Whose World, What Beat: The Transnational Music Industry, Identity, and Cultural Imperialism', *The World of Music*, 35, 2: 16–32.

Lewis, J. (2008) *Cultural Studies. The Basics*, 2nd edition, Los Angeles, CA: Sage, Chapter 10.

Robinson, D., Buck, E., Cuthbert, M., *et al.* (1991) *Music at the Margins: Popular Music and Global Diversity*, Newbury Park, CA: Sage.

Wallis, R. and Malm, K. (1984) *Big Sounds from Small Countries*, London: Constable.

Wallis, R. and Malm, K. eds (1992) *Media Policy and Music Activity*, London: Routledge.

CULTURAL INDUSTRIES

A term first coined and developed by Adorno, who referred to them as the 'culture industry', the cultural industries are economic institutions employing the characteristic modes of production and organization of industrial corporations to produce and disseminate symbols in the form of cultural goods and services, generally as commodities (Garnham, 1990). In analyses situated in business economics, they are referred to as the entertainment industries. Such industries are characterized by a constant drive to expand their market share and to create new products, so that the cultural commodity resists homogenization. In the case of the record industry, while creating and promoting new product is usually expensive, actually reproducing it is not. Once the master copy is pressed, further copies are relatively cheap as economies of scale come into operation; similarly, a music video can be enormously expensive to make, but its capacity to be reproduced and played is then virtually limitless.

The cultural industries are engaged in competition for limited pools of disposable income, which will fluctuate according to the economic times. With its historical association with youthful purchasers – though their value as a consumer group is not as significant as it once was – the music industry is particularly vulnerable to shifts in the relative size of the younger age cohort and their loss of spending power in the recent period of high youth unemployment worldwide (see **demography**). The cultural industries are also engaged in competition for advertising revenue, consumption time and skilled labour. Radio especially is heavily dependent on advertising revenue. Not only are consumers allocating their expenditure, they are also dividing their time among the varying cultural consumption opportunities available to them. With the expanded range of leisure opportunities in recent years, at least to those able to afford them, the competition among the cultural, recreational, and entertainment industries for consumer attention has increased.

Through the twentieth century, the music industry demonstrated most of the features identified as characteristic of the cultural/entertainment industries:

1. Profits from a very few highly popular products were generally required to offset losses from many mediocrities; overproduction is a feature of recorded music, with only a small proportion of releases achieving chart listings and commercial success, and a few mega sellers propping up the music industry in otherwise lean times.
2. Marketing expenditures per unit were proportionally large; this applied to those artists and their releases with a proven track record.
3. Ancillary or secondary markets provided disproportionately large returns; in popular music through licencing and revenue from copyright.
4. Capital costs remained relatively high, and oligopolistic tendencies prevailed; in the music industry, this was evident in the dominance

of the majors, in part due to the greater development and promotional capital they had available.

5. Ongoing technological development made it ever easier and less expensive to manufacture, distribute, and receive entertainment products and services. This is evident in the development of recording and distribution technologies.

6. Entertainment products and services have universal appeal; this is evident in the international appeal of many popular music genres and performers, enhanced by the general accessibility of music as a medium, no matter what language a song may be sung in.

Although these tenets remain in evidence (see the **music industry**), the advent of the Internet and digital music has altered the operation and relative importance of these features, reconfiguring the cultural industries in general, and the music industry in particular.

See: **Internet**; **mass culture**; **music industry**

Further reading:
Garnham, N. (1990) *Capitalism and Communication: Global Culture and the Economics of Information*, London: Sage.

CULTURAL INTERMEDIARIES

Bourdieu's notion of cultural intermediaries has been used to examine the role of personnel in the music industry in terms of their active role in the production of particular artists and styles of music, and the promotion of these: 'Although often invisible behind star names and audience styles, recording industry personnel work at a point where the tensions between artists, consumers and entertainment corporations meet and result in a range of working practices, ideological divisions and conflicts' (Negus, 1992; see also Toynbee, 2000). These personnel include artist and repertoire (A&R) staff responsible for finding new artists and maintaining the company's rosta of performers; the record producers and sound engineers, who play a key role in the recording studio; video directors; marketing directors and the associated record pluggers; press officers; record retailers; radio programmers and disc jockeys; concert and club promoters.

While there is an anarchic aspect of many of these industry practices, the result of the essential uncertainty endemic to the music business, the industry has come to privilege particular styles of music and working practices, and quite specific ways of acquiring, marketing and promoting performers. Such established modes of operating work against new artists, styles outside of the historically legitimated white **rock** mainstream, and the employment of women. The concept of cultural intermediaries is more useful than the related concept of gatekeepers, primarily because of its greater flexibility.

See: **marketing**; **producers**; **retail**

Further reading:
Toynbee, J. (2000) *Making Popular Music: Musicians, Creativity and Institutions*, London: Arnold.

CULTURAL STUDIES

The term 'cultural studies' became current in the late 1960s and early 1970s, initially associated with its institutional base at England's Birmingham University: the Centre for Contemporary Cultural Studies (BCCCS). Cultural studies represented a reaction against the high-culture tradition's strongly negative view of popular culture. Hall initially mapped the field according to a distinction between the paradigms of culturalism and structuralism, a neo-Gramscian synthesis of 'hegemony theory' and a series of post-structural variants. Cultural studies expanded and become more diverse, with developing international interest, especially in North America, and the establishment of further institutional bases. There in no sense exists a cultural studies orthodoxy, although there is a general recognition that cultural studies focuses on the relations between social being and cultural meanings. This embraces the analysis of institutions, texts, discourses, readings and audiences, with these understood in their social, economic and political context (for an overview of the development and scope of cultural studies, see Barker, 2002, and the contributions to Grossberg *et al.*; for a summary, along with coverage of associated concepts, Mikula, 2008).

Several key figures working within British Cultural Studies have been primarily concerned with the question of how the media actually undertake the production of 'consent' for social, economic and political structures which favour the maintenance of dominant interests. Their approach was markedly influenced by Gramsci's concept of ideological or cultural hegemony. This vein of cultural studies exerted considerable influence on popular music studies, primarily through the 1970s work on music and youth subcultures associated with the BCCCS (see **subcultures**), and critics who attempted to place popular music, especially rock, at the centre of oppositional ideology (Chambers, 1985; Grossberg *et al.*, 1992; Middleton, 1990). These writers emphasize the place of the individual in the determination of cultural meaning; for example, Chamber's theme is the constant interplay between commercial factors and lived experience:

> For after the commercial power of the record companies has been recognized, after the persuasive sirens of the radio acknowledged, after the recommendations of the music press noted, it is finally those who buy the records, dance to the rhythm and live to the beat who demonstrate, despite the determined conditions of its production, the wider potential of pop.
>
> (*Chambers, 1985: xii*)

Middleton similarly places popular music in the space of contradiction and contestation lying between 'imposed' and 'authentic', and also emphasizes the relative autonomy of cultural practices.

See: **subcultures**

Further reading:
Barker, C. (2002) *Making Sense of Cultural Studies: Central Problems and Critical Debates*, London: Sage Publications.

Chambers, I. (1985) *Urban Rhythms: Pop Music and Popular Culture*, London: Macmillan.

Grossberg, L., Nelson, C. and Treichler, P. eds (1992) *Cultural Studies*, New York: Routledge.

Grossberg, L. (1992) *We Gotta Get Out of This Place: Popular Conservatism and Postmodern Culture*, New York: Routledge.

Mikula, M. (2008) *Key Concepts in Cultural Studies*, Houndsmills: Macmillan.

CULTURE

The meaning and utility of 'culture', and the words used to qualify it, have been the subject of considerable discussion and debate. There is a general tendency to qualify 'culture', as a series of oppositions: the dichotomizing of 'high culture' against 'low culture', or 'elite' culture against 'popular culture'. A major focus, associated with the Frankfurt School, has been upon the culture industries and the shaping of 'mass culture'. The complexity of these concepts, and the difficulties posed by any straightforward application of them, is evident in their application to popular music.

Indeed, culture is one of the most difficult words in the English language, used in a variety of discourses, including fashion, the arts, nationalism and cultural studies, with each discursive context signalling a particular usage (see Williams, 1983; Mikula, 2008). Cultural and media studies, which have underpinned this volume, maintain a sociological rather than an aesthetic sense of culture, with a focus on popular culture rather than artistic pursuits associated with particular values and standards: elite or mass culture. In this approach, evident throughout popular music studies, culture is a sphere in which social inequalities are reproduced; a site of struggle over meanings. An aspect of this is the way in which music studies in education have historically largely stressed the classical musical tradition, seeing popular music as inferior and paying it little attention.

High culture

The high-culture tradition emerged during the nineteenth century; it was essentially a conservative defence of a narrowly defined high or elite 'culture' and its associated art forms: in critic Matthew Arnold's classic phrase: 'the best that has been thought and said' (1869). This asserted an artistic conception of culture: the only real and authentic culture is art, against which everything else is set. It views the valued civilized culture of an elite minority as constantly under attack from a majority or mass culture, which is unauthentic and a denial of 'the good life'. Its analytic emphasis is on evaluation and discrimination; a search for the true values of civilization, commonly to be found in Renaissance art, the great nineteenth-century novels and so on. The high-culture tradition includes cultural commentators such as F.R. Leavis, T.S. Eliot and Bloom; elements of it are also evident in Marxist-oriented critiques of mass culture, notably the Frankfurt School (see **mass culture**), and Raymond Williams 'left culturalism'.

The high cultural critique of popular culture has frequently vehemently attacked popular music. While such a view can be traced back to Plato, it emerged more forcefully with the massive social changes of the nineteenth century. For example, writing in 1839, Sir John Herschel claimed:

Music and dancing (the more's the pity) have become so closely associated with ideas of riot and debauchery among the less cultivated classes, that a taste for them, for their own sakes, can hardly be said to exist, and before they can be recommended as innocent or safe amusements, a very great change of ideas must take place.

(*Cited in Frith, 1983: 39*)

A succession of commentators regarded much popular music as mindless fodder, cynically manufactured for mindless youthful consumers. Bloom, for instance, claims that rock presents life as 'a nonstop commercial prepackaged masturbational fantasy' (1987) which he saw as responsible for the atrophy of the minds and bodies of youth.

Underpinning such views are assumptions about the potentially disruptive nature of 'the popular', and the need for social control and the regulation of popular pleasures. The high-culture view of popular culture has been criticized for failing to recognize the active nature of popular culture consumption; failing to treat the cultural forms seriously on their own terms; biased by aesthetic prejudices, which are rarely explicated; and resting on outmoded class-based notions of a high–low culture split. The traditionally claimed distinctions between high and low culture have become blurred. High art, including classical music, has become increasingly commodified and commercialized, while some forms of popular culture have become more 'respectable', receiving State funding and broader critical acceptance.

The high culture perspective remains evident in the application of aesthetics to popular music, and the tendency of musicology to ignore or dismiss popular music genres. It also underpins some State attitudes towards the funding and regulation of cultural forms. At an everyday level, it is implicit in the manner in which musicians, fans and critics make distinctions of value both between and within particular genres.

Popular culture

This was historically a term applied during the nineteenth century to the separate culture of the subordinate classes of the urban and industrial centres (see Storey, 1993). This culture had two main sources: a commercially oriented culture and a culture of and for the people (often associated with political agitation). While some subsequent usages of popular culture reserve it for the second of these, the term became more generally associated with the commercial mass media: print, aural, and visual communication on a large scale, including the press, publishing, radio and television, film and video, telecommunications and the recording industry. In considerations of popular music as a form of popular culture, the emphasis has been on texts and audiences, and the relationship between them – the way individuals and social groups use popular music within their lives.

Folk culture

The term folk culture has been applied to forms of culture which are tightly linked to particular social groups and which are not subject to mass distribution, even if electronically produced. The concept is some-times conflated with the notion of **roots** music and has been used in con-siderations of the musical characteristics and social dynamics of **folk music**. Often based in specific localities, early forms of popular music can be regarded as folk culture, including the pre-ska forms of Jamaican reggae, and the hillbilly styles which contributed to country & western and rockabilly.

See: **mass culture**

Further reading:
Arnold, M. (1869) *Culture and Anarchy*, Cambridge: Cambridge University Press,1986.
Bloom, A. (1987) *The Closing of the American Mind*, New York: Simon & Schuster.
Hall, S. and Whannell, P. (1964) *The Popular Arts*, London: Hutchinson.
Hoggart, R. (1957) *The Uses of Literacy*, London: Penguin.
Smith, P. (2001) *Cultural Theory: An Introduction*, Malden, MA: Blackwell.
Swingewood, A. (1977) *The Myth of Mass Culture*, London: Macmillan.
Williams, R. (1981) *Culture*, London: Fontana.
Williams, R. (1983) *Keywords*, London: Fontana.

DANCE; DANCING

As a social practice, dance has a long history, closely associated with music, ritual, courtship and everyday pleasure. Historically, social dancing dates back at least to the sixteenth century and the private balls of the aristoc-racy, with ballroom dancing popularized in the early nineteenth century (the waltz). Particular dance styles were part of Ragtime and early jazz music (e.g. the cakewalk). Dance is associated with the pleasures of physi-cal expression rather than the intellectual, the body rather than the mind.

At times, the closeness and implied sexual display of dance has aroused anxiety and led to attempts to regulate dance, or at least control who is dancing with whom. Forms of dance subject to considerable social criticism include the Charleston in the jazz age; jitterbugging, a popular and flamboyant form of dance in the 1940s; rock'n'roll in the 1950s; the twist in the 1960s and disco dancing in the 1970s. Adorno saw jitterbugging as a 'stylized' dance style whose performers had 'convulsive aspects reminiscent of St Vitus's dance or the reflexes of mutilated animals' (Adorno, 1991:46). As Negus (1996) observes, such responses reflected a distaste for overt expressions of sexuality, a racist fear of 'civilized' behaviour being undermined by 'primitive rhythms', and a concern that young people are being manipulated and effected by forms of mass crowd psychology (see **effects**).

Dance is central to the general experience and leisure lives of young people, and many adults, through their attendance at, and participation in, school dances, parties, discos, dance classes and club culture and raves. The participants in the dance break free of their bodies in a combination of 'socialised pleasures and individualised desires', with dancing operating 'as a metaphor for an external reality which is unconstrained by the limits and expectations of gender identity and which successfully and relatively painlessly transports its subjects from a passive to a more active psychic position' (McRobbie, 1991: 192, 194, 201). Dance also acts as a marker of significant points in the daily routine, punctuating it with what Chambers (1985) labels the freedom of Saturday night. These various facets of dance are well represented in feature films such as *Saturday Night Fever* (1977), *Flashdance* (1983) and *Strictly Ballroom* (1995).

Dance is associated with some popular musical genres to a greater extent from others, especially those included under the metagenre of dance/electronic dance music. Chambers (1985) documented the clubs and dance halls of English post-war urban youth culture, referring to 'the rich tension of dance' in its various forms, including the shake, the jerk, the Northern soul style of athletic, acrobatic dance and the break dancing and body-popping of black youth. There are forms of dance which are genre and subculture specific, such as line dancing in country, slam dancing and the pogo in punk, break dancing in some forms of rap, head banging in heavy metal and slam dancing and moshing at concerts by grunge and alternative performers.

The close link between dance and contemporary popular music is indicated in the title of a major documentary series on popular music, *Dancing in the Street* (1995), which shows changing dance styles and their associated musical genres, and in the very successful contemporary television show *Glee*.

Further reading:
McRobbie, A. (1991) *Feminism and Youth Culture*, Basingstoke: Macmillan.
Thomas, H. (1995) *Dance, Modernity and Modern Culture*, London: Routledge.

DANCE MUSIC

Dance bands and dance music came into general use as phrases from around 1910 onwards, with the advent of radio in the 1920s playing a major role in the popularization of dance. Dance bands, notably 'Big Bands', were a feature of many hotels and clubs during the interwar period and into the early 1950s. Dance music came to be used in a general sense, for those popular music genres capable of being danced *to* and, as such, includes music from a range of styles and genres. In the 1970s, 'dance music' became primarily equated with disco. In the late 1980s and through the 1990s, 'dance music' become associated with dance club scenes, rave culture in the United Kingdom and various genres/styles of electronic dance music.

See: **disco**; **EDM**; **rave** (and their suggested readings)

DANCEHALL

Jamaican dancehall was a subgenre of reggae that emerged during the mid-1980s. It placed the disc jockey (DJ) again at the centre of reggae, with deejays chatting in patois (toasting) over a digital rhythm ('riddim') loop, which emphasized percussion. The key producer in the evolution of the style was 'King Jammy' (Lloyd Jones), who had earlier worked under King Tubby (see **dub**). Dancehall was associated with sexually explicit lyrics, termed 'slackness' (Bradley, 2000), and, in later variants, a glorification of violence and gun culture. Stolzoff (2000) provides an extensive categorization of the various thematic styles of dancehall, primarily associated with particular DJ styles (including the rude boy rasta, the gangsta DJ and the loverman DJ).

Further reading: (see also the general studies of reggae, under that entry)
Manuel, P., and Marshall, W. (2006) 'The Riddim Method: Aesthetics, Practice and Ownership in Jamaican Dancehall', *Popular Music*, 25, 4: 447–70.

Stolzoff, N. (2000) *Wake the Town and Tell the People: Dancehall Culture in Jamaica*, Durham, NC: Duke University Press.

Further Listening: Various artists, *Dancehall: The Rise of Jamaican Dancehall Culture*, Soul Jazz, 2008 (double CD)

DELTA (COUNTRY) BLUES

Country blues, sometimes conflated with Delta blues, emerged in the still largely rural southern United States during the early 1900s, and became widely recorded during the 1920s. A significant factor here was the availability of lighter, portable electrical recording equipment to record companies, enabling them to record away from their main northern urban studios, in southern centres such as Atlanta and Memphis. There were strong regional variants, with Texas and the Mississippi Delta (Delta blues) the most prominent. Country blues fed into other forms of the blues, and strongly influenced later R&B, rockabilly, rock'n'roll and rock performers.

Country blues was characterized by its strong social realism, with many songs/recordings which are both beautiful and tortured, with a sense of anguish and desperation in their vocals. The country blues players developed the bottleneck or slide guitar technique, shaping the instrument's sound into another 'voice'. (A glass or metal tube is fitted over the guitarist's ring or little finger, stopping the strings of the guitar when it is slid up or down the fingerboard; the term comes from the use of the neck of a bottle that had been broken off and sanded down for the purpose.) Leading performers included Charlie Patton, Skip James, Robert Johnson and Bukka White.

Robert Johnson (1911–38) is regarded as 'the key transitional figure working within the Mississippi Delta's blues culture. He bridged the gap between the music's rural beginnings and its modern urban manifestations' (Barlow, 1989: 45). Johnson had limited commercial success during his short life, and his only recording sessions were held in San Antonio late in 1936 and in Dallas in early 1937, when he recorded a total of just 29 blues tracks. This small output was to have an influence out of all proportion to its size, not only on the blues, but also on the development of 'rock' in the 1960s, as British bands like the Rolling Stones and Cream covered songs by Johnson.

Johnson was strongly influenced by Son House's bottleneck slide guitar technique, which formed the core of his own playing style, and by other contemporary Delta bluesmen such as Charley Patton and Willie Brown. But Johnson assimilated a range of other influences, incorporating them into his own distinctive style. Contemporaries commented on the breadth of Johnson's musical tastes, and marvelled at his ability to

> pick a song right out of the air. He'd hear it being played on the radio and play it right back note for note. He could do it with blues, spirituals, hillbilly music, popular stuff. You name it he could play it.
>
> (*Robert Jr. Lockwood; cited Barlow, 1989: 46*)

Robert Palmer notes how Johnson made his guitar

> sound uncannily like a full band, furnishing a heavy beat with his feet, chording innovative shuffle rhythms and picking out high treble-string lead with his slider, all at the same time. Fellow guitarists would watch him with unabashed, open mouth wonder. They were watching the Delta's first modern bluesman at work.
>
> (*Palmer, 1981*)

Johnson recorded a number of strikingly original songs, which captured a timeless feeling of desperation and intensity. In songs like 'Rambling on My Mind', 'Dust My Broom' and 'Sweet Home Chicago' Johnson celebrated mobility and personal freedom; double entendres and sexual metaphors abound in 'Steady Rolling Man', 'Terraplane Blues' and 'Traveling Riverside Blues'; and in 'Crossroad Blues' and 'Hellhound on My Trail' Johnson encouraged the legend that he had flirted with the devil. Johnson's voice has an edge of desperation and hints at depths of experience. This is abetted by the use of repetition, and the interplay between the amplified acoustic guitar and the voice. His voice is particularly effective at conveying a fatalistic sense of the social and spiritual forces he saw arrayed against him. His vocal intonation is especially compelling in his poignant 'Love in Vain', with its themes of painful departure and separation.

The singer was widely thought to have sold his soul to the devil in return for the ability to be an outstanding blues singer and guitarist, since he disappeared for a short period and returned amazingly proficient. This, along with his early death and the lack of details about his life, created Johnson as a mythic figure. The force of this myth, and public and scholarly fascination with it, has led to a spate of books and documentaries on him (for an excellent review of these, and the creation of 'the Johnson myth', see Pearson and McCulloch, 2003). When one of only two known photos of him was used on a US commemorative stamp, the fact that it had been altered to remove the cigarette from Johnson's mouth created a good deal of controversy (Schroeder, 2004). There is continued interest in his recordings and his performing style.

The early 1960s saw the 'discovery' of the Delta blues by white middle-class youth. In the United States and the United Kingdom (and then internationally), artists such as Mississippi John Hurt and Skip James were recorded anew by such small folk-oriented labels as Vanguard, Prestige and Piedmont. These performers were embraced by folk music, then enjoying a boom period and appeared at the Newport Folk Festival in Rhode Island, and other **festivals**. Leading white rock musicians began to cover country blues songs, notably those by Robert Johnson (e.g. The Rolling Stones version of Johnson's 'Love in Vain', on *Let It Bleed*, ABKCO, 1989).

Interest in the country blues continues: a **box set** of Robert Johnson's complete recordings was a somewhat unexpected huge commercial success in the 1990s; other reissues have also done well with the advent of the CD.

Further reading:
Gioia, T. (2008) *Delta Blues. The Life and Times of the Mississippi Masters Who Revolutionized American Music.* New York: Norton & Company.
Palmer, R. (1981) *Deep Blue*, New York: Viking Press.
Pearson, B.L., and McCulloch, B. (2003) *Robert Johnson. Lost and Found*, Urbana: University of Illinois Press. Especially Chapter 13: 'who was he, really?'
Schroeder, P.R. (2004) *Robert Johnson, Mythmaking, and Contemporary American Culture*, Urbana: University of Illinois Press.
Wald, E. (2004) *Escaping the Delta: Robert Johnson and the Invention of the Blues*, New York: Harper Collins.

Listening: *Slide Guitar – Bottles Knives & Steel, Vols 1&2*, CBS; *Skip James Today!* Vanguard, 1991; Robert Johnson, *The Complete Recordings*, Columbia, 1990 (box set); Blind Lemon Jefferson, *Milestone*, 1974; Charlie Patton, *Complete Recordings 1929–1934*, (Box Set), JSP, 2002

Viewing: *The Search for Robert Johnson*, Sony, 1992 (DVD); *Can't You Hear The Wind Howl? The Life and Music of Robert Johnson*, Shout, 1997 (DVD)

DEMOGRAPHY

Demography is the study of human populations, primarily with respect to their size, their structure and their development. It includes aspects of the age structure and its relationship to social, economic and cultural structures. In popular music studies, research drawing on demography has been primarily concerned with examining the relationship between age structure and consumption, and the relevance of this to explaining the historical advent of particular genres and radio formats and their shifting popularity and market share.

An instructive example of such an approach is the explanation offered for the emergence of **rock'n'roll** in the mid-1950s, and the development of rock culture in the 1960s, as a combination of age-group demographics and individual musical creativity. The post-war baby boom was 'a crucial condition of the re-articulation of the formations of popular culture after the Second World War and the Korean War'; there were 77 million babies born between 1946 and 1964, and by 1964, 40 per cent of the population of the United States was under 20 (Grossberg, 1992: 172). The baby boom and the emergence of a youth market made the young a desirable target audience for the cultural industries: 'post-1945 American teenagers enjoyed an unprecedented level of affluence. Their taste in film, music, literature and entertainment was backed up by enormous purchasing power, which record producers and film-makers were quick to satisfy' (Welsh, 1990:3). One aspect of this search was the development of a young white audience for rhythm and blues.

American suburbia, where the baby boomers were concentrated, neither represented nor catered for the desires of American youth. As Grossberg (1992: 179) puts it: 'Rock emerged as a way of mapping the specific structures of youth's affective alienation on the geographies of everyday life'. This is to emphasize the point that the social category of youth 'is an affective identity stitched onto a generational history' (ibid.: 183); the particular configuration of circumstances in the 1950s forged an alliance of 'youth' and rock music as synonymous with that particular age cohort of young people. Authenticity, in Grossberg's sense of the term, is equated here with the ability of rock to resonate with youth's common desires, feelings and experiences in a shared public language. In the 1960s, the now teenage baby boomers elevated youth to a new level of social, political and economic visibility, and clearly the emergence and vitality of any cultural form is dependent on the existence of an audience for it. However, we must not over privilege such 'audience explanations' for the emergence of new genres of popular music: audiences are selecting their cultural/leisure texts from what is available to them, and the nature of the market is determined by much more than the constitutive qualities of its potential audience (see Peterson, 1990).

What demographic analysis can more convincingly show, is the changing audience for popular music over time. Goodwin observed at the end of the 1980s: '"older" music has become contemporary for audiences of *all* ages' (Frith and Goodwin, 1990: 259). The absolute numbers of young people entering the labour market in the United Kingdom and Europe had declined during the 1980s, and continued to fall in the 1990s. Similar demographic trends were observed in most other western countries. As an age cohort, seen usually as around 13–24 years of age, youth had historically been among popular music's major consumers, and young people continued to have considerable discretionary income for the leisure industries to tap. The straightforward historical association of popular music with youth, however, now needed qualifying.

By the late 1980s, Frith could accurately observe that 'In material terms, the traditional rock consumer – the "rebellious" teenager – is no longer the central market figure' (1988: 127). Nevertheless, particular generations of youth continued to be associated with the popularity of emerging cultures; in the 1990s, youth were constructed by the popular and academic media, and the advertising industry, as 'Generation X': a very media self-conscious group of youth, primarily associated with **grunge** as a style. At the same time, 'nostalgia rock' was prominent in popular music, with the release of 'new' Beatles material (*Live at the BBC*); the launch of *MOJO* magazine, placing rock history firmly at its core and with 35 per cent of its readers aged 35-plus; and successful tours by the Rolling Stones, Pink Floyd and the Eagles, among other ageing performers. This high level of interest in popular music's past was evident among both greying consumers and young people. Such repackaging and marketing of our collective musical memories was hardly new, but the scale was now different, and commentators raised questions about the vitality of popular music genres such as rock in the early twenty-first century.

The market for rock and pop music was increasingly extended to those who grew up with the music in the 1950s and 1960s, and who continued to listen to it and attend concerts. The proliferation of reunion tours, firmly established in the 1990s, has continued; in 2010, Bon Jovi were the highest concert earning performers. Research by the Demos think-tank in 2004, found that people in their forties and fifties are maintaining their interest in popular music; they represent a more profitable market then their teenage children because they have more disposable income and a greater desire for luxury goods (Press report, July 2004). Ageing along with their favoured surviving performers of the sixties, these older listeners largely account for the present predominance of 'golden oldies' radio formats and occupy an increasing market share of sales of record music, especially **back catalogue** releases (see RIAA data). These trends illustrate how demography continues to play a significant role in reshaping the cultural market place.

See: **audience**; **rock'n'roll**

Further reading:
Peterson, R.A. (1990) 'Why 1955? Explaining the Advent of Rock Music', *Popular Music*, 9, 1: 97–116.
Welsh, R. (1990, February) 'Rock'n'Roll and Social Change', *History Today*, 32–9.

DIASPORA

Originally used to refer to the dispersal of the Jews in the Greco–Roman period, diaspora has become applied to modern, often forced migrations of people. Diaspora is now commonly used in relation to contexts where cultural assimilation is incomplete and the culture of the originally displaced group, often ethnically identifiable, survives and is actively maintained in the new geographical locale.

Gilroy has been prominent in theorizing diaspora, primarily as a central concept to examine how dispersed black people are both unified and differentiated from each other ('the Black Atlantic'). Music provides a significant example of this process, through what Gilroy terms 'diasporic conversations'; as in 'the mutation of jazz and Afro-American cultural styles in the townships of South Africa and the syncretized evolution of Caribbean and British reggae music and Rastafari culture in Zimbabwe' (Gilroy, 1993: 199; see also the contributions to Whiteley *et al.*, 2004). Lipsitz (2007) also draws on the concept of diaspora, applying it to the contemporary global music industry, seeing dispersed peoples acting as 'cross cultural interpreters and analysts', especially through their use of music.

There has been considerable discussion of the nature of contemporary diasporic 'ethnic' identities and the musical styles associated with them. While such accounts can be celebratory of the resultant hybridized musical styles, they also seek to avoid the fetishization of marginality and the erosion of the frequent distinctions present within such communities. Negus, however, identifies a common problem that theorists of disapora have encountered: 'once in circulation, music and other cultural forms cannot remain "bounded" in any one group and interpreted simply as an expression that speaks to or reflects the lives of that exclusive group of people' (1996: 121; on this point, see **black music**).

See: **hybridity**; **globalization**

Further reading:

Gilroy, P. (1993) *The Black Atlantic: Modernity and Double Consciousness*, Cambridge, MA: Harvard University Press.

Gilroy, P. (1997) 'Diaspora, Utopia, and the Critique of Capitalism', in Gelder, K. and Thornton, S. (eds) *The Subcultures Reader*, London: Routledge.

Lipsitz, G. (2007) *Footsteps in the Dark: The Hidden Histories of Popular Music*, Minneapolis, MN: University of Minnesota Press.

DISCO

A term derived from French 'discotheque' – record library – referring to a club where you dance to records, disco became the dominant style of dance music in the period 1977–83. In the United States, the genre had a strong initial association with gay bars, and remained a cult there until the huge hit of film and soundtrack *Saturday Night Fever* (1977). A detailed history of American disco and dance music more generally during the 1970s, traces the development of 'a new mode of DJ'ing and dancing that went on to become the most distinctive cultural ritual of the decade' (Lawrence, 2003: Preface). Drawing in part on interviews with the key figures involved, Lawrence provides a narrative web of clandestine house parties and discotheques, traced back to legendary pre-disco New York dance clubs the Loft and the Sanctuary. Similar dance scenes were present around subsequent locales and musical genres. Internationally, disco became a pervasive and commercially highly successful genre, with prominent variants such as Eurodisco.

While most disco hitmakers were virtually anonymous, with **producers** to the fore (e.g. Giorgio Moroder), there were a few stars, notably Donna Summer, but also Labelle, Hot Chocolate, KC & The Sunshine Band, and, resurrecting their career, the Bee Gees. Although disco had faded by the early 1980s, its influence remained an integral part of chart pop, with performers such as the Pet Shop Boys celebrating the disco tradition and their place in it. Disco enjoyed something of a mid-1990s revival, helped by a renewed interest in Abba, whose music featured on several hit film soundtracks, such as *Muriel's Wedding*, (P.J. Hogan, 1994). In the United Kingdom, impetus for the Abba revival also came from various covers and tributes to their songs, such as Erasure's version of 'Take a Chance on Me' (on *Pop! The First 20 Hits*, Sire/Reprise, 1992), and the success of the **covers** band Björn Again. Disco has also been an element in the eclectic make up of the hybrid metagenre of contemporary dance music.

As a musical form and cultural practice, disco was frequently denigrated. Clarke describes it as a 'Dance fad of the '70s, with profound and unfortunate influence on popular music' … 'because the main thing was the thump-thump beat, other values could be ignored; producers used drum machines, synthesisers and other gimmicks at the expense of musical values' (1990: 344). Other commentators celebrated the forms vitality and emphasis on dance:

> Superficial, liberating, innovative, reactionary, sensuous, lifeless, disco emerged out of a subculture at the beginning of the 70s, dominated pop music for a few years at the end, and then shrank back… But during its brief dominance, it restored the dance groove as pop imperative.
>
> (*Smucker, 1992: 562*)

In an early academic treatment of disco, Dyer (1990) feels it necessary to entitle his analysis: 'In defence of disco'.

The genre has seen a resurgence of popular interest in the past 10–15 years, and undergone a positive critical reassessment (see Easlea, 2004; Echols, 2010).

See: **dance music**

Further reading:

Androite, J.-M. (2001) *Hot Stuff: A Brief History of Disco*. New York: Harper Collins.

Dyer, R. (1990) "In Defence of Disco", in Frith, S., and Goodwin, A. (eds) *On Record*, New York: Pantheon Books.

Easlea, D. (2004). *Everybody Dance: Chic and the Politics of Disco*. London: Helter Skelter.

Echols, A. (2010) *Hot Stuff: Disco and the Remaking of American Culture*. New York: W.W. Newton.

Jones, A., and Kantonen, J. (2005) *Saturday Night Forever: The Story of Disco*. Edinburgh: Mainstream.

Shapiro, P. (2006) *Turn the Beat Around: The Secret History of Disco*. New York: Faber & Faber.

Listening: Abba, *Abba Gold: Greatest Hits*, Polydor, 1992; Grace Jones, *Warm Leatherette*, Island, 1980; KC and the Sunshine Band, *Greatest Hits*, Rhino, 1990; Donna Summer, *Endless Summer: Donna Summer's Greatest Hits*, Polygram, 1994

DISCOGRAPHY

A discography is a systematic listing of sound recordings, usually in the form of a catalogue. Discographies vary widely in their comprehensiveness and level of detail, depending on the compiler's intent in producing the listing, the information available to them and their intended readership. Accordingly, they can include (or exclude) details of the recording artist; names of the recording personnel; composer credits; the date and place of the recording (along with the recording studio); the title of the musical work and issue details (the original release, issues for other markets and reissues); along with sales data, chart success and the market value of the recording. Specialist discographies are usually of individual artists, musical genres/styles or record labels.

The early recording companies were frequently very unsystematic in their cataloguing practices. There was a general lack of catalogues of released recordings, especially from the smaller companies, along with a failure to keep thorough records of releases. There was also the ephemeral nature of such material. This lack of systematic and accessible information on releases made record collecting a challenge, and fostered the growth of discography, especially among jazz enthusiasts and record collectors, who popularized the term in the 1930s. In 1934, the French critic Charles Delaunay was the first to publish a comprehensive discography, a word he coined. (His study *Hot Discography* was published in English in 1936). In 1935, the first such British compilation was published: *Rhythm on Record*, by Hilton Schelman, assisted by Stanley Dance. These two books were a basis for, and inspiration to, similar later works. Through the 1930s, hundreds of discographies of early jazz and jazz-related recordings were produced by collector enthusiasts, often in home-produced magazines, sometimes in the pages of *Melody Maker*, *Hot News* and *Swing Music*. At times, heated arguments raged over attribution and provenance of particular artists and recordings, and the intricacies of various label's notation/cataloguing practices. This vernacular scholarship provided an essential resource for later major compilations, for instance, those by Brian Rusk in the United Kingdom.

Painstaking research into and publication of discographies was also central to the initial collecting of blues and other 'race' music, and to popular dance music of the 78 rpm era. Jazz and blues discography informed and was extended into rock'n'roll, rock music and various other genres from the 1960s onward. Examples of contemporary 'rock' discography include the series of volumes by Strong in the United Kingdom. There are different emphases present in these, compared with their jazz and blues counterparts, with rock and pop discographies more concerned with the chart history of recordings.

Popular music magazines frequently include extensively researched artist, label or genre retrospectives with accompanying discographies. This is especially evident in those aimed at collectors: for example, the US-based *Goldmine* (1974–) and the UK published *Record Collector* (*c.* 1978–). There is also now also a plethora of record collecting guidebooks, often 'doubling' as discographies. Another form of discography are 'best of' volumes, such as the *MOJO* collection edited by Irwin (2000); these contribute to **canon** formation: the identification of which artists/recordings/genres are 'worthy' of being collected and the relative status of these.

See **record collecting**; **music press**

DISCOURSE ANALYSIS

At a popular level, discourse refers to a body of meaning associated with a particular topic or field, regardless of the form of its transmission, for example, medical discourse. Discourse is the domain of language use, especially the common ways of talking and thinking about social issues. Discourse analysis is a method of analysing such patterns of language use and their social function. While discourse is often manifested in language, it is embedded in organizational and institutional practices. Accordingly, discursive practices are real or material, as well as being embodied in language, and function as a form of ideology. They help constitute our personal, individual identity our subjectivity.

In social science, discourse analysis seeks to tease out the underlying assumptions and belief systems, and their associated meanings, embedded within a particular discourse. This is undertaken through an analysis of various forms of **text**, including documents such as policy statements, novels and interview transcripts. In post–structuralist social theory, discourse refers to a historically, socially and institutionally specific structure of meaning(s); statements, terms, categories, concepts, about the nature of individuals and the world they inhabit. While there are dominant discourses, what Foucault terms 'truth generating discourses', discourses are multiple; they offer competing and frequently contradictory ways whereby we give meaning to the world and our social existence within it.

As with other forms of discourse, popular music contains meanings that both reflect and help constitute wider social systems and structures of meaning. There are discourses around many of the terms used to describe the field and its constituent genres (see the discussion under **popular music**). More specifically, discourse analysis has been utilized, at times implicitly rather than directly, to examine popular music: song lyrics as performed language; discourses around musical styles and stars, especially in relation to sexuality (e.g. on heavy metal as a masculine/male form), DJ talk and music video. There is also a debate about whether music itself can be analysed as a discourse (Shepherd and Wicke, 1999: 144–9).

To take an early example of the value of such an approach, Gill used discourse analysis to provide 'a thorough and principled approach to analysing *talk*' (1996: 210); in this case, the responses of male DJs and programme controllers from two commercial radio stations in the United Kingdom, to a question about the lack of female DJs, a pertinent issue given male DJs domination of the airwaves. She observes that a traditional approach to this issue would use attitude surveys, questionnaires or structured interviews with those responsible for appointment decisions; trying to pinpoint a single answer to why there are so few female DJs. 'Discourse analysis, in contrast takes variability seriously, as something interesting in its own right' (213). This is facilitated by the use of informal interviews, and an analytical approach which sought to tease out the practical ideologies through which the employment of women DJs are understood and legitimated. The interviewees used a range of reasons to account for the lack of women DJs, including women not applying to become DJs; listeners' preference for male presenters; women's lack of the necessary skills and the unsuitability of women's voices. 'It is important to note that these were not alternative accounts … each was drawn on by the all or most of the broadcasters at different points in the interviews'. Utilizing discourse analysis, Gill sought not simply to identify the different accounts selectively drawn upon, but 'to examine how they were constructed and made persuasive' (ibid.). Her analysis showed how the broadcasters constructed the problem as lying in women themselves or in the particular wants of the audience. Both of these discursive practices – the way the broadcaster's accounts were organized – enabled the broadcasters to present themselves as non-sexist: 'The role of the radio station was made invisible, and discussions of employment practices and institutionalized sexism were conspicuous by their absence' (1996: 217). Several researchers into music-based subcultures have drawn on discourse analysis (e.g. Kahn-Harris on *Extreme Metal*).

Further reading:
Gill, R. (1996) "Ideology, Gender and Popular Radio: A Discourse Analytic Approach", in Baehr, H. and Gray, A. (eds) *Turning It On: A Reader in Women and Media*, London: Arnold.

DJ; DJ CULTURE

The DJ is the person responsible for presenting and playing the music which is a part of radio and music videoprogramming, and central to many clubs, dances, discos, etc. Popular music studies have concentrated on (i) the role of the DJ in the history of radio, especially the emergence of personality radio and the elevation of DJs to star status in the 1950s and (ii) DJs as central figures in contemporary dance music and club culture. In each case, the notions of **gatekeeper** and **cultural intermediary** have been used to examine the influence of DJs.

(i) *DJs and the history of radio*: Initially, music radio announcers were primarily responsible for cuing records and ensuring smooth continuity, and had little input into the determination of radio playlists. The reshaping of radio in the 1950s was a key influence in the advent of rock'n'roll, while radio airplay became central to a performer's commercial success. The DJ emerged as a star figure, led by figures such as Bob 'Wolfman Jack' Smith, Dick Clark, Alan Freed and Dewey Phillips (with his 'Red Hot and Blue' show the earliest of its kind), helped introduce black R&B music to a white audience. Freed's *Morning Show* on WJW in Cleveland in the early 1950s, and his subsequent New York radio programmes and associated live shows, popularized the very term rock'n'roll. The considerable influence wielded by DJs on music radio playlists, and the associated pay to play practices, led to official investigations of payola. Personality radio and the cult of the DJ was very much part of pirate radio in the 1960s. The role and status of contemporary radio DJs depends very much on the type and format of the radio station.

Further reading:
Ennis, P.H. (1992) *The Seventh Stream*, Hanover: Wesleyan University Press, Chapter 5: 'The DJ takes over, 1946–1956'.

(ii) *DJs and club culture*: When DJs became mixers, they entered the world of musicianship. For example, DJs played a major role in the emergence of the 12-inch single as a standard industry product among United States, then British, record companies in the 1970s. American DJs began mixing seven-inch copies of the same record for prolonged play, then recording their own mixes, first on tape then on vinyl, to play in clubs. The practice became sufficiently widespread to make it worthwhile for record companies to cater for this new market. Initially produced for public performance only, 12-inch singles became retail products from 1978 on, and by the early 1990s represented some 45 per cent of the singles sold (Thornton, 1995). In the process of mixing, DJs created new music, becoming 'turntable musicians'.

The role of the DJ is vital to dance **club culture**. The club atmosphere, mood, or 'vibe' is created in the interaction between the DJ, the crowd and the physical space which they share. The DJ's choice and sequencing of records, in a dialectic with the mood of the clubbers, is central to this interaction. **House** DJs in the late 1970s took 'the first tentative steps of a development which would eventually transform the DJs role from one of "human jukebox" to a position as the central creative focus of dance music culture' (Kempster, 1996: 11).

See: **dance music, radio**; **payola**

Further reading:
Haslam, D. (2001) *Adventures on the Wheels of Steel: The Rise of the Superstar DJ*, London: Fourth Estate.
Kempster, C. (1996) *History of House*, London: Sanctuary.

DOCUMENTARY

'Constructed as a genre within the field of nonfictional representation, documentary has, since its inception, been composed of multiple, frequently linked representational strands' (Beattie, 2004: 2). Popular music documentaries include concert, tour and festival films; profiles of performers and scenes and ambitious historical overviews. Such documentaries can be produced for either film or television (as both 'one-offs' and series). The various forms of popular music documentary have served a number of economic and ideological functions. As a form of programming, they create income for their producers and those who screen them, via rights and royalties. They validate and confirm particular musical styles and historical moments in the **history** of popular music as somehow worthy of more 'serious' attention. While celebrating 'youth' and the mythic status of stars, they also confirm their status as 'the other' for critics of these sounds and their performers.

Concert/tour/festival/scene documentaries demonstrate a close link between the documentation of musical performance and observational modes of documentary film-making. Referred to in the United States as 'direct cinema', and evident from the early 1960s, these documentaries have a well-established tradition, exemplified in the work of director D.A. Pennebaker (*Don't Look Back*, 1966; *Monterey Pop*, 1968 and *Down From the Mountain*, 2002). Direct cinema has recently mutated into 'docusoap' and other variants of **reality television**, as in MTV's *The Real World* series (which frequently featured participants who were seeking musical careers), and *Meet the Osbournes*, a fly on the wall depiction of the family life of ageing heavy metal rocker Ozzy Osbourne.

Films of music festivals have consolidated the mythic status of events such as Monterey Pop (1968) and, especially, Woodstock (1969), with the 1970 film a major box office success. A number of other concert and concert tour films have had a similar but more limited commercial and ideological impact. See, for example, *The Last Waltz* (Martin Scorsese, 1978), a record of The Band's final concert; *Hail, Hail Rock and Roll* (Taylor Hackford, 1987), featuring Chuck Berry and other seminal rock'n'roll performers; *Stop Making Sense* (Jonathon Demme, 1984), featuring Talking Heads; Prince's *Sign O' The Times* (Prince, 1987) and Neil Young and Crazy Horse in *Year of the Horse* (1998, directed by Jim Jarnusch). Such films capture particular moments in 'rock history', while at the same time validating particular musical styles and performers.

Other documentaries consolidate particular historical moments like the Beatles first tour of America (*What's Happening! The Beatles in the USA'*, 2004, directed by Albert and David Maysles); the Rolling Stones Altamont concert of 1969 (*Gimme Shelter*, 1970); and Julien Temple's examination of the Sex Pistol's phenomenon, including the television interview' that sparked off controversy (*The Filth and the Fury*, 2000). Documentaries have also been important in exposing particular scenes, sounds, and performers to a wider audience, as in *The Decline of Western Civilization, Part One* (1981) on the Los Angeles **punk/hardcore** scene circa 1981, featuring Black Flag, the Circle Jerks, X, and the Germs; its 'sequel', *The Decline of Western Civilization, Part Two: the Metal Years* (1988), featuring Aerosmith, Alice Cooper, Ozzy Osbourne, Kiss, Metallica, and Motorhead; and *Hype* (1996) on the Seattle grunge scene. The success of *Buena Vista Social Club* (1999) introduced Cuban music to an international audience, and led to massive sales of the accompanying soundtrack album (which had initially gone largely ignored following its first release in 1996). *Down From the Mountain* (D.A. Pennebaker, 2002) consolidated the audience for contemporary **bluegrass**. Documentaries have reminded us of the role of largely forgotten session musicians and 'house bands', for example, the Funk Brothers in *Standing in the Shadows of Motown* (Paul Justman, 2002). Other popular music documentaries have celebrated major performers; for instance, The Who in *The Kids Are Alright* (Jeff Stein, 1979; released as a *Special DVD Edition*, 2004). As with any genre, the ultimate accolade is parody, best represented by *This is Spinal Tap* (Rob Reiner, 1984).

Documentary series on the history of popular music, made for television, include the joint BBC and US co-production *Dancing in the Street* (1995); *Walk on By* (2003) a history of songwriting; Ken Burns *Jazz* (2001) and the Australian series *Long Way to the Top* (ABC, 1997). In addition to the income from their initial screenings and international licencing, such series have produced accompanying books, soundtracks and 'sell through' video/DVD **boxed sets**. Through their selection of material depends heavily on the nature and quality of what is available, these programmes visually construct particular historical narratives, reframing the past. In the case of *Dancing in the Street*, for example, the emphasis is on 'authentic artists' rather than commercial performers: in the episode *Hang on to yourself*, Kiss get barely a minute, while 'punk icon' Iggy Pop features throughout. In sum, music documentary history is situated primarily around key performers and styles, a form of **canonization**.

Further reading:
Beattie, K. (2004) *Documentary Screens: Non-Fiction Film and Television*, London: Palgrave Macmillan.
Most of the titles mentioned above are now available in DVD format; some are also on YouTube.

DOO-WOP

Doo-wop is derived from two of the many nonsense syllables sung by back-up vocalists. As a **genre**, doo-wop is primarily equated with the mainly black vocal harmony music of the 1950s, although its origins were in the late 1930s and the ballad style of the Ink Spots. Doo-wop evolved out of the gospel tradition, and was characterized by close (four part ballad) harmonies. As essentially an '**a cappella**' style, doo-wop was developed by New York groups, often originally singing on street corners, in the period 1945–55. The songs were relatively simple and extremely formulaic, with a sentimentalized romance as the dominant theme. Pioneer performers included the Ravens, and the Orieles, with their single 'Crying in the Chapel' (1953) the first doo-wop release to gain acceptance with white listeners. Doo-wop spread to other US cities, reaching its zenith in the late 1950s, with The Platters, The Clovers, The Coasters, and Dion and the Belmonts.

Gribin and Schiff argue that doo-wop deserves greater recognition for its contribution to rock music's development during the 1950s. Groups

such as the Drifters and the Coasters added a stronger beat and more pro-
nounced gospel elements, providing a bridge to what became known as
soul music. The genre did not survive the **British Invasion** of the early
to mid-1960s, although it remained influential on soul (The Miracles and
the Impressions) and was evident in the work of pop artists such as The
Four Seasons, who enjoyed considerable chart success in the mid- to late
1960s. The genre enjoyed a brief, nostalgic revival in the 1970s, with the
popularity of groups such as Manhattan Transfer and Sha-Na-Na, whose
name is taken from the background harmony of the Silhouettes earlier
doo-wop classic 'Get a Job' (1958). In the 1990s, the influence of doo-
wop was evident in the work of performers such as Boys 2 Men (sometimes referred to as 'hip hop doo wop') and in several of the **boy bands**.
It continues to be present in various styles popular music emphasizing
close harmony.

Further reading:

Gribin, A.J and Schiff, M. (1992) *Doo-Wop: The Forgotten Third of Rock'N'Roll*,
    Iola, WI: Krause Publications, (Includes a substantial 'sonography').
Hansen, B. (1992) 'Doo-Wop', in *The Rolling Stone Illustrated History of Rock and
    Roll*, 3rd edition, New York: Rabdom House. (Includes a useful discography).

Listening: The Four Seasons, *Anthology*, Rhino, 1988; *The Best of Doo Wop Up
Tempo*, Rhino, 1989; Boys 2 Men, *Cooleyhighharmony*, Motown, 1991

DRUM'N'BASS

A variant of electronic dance music, drum'n'bass achieved a high profile
in the UK music press in the mid-1990s. Originally, the style was called
'jungle', but the racist connotations of this led to the term's displacement.
An eclectic style, 'brought on by the advances and prevalence of digital
sampling technology' (Sicko, 1998), drum'n'bass was an example of the
increasing eclecticism and hybridity of contemporary dance music. It
drew variously on funk, techno, jazz fusion, house, reggae and hip hop.
With its high beats per minute (175–85), drum'n'bass was an accelerated
form of hip hop, and regarded as a 'harder' descendant of house and
techno music (Sicko, 1998). Leading practitioners included Goldie and
Roni Size, while the style was associated with specialist record labels
Moving Shadow, Prototype, and, especially significant, Metalheadz.

See: **electronic dance music** (and the suggested readings there)

Listening: *Breakbeat Science vol. 1*, Volume/Vital, 1996; Roni Size, Reprazent, *New Forms*, Talkin Loud, 1998; Goldie, *Timeless*, FFRR, 1995

DUB

'Dub' refers to 'a process of deconstruction by which the engineer strips music down to its basic rhythm components, introduces novel elements, and thereby provides a new interpretation of material' (Partidge, 2007: 309). The early history of dub is complex, but its origins are usually traced to the ska and reggae sound systems that emerged in Jamaica in the 1960s.

Dub music initially flourished during the era of 'roots reggae', approximately 1968–85, and was pioneered by recording studio producers such as King Tubby (Osbourne Ruddock), Errol T. (Errol Thompson), and Lee 'Scratch' Perry. The demand for exclusive unreleased music in the Jamaican sound system encouraged the production of 'dub plates', a metal plate with a fine coating of vinyl. Partidge (2007) and Veal (2007) both trace the emergence of dub and its wider significance, providing extensive discussion of the recording techniques involved, which produced a style 'built around fragments of sound over a hypnotically repeating reggae groove' (Veal, 2007: 2). Dub was subsequently very influential on electronic dance music: Indeed, the term dub is now used rather indiscriminately by producers of dance and ambient music:

> Today, the sounds and techniques of classic dub have been stylistically absorbed into the various genres of global electronic popular music (such as hip hop, techno, house, jungle, ambient, and trip hop), and conceptually absorbed into the now commonplace practice of song remixing.
>
> (*Veal, 2007: 2*)

A recent variant of dub is 'dubstep', popularized by UK-based labels such as Hyperdub.

Further reading: (see also the general studies of reggae, under that entry)

Katz, D. (2000) *People Funny Boy: The Genius of Lee 'Scratch' Perry*, Edinburgh: Payback Press. (Perry received a Grammy Award in 2003).

Partidge, C. (2007) "King Tubby Meets the Upsetter at the Grass Roots of Dub: Some Thoughts on the Early History and Influence of Dub Reggae", *Popular Music History*, 2, 3: 309–31.

Veal, M.E. (2007) *Dub. Soundscapes and Shattered Songs in Jamaican Reggae*, Middletown, CT: Wesleyan University Press.

Listening: Glen Brown and King Tubby, *Termination Dub 1973-1979*, Blood & Fire/Chant, 1996; Joe Gibbs and Errol Thompson, *African Dub All-Mighty*, Lightning, 1975 (the first in a series of compilations; Lee Perry, *The Producer Series/Words of My Mouth*, Trojan, 1996 (compiles Perry's 1970s work); *5: Five Years of Hyperdub*, Various Artists, Hyperdub/Southbound, 2009

EDM (ELECTRONIC DANCE MUSIC)

In the late 1980s and through the 1990s, 'dance music' become associated with dance club scenes, rave culture in the United Kingdom, and various genres/styles of electronic dance music (EDM). The boundaries and constitution of this metagenre are highly fluid: EDM demonstrates a postmodern aesthetic of creating a **bricolage** of previous styles, along with a continuing underpinning reliance on technology and beat.

In the 1980s and through the 1990s, EDM mutated into a number of identifiable styles, with associated scenes and loose subcultures. These were broadly characterized by their extensive use of state-of-the-art technology and samples, musical eclecticism and links to dance/club scenes. As music press reviews and articles, and marketing hype indicate, there is considerable overlap between the various forms, with shifting and unclear boundaries present, and subgenres splintering off. As Straw observed,

> the growth and fragmentation of dance club music culture has meant that almost all of [these styles] now continue to develop, each with its specialized clubs and record labels, and each allotted a different review section in the dozens of magazines which have merged to catalogue and evaluate new dance records.
>
> *(2001: 172)*

This process has continued, along with increased academic interest in EDM and its associated culture, with researchers often adopting an ethnographic approach to local case studies (Montano, 2010). Much of this work situates EDM and its associated club cultures as a form of contemporary counter-culture, a platform for protest and activism (St. John, 2009, provides an excellent survey of the global scope of EDM and club culture). The **sampling**, which is a major part of EDM, raises questions around authorship and the ownership of sounds.

Following several standard histories and overviews (especially Reynolds, 1998; Gilbert and Pearson, 1999; Woodstra and Bogdanov, 2001), the following EDM genres have been accorded separate treatment:

- House (including major variants, such as Acid House, Trance)
- Drum'n'Bass/Jungle
- Madchester
- Techno (including major variants, such as Detroit Techno; New York Garage)
- Trip-hop

Related styles include ambient and folk psychedelia.

EDM remains a prominent part of the global music industry and popular music culture, closely tied to clubs, club culture and subcultural styles; it has substantial sales, its own charts, key venues and star DJs. The establishment of a journal on EDM, DANCECULT, in 2010, was indicative of the current academic interest in the metagenre.

See also: **clubs**, **club culture**; **DJ**; **raves**, **rave culture**

Further reading:

DANCECULT. *Journal of Electronic Dance Music.*

Garratt, S. (1999) *Adventures in Wonderland: A Decade of Club Culture*, London: Headline.

Gilbert, J. and Pearson, E. (1999) *Discographies: Dance Music, Culture and the Politics of Sound*, London and New York: Routledge.

Lawrence, T. (2003) *Love Saves the Day: A History of American Dance Music Culture, 1970-1979*, Durham and London: Duke University Press.

Montano, E. (2010) 'How do you know he's not playing Pac-Man while he's supposed to be DJing?: technology, formats and the digital future of DJ culture' *Popular Music*, 29/3: 397–416.

Reynolds, S. (1998) *Generation Ecstasy: Into the World of Techno and Rave Culture*, Boston: Little, Brown & Company.

St. John, G. (2009) *Technonomad: Global Raving Subcultures*, London: Equinox.

Straw, W. (2001) 'Dance Music' in Frith, S., Straw, W. and Street, J. (eds) *The Cambridge Companion to Pop and Rock*, Cambridge, MA: Cambridge University Press, pp. 158–75.

Woodstra, C. and Bogdanov, V. eds (2001) *All Music Guide to Electronica: The Definitive Guide to Electronic Music*, San Franciso, CA: Backbeat Books.

EDUCATION

There has been a good deal of discussion of educational issues in popular music studies: the validity and place of popular music within the school and tertiary curriculum; how the study of popular music can best be approached, especially the role of 'theory'; and the professional training of musicians and music industry personnel, notably the continuum between formal and informal learning.

The curriculum status of popular music studies

Popular music can be a subject in its own right, but is more commonly found as a component of other courses. For example, in the school systems of Canada, the United Kingdom, the United States and Australia, popular music may be studied within music, social studies, and media studies. In the tertiary sector, it is usually found within departments of music, media/communication studies and cultural studies. Such courses usually emphasize Anglo-American pop/rock music and its associated genres, representing a form of musical hegemony.

At all levels, the subject historically had to struggle to be accepted as a legitimate educational study. Writing in 1982, Vulliamy and Lee argued that the majority of young people faced a clear opposition between music that is acceptable to the school, usually based in the classical tradition, set against their own (usually popular) musical preferences, which by inference they were led to see as of little value or significance. This situation exacerbated the conflict between the cultural values transmitted through schools and the cultural values of young people. Vulliamy and Lee argued that forms of musical analysis through notation are inappropriate to popular music, which can be legitimated in school by establishing different evaluative criteria (from traditional musicology). This is in line with the view that all music is bounded by particular styles and traditions and occurs within a sociocultural context. These views have continued to be debated (see the journal *Music Education*, published by Cambridge University Press; Green, 2001).

The academic study of music at tertiary level includes musicology; ethnomusicology and the anthropology of music; sociology and semiotics; media and cultural studies; and, since the 1980s, drawing variously on these earlier approaches and traditions, popular music studies (Tagg and Clarida, 2003: Chapter 3). I concentrate here on the last of these; see the separate entries on **musicology, ethnomusicology, semiotics** and **cultural studies**. By the 1980s, the attainment of a certain level of academic credibility for the field was indicated by the appointment of professors of popular music studies; the creation and growth of specialist research centres and research archives (notably The Institute of Popular Music at Liverpool University); the proliferating tertiary level courses, both industry oriented and of a more general media and cultural studies nature; the existence of a number of now well-established academic journals on popular music, considerable cultural journalism in the commercial music press and in fanzines, and an explosion of the critical literature; and the existence, since 1981, of the International Association for the Study of Popular Music.

Pedagogy

Attempts to teach popular music studies are seen to confront a number of difficulties, both theoretical and practical in nature. There is a tendency to either over-theorise, or not to theorise: 'Theoretical abstractions and rote memorization tends to take students further away from the music itself, while musical transcriptions and technical analyses are scarcely more effective at getting the energy that made the music so exciting to begin with' (Gass, 1991: 731). Accordingly, many commentators consider it necessary to begin with students' own consumption, the context within which it occurs, and the meanings they attach to it. However, to neglect theoretical concerns and terminology is to risk the danger of turning popular music studies into a nostalgic form of populism, largely focused on the products of the record industry and viewing their history as one of shifts in genre popularity and the relative status of musicians. While it is necessary to engage with theory, constantly seeking to demonstrate its links with students' own lives and experiences, this creates its own problems, especially the difficulty of opening popular music up for critical discussion. The relative emphases to be accorded to musicological analyses and approaches derived from sociology and cultural studies, have also been an ongoing issue.

Discussion around these questions and issues, begun in the 1980s, has been on-going and is often evident at popular music studies conferences. A further issue is the balance in tertiary courses, especially those with a vocational aspiration (industry training), between 'academic' knowledge and 'practical' work. This is related to the continuum that exists between formal and informal learning, and the manner in which musicians are socialized into their practices (Green, 2001). A new edited study (Green, 2011) situates these issues internationally, considering how individuals in a number of national and regional settings construct their musical identities in relation to their experiences of formal and informal music learning and teaching.

Further reading:
Gass, G. (1991) "Why Don't We Do It in the Classroom?" *South Atlantic Quarterly*, 90, 4.
Green, L. (2001) *How Popular Musicians Learn: A Way Ahead for Music Education*, Aldershot: Ashgate.

Green, L. ed. (2011) *Learning, Teaching and Musical Identity. Voices across Cultures*, Bloomington, IN: Indiana University Press.
The International Association for the Study of Popular Music: www.iaspm.net

School commitment and music preferences

During the 1980s, a number of studies established an association between commitment to school and preferences in popular music. Tanner (1981) is typical of this early work; he found that students with a low commitment to school (an attitudinal scale of six items was used to judge this) were more likely to favour 'heavy' rock than those with a high school commitment, were correspondingly less committed to 'top 40' rock, and were, as a group, predominantly working class; they were also more likely to be associated with delinquent activity. This relationship between delinquent activities, social class and school commitment, on the one hand, and the predilection for 'heavy rock' on the other, was 'the clearest association' uncovered by Tanner's study. He plausibly suggested that **heavy metal** provided 'a symbolic rejection of the prevailing values and assumptions of the schooling process' and indicated 'a correspondence between "heavy metal" and a subcultural solution rooted in action physicality and collective solidarity' (Tanner, 1981). In his wider study of Scandinavian adolescents, Roe (1983) similarly concluded that music functions to symbolically express 'alienation from school' and that low school achievement and a greater preference for 'socially disapproved music' were strongly linked. Subsequent studies largely confirmed these findings, especially in relation to heavy metal (Christenson and Roberts, 1998).

Further reading:

Christenson, P.G. and Roberts, D.F. (1998) *It's Not Only Rock & Roll: Popular Music in the Lives of Adolescents*, Cresskill, NJ: Hampton Press, Inc.
Roe, K. (1983) *Mass Media and Adolescent Schooling*, Stockholm: Almqvst and Wiksell.
Tanner, J. (1981) "Pop Music and Peer Groups: A Study of Canadian High School Students Responses to Pop Music", *Canadian Review of Sociology and Anthropology*, 18, 1: 1–13.

EFFECTS; 'ROCK SUICIDES'

A major tradition in American media research seeks to identify the specific effects of the media on behaviour, attitudes and values. This approach is most evident in studies of television, but is also seen in many of the claims made for the negative influence of popular music. Groups such as the Parents Music Resource Center in the United States (see **censorship**) have used 'effects' research to support their arguments.

The effects tradition is based on behaviourism: a major school of psychology, based on stimulus–response theory and the work of B.F. Skinner, behaviourism was developed in the 1920s in the United States. Although remaining influential, it has been strongly criticised for its lack of attention to the importance of the complex social situation in which media consumption occurs, the absence of any satisfactory theory of personality, and the neglect of the particular self of the individual consumer. The behaviourist approach reduces the interaction between medium and recipient to a simple communication flow model, and accordingly fails to offer a satisfactory explanation for the operation of the popular media (Ross and Nightingale, 2004; Chapter 3, provides a useful historical overview and informed discussion of effects research).

Effects research has been prominent in the study of 'television violence', including the analyses of **music video**. Aikat (2004) surveys this body of work, to situate his own investigation of the incidence and extent of violent content in music videos on four leading music television web sites (BET.com; Country.com; MTV.com and VH1.com). He found that 'audiences for hip-hop/rap and hard-rock videos are the most likely to be exposed to violence, while audiences for adult-contemporary, country, and R&B music videos are least likely to see violence when viewing online music videos' (ibid.: 235). This was a finding 'of particular concern when considering that music videos generally are targeted toward younger audiences' and music video content may be capable of guiding adolescent behaviour (ibid.: 234). However, the qualified nature of his conclusions illustrates the limitations of studies drawing primarily on content analysis: 'The results here suggest that *at least some* young audience members who are frequently exposed to music videos could be adversely affected by their exposure, as previous effects research has concluded' (ibid.; my emphases).

'Rock suicides'

A further example of the use of 'effects research', and the assumptions underpinning it, is the debates surrounding the relationship between popular music and adolescent suicide. During the 1980s, there were several celebrated court cases in the United States, in which unsuccessful attempts were made to hold popular music responsible for teenage 'rock suicides'. The main targets were heavy metal performers Ozzy Osbourne (especially his song 'Suicide Solution', on *Blizzard of Ozz*, Jet, 1981), and Judas Priest, (and their album *Stained Glass*, Columbia, 1978). Similar arguments resurfaced following a spate of teenage suicides in the New York–New Jersey areas, and 'copycat' suicides after Kurt Cobain's suicide in 1994. These featured prominently in the popular press, where objective reasons for such tragedies were ignored in favour of more sensational accounts. Heavy metal and Gothic rock were the main genres held accountable by critics. While they did not always reach the courts, similar claims and arguments about a connection between adolescent suicide and genres such as heavy metal have been evident in other countries.

The relationship between popular music and behaviour in such cases, and the public/press response to them, has been considered in a number of academic studies (on the US cases, see Weinstein, 1991; Shuker, 2008, gives an account of the New Zealand experience of 'Gothic suicides'). These consider how the press coverage of such tragedies has treated them as a form of **moral panic**; and critically examine the claims of causality, perceived subliminal messages in the music, and the preferred readings of songs such as Osbourne's 'Suicide Solution' present in such cases. These studies largely conclude, along with more balanced press accounts, that popular music could hardly be held accountable (at least solely) for such suicides. Teenagers attempt suicide for complex and frequently interrelated reasons: growing unemployment, family breakdown, lack of communication in families, peer pressure, sexuality and low self-esteem. In the case of the suicides picked up on by the press, it is possible that the music may have acted as a final catalyst, contributing to depression. More likely, however, is that the youth involved were already depressed or psychotic.

See: **audiences**; **moral panic**

Further reading:

Aikat, D.D. (2004) "Streaming Violent Genres Online: Visual Images in Music Videos", *Popular Music*, 27, 2: 221–40.
Weinstein, D. (2000) *Heavy Metal: The Music and its Culture*, Boulder, CO: Da Capo Press.

ELECTRONIC DANCE MUSIC

see **EDM**

EMO

Emo is a US-based genre of indie rock music, characterized by strong melodies and expressive confessional lyrics, and associated with a teenage cultural style.

Emo developed out of the Washington, D.C., hardcore punk scene of the mid-1990s, where it was termed 'emotional hardcore' or 'emcore', and identified with bands such as Rites of Spring (Greenwald, 2003, provides a detailed exposition of the development of the genre and its associated youth culture). Emo then took on stylistic elements of 1990s pop punk and indie rock, in what some commentators labelled a 'second wave' of performers (e.g. Jawbreaker). By the late 1990s, several indie labels specialized in the genre, which shifted towards the mainstream with the success of Dashboard Confessional and The Promise Ring. Greenwald considers The Promise Ring's 1997 album, *Nothing Feels Good*, 'the pinnacle of its generation of emo: a convergence of pop and punk, of resignation and celebration, of the lure of girlfriends and the pull of friends, band mates, and the road' (ibid.: 44). Relentless touring by emo bands and a respect for their fans are seen as an essential part of the emergence and consolidation of the genre.

In the 2000s, emo diversified, with more aggressive styles such as 'screamo', defined as having 'roots in and similarities to emo, while hinting at the extra kick that comes from its traces of thrash and metal' (Jim DeRogatis, in *Guitar World*, November 2002, Refused, *The Shape of Punk To Come*, Burning Heart Records, 1998, is seen as a key screamo album). Emo continued to consolidate its place in the mainstream commercial music market, with a 'third wave' of successful bands, including My Chemical Romance, Fall Out Boy and Panic at the Disco. Emo remains commonly used by journalists to describe a wide range of bands, whose members often reject the label.

Greenwald (2003) argues that emo is more than a musical genre, with fan's focus on fashion and dress styles making it 'an essential rite of teenage-hood', although it is one that has been criticized for its male orientation (Hopper, 2004). One of the most interesting aspects of emo culture is the manner in which it has formed around and through the Internet. Myspace, the online networking site has become synonymous with the emo scene, and a key site for the marketing and popularization of emo bands.

See: **indie**; **social network(ing)**

Further reading:
Greenwald, A. (2003) *Nothing Feels Good: Punk Rock, Teenagers, and Emo*, New York: St Martin's Press. (His main title is taken from *The Promise Ring* album).

Hopper, J. (2004) "Emo: where the girls aren't", in Hart, M. (ed.) *Da Capo Best Music Writing 2004*, Cambridge, MA: Da Capo.

Listening: Jawbreaker, *24 Hour Revenge Therapy*; Weezer, *Pinkerton*, Geffen, 1996; The Promise Ring, *Nothing Feels Good*, 1997; Fall Out Boy, *From Under the Cork Tree*, 2006; My Chemical Romance, *The Black Parade*, Reprise, 2006.
On contemporary emo performers and the general culture, see music magazines such as *AP* and *Kerrang!*

ETHNICITY; RACE

The term 'race' is still widely used in popular discourse and in some academic work. 'Race' has historically often been considered as a biological concept, whereby humans can be classified according to a number of physical criteria. Sociologists/cultural theorists now generally regard this as an untenable and ideologically motivated view, associated with *racism*. The alternative term 'ethnicity' is defined on the basis of shared cultural characteristics for a group of people, based in part on cultural self-identification, but can also include an overlay of cultural criteria on to perceived racial characteristics. There is considerable debate around both terms, which should be considered *social* categories.

Ethnicity has been an important consideration in virtually all aspects of popular music studies, particularly in regard to **African–American/black music** in the United States. For the sake of brevity and focus, I have concentrated on the American debates, but popular music is involved in the social processes of 'racialization' internationally, and can both cross and reinforce ethnic/racist boundaries. (The following topics are covered separately and only summary reference is made to them here – see the related entries.)

1. The lack of black ownership of record companies (with a few exceptions, notably Berry Gordy and **Motown**; Russell Simmons at Def Jam), or representation in management, has been critiqued and debated, along with the **marketing** of black music, and the use of the term 'race music' to historically describe **R&B**.
2. The **appropriation** of black music is a contentious issue, as is the status of **crossover**. A considerable body of writing, much of it historical, has examined these issues in the **history** of American popular music.
3. The use of the term **black music**, and the associated notion of an identifiable 'black voice' in vocal styles, is sharply contested.

4. Studies of the **consumption** of popular music in ethnically mixed or diverse populations and communities, show that 'blacks' are more likely (then their white or Asian counterparts) to favour 'black' music genres, most notably **soul**, **R&B**, **blues**, **reggae** and **rap**. These genres have become virtually synonymous with 'black music' and black culture, notably among black adolescents and young adults. However, as the mainstreaming of reggae, rap and hip hop demonstrates, their following is hardly confined to black populations alone.

Further reading:

Neal, M. (1999) *What the Music Said: Black Popular Music and Black Public Culture*, New York and London: Routledge.

Ramsey, G.P., Jr. (2003) *Race Music. Black Cultures from Bebop to Hip-Hop*, Berkeley, CA, and London: University of California Press.

ETHNOGRAPHY

A research method initially developed in social anthropology, ethnography has been utilized in a variety of disciplines. In the anthropological sense, ethnography refers to the description and analysis of a way of life, or culture, and is based on direct observation of behaviour in particular social settings. In contemporary usage, ethnography has become a broad term, associated with a range of methods, including case study, participant observation, life history and symbolic interactionism. There is considerable debate over the status of ethnography as a form of knowledge, and the various approaches to 'field work'. In the traditional, anthropological sense, ethnography involves extensive and intimate involvement in the community studies, but much contemporary 'ethnography' is limited to forms of participant observation. Ethnography was increasingly utilized in the **cultural studies** 'turn' towards the study of the 'active' audience in the 1980s.

In 1993, Cohen argued that popular music studies (at least in Western contexts) lacked ethnographic data and micro-sociological detail, especially in relation to the grassroots of the industry, 'the countless, as yet unknown bands struggling for success at a local level' and the actual process of music making. Since then, there have been a variety of studies along such lines, drawing on various forms of ethnography: community and urban studies, such as those in Liverpool; studies of the geographic popularization of specific genres, along with their local music scenes; investigations of popular music and youth cultures and **subcultures**) and studies of the process of music making and becoming a musician, notably the classic studies by Becker on **jazz** musicians and Bennett on the musical socialization of rock musicians (see **making music**).

Accounts of music-making in non-Western settings are more numerous, and there is a rich tradition of ethnography within ethnomusicology (see below).

Recent interest in ethnographic approaches, and qualitative approaches, marks the continued shift within cultural and media studies, from the global to the local, and to an emphasis on the study of consumption and audiences. An example of current work on urban space, drawing on ethnographic approaches, is the 2-year project, 'Popular Musicscapes and the Characterization of the Urban Environment', based at Liverpool's Institute of Popular Music (see the Special Edition of *Popular Music History*, 4, 2, 2010).

Several large-scale studies are international.

See: **making music**; **scenes**; **subcultures**

Further reading:
Cohen, S. (1993) "Ethnography and Popular Music Studies", *Popular Music*, 12, 2: 123–38.
Kirschner, T. (1998) "Studying Rock: Towards a Materialist Ethnography", in Swiss, T., Sloop, J. and Herman, A. (eds) *Mapping the Beat: Popular Music and Contemporary Theory*, Malden, MA and Oxford: Blackwell, pp. 247–68.

ETHNOMUSICOLOGY

The academic study of music in its cultural context: the anthropology of music. The term ethnomusicology gained currency in the mid-1950s, replacing the traditional descriptor: 'comparative musicology'.

> Ethnomusicology includes the study of folk music, Eastern art music and contemporary music in oral tradition as well as conceptual issues such as the origins of music, musical change, music as symbol, universals in music, the function of music in society, the comparison of musical systems and the biological basis of music and dance.
>
> (*Myers, 1992*)

This broad scope aside, the main areas of study in ethnomusicology have been music in oral tradition and living musical systems, usually in non-Western settings or in relation to indigenous people in Western societies, for example, the American Indians, Australian Aboriginals and the

New Zealand Maori, with particular interest in the relationship of cultural context and musical style. Fieldwork has been the main research method, using various forms of ethnography, and with considerable use of recordings and written notation. While historically the field was split between musicology and anthropology, the two strands fused in the 1980s, as 'interest shifted from pieces of music to processes of musical creation and performance – composition and improvisation – and the focus shifted from collection of repertory to examination of these processes'(Myers, 1992). Lysloff and Gay (2003: Chapter 1) have argued for a more contemporary oriented 'ethnomusicology of technology, an ethnographic study with emphasis placed on technological impact and change'.

A fascinating example of ethnomusicology is Neuenfeldt's edited collection (1997), tracing the changing place of the didjeridu in Australian Aboriginal culture, from a range of musical, cultural and sociological standpoints.

See: **ethnography**

Further reading:
Ethnomusicology (journal).
Lysloff, R. and Gay, Jr. L. eds (2003) *Music and Technoculture*, Middletown, CT: Wesleyan University Press.
Myers, H. (1992) *Ethnomusicology: An Introduction*, London: Macmillan.
Neuenfeldt, K. ed. (1997) *The Didjeridu: From Arnham Land to Internet*, London and Sydney: John Libbey/Perfect Beat Publications.
Post, J.C. (2004) *Ethnomusicology: A Guide to Research*, New York and London: Routledge.
Post, J.C. (2006) *Ethnomusicology. A Contemporary Reader*, New York and London: Routledge.

EXPERIMENTAL

see **avant garde**

EXTREME METAL

An umbrella term for heavy metal's most transgressive genres, including death metal, grindcore, doom metal and black metal.

Harris observes that on the edge of metal culture, forms of metal that are much more obscure and that attract far less attention than contemporary mainstream heavy metal are thriving: 'These forms of metal represent the most diverse, the most artistically vibrant, the most dynamic and also the most problematic aspects of metal culture. Collectively they are known as extreme metal.' (2007: 20). These ambitious claims are convincingly elaborated in his comprehensive and very readable study, which I have primarily drawn on for the following overview (bracketed page numbers refer to Harris).

Black metal was arguably the first form of extreme metal to appear, popularised by the British band Venom, whose 1982 album *Black Metal* gave the style a label and inspired a new generation of metal bands. Venom presented 'more extreme occult imagery than other metal bands' and 'a speeded up and stripped-down version of the genre', which helped shape thrash metal. In the mid-1980s, death metal developed out of thrash, with bands such as Cannibal Corpse and Morbid Angel featuring fast growled vocals, lyrics that dealt with themes such as war, violence, and the occult, and complicated guitar work (although with few solos). Grindcore represented a 'punk-influenced radicalisation of death metal' (3), utilizing extreme speed, and featuring short songs. Doom metal also emerged in the 1980s, as 'an extremely slow form of metal with long epic song structures and melancholic lyrics' (4). Variants of these styles developed; these were often nationally based, as with Norwegian black metal in the early 1990s (in addition to Harris, see Soderlind, 2003). These genres 'share a musical radicalism that marks them out as different from other forms of heavy metal' (5) and are disseminated through small-scale but global 'underground' networks, rather than mainstream commercial modes of distribution.

In summary, extreme metal demonstrates the process of intensification that occurs with the ongoing maturation of popular music genres. Although extreme metal 'frequently teeters on the edge of formless noise' (5), it has been influential in providing 'a crucial motor of innovation within metal' (6). Extreme metal exercises a fascination for both its fans and academics, with several substantial studies of the 'genre' (in addition to Harris, see Purcell, 2003; Soderlind, 2003).

Further reading:

Harris, K. (2007) *Extreme Metal. Music and Culture on the Edge*, Oxford and New York: Berg. (Harris uses the concepts of transgression to consider the different styles of extreme metal, and Bourdieu's cultural capital and habitus to examine hierarcy, status and power within the metal scene.)

Purcell, N.J. (2003) *Death Meets Music: The Passion and Politics of a Subculture*, Jefferson, NC: McFarland. (Purcell usefully situates her approach in subcultural studies, and her focus on the United States is valuable, but her discussion is heavily and rather uncritically reliant on her metal informants.)

Soderlind, D. (2003) *Lords of Chaos: The Bloody Rise of the Satanic Metal Underground*, Los Angeles, CA: Feral House.

FANS; FANDOM

Popular music fans are people who avidly follow the music, and lives, of particular performers and specific genres, with various degrees of enthusiasm and commitment. Fandom is the collective term for the phenomenon of fans and their practices: attending concerts, collecting recordings, putting together scrapbooks, filling bedroom walls with posters and discussing about the star with other fans. Music industry practices help to create and support fandom; record labels and the artists themselves have frequently supported official fan clubs and appreciation societies. Many fan clubs (especially those associated with the Beatles and Elvis Presley) conduct international conventions, even well after the performers celebrated are dead or groups have disbanded. Pop fans' commitment may last only as long as an often brief career, as with the Spice Girls, whereas the fans of performers such as Bruce Springsteen maintain their fandom over time, as do the Deadheads and fans of Elvis Presley (Doss, 1999; Marcus, 1991).

In 1991, Lewis could correctly observe that while fans are the most visible and identifiable of audiences, they 'have been overlooked or not taken seriously as research subjects by critics and scholars' and 'maligned and sensationalized by the popular press, mistrusted by the public' (Lewis, 1992: 1). Fan behaviour was often described as a form of pathology, and the terms applied to it had clear connotations of condemnation and undesirability: 'Beatlemania', 'teenyboppers' and 'groupies'. The last form was considered an extreme form of such fan, moving beyond vicarious identification and using their sexuality to get close to the stars – even if the encounter is usually a fleeting one. Since then, studies of fandom have been a growth point in popular music studies. However, while academic discussions emphasize a less-stereotyped image, the popular view of fans has arguably not changed much. This continues to reflect the traditional view of fandom, situates it in terms of pathology and deviance, and using 'fans' primarily for teenagers who avidly and uncritically follow the latest pop sensation.

Current academic studies of popular fans and fandom reflect the increased theoretical and conceptual diversity of fan studies more generally (see, for example, the contributions to the edited volume: Gray, Sandvoss, Harrington, 2007). Fandom is now regarded as an active process and a complex phenomenon, related to the formation of social identities, especially sexuality, and offering its participants membership of a community not defined in traditional terms of status. There have been significant reappraisals of the negative views formerly applied to fans such as the 'bobby soxers', Frank Sinatra's adolescent female fans in the 1940s (Scrum, 2004) and the groupies of the 1960s (Rhodes, 2005). Hills distinguishes 'cult fandom' as a form of cultural identity, partially distinct from that of the 'fan' in general, related to the duration of the fandom concerned, especially in the absence of new or 'official' material in the originating medium or personna (Hills, 2002; Preface: x). A distinction can also be made between fans and aficianados, with the latter more focused on the music and with different affective investments present (Shuker, 2008: 183).

In fandom,

> moods and feelings become organized and particular objects or personas take on significance. By participating in fandom, fans construct coherent identities for themselves. In the process, they enter a domain of cultural activity of their own making which is, potentially, a source of empowerment in struggles against oppressive ideologies and the unsatisfactory circumstance of everyday life.
>
> (*Lewis, 1992: 3*)

Most fans see themselves as part of a wider community, even if their own fan practices are 'private' and individual activities alone were undertaken. Examples of such empowerment are as diverse as 'metalheads', 'deadheads' (fans of the Grateful Dead) and Bruce Springsteen (Cavicchi, 1998). There is an assertion of female solidarity evident in the activities of female fans, for example, those of the Spice Girls (see **dance pop**).

Beyond possible empowerment, popular music fandom as a form of cultural activity has a number of pleasurable dimensions common to both fans and afficianados: dance and its associated rituals of display and restraint; the anticipatory pleasure of attending a concert or playing a new purchase; the sheer physical pleasure of handling records/tapes/CDs; the pleasure of finding that rare item in a second-hand store bin; and the intellectual and emotional pleasures associated with 'knowing' about particular artists and genres valued by one's peers and associates. Fans actively interact with texts 'to actively assert their mastery over the mass-produced texts which provide the raw materials for their own cultural productions and the basis for their social interactions', becoming 'active participants in the construction and circulation of textual meanings' (Jenkins, 1997: 508). This active engagement with texts has been termed 'textual poaching', drawing on the work of de Certeau, who applied the term 'poaching' to such practices by readers.

Fandom is a central theme in some popular music fictional narratives, and features strongly in many films with a popular music theme or focus, for example *Almost Famous*. Memoirs and studies that document the perspective of the fans themselves offer considerable insights (Aizelwood, 1994; Klosterman, 2002; Vermorel and Vermorel, 1985).

The rise of interactive media (e-mail, listservs and the Internet) have added a new dimension to fandom, aiding in the formation and maintenance of fan bases for performers and musical styles (see Gray, Sandvoss, and Harrington, 2007).

See: **cultural capital**

Further reading:
General:
Gray, J., Sandvoss, C., and Harrington, C.L. (2007) *Fandom: Identities and Communities in a Mediated World*, New York and London: New York University Press.
Hills, M. (2002) *Fan Cultures*, London and New York: Routledge.
Jenkins, H. (1997) "Television Fans, Poachers, Nomads", in Gelder, K. and Thornton, S. (eds) *The Subcultures Reader*, London and New York: Routledge.
Lewis, L. ed. (1992) *The Adoring Audience: Fan Culture and the Popular Media*, London: Routledge.
Rhodes, L.L. (2005). *Electric Ladyland: Women and Rock Culture*. University of Pennsylvania Press.
Cass studies and personal accounts:
Aizlewood, J. ed. (1994) *Love is the Drug*, London: Penguin.
Carvicchi, D. (1998) *Tramps Like Us: Music and Meaning Among Springsteen Fans*, New York: Oxford University Press.
Doss, E. (1999) *Elvis Culture: Fans, Faith and Image*, Lawrence, KS: University Press of Kansas.
Klosterman, C. (2002) *Fargo Rock City: A Heavy Metal Odyssey in Rural North Dakota*, London: Simon & Schuster UK Ltd.
Marcus, G. (1991) *Dead Elvis: A Chronicle of a Cultural Obsession*, New York: Penguin.
Vermorel, F. and Vermorel, J. (1985) *Starlust. The Secret Fantasies of Fans*, London: W.H. Allen.

FANZINES

Fanzines are distinguished from the bulk of the **music press** because of their largely non-commercial nature. Fanzines are part of alternative publishing, which is characterized by the centrality of amateurs, readers as writers; no mainstream channels of distribution; a non-profit orientation; and a network based on non-professional expertise from a wide base of enthusiasts.

Produced by one person, or a group of friends, working from their homes, popular music fanzines are usually concentrated totally on a particular artist or group and are characterized by a fevour bordering on the religious: 'Fanzines accumulate rock facts and gossip not for a mass readership but for a small coterie of cultists, and they are belligerent about their music' (Frith, 1983: 177). This stance can be a reactionary one, preserving the memory of particular artists/styles, but is more usually progressive. As Savage acutely observes, fanzines were historically tied to the English radical tradition of pampleteering. Many of the original punk fanzines were characterized by a broadly leftist cultural politics, challenging their readers to take issue with the views presented by bastions of the status quo and reasserting the revolutionary potential of rock. Fanzines like *Crawdaddy* in the 1960s and *Sniffin' Glue* in the 1970s had tremendous energy, reflecting the vitality of live performances and emergent scenes.

The initial impact of **punk rock** was aided by a network of fanzines and their enthusiastic supporters. Savage argues that in the early days of punk in the United Kingdom, nobody was defining 'punk' from within:

> the established writers were inevitably compromised by age and the minimal demands of objectivity required by their papers. The established media could propagandize and comment, but they could not dramatize the new movement in a way that fired people's imagination.
>
> (*1991: 200*)

With photocopying cheap and accessible for the first time, the fanzines were a new medium tailor made for the values of punk, with its do-it-yourself ethic and associations of street credibility, and there was an explosion of the new form. These fanzines provided a training ground for a number of music journalists (including Paul Morley, Jon Savage, and Lester Bangs), and in some cases useful media expertise for those who, taking to heart their own rhetoric of 'here's three chords, now form a band', subsequently did just that. Fanzines producers/writers did not have to worry about deadlines, censorship or subediting, and 'even the idea of authorship was at issue, as fanzines were produced anonymously or pseudonymously by people trying to avoid discovery by the dole or employers' (Savage, 1991: 279). Fanzine readers tend to actively engage with the publication: they debate via the 'letters to the editor', contribute reviews of recordings and concerts, provide discographies, and even interviews with performers.

A number of studies have demonstrated the value of fanzines to producing and maintaining particular musical styles and scenes. The growth of the audience for **heavy metal** in the 1980s was accompanied by a proliferation of metal fanzines, which played an important commercial role in the absence of radio airplay for metal and the hostility of the mainstream press toward it. These metal fanzines create an information network connecting fans and bands globally. As with fanzines in other youth subcultures, they were 'characterized by a passionate, almost proselytizing, tone. Fanzine editors adhere *fanatically* to the metal conventions, standards, and practices' (Weinstein, 1991: 178). Fanzines have been integral to the development and popularization of alternative scenes, as with Seattle in the early 1990s. In the case of **progressive rock**, fanzines maintain interest long after the genre had been discarded by the mainstream music press. There was a mushrooming of UK dance club fanzines in the early 1990s, linking a network stretching from Manchester to London.

Despite their essentially non-commercial and often ephemeral nature, fanzines remain a significant part of the popular music scene. They represent a cultural space for the creation of a community of interest. The **Internet** has provided a new medium for the international dissemination of fanzines; through their 'printing' of contemporary concert reviews and tour information, such 'e zines' have an immediacy that provides a form of virtual socialization for fans. Music blogs can also be considered a form of fanzine.

See: **music press**

Further reading:
Atton, C. (2010) "Popular Music Fanzines: Genre, Aesthetics, and the Democratic Conversation" *Popular Music and Society*, 33, 4: 517–31.
Savage, J. (1991) *England's Dreaming: Sex Pistols and Punk Rock*, London: Faber and Faber.
Weinstein, D. (1991) *Heavy Metal. A Cultural Sociology*, New York: Lexington.
For reviews of current fanzines, see *Record Collector* magazine (UK).

FASHION

Fashion is central to popular music. Music preferences and the status of genres are subject to fluctuation in critical and commercial popularity, with changing fashions' related to shifts in the constitution of the genre, its audience, the music industry and social trends. The music aside, genres are, to varying degrees, based around fashions and style, and the performers who establish them. Examples include **glam rock** (see Bracewell, 2007, on Roxy Music), the **New Romantics** in the 1980s and **emo**, more recently. Their performers and their fans present, adopt and popularize particular clothing and hair fashions. A similar process is clearly evident in the styles of youth **subcultures**. While fashion and style are indicative of individual and group subjectivities, and serve to demarcate them from other styles and the 'mainstream', they are subject to commodification: the 'grunge look' was the subject of major spreads in the fashion press in 1992–3. Particular historical moments and locations can be closely identified with fashion, as in 'Swinging London' in the 1960s (Levy, 2003), centred around a scene including rock stars (notably The Beatles and The Rolling Stones), film directors, fashion designers (Mary Quant) and photographers (David Bailey).

Further reading:
Bracewell, M. (2007) *Re-Make/Re-Model: Art, Pop, Fashion and the Making of Roxy Music 1953–1972.* London: Faber & Faber.
Levy, S. (2003) *Ready, Steady, Go! Swinging London and the Invention of Cool*, London: Fourth Estate.

FEMININITY

see **gender**

FESTIVALS

A festival is a concert, usually outdoor, often held over several days. There is an established historical tradition of popular music festivals, with regular events such as the Newport Folk and Jazz Festival and the New Orleans

Mardi Gras in the United States, and the UK's Cambridge Folk Festival. Festivals play a central role in popular music mythology. They keep traditions alive, maintaining and expanding their audience base, legitimating particular forms of that tradition, and giving its performers and their fans a sense of shared, communal identity. This role has been maintained through historical retrospectives and anniversary celebrations, as with the recent 40th anniversary of the 1969 Woodstock festival, which saw the (re-)release of a number of celebratory books, documentary films and recordings.

A number of festivals at the end of the 1960s and in the early 1970s helped create the notion of a youth-oriented rock **counter-culture**, while confirming its commercial potential: Monterey, 1967; Woodstock, 1969; and the Isle of Wight, 1970. The other side of the 1960s rock ideology was revealed in the violence at the Rolling Stones free concert at Altamont, near San Francisco, at the end of their 1969 tour of the United States. The 1980s saw the reassertion of the music festival, with the success – both financially and as ideological touchstones – of the politically motivated 'conscience concerts': Live Aid, 1985, and the various Amnesty International concerts. A summer festival season is now a feature of the United Kingdom, Europe, and North American music calendar. The festivals usually include a range of performers, often spread across several days on multiple stages. In the face of an attractive range of choices facing fans, festivals often place an emphasis on a particular musical style, a grouping of artists aimed at attracting a particular fan constituency. A prominent example is the WOMAD (the World of Music, Arts and Dance) concerts, which have become an established feature of the UK popular music scene since they began in 1982. WOMAD has also been successfully exported internationally as far as Australia and New Zealand, where it forms a key event within a southern summer of music festivals. WOMAD has helped world music gain mainstream exposure, although in a commodified manner: 'a kind of commercial aural travel-consumption, where the festival, with its collections of "representative" musicians, assembled from "remote" corners of the world, is a (very) late twentieth-century version of the Great Exhibitions of the nineteenth century' (Hutayk, 1997: 108).

In the United Kingdom, the iconic Glastonbury Festival (known initially as the Pilton Festival) was first held as a musical festival in the early 1970s. Since then, it has been held annually, with several fallow years, in the June Summer solstice. Early festivals were closely associated with traditional English mysticism and new age philosophies, and the hippie counter-culture, a tradition that continues but in more muted and commercialized forms. The second, known as the Glastonbury Fair, was held in 1971, with a pyramid-like stage built over a 'blind spring' for the release and absorption of energies. This free festival was attended by an audience of 12,000 and musicians included David Bowie, Hawkwind, Melanie and Brinsley Schwarz. Glastonbury Festivals continued to celebrate alternative life styles and, in the 1990s, included political 'new folk' bands, such as The Levellers. At the same time, since the 1980s it has been put on an increasingly larger-scale commercial footing, with recent festival tickets rapidly being sold out (the 2009 festival was attended by 137,500). In 2011, UK Music published a report stating that the Glastonbury Festival contributes over 100 million pounds annually to the UK economy. Glastonbury has been the subject of several documentary films and celebratory books (see McKay, 2000).

Within popular music studies, there is a small, but growing, body of literature on festivals. The contributors to Bennett (ed., 2004) reevaluate aspects of Woodstock (1969), the most famous festival of all; Silverman (2007) examines North American 'world music' festivals; and Lebrun (2009) considers the role of popular music festivals in the process of constructing 'anti-mainstream' discourses and practices in France.

Lebrun's study is particularly informative, not least as France, since the early 1990s, has been the European leader in terms of the number and scale of festivals, including a variety of music, dance and theatre events. In 2006, French rock and pop music festivals had a combined audience of over 1.6 million people, including upwards of 650,000 at the Festival Interceltique de Lorient, an 'ethnic' Celtic event launched in 2001 in Brittany (Lebrun, 2009: 137). Lebrun draws on extensive fieldwork, including interviews, to show how the festival goers at such events enjoyed the festival experience as a disruption of their everyday lives, through 'the destabilization of dominant media and dominant social conventions' (ibid.: 135). At the same time, however, she identifies a tight regulatory system that codifies such festivals, 'whose structural and economic rigidity is somewhat at odds with the experience of them by audiences (and artists and critics) as places of instability' (ibid.: 136). As her analysis demonstrates, popular music festivals are subject to a series of contradictions and inconsistencies, placing them at the intersection of commercial imperatives and 'alternative' authenticity.

The major festivals, such as Glastonbury and Knebworth (now Sonisphere) in the United Kingdom, are big business, while local communities are using (usually smaller scale) music festivals as a form of cultural tourism. In addition to their economic importance, music festivals, as a form of extended **concert**, reinforce popular music personnas, creating icons and myths in the process. The performers are made 'accessible' to those attending the concert, and, increasingly with large-scale festivals via satellite television and document art films, to a national and even a worldwide audience. At the same time as it forms a temporary community, joined in celebration and homage to the performers/the genre, the festival audience is being created as a commodity. If it attracts the projected audience, the festival is a major commercial enterprise, with on-site sales of food and souvenirs, the income from the associated television broadcasts via satellite to a global audience/market, and the subsequent 'live' recordings, for example from Knebworth and Rock in Rio. In summary, music festivals are sites where commerce and popular ideology interact to produce historically significant musical meanings.

See: **concerts**; **documentary**

Further reading:

Bennett, A. ed. (2004) *Remembering Woodstock*, Aldershot: Ashgate.

Hutayk, J. (1997) "Adorno at WOMAD: South Asia Crossovers and the Limits of Hybridity Talk", in Werbner, P. and Madood, T. (eds) *Debating Cultural Hybridity*, London and New Jersey: Zed Books, pp. 106–36.

Lebrun, B. (2009) *Protest Music in France. Production, Identity and Audiences*, Farnham (UK) and Burlington (USA): Ashgate; Chapter 6.

McKay, G. (2000) *Glastonbury: A Very English Festival*, London: Victor Gollancz.

Schowalter, D. (2000) "Remembering the Dangers of Rock and Roll: Toward a Historical Narrative of the Rock Festival", *Critical Studies in Media Communication*, 17, 1.

Listening: *Woodstock 40 Years On: 3 Days of Peace and Music*, box set (6 CDs; 78 pp. booklet), US: Rhino records

FILE SHARING

see **peer to peer**

FILM

Film has had an important relationship to popular music. Early silent films often had a live musical accompaniment (usually piano); and with the 'talkies' musicals became a major film genre of the 1930s and continued to be important in the 1960s. Composers and musicians, primarily **stars**, provided a source of material for these films, as did Broadway musicals. A new form of musical, the 'rock musical', played an important part in establishing rock and roll in the mid-1950s. The various genres of popular music, its fans and performers have continued to act as a rich vein of colourful, tragic and salutary stories for filmmakers. There have been a number of significant one-off music documentaries and series. Since the late 1980s, considerable synergy has been created between the music and film industries, with film soundtracks representing another avenue of revenue for recordings, including the back catalogue, and helping to promote contemporary releases.

The discussion here deals with popular music, thematic elements and plots present in mainstream feature film, given their importance, separate entries consider:

- Biopics
- Musicals: classic Hollywood musicals, and the popular/rock musicals that followed.
- Documentaries
- Soundtracks

The historical development of each form or genre is briefly sketched, and an attempt made to establish its central themes and conventions, and the significance of these for the viewing/listening audience.

Films dealing in some way with popular music, and often also drawing on it for their soundtrack, are frequently treated as a generic group, as 'rock films'. There is now a substantial body of such films, including a number of identifiable subgenres (see Shuker, 2008: Chapter 8). During the 1950s, the decline of the Hollywood studio system and a dwindling cinema audience led Hollywood linking up with the record industry to target youth, with a spate of teenage musicals. Many of these served primarily as contrived vehicles for their real life stars, notably those starring Elvis Presley.

In helping to establish an identity for rock'n'roll, these films placed youth in opposition to adult authority, and for conservatives confirmed the 'folk devil' image of fans of the new genre, associating them with juvenile delinquency, a major concern internationally through the 1950s. Thematically, however, they actually stressed reconciliation between generations and classes, with this acting as a point of narrative closure at the film's ending. They also helped create an audience and a market for **rock and roll**, particularly in the United Kingdom, but also in countries even more distant from the initial developments in the United States.

These related roles continued to be in evidence in the subsequent development of the relationship between film and popular music, with developments such as British/Mersey beat and the musical 'British Invasion' (of the United States) in the early 1960s providing narrative vehicles for performers such as The Beatles. In the mid–late 1960s, with the emergence of the counter-culture, popular music was a necessary backdrop and a cachet of cultural authenticity for films such as *Easy Rider* (Dennis Hopper, 1969), which fused an effective rock soundtrack with thematic youth preoccupations of the day: the search for a personal and cultural identity in contemporary America.

There has continued to be a profusion of 'rock films', often based in emerging musical genres and scenes, and exploring a range of themes: youth subcultures; adolescent and young adult sexuality and gender relationships; class and generational conflict; nostalgia; stardom and the rock lifestyle; and fandom and the joy of making music (Shuker, 2008: 149–50). The story lines of these rather loosely grouped films, involve popular music to varying extents, ranging from its centrality to the narrative theme, to its use as soundtrack. These films articulate with the hopes and dreams, and fantasy lives, which popular music brings to people. When an actual artist is drawn on, or featured, such films help the process of mythologizing them, as with Elvis Presley. Dominant themes include youth/adolescence as a rite of passage, frequently characterized by storm and stress, and using subcultural versus 'mainstream' affiliations to explore this; reconciliation, between generations, competing subcultures, and genders, frequently expressed through the emergence of couples; and the search for independence and an established sense of **identity**. Given such themes are ones identified in the literature as central adolescent 'tasks' and preoccupations, they clearly appeal to youthful cinema audiences and to filmmakers looking for box office appeal.

Further reading:

Doherty, T. (1988) *Teenagers & Teenpics: The Juvenilization of American Movies in the 1950s*, Boston: Unwin Hyman.

Mundy, J. (1999) *Popular Music on Screen: From the Hollywood Musical to Music Video*, Manchester: Manchester University Press.

Romney, J. and Wootton, A. (1995) *Celluloid Jukebox: Popular Music and the Movies Since the 50s*, London: British Film Institute.

FOLK MUSIC

International in scope, with a long history and a variety of associated genres/styles, folk music is best regarded as a **metagenre**. Folk music was historically regarded as a more valid, or 'respectable' form of popular music, reflecting its perceived roots in people's common experience, its general lack of mass commercialization, and the associated connotations of authenticity. This status is evident in the activities of several early song collectors, who sought to preserve rural based forms of folk music as part of a conservative project of cultural uplift (see **song collecting**).

While in a sense, it can be argued that all popular music is a form of folk music, more specifically, and historically, the term was originally reserved for music passed from person to person or generation to generation without being written down. This 'folk' is regarded as simple, direct, acoustic-based music, drawing upon the experiences, concerns and customs (folklore) of 'common people' and their communities. As such, folk music includes ethnic music, such as the social and religious ceremonial music of Africans or American Indians; African-American spirituals and blues; work songs (e.g. sea shanties), political and protest songs (broadsides) and love songs. Its form and variants exist in every country and are often regionally based (e.g. the Appalachians in the United States). Considerable mixing and mingling of different traditions, song structures, and instrumentation is evident. Since the 1950s, commercial forms of folk music have become more evident, and expanded the definition of what counts as 'folk'. This has not been without controversy: the genre's history is one of the debates around **authenticity**, and its role in the **enculturation** of folk culture (Frith, 1981). Folk music has taken differing paths in the United Kingdom and the United States, and in other national contexts, as a shifting signifier that continuously mutates in meaning (for an instructive national example, see Smith, 2005, on its development in Australia).

Folk music experienced a strong revival in the United States and the United Kingdom in the late 1950s through to the early 1960s (Cantwell, 1995; Brocken, 2003). The Folkways compilation by Harry Smith, *Anthology of American Folk Music*, released in 1952, was a major influence on this. The three disc, 84 song collection drawn from Smith's collection of 78s, included blues, coalmining ballads, Baptist spirituals, Appalachian and Arcadian folk music, making these available to a wider public for the first time (Skinner, 2006; see also **collecting**).

In the United States, there were influential local scenes in Greenwich Village in New York (for an insiders account of this, see the entertaining memoir by Van Ronk) and Cambridge, Boston. Leading performers included Bob Dylan, Joan Baez and Phil Ochs, who built on the radical activist, popular traditions developed by Woody Guthrie and Pete Seeger in the 1930s. Several folk performers went on to commercial success as singer, songwriters and as members of folk rock groups in the 1960s. The British folk scene of the 1960s was oriented more towards a folk club circuit, and regular major festivals. Leading performers included John Renbourne, Davy Graham, Bert Jansch, Sandy Denny and John Martyn; many were influential on the development of British electric folk (or folk rock) styles.

Contemporary folk music continues to be a very active genre in its own right. There are important folk music archival collections, associated magazines and record companies (e.g. Folkways). Annual festivals, such as Newport in the United States and Cambridge in the United Kingdom, have been central to the continued vitality of the music, while helping to maintain what counts as 'folk music'. Folk is an element in various styles of the blues, country, and reggae, and in contemporary hybrid styles such as 'psychedelic folk': a label applied to performers such as Devendra Banhart, Joanna Newsome and Will Oldham, who fuse indie/punk aesthetics and folk influences (Encarnacao, 2009). I have included in this volume one of the hybrid genres that has been an important part of more 'mainstream' commercial popular music: folk rock.

See: **folk rock; singer songwriters**

Further reading:
Brocken, M. (2003) *The British Folk Revival, 1944–2002*, Aldershot: Ashgate.
Cantwell, R. (1996) *When We Were Good. The Folk Revival*, Cambridge: Cambridge University Press.
Cohen, R. (2006) *Folk Music. The Basics*, London: Routledge. An accessible concise history, with a good discography of issues on CD, and a comprehensive bibliography.
Encarnacao, J. (2009). *Punk Aesthetics in Independent "New Folk", 1990–2008*, Sydney, MA: University of Technology.
Frith, S. (1981) '"The magic that can set you free": the ideology of folk and the myth of the rock community', collected in Frith, S. *Taking Popular Music Seriously (2007)*, Aldershot: Ashgate.
Skinner, K. (2006) '"Must Be Born Again": resurrecting the Anthology of American Folk Music", *Popular Music*, 25/1: 57–75.
Smith, G. (2005) *Singing Australian. A History of Folk and Country Music*, Melbourne: Pluto Press.
Van Ronk, D. with Elijah Wald (2005) *The Major of MacDougal Street*, Cambridge, MA: Da Capo Press.
Magazines: *Sing Out! Dirty Linen. FRoots*

Listening: (see also the discographies in Cohen and Cantrill, above) Harry Smith, *Anthology of American Folk Music*, Folkways 1952; reissued as a six CD box set in 1997; Joan Baez, *Joan Baez*, Vanguard, 1960; Bob Dylan, self titled debut, Columbia, 1962; Woody Guthrie, *The Legendary Performer*, RCA, 2000; Joan Tabor, *Ashore*, Southband, 2011; Devendra Banhart, *Cripple Crow*, XL Recordings, 2005

FOLK ROCK

Folk music provided the basis for folk rock in the mid–1960s: a genre built around folk song structures and topical themes, adapting instruments and techniques associated with folk styles while using amplified instrumentation and rock and, to a lesser degree, pop conventions. Folk rock also had links with country and psychedelic rock (the early Grateful Dead, Jefferson Airplane, and Country Joe and the Fish). The new genre arguably first came to wider attention with Bob Dylan's famous double set (half acoustic, half electric) at the Newport Festival in 1965, and subsequent 'electric' tour. As Dylan's hostile reception from some of his audience indicated, such innovations were not always welcomed by folk purists. In the United States, leading exponents of folk rock included the Byrds, The Flying Burrito Brothers, and the Loving Spoonful. The Byrd's recoding of Dylan's 'Mr Tambourine Man' (1966) is often regarded as the archtypal folk rock record. During the 1970s, performers such as Jackson Browne, Tom Rush, Tim Hardin, Joni Mitchell and James Taylor combined folk styles and a rock ambience, with personalized lyrics which listeners could identify with.

In the United Kingdom, the hybrid form was often termed electric folk (see Laing, 1975), as exponents added new instruments to traditional ones, reworking many standard songs. Leading performers included Lindisfarne, Steeleye Span, Pentangle, Donovan and Fairport Convention; the last continue to perform. The genre became part of the guitar-based sound of much mainstream rock music through the 1980s (e.g. the Long Ryders), and in alternative and indie bands such as REM.

Further reading:

Laing, D. *et al.* (1975) *The Electric Muse: The Story of Folk into Rock*, London: Methuen.

Unterberger, R. (2002) *Turn! Turn! Turn! The 60s Folk-rock Revolution*, San Francisco, CA: Backbeat Books. (Includes an extensive discography).

Viewing: *Dancing in the Street*, episode 3

Listening: The Loving Spoonful, "Do You Believe in Magic?", 1965; Bob Dylan, "Like A Rolling Stone", 1965; The Byrds, "Turn! Turn! Turn!" 1965, on *Turn! Turn! Turn!* CBS, 1966; *Portfolio - Steeleye Span*, Chrysalis, 1988; REM, Murmer, RS, 1983; Richard and Linda Thompson, *I Want To See the Bright Lights Tonight*, Island, 2004 (CD reissue)

FORMATS

The major record(ing) formats are the shellac 78; various forms of vinyl: albums, singles and EPs; the compact disc (CD); cassette audio tape and MP3s. Formats are a significant part of popular music, providing empirical data for historical studies of market cycles, shifting consumer tastes and changing opportunities for musicians. Formats have exercised a significant influence on the marketing of particular genres and their associated artists and audiences. Changing technologies and their associated formats usually appeal to consumers wanting better sound, and to those who possess a 'must have' consumerist orientation to such new technologies, thereby creating fresh markets as older consumers upgrade both their hardware and their record collections.

The first major recording/phonograph companies (Columbia, established in 1889; RCA, 1929, incorporating Victor formed in 1901; and Decca, 1934, in the United States) were engaged from the inception of the industry in a battle over alternative recording and reproducing technologies. At stake was the all important market share. The 10-inch 78 rpm shellac disc emerged as the standard by the 1930s, but experimentation and research continued. Not only was sound quality a consideration, arguably even more important was the amount of music that could be placed on a record, offering the consumer 'more value for money'. In the early post-war years, Columbia developed a long-playing hi-fidelity record using the newly developed vinyl. In 1948, Columbia released its 12-inch 33-and-a-third rpm LP. Refusing to establish a common industry standard, RCA responded by developing a 7-inch vinyl record, with a large hole in the middle, that played at 45 rpm. After several years of competition between the two speeds, the companies pooled their talents and agreed to produce in both formats. By 1952, the LP had become the major format for classical music and the 45 the format for single records for popular radio airplay, jukeboxes and retail sales. Since the 1950s, there have been marked shifts in the popularity of various recording formats (Shuker, 2008: 38–40; Hull et al., 2010).

(A fuller discussion of the historical development of each format, and their subsequent relative economic and cultural significance, is not possible here: see further reading, below).

Further reading:

Chanan, M. (1995) *Repeated Takes: A Short History of Recording and its Effects on Music*, London: Verso.

Millard, A.J. (2005) *America on Record: A History of Recorded Sound*, 2nd edition, Cambridge: Cambridge University Press.

FRANKFURT SCHOOL

see **mass culture**

FUNK

The terms 'funk' and 'funky' were in use in the 1950s among urban black musicians, primarily to describe forms of modern **jazz** and R&B concentrating on 'swing' and 'soul' – the latter being equated with authenticity and sincerity. Funk was also used in a more negative sense to refer to music considered low down, earthy, or crude. Subsequently, funk was applied to the 'anarchic and polyrhythmic' late 1960s and 1970s derivatives of soul: 'High energy, mind-expanding black rock & roll, a soulful psychedelic reaction' (DeCurtis, 1992: 268). Musically, funk tends to have little melodic variation, and rhythm – 'the groove' – is all important. Major performers included James Brown, Sly and the Family Stone, George Clinton, (Parliament, Funkedelic), Kool & the Gang, and Earth, Wind and Fire. Funk was an element in subsequent black-oriented genres, such as hip-hop and techno-funk, and the eclectic work of artists like Prince and bands such as Living Colour. It also made a major contribution to disco (the Ohio Players), rap and hip hop. As even this short list indicates, funk encompasses a variety of associated musical styles, and Vincent (1996) comprehensively identifies a succession of 'Funk Dynasties', extending from the late 1960s to the 1990s.

In what seems to be the only book-length academic exploration of funk, Danielsen (2006) concentrates on its 'golden age' of the 1960s and two of its major artists, James Brown and Parliament/George Clinton. She argues that funk is a distinct musical style, one that must be regarded as both a musical text and a lived experience. A major focus of her study is on the role of race in the construction and consumption of the genre, its crossover success and how African-American music remains a means of catharsis and dealing with the pleasures of the body.

Further reading:

Danielsen, A. (2006) *Presence and Pleasure. The Funk Grooves of James Brown and Parliament*, Middletown, CT: Wesleyan University Press.

Vincent, R. (1996) *Funk: The Music, the People, and the Rhythm of the One*, New York: St Martin's/Griffin.

Listening: James Brown, *Cold Sweat*, King, 1967; Funkadelic, *One Nation under a Groove*, WB, 1978; Parliament, *Mothership Connection*, Casablanca, 1976; Michael Jackson, "Billy Jean", on *Thriller*, Epic, 1983; Prince, *1999*, WB, 1984

GANGSTA RAP

Gangsta rap was the label applied to a style of rap in the early to mid-1990s, characterized by violent and misogynist lyrics, which attracted considerable controversy and was the subject of several high-profile legal cases. Gangsta rap was regarded by some commentators (Price, 2006) as too extreme to be considered a genuine part of 'hip hop culture', but presented conservative critics of the new music with a caricatured image of the genre as a target for censorship.

Rap had already been attacked from the political left for its sexism and homophobia and was now criticized for its profanity and obscenity (see the discussion of the contradictions at work here, in George, 1999). A judge in Florida declared the rap group 2 Live Crew's album *As Nasty as they Want to Be* (1990) to be obscene, the first such ruling for a recorded work in US history. In the United Kingdom, in October 1990, the Los Angeles group Niggaz with Attitude (NWA) released a single with a B-side 'She Swallowed It', dealing with oral sex. Many of the major department store chains, and some music retailers, refused to stock the record, conscious of the lack of clarity surrounding the 1959 Obscene Publications Act and fearing prosecution. In June 1991, NWA released their second album, *Efil4zaggin* (Niggaz 4 life, backwards) in the United Kingdom, after it had already topped the American *Billboard* chart and sold nearly a million copies in its first week of release. The album contained a number of tracks featuring sexual degradation and extreme violence towards women, along with considerable swearing. The police raided the premises of Polygram, the record's UK distributor, and seized some 12,000 copies of the album, and shops withdrew the album from sale. A prosecution followed, using the Obscene Publications Act's definition of an 'obscene article' as one which 'tend(s) to deprave and corrupt'. The high-profile court case revolved around free speech arguments versus claims that the record was obscene, especially in its portrayal of women. The magistrates who judged the case ruled that the album was not obscene under the terms of the Act; the seized stock was returned and the album went back on sale (see Cloonan, 1995, for a detailed treatment of this episode, and the associated issues).

The anti-authority political attitudes and values in gangsta rap also attracted the attention of the New Right in the United States, and internationally. The NWA song 'Fuck the Police' and Ice-T's song 'Cop Killer' (on the album *Body Count*) both created controversy and calls to ban their performers' concerts and records. In New Zealand, in July 1992, the Police Commissioner unsuccessfully attempted to prevent an Ice-T concert in Auckland, arguing that 'Anyone who comes to this country preaching in obscene terms the killing of police, should not be welcome here' (Shuker, 2008: 235–7). 'Cop Killer' is a revenge fantasy of the disempowered, in which the singer recounts getting ready to 'dust some cops off'. President Bush and Vice President Dan Quayle sided with law-enforcement groups in protesting Time Warner's release of the record. Several US national record-store chains stopped selling *Body Count*, and in July 1992 Time Warner pulled the song at Ice-T's request after police groups picketed the media conglomerate's shareholders meeting in Beverley Hills. Anxious to avoid governmental regulation, in September, Warner Music Group executives met with several of the rappers on the label, including Ice-T, and warned them to change their lyrics on some songs or find another label for their work. Time Warner's Sire Records delayed the release of Ice-T's *Home Invasion* album; the performer eventually changed labels, and the album was released on Rhyme Syndicate/Virgin in 1993.

Gangsta rap was a factor in recording companies, music retail, and radio in the mid-1990s beginning to use the designation 'hip hop' for rap music, to avoid negative connotations. Similarly contentious lyrics, however, continued to be evident in the recordings and music videos of later performers such as Nelly (Shuker, 2008: 115–6) and Eminem.

See: **censorship**; **rap**

Further reading: (see also the general studies in the entry on **rap**)

Cloonan, M. (1995) *Banned! Censorship of Popular Music in Britain*, Aldershot: Arena.

George, N. (1999) *Hip Hop America*, New York: Penguin Books. Chapter 13: Too Live.

Listening: Ice-T. 'Cop Killer', on album *Body Count*; 2 Live Crew, *As Nasty as They Want to Be*; NWA, 'Fuck the Police'

GARAGE BANDS; GARAGE ROCK

The garage bands of the late 1960s, so-called as exponents made the music in the garage or basement, were especially prominent in the United

States. Although some performers had already developed a raw rock sound (see Gillet, 1983: 312–3), most garage bands were a response to the **British Invasion** of the American market, and their music was heavily influenced by The Yardbirds, The Kinks and The Who. Playing rock music with lots of enthusiasm, these performers are largely notable for producing some classic one-hit wonders. Some bands were more enduring, including the Standells, the Electric Prunes and the Count Five. In the United Kingdom, garage was best represented by the proto-punk of the commercially successful Troggs ('Wild Thing', 1966).

Garage rock was characterized by enthusiasm, commitment and energy, rather than technical ability. Garage rock made a virtue out of limited musicianship and associated notions of authorship. Covers were central to most repertoires, and frequently covered standards were 'Gloria' (originally a single B-side for Them in the United Kingdom in 1966), 'Hey Joe' (The Leaves) and 'Louie, Louie' (The Kingsmen). Musical characteristics were 'a premium on sheer outrageousness, over-the-top vocal screams and sneers, loud guitars that almost always had a fuzztone' (Erlewine, 1995). Although the basic sound was created for effect, it also reflected the limited instrumentation and recording facilities available to the groups.

The genre was the province largely of white, teenage, suburbanites. It first emerged around 1965, predominantly on tiny, local record labels, linked to strong regional scenes (especially Texas, CA), each with a distinctive style. The genre declined through 1967–8 with the impact of the Vietnam War draft/college attendance on band members, and the performers' general lack of commercial success. The surviving garage bands moved towards more progressive, **psychedelic** sounds, with some success: The Electric Prunes, The Blues Magoos and the Chocolate Watchband.

In 1972, a compilation of garage band releases, *Nuggets*, by Lenny Kaye, created new interest in their work, spawning a whole series of reissues (*Nuggets*, vols 1-12, Rhino; and *Pebbles*, vols 1-10, AIP). In his liner notes, Kaye termed the genre 'punk rock', a prescient acknowledgement of garage rock's subsequent influence: the advent of **punk rock** in the late 1970s and 1980s saw a revival of interest in the garage bands, whose sound is not dissimilar.

Garage rock and its sixties performers received some coverage in the music press, where it was supported by Lester Bangs and Greg Shaw, the editor of the influential *Bomp* ganzine, but remained strangely neglected in otherwise comprehensive American rock histories (Garofalo, 2011; Starr and Waterman, 2003). The genre retained a cult following, including fanzines and web sites, and several reissue labels covering it. Following its classic 1960s period, garage rock remained intermittently present on indie labels through the 1980s, and was an influence on grunge. More extended academic treatments of 1960s garage rock are provided by Hicks (1999), who, somewhat ambitiously, sees the genre as a form of avant garde music, and Abbey (2006).

In 2000–3, there was an international revival of the style, identified with bands such as the White Stripes and The Strokes in the United States, The Hives (Sweden), The Vines (Australia) and The Datsuns (New Zealand). Abbey (2006) traces the origins of the new garage rock to Detroit, with the White Stripes at the centre of a local scene that coalesced around 2000–1. The music press gave this 'new garage rock revolution' (*NME* 8 March, 2003: 38) considerable coverage, according to a stylistic coherence that is difficult to validate. The associated bands displayed similar characteristics to their 1960s predecessors: a preference for 'stripped back' rock'n'roll, but with a range of inflections; an emphasis on energetic live performance; and personal styles (hair, clothes) aligned with those of their fans. These cohered around a conception of 'rock authenticity', appealing traditional fans of that style who were disenchanted with commercialized and MTV oriented nu-metal and hip hop, and electronic dance music.

The term garage continues to be used by rock critics for bands drawing on the earlier traditions, such as The Black Keys ('primal garage blues': *Brothers*, 2010).

Further reading:

Abbey, E.J. (2006) *Garage Rock and Its Roots. Musical Rebels and the Drive for Individuality*, Jefferson, North Carolina, and London: McFarland.
Bangs, L. (1992) "Protopunk: the Garage Bands", in DeCurtis and Henke (eds) *The Rolling Stone Illustrated History*, pp. 452–4 (includes discography).
Gillet, C. (1983) *The Sound of the City*, revised edition, London: Souvenir Press.
Hicks, M. (1999) *Sixties Rock: Garage, Psychedelic and Other Satisfactions*, Urbana and Chicago: University of Illinois Press, Chapter 3.
MOJO, June 2003; with an accompanying "Instant Garage" CD compilation.

Listening: *Nuggets Volume One: The Hits*, Rhino, 1984; The Strokes, *Is This It*, RCA, 2001; *The Best of the Troggs*, Polygram, 1988; *The Best of the Chocolate Watch Band*, Rhino, 1983; The White Stripes, *Elephant*, XL Records, 2003; The Vines, *Highly Evolved*, Capitol Records, 2002

GATEKEEPERS

A media studies term initially applied to how telegraph wire editors selected items for inclusion in local papers, gatekeepers became an established approach to analyse the way in which media workers select, reject and reformulate material for broadcast or publication. Based on a filter-flow model of information flow, gatekeepers' open the gate for some texts and information, and close it for others.

The music industry has a number of gatekeepers, making the initial decision about who to record and promote, and filtering material at each step of the process involving the recording and marketing of a song. Studies of radio have been the main users of the concept; for example, Rothenbuhler (1985) examined one US radio station in depth to determine how, within a given airplay format, the programmer decides which songs to play. The main gatekeepers were the station's programme director and music director, or outside consultant. Subsequent studies of radio have confirmed this finding in various national settings. Decisions on which releases, artists and genres to accord airplay or screen time help shape consumption preferences and can consolidate new genres; for example, US College radio and alternative rock, and MTV and heavy metal, in the late eighties. This process can also serve to privilege imported musical repertoire at the expense of local music (see Neill, 2005, on New Zealand radio).

Organizations involved in industry regulation (e.g. the various performing rights collecting bodies), and government regulatory agencies act as gatekeepers. The editors of music trade publications, and the popular music press, can also be considered a form of gatekeeper, since reviews, artist profiles, chart lists and publicity information help shape radio programmers choices.

The concept became critiqued for being too mechanistic, as oversimplified and of little utility. Nevertheless, it remains useful if used in conjunction with considerations of how musical forms 'arrive' at a 'gate', and how they are subsequently modified.

See: **radio**; **censorship**; **music industry**; **music press**

Further reading:
Neill, K. (2005) in Neill, K. and Shanahan, M. (eds) *The Great New Zealand Radio Experiment*, Palmerston North: Dunmore Press.
Rothenbuhler, E (1985) "Commercial Radio as Communication", *Journal of Communication*, 1: 125–44.

GENDER; FEMININITY; MASCULINITY

The term 'sex' is used to refer to biological differences between male and female. Gender is used for everything that is socially constructed and culturally transmitted. Masculine and feminine are characteristics of men and women, respectively. The major debate in gender studies, sociobiology and sociology, more generally, is between those who believe that these characteristics are indicative of biological natures (essentialists) of men and women, and those who argue that masculine and feminine are ascribed roles, and masculinity and femininity are cultural, shaped by socialization rather than biology (Roberts, 2009; 96, 108; for a fuller introduction, see Mac an Ghaill and Haywood, 2006).

Much of the work around gender issues in popular music has focussed on girls and women. It has been forcefully argued that the dominant ideologies and discourses throughout popular music generally privilege males, while at the same time constructing a normative masculinity. There is rather less literature on male gender issues in popular music and the construction of masculinity. The dominance of male–female binaries in popular music's analysis of gender has been challenged by studies of 'queer music', a term appropriated by gays and lesbians. The significance of gender is evident in a number of areas of popular music studies, which can only be briefly alluded to here. I have further addressed several of these topics in the specific entries indicated (in bold).

There is a lack of women in the male-dominated music industry; traditionally, they are largely in stereotypically 'female' roles, for example, press, office personnel. There are few women working in A&R, or as producers, managers, and sound mixers, all spheres that are male dominated, a situation partly related to technologies as masculinist. The **history** of popular music is largely constructed around male performers and male-dominated genres. While women's contribution to gospel, the blues, and soul are generally recognized, there is a tendency to marginalize their place in the development of rock, metal and dance music. Even when they are credited, their contributions are seen in stereotypical terms: divas, rock chicks (e.g. Suzi Quatro, Janis Joplin), men-pleasing angels (Doris Day), victims (Billie Holiday) or problem personalities (Judy Garland). These narratives have been challenged by popular music histories focussed on women, and through reevaluations of phenomena such as **girl groups** and **fandom**. Linked to this, both traditional **musicology** and the popular **music press** have constructed a male-dominated musical **canon**, with this challenged by feminist scholars and music critics.

The perceived masculine or feminine nature of particular genres has been identified and debated. For example, pop is generally seen as 'a girls' genre', while hard rock and heavy metal are regarded as primarily male-oriented genres: encoded as signifying masculinity. Even genres which, at least at the level of rhetoric, challenge gender stereotyping, such as indie and punk, demonstrate considerable sexism. Women performers predominate in a cappella and gospel music, and are prominent in folk and country and among singer songwriters. These are socially constructed patterns, reflecting differential expectations and resources, including access to musical knowledge and equipment (see, for example, Whiteley, 1997). There has been considerable discussion of the treatment of gender and sexuality in song lyrics and performance styles, and in music videos, with some genres having a clear misogynist strain; for example, hard rock ('cock rock'), and glam metal.

In relation to audiences and consumption, girl **fans** and their musical tastes are often denigrated (e.g. pop's teenyboppers), while male fans are validated (especially in legitimating non-mainstream musical styles); record **collecting** presents itself as a highly gendered practice; and youth **subcultures** have been historically a male preserve, with girls generally absent, 'invisible', or socially insignificant.

A number of historical and contemporary studies have investigated these topics. In relation to rock, for example, in a classic early investigation, Cohen found that, in the Liverpool rock music scene she studied, women were not simply absent, but were actively excluded. All-male bands tended to preserve the music as their domain, keeping the involvement of wives and girlfriends at a distance. This situation reflects the more restricted social position of women, with greater domestic commitments and less physical freedom; the lack of encouragement given to girls to learn rock instruments and rock sexuality as predominantly masculine. Consequently, there are few women bands in rock, or women instrumentalists, and, most women rock performers are 'packaged as traditional, stereotyped, male images of women' (Cohen, *Rock Culture in Liverpool*, 1991: 203). In the early 1990s, the situation Cohen identified was challenged by the **Riot Grrrl** movement. More recent studies of rock genres and scenes, along with populist biographical accounts, show a complex set of influences at work (see **indie**).

See: **girl groups**; **fandom**

Further reading:
General: Mac an Ghaill, M. and Haywood, C. (2006) *Gender Culture and Society: Contemporary Femininities and Masculinities*, Basingstoke: Palgrave Macmillan.
Popular Music: The following are useful introductions to gender issues in popular music studies, along with several general studies of women in popular music; more specific references to the aspects summarized above can be found in their respective entries. In addition to 'academic' studies, popular **biographies** and autobiographies of women performers can provide considerable insights, as in Pat Benatar (2010) on her career as a female 'rock' artist in the 1980s.

Benatar, P., with Patsi Bale Cox (2010) *Between a Heart and a Rock Place. A Memoir*, New York: HarperCollins.

Carson, M., Lewis, T., and Shaw, S.M. (2004) *Girls Rock! Fifty Years of Women Making Music*, Lexington, KY: The University Press of Kentucky.

McClary, S. (1991) *Feminine Endings: Music, Gender, and Sexuality*, Minnesota, MN: University of Minnesota Press.

Press, J. and Reynolds, S. (1995) *The Sex Revolts, Gender, Rebellion and Rock 'n' Roll*, London: Serpents Tail.

Whiteley, S. ed. (1997) *Sexing the Groove: Popular Music and Gender*, London: Routledge.

Whiteley, S. (2005) *Too Much Too Young. Popular Music, Age and Gender*, London: Routledge.

GENRE; METAGENRES

Genre can be basically defined as a category or type. A key component of textual analysis, genre is widely used to analyse popular culture texts, most notably in their filmic and popular literary forms (e.g. thrillers, science fiction and horror).

Genre is central to popular music culture. Some accounts, wanting to ground the discussion more in musicology, prefer the term style to genre (Charleton, 1994). Identifiable genres of popular music are understood as such by musicians, the music industry and by consumers. At the same time, there is considerable argument about the historical location and development of particular genres, their characteristics and the boundaries between them. Genres are constantly debated and contested; while they may share formal musicological characteristics and histories, they are situated in a commercial and cultural nexus. As Holt (2007: Chapter 1) claims, the complex cultural work associated with genre, and the multiplicity of sites where it is active, mean that genre is not a simple concept amenable to easy definition. That said, there have been a number of substantive attempts to develop a broadly applicable definition of music genre (Fabbri, 1991; Frith, 1996; Negus, 1999), while numerous studies of particular genres have been forced to grapple with the issue.

Genre categories are evident in the A&R and marketing practices of sound recording companies; the data collected by recording industry organizations (e.g. the RIAA's consumer profile statistics); industry publications such as *Billboard*, especially its chart listings; the formats of radio stations and MTV channels; music retail and the music press. Fans will frequently identify themselves with particular genres, often demonstrating considerable knowledge of the complexities of their preferences (sub-genres). Similarly, musicians will frequently situate their work by reference to genres and musical styles. The various popular music encyclopaedias, the standard histories, journalistic and academic analyses, all use genre as a central organizing concept.

Lena and Peterson (2008) provide a useful survey (and references) on what they see as two dominant approaches to the study of musical genre: those grounded in musicology, which identify genre as music sharing distinctive musical characteristics, and accounts that place genre study more firmly in a social context, which they see as having greater explanatory power. Following the 'social context' approach, Lena and Peterson define music genres as 'systems of orientations, expectations, and conventions that bind together an industry, performers, critics, and fans in making what they identify as a distinctive sort of music.' (2008: 698). This situates genre is a process: as Frith has observed, for musicians genre categories constitute an effective shorthand for discussing and making music; for listeners, genre helps organize the listening process and for the industry, genre combines musical style (the sound) and the marketing of it (Frith, 1996: 79–95).

In part, critical analysis has concentrated on the tension between an emphasis on 'standardized codes that allow no margin for distraction' (Fabbri, 1999), and the fluidity of genres as these codes are elaborated on and challenged and displaced by new codes. Currently, while musical genres continue to function as marketing categories and reference points for musicians, critics and fans, particular examples clearly demonstrate that genre divisions must be regarded as highly fluid. No style is totally independent of those that have preceded it, and musicians borrow elements from existing styles and incorporate them into new forms. Kronengokld (2008) provides an insightful example of this, in his discussion of the links between three late-seventies genres – disco, new wave and album-oriented rock – normally viewed as distinct, but that 'overlap in varying degrees with respect to their historical moment, modes of dissemination, institutional frames (like record labels), musical materials, personnel, and audiences' (ibid.: 43). He observes that:

> When you study these genres you can't entirely abandon the notion of genre as a set of rules and constitutive features; but these and other genres of the seventies can often be better referenced to their internal variety and proliferation of subgenres, their modes of revision and transformation, and their movement towards other genres.

> *(Ibid.)*

Drawing on this literature, I would suggest that several distinguishing characteristics of genres can be identified and applied to the study of meta-genres. First, there are the stylistic traits present in the music: their musical characteristics, that produce an identifiable sound, are according to conventions of composition, instrumentation and performance. These may vary in terms of their coherence and sustainability, particularly within metagenres. Along with other aspects of genre, particular musical characteristics can be situated within the general historical evolution of popular music.

Second, there are other, essentially non-musical, stylistic attributes, most notably image and its associated visual style. This includes standard iconography and record cover format; the locale and structure of performances, especially in concert, and the dress, make-up and hair styles adopted by both the performers and their listeners and fans. Musical and visual stylistic aspects combine in terms of how they operate to produce particular ideological effects, a set of associations that situate the genre within the broader musical constituency.

Third, there is the primary audience for particular styles. The relationship between fans (and subcultures) and their genre preferences is a form of transaction, mediated by the forms of delivery, creating specific cultural forms with sets of expectations. Genres are accorded specific places in a musical hierarchy by both critics and fans, and by many performers. This hierarchy is loosely based around the notions of authenticity, sincerity and commercialism. The critical denigration of certain genres, including disco, dance pop and the elevation of others, such as alt. country, reflects this, and mirrors the broader, still widely accepted, high/low culture split. We must acknowledge the ultimately subjective nature of these concepts, and the shifting status and constituency of genres. This point becomes clear when we check the genres listed here against those included in the major encyclopaedias, compendiums and histories of popular music. Furthermore, genres are historically located; some endure, others spring briefly to prominence then fade.

Fourth, there are the institutional frames and practices, especially within the music industry practices, which help shape genres.

In this volume, drawing on 'standard' histories, guidebooks and studies of particular genres, I have adopted the concept of **metagenres** as a starting point for further discussion. The metagenres included:

- Blues (including R&B and gospel).
- Country
- EDM: electronic dance music
- Folk

- Heavy metal
- Jazz
- Pop
- Hip Hop
- Reggae
- Rock
- Soul
- World music

Obviously, especially given the fluidity of genres mentioned earlier, these designations are open to debate. For example, should R&B and gospel be 'lumped in' with blues, or is the latter more appropriately placed with soul? World music is more of a marketing ploy, as its various nationally based genres have only limited musical coherence. These metagenre categories are, in part, necessary heuristic devices to give some structure to the various genre entries included in this guide.

These general umbrella terms are each characterized by having a specific geographical, social and cultural and a historical point of origin; a broad musicological identity; and a subsequent history of stylistic and international diffusion, with emergent associated major genres and subgenres. It needs to be stressed that each of these aspects is often debated, and I have tried to indicate the associated issues in the specific entries. In moving beyond each to examine major genres/subcultures that are associated with them, I have largely focussed on those which have had a greater impact on Anglo-American/Western commercial/mainstream popular music. For example, in the case world music, I have included entries on bhangra, bossa nova, Celtic, salsa and Tejano. In the case of jazz, I have identified the popular styles of ragtime and jazz rock fusion, for separate treatment.

Further reading:

Borthwick, S. and Moy, R. (2004) *Popular Music Genres: An Introduction*, Edinburgh: Edinburgh University Press.

Charlton, K. (1994) *Rock Music Styles: A History*, 2nd edition, Madison, WI: Brown & Benchmark.

Fabbri, F. (1999) *Browsing Music Spaces: Categories and the Musical Mind*. Reproduced online by permission of the author at www.tagg.org

See also Fabbri's essay in Moore, A. (ed.) (2007) *Critical Essays in Popular Musicology*.

Frith, S. (1996) *Performing Rites: On the Value of Popular Music*, Cambridge: MA: Harvard University Press.

Holt, F. (2007) *Genre in Popular Music*, Chicago, IL: The University of Chicago Press.

Kronengokld, C. (2008) "Exchange Theories in Disco, New Wave, and Album-Oriented Rock", *Criticism*, 50, 1: 43–82.

Lena, J. And Peterson, R. (2008) "Classification as Culture: Types and Trajectories of Music Genres", *American Sociological Review*, 73, 5: 697–718.

GIRL GROUPS; GIRL GROUP SOUND

While often the studio creations of producers such as Phil Spector, girl groups were on the cutting edge of early 1960s pop music. Leading performers included Darlene Love, who sang lead vocals on a number of group's records; the Ronnettes, the Supremes and the Crystals. The girl groups had a clearly identifiable sound: 'girlish vocals fraught with adolescent idealism and pain, plus quirky arrangements embellished by strings and a dramatic drumbeat' (O'Brien, 2002). The vocals were a combination of qualities: nasal, high-pitched, humming and husky, they owed much to soul and gospel, yet were at the same time unique. Their song narratives were morality tales about the attractions and perils of 'first love', especially of the forbidden variety, primarily written by several youthful songwriting teams, including Gerry Goffin and Carol King. Many girl group releases were on independent labels, including Red Bird, Phillies, Scepter, and an ascendant Motown. The girl groups had considerable impact, articulating the optimism present in the United States under the Kennedy administration, and providing the basis for the success of the 1960s British beat groups, including the Beatles. By the mid-1960s, the girl group sound had been assimilated into mainstream pop, but they have continued to exercise a fascination for fans and popular journalism, linked to a mythic status associated with innocence and optimism (Greig, 1989). The place of the girl groups in the history of pop music and the dynamics of their production have been recently subject to a critical reassessment, according them with greater significance within popular music culture (Warwick (2007).

Further reading:

O'Brien, L. (2002) *She Bop II: The Definitive History of Women in Rock, Pop, and Soul*, London: Continuum.

Greig, C. (1989) *"Will You Still Love Me Tomorrow?" Girl Groups from the 50s on*, London: Virago Press.

Warwick, J. (2007) *Girl Groups, Girl Culture: Popular Music and Identity in the 1960s*, New York: Routledge.

Listening: Girls Aloud, *Chemistry*, Polydor, 2005; *The Best of the Crystals*, ABKCO, 1992; *The Best of the Ronnettes*, ABKCO, 1992; The Supremes, *Anthology*, Motown, 1974
There are a number of good compilations; see those issued by Rhino.

Viewing: *Dancing in the Street*, episode 2

GLAM METAL

A more commercial style of metal, based in hard rock and with a strong visual impact. Musically, the emphasis in glam metal was on accessibility and hooks: 'tuneful hard rock' (Berelian, 2005: 137), with often gratuitously salacious lyrics reflecting indulgence and partying (see Spheeris's 1988 documentary). Glam metal drew on and intersected with earlier **glam rock**, and image was as important as the music itself.

The style emerged in Los Angeles in the early 1980s, with bands such as Mötley Crüe, Twisted Sister and Poison. Other glam metal bands included WASP (an acronym for 'We Are Sexual Perverts'), whose controversial debut single for Capitol Records, 'Animal (Fucks Like A Beast)' 1984, was attacked by the Parent's Music Resource Centre (see **censorship**). Mötley Crüe were the key band, epitomizing the sex, drugs and rock and roll lifestyle projected in L.A. glam metal (see drummer Tommy Lee's autobiography). Their album *Dr Feelgood* (Universal 1984) topped the US charts and was top 5 in the United Kingdom, with producer Bob Rock playing a major role in shaping the band's hard rock for a mass market. Several singles from the album, and their music videos, also charted (notably 'Kick Start My Heart'). Guns N'Roses, formed in L.A. in 1985, took the glam metal template to its extreme, and in the late 1980s were one of the world's most successful (and notorious) bands, Bands such as Bon Jovi (USA) and Def Leppard and Whitesnake (UK) were lumped into the glam rock category, primarily as they shared aspects of the image (long hair and spandex), but were more part of commercial hard rock.

Glam metal had considerable commercial success in the late 1980s, although it was frequently treated with disdain by the music press and fans of earlier traditional metal of the 1970s and was responsible for breaking heavy metal with American radio and music television. The public and fan fascination (see Klosterman, 2002) with the 'wasted' image and visual aesthetic of the bands, and the commercial success of their music, made them appealing to MTV, who included many glam metal band music videos on high rotation. Glam metal, despite its frequent sexism, was also important for the 'feminization' of metal fandom during the 1980s, expanding the appeal of heavy metal beyond its established male following.

The rise of grunge rock in the 1990s, which situated itself in marked contrast to the hedonistic lifestyles of the LA bands, saw a decline in the popularity of glam rock, abetted by the band's self-destructive tendencies. The style has remained evident, however, with band reunion tours (e.g. Mötley Crüe in 2005), documentaries, biographies from/of several band members and compilations and rereleases of key recordings. The rock press, especially *Classic Rock* and *Rolling Stone* magazine, has consistently featured glam rock bands and their members, notably Axel Rose and Slash from Guns N'Roses (see **Classic Rock**).

Further reading:

Berelian, E. (2005) *The Rough Guide to Heavy Metal*, London: Rough Trade Publications.

Christe, I. (2004) *Sound of the Beast: The Complete Headbanging History of Heavy Metal*, New York: Harper Entertainment.

Klosterman, C. (2002) *Fargo Rock City: A Heavy Metal Odyssey in North Dakota*, New York: Scribner.

Viewing: *Seven Ages of Rock*, episode 4: 'Never Say Die'; *Decline of Western Civilization - Part Two: The Heavy Metal Years* (Penelope Spheeris, 1988)

Listening: *Classic Mötley Crüe*, The Universal Master Collection, 2004; Bon Jovi, *Slippery When Wet*, Mercury, 1986; Guns N'Roses, *Appetite For Destruction*, Geffin, 1987

GLAM ROCK; GLITTER ROCK

Also referred to as glitter rock, glam rock was a musical style/genre, and an associated subculture, which flourished in the early 1970s. Glam was especially prominent in the United Kingdom, but had its performers internationally, including the United States, Australia, and New Zealand (Chapman, 2009). Glam was both a reaction against the seriousness of late 1960s progressive rock and the counter-culture, and an extension of it. It strongly emphasized the visual presentation of performers and their concerts, with vividly coloured hair, outrageous costumes, heavy make-up and fire breathing (in the case of Kiss). In glam, the music was almost secondary to the act itself, leading Frith (1988: 42) to observe that 'the image of rock star – previously taken to be quite natural (rock was sincere) or entirely false (a cynical sales device) … became part of musicians' creative effort'.

British glam pioneers were early period David Bowie and Garry Glitter, who had three British number one chart singles in the mid-1970s: 'With its mammoth drum beat, growling guitar, dumb instrumental hook, and incessant chorus of "hey"', his debut single 'Rock and Roll, Part Two' was a huge hit' (Erlewine, 1995: 342). In the United States, glam was represented by performers such as Kiss, with a huge fan following ('the Kiss Army') for their highly theatrical concerts, the punkish New York Dolls, and light heavy metal bands such as Bon Jovi. Other glam rockers included the more prosaic pop-oriented styles of Sweet and Slade, and the more art rock–oriented Roxy Music and Queen ('Bohemian Rhapsody', 1975).

As the above list indicates, males dominated glam. The few prominent female performers, such as Suzi Quatro, adopted a blend of masculine and androgynous musical and performance styles. Elements of androgyny and bisexuality (see Auslander, 2006) were a central part of glam's image and appeal. The style of glam performers and their fans combined hippy sartorial elegance and skinhead hardness: 'Reminiscent of mods in their extravagant clothes, high heels and make-up (often offset with tattoos), hard-working lads masculinized their decadent image composed of a collage of Berlin thirties and New York gay' (Brake, 1985: 76). Glam was part of the 1970s embourgeoisement of leisure in the United Kingdom, with new city centre leisure centres and influenced and merged into the new romantics; for example, Adam and the Ants.

See: **heavy metal**; **new romantics**

Further reading:

Auslander, P. (2006). *Performing Glam Rock: Gender and Theatricality in Popular Music*. Ann Arbor: University of Michigan Press.

Chapman, I. (2009) *Glory Days: From Gumboots to Platforms*. Auckland: HarperCollins.

Glam! Bowie, T. Rex, Queen and the Glory years of Glam Rock. 1970-1975. (2004) London: IPC. NME special edition.

Lenig, S. (2010) *The Twisted Tale of Glam Rock*. Santa Barbara: Praeger.

Thompson, D. (2000) *Glam Rock*. Ontario: Collectors Guide Publishing.

Listening: David Bowie, *The Rise and Fall of Ziggy Stardust*, Rykodisc, 1972; Kiss, *Double Platinum (Greatest Hits)*, Casablanca, 1978; New York Dolls, *Rock & Roll*, Mercury, 1994 (contains their 1973 and 1974 albums); *Rock'n'Roll: the Best of Gary Glitter*, Rhino, 1990; T Rex, *Electric Warrior*, Reprise, 1972; Suzi Quatro, *Greatest Hits*, EMI, 2002; *The Best of Sweet*, Capitol, 1993

GLOBALIZATION

Refers to the increasing economic, social, cultural and political global connections present internationally; the result of the world being shrunk into one communications system, dominated by international media conglomerates. Globalization emerged as a critical concept in the late 1980s. 'Patterns of population movement and settlement established during colonialism and its aftermath, combined with the more recent acceleration of globalization, particularly of electronic communications, have enabled increased cultural juxtaposing, meeting and mixing on a global scale' (Barker, 2002). It was often used to argue that regional and local cultures are squeezed out, overwhelmed, or colonized and 'watered down' and commercialized for 'mainstream' global consumption. Although globalization was frequently used in association with **cultural imperialism**, it was distinguished from it as a more complex and less deterministic or predictable process (see Crowthers, 2007; Hesmondhalgh, 2007: Chapter 6).

In relation to popular music, globalization has an economic and a cultural dimension, with the two closely linked. The dominance of the popular music industry and market by the **major** recording companies, and the internationalization of music genre as global repertoire (Negus, 1999) can be viewed as examples of globalization.

An important aspect of the role of the majors in national popular music markets is the question of the possible conflict between the local and the global, in relation to national musical vitality. The basic concern is that the transnationals will promote their international artists at the expense of local artists, and international preferences and genres at the expense of more 'authentic' local popular music, and only develop those local talents and genres with global sales potential. At a more general level, it is noteworthy that English is the dominant language of popular music, arguably a form of linguistic globalization. Do the policies and activities of the multinationals inhibit the development of indigenous music in local markets? The response is complex and varies from country to country.

The musical interplay of the global and the local has been a central theme in recent scholarship. This has engaged with notions of **appropriation**, **hybridity** and **syncretism** to demonstrate that the relationship is a negotiated rather than a deterministic one (see Born and Hesmondhalgh, 2000; and the related entries here). The playing out of such negotiations is particularly evident in diasporic communities, the internationalization of genres such as hip hop and reggae, and in world music more generally. The term 'glocalization' has become utilized to show how sharp distinctions between global and local are difficult to maintain (e.g. Taylor, 2007).

See: **cultural imperialism**; **diaspora**

Further reading:
Crowthers, L. (2007) *Globalisation and American Popular Culture*, Plymouth, UK: Rowan & Littlefield.
Lewis, J. (2008) *Cultural Studies. The Basics.* 2nd edition. Los Angeles, London: Sage. Chapter 10. Globalization and Global Spaces: Local Transformations.

GOSPEL

While its religious content has generally kept gospel from enjoying significant commercial success in the mainstream of popular music, it has been hugely influential, especially on soul and R&B: Garofalo (1997) refers the genre as 'sanctified R&B'.

Black slaves in the United States adapted the spiritual as part of the Protestant revival at the beginning of the nineteenth century, and gospel arose from the upsurge in fundamentalist church going in black urban communities in the 1920s. Thomas Dorsey (b. 1899), a major composer and choir leader, is credited with inventing the term 'gospel'. Vocal call and response was an important element of gospel: the practice of singing in which the solo vocalist, the caller, is answered by a group of singers (for more contemporary examples, see the recordings of The Staples Singers). An intense spiritual 'feeling' was central to early gospel music, while the moaning, pleading and supplicating vocals became part of the repertoire of jump blues and early soul singers. Gospel was an important part of the upbringing of many early rockabilly singers, and is evident in their vocal style; for example, Elvis Presley. During the late 1950s, Sam Cooke and Ray Charles performed gospel tunes with secular lyrics, or adapted gospel tunes, anticipating soul music. Other leading gospel performers were Mahalia Jackson, America's most popular gospel artist in the 1950s, and Aretha Franklin, who was a gospel star before singing more secular material.

Gospel is clearly influential on the smooth harmonies and lead vocals of contemporary R&B and hip hop, and gospel choirs continue to flourish; gospel continues to be a *Billboard* chart category, and feature among the Grammy awards.

See: **doo-wop**; **R&B**; **soul**

Further reading:
Bogdanov, V., Woodstra, C. and Erlewine, S. eds (2003) *All Music Guide to the Blues*, 3rd edition, San Franciso AMG. Backbeat Books.

Cusic, D. (1990) *The Sound of Light: A History of Gospel Music*, Bowling Green, OH: Bowling Green State University Press.

Moore, A. ed. (2002) *The Cambridge Companion to Blues and Gospel*, Cambridge: Cambridge University Press. An excellent collection of essays, with extensive notes, a substantial bibliography (pp. 194–201), and a selected discography and videography.

Listening: Aretha Franklin, *Amazing Grace*, Atlantic, 1972; *Goodbye Babylon*, (six CD box set), Dust-To-Digital, covers first three decades of recorded rural gospel music, black and white; Mahalia Jackson, *Gospels, Spirituals, Hymns*, CBS; Ray Charles, *The Right Time*, Atlantic, 1987 (especially 'I Got A Woman'); *Sam Cooke with the Soul Stirrers*, Specialty CD, 1991

GOTH/GOTHIC ROCK; GOTHS

Goth is a musical genre and an associated subcultural style, which have attracted considerable journalistic and academic attention. 'Goth', or 'Gothic rock', emerged as a part of post-punk alternative and 'indie' rock in the United Kingdom in the late 1970s. Its origins in cities such as Manchester in the English Midlands, and in London's suburbia, reflected a broader urban malaise, and the indie scene's disenchantment with contemporary politics and culture. As such, Goth was also a rejection of the utopian sentiments and commercialism of glam rock, disco, and British New Pop that had dominated commercial music and associated street fashion through the 1970s and into the early 1980s. At the same time, however, Goth had clear debts to the visual sense and theatricality of both glam and of New Romantics performers such as Adam and the Ants. Goth bands commonly adopted names with Gothic and general Romantic artistic connotations. Singer Siousie Sioux used the term 'gothic' to describe the orientation of her band and may be the originator of the term.

The Goth bands initiated and did much to popularize a Goth 'look', especially through the image and style of charismatic and striking looking band leaders such as Peter Murphy (Bauhaus), Ian Ashbury (Southern Death Cult), Siouxie Sioux (Siouxie and the Banshees) and Nick Cave (The Birthday Party; The Bad Seeds). Along with the music, fashion was at the heart of an emergent subcultural style (Brill, 2008; Spooner, 2006). Goths were initially characterized by their wearing of black clothes, with a taste for 'rich' fabrics such as velvet, lace and leather; the extensive use of silver jewellery; long, black dyed hair, and the heavy use of dark eye/

face make-up. To begin with, Goth was primarily an English phenom-enon, although it quickly developed internationally, particularly in Germany and the United States.

The development of Goth was underpinned by an interlinked net-work of clubs and other live venues, record labels and specialist music magazines and fanzines; today, these have a strong Internet presence. Both the music and the associated subculture have maintained them-selves in various national contexts and urban scenes. Goth is now an international phenomenon, with well-established performers and scenes, most notably in the United States, Europe, Japan, and New Zealand. As with other well-established musical genres, Goth has mutated into a range of subgenres, most notably Dark Wave, Goth Metal and Techno Goth. The Goth subculture has also developed a number of distinct styles, usually linked to its musical variants (Hodkinson, 2002; Brill, 2008).

Early Goth was influenced by the proto-punk music of American band the Velvet Underground, the sound experiments of the rock avant garde and the Goth tradition in literature and the arts. Simon Reynolds regards Bauhaus, The Banshees, The Birthday Party, and Killing Joke as the cru-cial 'proto-Goth' groups (Reynolds, 2006: 433). The label Goth, or Gothic Rock, was applied in the music press in the early 1980s to the music of Joy Division, Bauhaus, Siousie and the Banshees, and Southern Death Cult, notably in several influential *NME* cover stories. Bauhaus' debut EP, *Bela Lugosi's Dead* (1979) is often credited with introducing the genre in the United Kingdom; the 9.5-minute title track, with its lengthy haunting electronically produced sound effects, became a gothic rock anthem. The thematic gothic connection lay in the fact that Lugosi played the lead part in the original *Dracula* film, 1931.

The Goth bands provided a dark, angst-ridden and introspective alter-native to the musical mainstream of disco and chart pop. Thematically, their music drew on the historical use of Goth in relation to architecture, art, literature, and film and television, combining gothic images (gloomy medieval castles, etc.) with a negative view of contemporary society. As Brill observes (2008: 3): 'Song lyrics revolved around the dark recesses of the human soul: death, suffering and destruction as well as unfulfilled romance and isolation, but also the more arcane, taboo aspects of magic and technology (e.g. ancient rituals, vampires).'

While there was a variety of gothic bands and instrumental line-ups, the basic characteristics of the music remained fairly constant: a low–bass pulse, slow, repetitive drums, electronic sound effects, low–pitched vocals, often spoken rather than sung, and with deep, dramatic vocal timbre (e.g. Joy Division 'Love Will Tear Us Apart', on *Closer*, Qwest, 1980).

As a retrospective celebration of Goth (*UNCUT*, 2004) demonstrates, through the period 1976–92, UK Goth covered a broad spectrum of music, including Robert Smith and the Cure; Nick Cave and the Bad Seeds; the Cocteau Twins; Sisters of Mercy, Southern Death Cult, Bauhaus, and the Jesus and Mary Chain. It should be noted that several of the musicians involved were not always comfortable with being associated with the 'Goth' label, which they regarded as a convenient but misapplied journalistic convenience. With considerable justification, Reynolds sees 1982–3 as 'the crucial moment for Goth's emergence' in the United Kingdom, with numerous bands performing and recording – with some commercial successes – indie labels (notably 4AD, Beggar's Banquet, Factory), and thriving clubs and festivals. Indicating the tendency to valorize the cult aspect of Goth, The Cure, the most commercially successful Goth band, were criticized by some journalists as 'Light Goth'. Subsequently, several UK Goth bands mutated into post–punk hybrids of Hard Rock/Heavy Metal, notably The Sisters of Mercy and The Cult (formerly Southern Death Cult).

As Brill documents, 'In the early 1990s the second wave of Goth shifted its impetus from Britain to Germany, which has since been the unrivalled epicentre of the scene' (2008: 4). A network of independent record labels, magazines, clothing companies and events promoters specializing in Goth had developed in Germany through the 1990s. This network included *Orkus* and *Sonic Reducer*, which established themselves as news–stand Goth magazines; 'Black' summer festivals such as M'Era Lune, which routinely drew audiences of 15–20,000 people; and record labels (e.g. Trisol, Out of Line) and numerous professional bands. By the early 2000s, Brill estimates that there were 70–90,000 Goths in Germany, compared with roughly 15,000 in the United Kingdom (2008: 187; notes 2 and 3). In Germany, members of the Goth subculture were often called Gruftis (English: tomb creatures).

There are also significant Goth music scenes and bands in Scandinavia, especially Finland (Nightwish); Italy (Ataraxia); Austria (L'Ame Immortelle) and Switzerland (Lacrimosa). Smaller Gothic club scenes are present in cities such as Paris, Rome and Barcelona, and in Eastern Europe. Even countries with relatively small Goth scenes have produced prominent Goth bands; these include Portugal (Moonspell) and the Netherlands (the Gothic Metal band Within Temptation), although it is noticeable that they frequently record on German–based record labels. In order to reach a wider audience, most European Goth bands sing at least some of their recordings in English. Many of the leading Goth bands and their fans congregate at the well-organized music festivals in Germany and Britain.

The continued vitality of Goth was indicated by the commercial impact of Evanescence's album *Fallen* (2003) and remains evident in the success of specialist record labels and retrospective compilations and on-going record collector interest in the genre (Ogg, 2007). Much of con-temporary (post-2000) Goth music in Europe (and internationally) is largely present in hybrid genres, including Cyber Goth: an upbeat, melo-dic style of electronic music, which originated in South East England in the 1990s, and 'Middle Ages Goth', a crossover between rock and secular medieval music, which is a significant part of the German Goth scene.

As part of the increased cyberspace orientation of contemporary pop-ular music, Goth bands and Goth subcultures can be found on Myspace, YouTube and the Internet more generally.

Further reading:
Brill, D. (2008.) *Goth Culture*, Oxford: Berg.
Goth (2004) *UNCUT Presents NME Originals*: Vol. 1, issue 7, Manchester: Manchester University Press.
Hodkinson, P. (2002) *Goth: Identity, Style and Subculture*, Oxford: Berg Press.
Ogg, A. (2007) "Goth. Back In Black. The top 50 rarities", *Record Collector*, December: 63–7.
Reynolds, S. (2006) *RIP IT UP AND START AGAIN. Post-punk 1978–84*, Chapter 22.
Spooner, C. (2006) *Contemporary Gothic*, London: Reaktion Books.
Thompson, D. (2003) *The Dark Reign of Gothic Rock; in the Reptile House with the Sisters of Mercy, Bauhaus and the Cure*, London: Helter Skelter.

Listening: Bauhaus, "Bela Lugosi's Dead", single, 1979; on album *In the Flat Fields*, 4AD, 1980; Cocteau Twins, *Stars and Topsoil. A Collection 1982-1990*, Shock Records, 2000; Evanescence, *Fallen*, Wind Up, 2003; Joy Division, *Unknown Pleasures*, Factory/Virgin, 1980; Nightwish., *Dark Passion Play*, Nuclear Blast/Roadrunner, 2007; Siousie and the Banshees, *Once Upon a Time. The Singles*, Geffin, 1984; The Sisters of Mercy, *God's Own Medicine*, Elektra, 1987
Compilations: Goth Box. Cleopatra, (4 CDs), 1996; *A Life Less Lived. The Gothic Box*, Rhino Records, 2006. (3 CDs, plus a DVD)

GRAMOPHONE CULTURE

The Edison phonograph, a 'talking machine' he first publically demon-strated in November 1877, represented the true beginning of recorded sound. In 1896, the first machines aimed at the home entertainment mar-ket were introduced by Edison and the Columbia label in the United

States. By 1900, the gramophone (the term gradually replaced the 'phonograph', coming to denote all forms of 'record player') had emerged as the fashion accessory of the day. The phonograph was originally intended primarily as a business tool, but moved into entertainment initially through coin-operated phonographs (from 1889). With the development of pre-recorded cylinders in the early 1900s, the phonographic industry took off: while in 1897 only about 500,000 records had been sold in the United States, by 1899 this number had reached 2.8 million, and continued to rise.

Along with recorded sound, the phonograph, played a role in defining modernity, being used in ways that sharply changed the culture of music in the home and turning music into a 'thing', a physical commodity for sale and exchange in the market place. The domestication of recorded sound increased the musical repertoire available to the domestic home listener, while freeing up the experience of music from its physical location. It replaced 'the shared Victorian pleasures of bandstand and music hall with the solitary delight of a private world of sound' (Millard, 1995: 1). The result was a pervasive 'gramophone culture', which embraced a number of sites: physical and social spaces and institutions that shaped the production and consumption of recorded music.

As several historians have comprehensively demonstrated, the sound recording did not exist solely as an aural artefact; rather, it must be placed in a wider context of a variety of advertising and critical texts, along with the social practices these both engender and sustain (Chanan, 1995; Day, 2000; Syme, 2004). Syme draws on what he terms an 'elastic' sense of discourse analysis, underpinned by the view that 'cultural practices – including those associated with the phonograph – are social constructions' (Syme, 2004: 7), to provide a fascinating cultural history of the recording. He usefully distinguishes between 'on the record' texts, such as album covers and liner notes, and 'off the record texts', such as magazines and advertisements, reviews, and record company catalogues: 'The aggregate effect of these discourse maneuvers associated with the phonograph helped create a community of interest across the globe, a constituency of specialized phonographic subjects: record producers, cover designers, reviewers, performers, journalists, listeners, collectors, and hobbyists' (ibid.: 8).

The gramophone helped democratize classical music by enabling it to be heard away from the concert setting and in the home. The listening habits associated with classical records and recording were produced and naturalized through a magazine culture, which conveyed the idea that collecting and listening to records were legitimate pastimes. *The Gramophone* (1923–), published by the UK Gramophone Society, facilitated this process.

See: **sound reproduction**

Further reading:

Chanan, M. (1995) *Repeated Takes: A Short History of Recording and its Effects on Music*, London: Verso.

Day, T. (2000) *A Century of Recorded Music. Listening to Musical History*, New Haven: Yale University Press.

Eisenberg, E. (1988) *The Recording Angel: Music, Records and Culture From Aristotle to Zappa*, London: Pan Books.

Symes, C. (2004) *Setting the Record Straight. A Material History of Classical Recording*, Middletown, CT: Wesleyan University Press.

GRUNGE

Grunge represented the mainstreaming of the North American indie rock ethic and style of the 1980s (Azerrad, 2001). As much a marketing device as an identifiable 'sound' (cf. **alternative** music, which it is often conflated into), grunge initially developed in the Seattle area (USA) in the late 1980s, associated with the influential indie label, Sub Pop. Pearl Jam and Nirvana were the two most influential bands, credited as leading the commercial break though of grunge/alternative rock into a relatively moribund music scene in the early 1990s. Grunge became part of an international phenomenon (e.g. Britain's Bush, and Australia's silverchair), which briefly dominated the global music market in the mid-1990s.

The enormous worldwide response to the 1994 suicide of Kurt Cobain, Nirvana's lead singer, indicated the impact of grunge. The popularity of grunge was displaced by hip hop and electronica at the end of the decade, with the 'death' of the style being heralded by the music press with the break up of Soundgarden in April 1997.

Grunge eschewed polished technique in favour of raw, angry passionate songs that articulated the pessimism and anxiety of young people, underpinned by a broadly anti-establishment attitude. A series of compilation grunge/alternative albums, *The Trip*, show grunge to be musically a disparate genre, with noticeable differences in tempo, rhythm and melody within a core structure of dominant guitar sounds and pessimistic lyrics. Many later grunge performers straddle genres; for example, Green Day are on the border between grunge and punk. While there was usually no 'grunge' category at the various music awards, those for alternative music were frequently won by bands identified with the genre (Pearl Jam at the 1995 MTV Awards). Grunge embraces clothing and attitude as well as music, and the 'grunge look' includes flannel shirts, big baggy shorts and opportunity shop clothing. But in reacting against commercialism and capitalism, grunge arguably established a new conformity, as both the music and clothing styles were soon commodified.

Grunge and its main figure, Kurt Cobain, continue to exercise a fascination for the popular music press and academic analysis.

See: **alternative**; **scenes**

Further reading:

Anderson, K. (2007) *Grunge. The End of Rock and Roll*, London: Aurum. Includes and extensive discography.

Azerrad, M. (2001) *Our Band Could Be Your Life: Scenes from the American Indie Underground, 1981-1991*, Boston: Little, Brown and Company.

Nirvana & The Story of Grunge, (2005) MOJO Classic: London.

Listening: Nirvana, *Nevermind*, Geffen (US #1 album 1991); Pearl Jam, *Ten*, Epic, 1991; *The Trip*, Vols 1–8

HARD (HEAVY) ROCK

A loose, amorphous genre/style; hard rock is also variously referred to as heavy rock, stadium (or arena) rock or cock rock. The term has been applied since the late 1960s (The Who, Led Zeppelin) and early 1970s (Bad Company) to a variety of performers whose music was characterized by hard, driving rhythms, strong bass drum and use of backbeat (on snare), and short melodies, limited in pitch range. The formal structure of hard rock songs is largely verse–chorus–verse–chorus–solo section (usually played by the lead guitar) –verse–chorus (see Moore, 2001). It is a male-dominated genre, with a largely male following.

Hard rock is also characterized by loud volume and assertive masculinity; evident in the persona of performers, especially vocalists (e.g. Roger Daltrey, Robert Plant, Axl Rose) and lead guitarists, and the genre's predominantly male following. Cock rock has been used as an alternative term for hard rock, highlighting the genre's often explicit and aggressive expression of male sexuality, its at times mysogynist lyrics and its phallic imagery. Cock rock performers were regarded as aggressive, dominating and boastful, a stance, it was argued, evident in their live shows (see Frith and McRobbie, 1978).

Early hard rock styles drew on R&B (The Who), and overlapped with early forms of heavy metal (Deep Purple). The Who fused melody and raw percussive power, extending the structural limitations of early rock'n'-roll. In the United States in the 1980s, hard rock became associated with arena rock, so-called because of large-scale concerts, held in sports arenas, by bands such as Grand Funk Railroad, Kiss, Journey and Foreigner (Waksman, 2009). Other leading hard rock performers in the 1980s and 1990s included Bruce Springsteen, Australia's Cold Chisel (and a solo Jimmy Barnes), Van Halen, The Cult, Bon Jovi and Aerosmith.

Hard rock is now a global genre, with many national examples. It is evident in the music of a range of current performers (e.g. Velvet Revolver) and styles such as contemporary garage rock, and it is a staple part of the play-list for 'Classic Rock' radio.

See: **classic rock**; **garage rock**; **heavy metal**

Further reading:
(The main histories of rock all include discussion of the genre and its performers; see the suggestions in **rock**)
Frith, S. and McRobbie, A. (1990) "Rock and Sexuality", in Frith and Goodwin (eds) *On Record*. New York: Pantheon Books.
Waksman, S. (2009) *This Ain't the Summer of Love*, Berkeley, CA: University of California Press.

Listening: Deep Purple, *Smoke on the Water. The Best of Deep Purple*, EMI, 1994; The Who, *Live at Leeds*, MCA, 1970; CD 1995; Guns N'Roses, *Appetite for Destruction*, Geffin, 1987; Bad Company, *10 From 6*, Atlantic, 1986; Black Country Communion, *Communion*, Warner Music, 2010

Viewing: *The Song Remains the Same* (Peter Clifton and Joe Massot, 1976, on Led Zeppelin); *The Kids Are Alright* (Polygram, 1984, on The Who); *Seven Ages of Rock*, episode 5: 'We Are The Champions' (The Age of Stadium Rock)

HARDCORE

In a general sense, hardcore is used to signify more extreme variants of a cultural form (e.g. hardcore pornography, with its explicit sexuality). Sometimes it is abbreviated to 'hard', as in 'hard trance', electronic music with higher beats per minute. Several extreme styles of heavy metal also draw on the concept (e.g. grindcore). Its more general use in popular music has been in relation to various styles of alternative and indie music. Part of the US underground in the late 1970s, hardcore developed out of punk and was linked with grunge and alternative rock. By the late 1990s, the label had become a cliché, although it remains widely used.

'Uncompromising' is the word often used to characterize the genre. Originally harder and faster than its direct ancestor, punk rock, hardcore took punk music and 'sped up the tempos as fast as humanely possible, sticking largely to monochrome guitars, bass and drums, and favoring half-shouted lyrics venting the most inflammatory sentiments the singers and songwriters could devise' (Erlewhine, 1995: 917). While internationally in evidence, hardcores's chief breeding ground was the United States. The genre was strongest in the San Francisco Bay area (the Dead Kennedys, Black Flag, the Circle Jerks), and Washington DC (Minor Threat, the Bad Brains). British hardcore/post-punk bands were noted for their melodically minimal, percussive structures (Wire, The Fall). Politics were left of centre, but enmeshed in a mass of contradictions, for instance that hardcore was against sexism and racism, but its performers were generally white and male. Nearly all (early) hardcore bands were on small, independent labels. A number of alternative bands had their roots in hardcore, before broadening the scope of their music and signing with major labels; for example, Hüsker Dü, X, and the Replacements. Some local alternative scenes cohered around hardcore musicians and their fans, notably the 'Straightedge' subculture in Washington DC.

See: **alternative**; **indie**; **punk**

Further reading:
Blush, S. (2001) *American Hardcore: A Tribal History,* Los Angeles, CA: Feral House.
Fairchild, C. (1995) '"Alternative" Music and the Politics of Cultural Autonomy: The Case of Fugazi and the D.C. Scene', *Popular Music and Society*, 19, 1: 17–36.

Listening: The Dead Kennedys, *Fresh Fruit for Rotting Vegetables*, Alternative Tentacles, 1980; Black Flag, *Damaged*, SST, 1981; Wire, *Pink Flag*, Restless, 1977

Viewing: *The Decline of Western Civilization, Part One*, Penelope Spheeris, 1981; the Los Angeles punk/hardcore scene circa 1981, featuring Black Flag, the Circle Jerks, X, and the Germs

HEAVY METAL

Heavy metal (HM), now often referred to simply as metal, can be considered a metagenre. It has a substantial history, distinctive fans and encompasses a wide range of subgenres. The musical parameters of HM as a genre cannot be comfortably reduced to formulaic terms. It is usually louder, 'harder' and faster-paced than conventional rock music, and remains predominantly guitar oriented. The main instruments are electric guitars (lead and bass), drums and electronic keyboards, but there are numerous variants within this basic framework (see Charleton, 1994; Walser, 1993). Some forms of the genre have enjoyed enormous commercial success and have a large fan base; other, 'harder' extreme subgenres have a cult following.

Some critics see HM as beginning in the late 1960s, its origins variously being traced to several key recordings: Blue Cheer's 1968 reworking of Eddie Cochran's 1950s hit 'Summertime Blues', which turned Cochran's great acoustic guitar riff into distorted metallic sounding electric guitar chords, accompanied by a thumping percussion, and Steppenwolf's 'Born To Be Wild' (1967) with its reference to 'heavy metal thunder' (from the William Burroughs' novel Naked Lunch) in the song's second verse. HM was a logical progression from the power trios of 1960s groups such as the Jimi Hendrix Experience and Cream, who played blues-based rock with heavily amplified guitar and bass reinforcing each other.

However, histories of the genre generally see the release of Black Sabbath's eponymous debut album (1970), which reached number 8 in the UK album chart and spent three months on the US album chart, and their follow-up album Paraniod (1970) as establishing the early parameters of HM. The band's origins in industrial Birmingham were reflected in their music, characterized by Tony Iommi's style of guitar playing (born of necessity following an industrial accident; see his interview in the documentary Seven Ages of Rock), singer Ozzy Osbourne's vocal wail, and lyrics drawing on black magic and the occult (see the contemporary reviews and interviews in Hoskyns, 2004; also Christe, 2004). Also important contributors to shaping the new genre were albums from Deep Purple (Deep Purple in Rock) and Uriah Heap (Very 'eavy, Very 'umble in the United Kingdom, self-titled in the United States), both were also released in 1970. Christe (2004), writing from the viewpoint of a sympathetic critic, sees metal's early success as based on its devoted fans: an audience linked by tape trading and established by heavy touring and a strong commitment to the live concert event by bands such as Sabbath.

The commercial success of the British bands Black Sabbath, Deep Purple and, above all, Led Zeppelin, and Grand Funk and Mountain in the United States – despite the general critical 'thumbs down' for their efforts – consolidated HM as a market force in the early 1970s and established a HM youth subculture. Even this short list of performers demonstrates the difficulties of bounding the genre, and there are differences in their treatment in the various histories and commentaries on metal. Led Zeppelin performed more traditional blues-based material and combined acoustic outings with electric guitars, yet are accorded the HM tag chiefly because they played at a very loud volume. Although Deep Purple and their American counterparts are often considered as HM bands, they have also been classified as 'hard' or 'heavy' rock (see, among others, Christe, 2004: 12–17; Popov, 1997; Weinstein, 1991). In the 1980s, there was a clear distinction possible between the more overtly commercially oriented MTV friendly HM bands, such as Bon Jovi and Poison with their glam rock images, and mainstream HM bands, whose styles merge into hard rock, such as Guns N'Roses, and Aerosmith.

HM was (and still is) frequently criticized as incorporating the worst excesses of popular music, notably its perceived narcissism and sexism, and it was also often musically dismissed. The genre was one of the main targets of moves to censor popular music in the 1980s in the United States (see **censorship**). Even Lester Bangs, one of the few rock critics to view the emergence of HM favourably, wrote:

> As its detractors have always claimed, heavy-metal rock is nothing more than a bunch of noise; it is not music, it's distortion – and that is precisely why its adherents find it appealing. Of all contemporary rock, it is the genre most closely identified with violence and aggression, rapine and carnage. Heavy metal orchestrates technological nihilism.
>
> (*1992*)

A much-debated question is why a genre generally panned by the critics (and many other music fans) as formulaic noise, associated with a negative social stance and consequent public controversy, became so popular? HM fans are attracted by its sheer volume, the 'power' of the music; the genre's problem-oriented lyrics, at both the global and personal levels; and by its performers general lack of a commercialized image. This is a form of **authenticity**, with metal fans seeking greater 'substance' than available through mainstream chart-oriented music.

Until the publication of Weinstein's comprehensive sociological study (1991, 2000), Walser's more musically grounded treatment (1993), and Arnett's study of its fans (1996), there were few attempts to seriously discuss the genre. Yet, as these studies showed, HM displayed a musical cogency and enjoyed a mass appeal, existing within a set of social relationships. There was a well-developed HM subculture, predominantly working class, white, young and male, identifying with the phallic imagery of guitars and the general muscularity and oppositional orientation of the form. The symbols associated with HM, which include Nazi insignia and Egyptian and Biblical symbols, provided a signature of identification with the genre, being widely adopted by metal's youth cult following (see Arnett, 1996).

Once established, HM demonstrated the common pattern of genre fragmentation and hybridization. There are a number of identifiable HM subgenres or closely related styles. Although historically specific, each has continued to be represented in the wide variety of contemporary metal performers. The following have been accorded separate treatment:

- NWOBHM (the New Wave of British Heavy Metal)
- Glam metal (also referred to as lite, hair or pop metal)
- Thrash/speed metal
- Extreme metal (including death metal, black metal, grindcore and doom metal)
- Nu-metal

Metal has also been part of several hybrid styles, notably prog metal and rap-metal, and been drawn on by performers who are largely situated in mainstream commercial rock, such as the 'funk metal' of the Red Hot Chilli Peppers (*Blood Sugar Sex Magic*, WB, 1991). 'Christian metal' features lyrics drawing on the Bible and Christian values, but within a metal framework; for example, Stryper, *In God We Trust*, Hollywood, 1991. (The band take their name from Isaiah 53:5: 'and with his stripes we are healed'.) In addition, metal has interacted with related genres, notably punk (see Waksman, 2009) and grunge (Weinstein, 2000: Chapter 8).

HM has maintained a high market profile, despite frequent critical derision and a negative public image. The success of Metallica, and newer bands such as Godsmacked and Disturbed, has consolidated metal as part of mainstream commercial popular music. At the same time, the intensification of the genre has created sub-styles on the margins of metal itself (e.g. Swedish death metal).

Further reading:

Arnett, J. (1996) *Metalheads. Heavy Metal Music and Adolescent Alienation*, Boulder, CO: Westview Press.

Bangs, L. (1992) 'Heavy Metal', in DeCurtis, A. and Henke, J. (eds) *The Rolling Stone Illustrated History of Rock and Roll*, 3rd edn, New York, NY: Random House, pp. 459–64.

Berelian, E. (2005) *The Rough Guide to Heavy Metal*, London: Rough Trade Publications.

Christe, I. (2004) *Sound of the Beast: the Complete Headbanging History of Heavy Metal*, New York, NY: Harper Entertainment.

Hoskyns, B. ed. (2004) *Into the Void: Ozzy Osbourne and Black Sabbath. A Rock's Backpages Reader*, London and New York, NY: Omnibus Press.

Popoff, M. (1997) *A Collector's Guide to Heavy Metal*, Toronto, ON: Collectors Guide Publishing.

Walser, R. (1993) *Running With the Devil: Power, Gender and Madness in Heavy Metal Music*, Middletown, CT: Wesleyan University Press.

Weinstein, Deena (1991, 2000) *Heavy Metal. The Music and Its Culture, Revised Edition*, USA: Da Capo Press. (The 2000 edition adds a chapter on the 1990s).

Magazines: *Metal Hammer*; *Kerrang!*; *Blunt*; *Classic Rock*

Viewing: *Dancing in the Street*, episode 7, 'Hang On To Yourself'; *Decline of Western Civilization – Part Two; The Heavy Metal Years* (Penelope Spheeris, 1988); *Seven Ages of Rock*, BBC, 2007: episode 4: 'Never Say Die'; *Metal. A Headbanger's Journey*, Directed and produced by Sam Dunn, Scot McFadyen, Jessia Wise, Canada, 2006

Website: Keith Kahn-Harris provides an extensive bibliography on metal and related genres, and his own work on death metal www.kahn-harris.org

HEGEMONY

Italian Marxist theoretician Antonio Gramsci's concept of ideological (or cultural) hegemony was advanced to explain how a ruling class maintains its dominance by achieving a popular consensus mediated through the various institutions of society, including the mass media. Hegemony mystifies and conceals existing power relations and social arrangements. Particular ideas and rules are constructed as natural and universal 'commonsense' and the popular media play a leading role in this process. Hegemony operates in the realms of consciousness and representations, making popular cultural forms important contributors to its formation and maintenance (Mikula, 2008; Roberts, 2009; see Barker, 2002: Chapter 3, gives a fuller discussion of the concept).

In relation to popular music, hegemony has been utilized to examine the manner in which song lyrics and music videos underpin dominant conceptions of gender, sexuality and ethnicity; to investigate the cultural symbolic challenge offered by youth subcultures to mainstream, dominant society, and, most significantly, to analyse the Anglo-American international dominance of the music industry and its styles. This dominance has waned in recent years, with the reassertion of the European market and the emergence of Japanese media conglomerates as major players in the music industry, but the Anglo-American market remains of major importance, not least for its commercial legitimation of emergent trends. Aside from its market share, the Anglo-American music industries established and continues to privilege particular formats and working practices as 'natural' and accepted, especially those associated with 'international repertoire' (Negus, 1999).

See: **cultural imperialism; globalization; subcultures**

HERITAGE; 'ROCK MUSEUMS'

Heritage has traditionally referred to the 'representations of custom, tradition and place that coalesce within the cultural memory of a particular national or regional context and fundamentally contribute to the shaping of the latter's collective identity' (Bennett, 2009: 476–7). As traditional dichotomies between 'high' and 'low' culture have been eroded, forms of contemporary culture, including popular music, have increasingly become part of this discourse. The concept of heritage is now multi-faceted, increasingly fragmented and highly contested (Atkinson, 2008). In relation to popular music, the cultural dominance of the baby boomer generation has fostered a collective remembering and celebration of **rock** as an art form, with an associated **canon** of performers and recordings, as well as physical and electronic sites. This process of what Schmutz (2005) terms 'retrospective cultural consecration', produces a hegemonic view, although this is contested by counter discussions that emphasize a different set of cultural memories, while also situating these in terms of cultural heritage.

Aspects of popular music as cultural heritage include the canonization of performers, scenes and styles/genres through the music press, film and television documentaries and features, and the tribute band phenomenon. A further aspect, considered here, is dedicated to popular music museums – sometimes collectively referred to as 'rock museums' – and temporary museum exhibitions. The creation of a number of museums devoted to the history of popular music is part of the now prominent 'heritage industry'. Leading examples in the United State include the Rock and Roll Hall of Fame (Cleveland), the Experience Museum (Seattle, Washington) and the Delta Blues Museum (Clarkesdale). Graceland, Elvis Presley's mansion and grave site, can also be considered a form of museum. It is among the leading tourist attractions in the United States. Also significant, have been temporary exhibitions on popular music, such as 'The

Beat Goes On' in National Museums Liverpool, in 2008–9. As do 'main-stream' museums, popular music museums and exhibitions raise questions on the selection of the material for inclusion (such as which artists, periods, styles and artefacts) and the manner in which these are to be contextualized and displayed. In general, the narratives constructed frequently reinforced standard (hegemonic) views of who, what and where have been historically significant (see **history**).

The Delta Blues Museum, established in 1979, is typical of the approach and displays here, featuring vintage instruments and recording equipment, early recordings, and memorabilia. It has a library, a record collection, and an archive, including letters and photographs. Supported by performers such as ZZ Top, and the magazine *Living Blues*, the Delta Blues Museum seeks to preserve the music, and to raise the self-esteem of local people by reminding them of the important role the area has played in the development of the music.

Temporary museum exhibitions have also been significant in creating and representing narratives of popular music. As part of Liverpool's year as European Capital of Culture, 'The Beat Goes On' exhibition, which ran from 12 July 2008 to 1 November 2009, examined aspects of Merseyside's popular music history from 1945 to the present day. As the souvenir booklet produced for the exhibition noted: 'The Beat Goes On celebrates Liverpool's popular music heritage and identity, its successes and its evolution over the past 60 years', and 'draws on a wealth of material from record companies, institutions and private collectors as well as fascinating objects from National Museums Liverpool's own collection'. In addition, the exhibition relied heavily on the collections of the Institute of Popular Music at the University of Liverpool (see Strachan, 2008), whose staff member Marion Leonard was seconded for two years to act as lead curator on the project. On display were numerous sound recordings, including rare shellac 78s, demo tapes by later famous musicians, accompanied by their hand written notes, and vinyl albums by obscure Liverpool bands. Listening stations with 45s were part of a sonic timeline that enabled visitors to trace shifts in musical styles and their performers, illustrating the range of musical influences that had shaped the city's musical landscape: country, jazz, blues, calypso and folk were all present by the end of the 1940s, followed by rock and roll and skiffle in the 1950s, Merseybeat in the 1960s, and later club scenes and sounds. Items from the music press included magazines and xeroxed fanzines. A feature of the exhibition was the attention paid to the role of image and design, featuring local contributions to album artwork, photography, music video and costume.

Leonard has insightfully reflected on the construction of the exhibition, along with similar recent exhibitions:

> In effect, the institutional logic of museums and art galleries mean that the conceptual underpinning of popular music exhibitions tends to take the form of either canonic representations, the contextualization of popular music artefacts as art or the presentation of popular music as local or social history.
>
> (*Leonard, 2007: 147*)

She argues that 'these types of approach represent a problem for the researcher/curator attempting to reconstruct a truly social history of popular music as they tend to replicate dominant hegemonic versions of history'. (In the case of Liverpool, this means a focus on Merseybeat in the sixties, especially The Beatles.) The recollections of private collectors, along with their loaned artefacts, she suggests, offer a way forward to a 'more balanced representation of a variety of popular music practices'.

See: **canon**; **classic rock**; **collecting**; **history**; **music press**; **tribute bands**

Further reading:

Atkinson, D. (2008) "The heritage of mundane places", in B. Graham and P. Howard, (eds) *The Ashgate Research Companion to Heritage and Identity*, Aldershot: Ashgate, pp. 381–95.

Bennett, A. (2009) "'Heritage rock": rock music, representation and heritage discourse', *Poetics*, 37: 474–89.

Burgoyne, R. (2003) "From contested to consensual memory: the rock and roll hall of fame museum." K. Hodgkin and S. Radston (eds) *Contested Pasts: The Politics of Memory*, London: Routledge, pp. 208–20.

Leonard, M. (2007) "Constructing histories through material culture: popular music, museums and collecting", *Popular Music History*, 2, 2: 147–67.

Santelli, R. (1999) "The Rock and Roll Hall of Fame and Museum: Myth, Memory, and History", in K. Kelly and E. McDonnell (eds) *Stars Don't Stand Still in the Sky*. Washington Square, NY: New York University Press, pp. 237–43.

Schmutz, V. (2005) "Retrospective cultural consecration in popular music", *American Behavioral Scientist*, 48: 1510–23.

Websites: Rock and Roll Hall of Fame: www.rockhall.com; Delta Blues Museum: www.deltabluesmuseim.org; Graceland: www.graceland

HIP HOP; RAP

Rap music, and the hip hop culture that it is a part of, can be considered a **metagenre**. Initially part of a dance style that began in the late 1970s among black and Hispanic teenagers in New York's outer boroughs, rap became the musical centre of the general cultural phenomenon of hip hop: the broad term that encompassed the social, fashion, music and dance subculture of American's urban, black and Latino youth of the 1980s and 1990s (Price, 2006: Chapter 2: The Elements). Potter regarded hip hop culture as constituting a 'highly sophisticated postmodernism' (Potter, 1995: 13), a self-conscious political practice, reclaiming, recycling and reiterating the past, for the common people, and a 'cultural recycling center' and a 'counter-formation' of capitalism (ibid.: 108). The central reference point here is the idea that consumers trace their own paths through the commodity relations with which they are presented. Other observers critiqued such grand claims being made (often by white intellectuals) for early hip hop, seeing it in more prosaic terms as a form of black street culture. Hip hop moved from New York in the late 1970s, with a local following, to attract a wider audience, including white youth, and, by the late 1990s, was a part of mainstream musical culture.

Some commentators claim that the antecedents of rap lie in the various earlier story-telling forms of popular music, particularly talking blues, call-and-response in blues and gospel, but such links are not that evident. There is a stronger argument for a connection with the spoken political edged verses of Gil Scott-Heron and The Last Poets in the late 1960s and early 1970s. However, hip hop's more direct formative influences were with reggae's DJ toasters and stripped down styles of funk music, notably James Brown's use of stream-of-consciousness raps over elemental funk back-up (see John Szwed, "The Real Old School", in Light, 1999).

Studies of hip hop identify roughly four periods in its development: (1) its origins in the mid-1970s; (2) a 'break-out' period 1979–1988; (3) its commercialization, diversification and the rise of gangsta rap; and (4) since the late 1990s, the consolidation of hip hop as a central part of mainstream culture; this has included further stylistic diversification and the emergence of a number of major stars. (For a good overview of rap through 2000, along with discographies, see Light, 1999. Chang, 2005, is a much-acclaimed history, which foregrounds the voice of the artists; there is a useful 'hip-hop culture chronology' in Price, 2006.)

Until 1979, hip hop was primarily a local New York phenomenon. Rappers made their own mixes, borrowing from a range of musical sources and talking over the music in a form of improvised street poetry (rapping). This absorption and re-contextualizing of elements of popular culture marked out rap as a form of pop art or postmodern culture (Potter, 1995). The style was commercially significant, as black youth were 'doing their own thing', bypassing the traditional music industry.

Early hip hop transformed the turntable from a technology for playing back recorded sound into a musical instrument. Performers placed two copies of the same record on adjacent turntables, switching back and forth between these they could use their hand to 'backspin' one counter clockwise, while continuing to play the other through the loud-speakers. This technique enabled the rapper/DJ to repeat a particular 'break' over and over. A further innovation which became a central part of rap recordings was 'scratching', along with the reciting of rhyming phrases (rapping) over the 'breakbeats' produced on the turntables (see Schloss, 2004). These practices, pioneered by Grandmaster Flash, Kool Herc and others in the mid-1970s, became associated with what is now termed 'old school' rap.

Many early rappers recorded on independent labels, initially on 12 inch singles, most prominently Sugar Hill Records in New York (see Shapiro, 2004: 351–2). The Sugarhill Gang, 'Rapper's Delight' (1979) and Grandmaster Flash and the Furious Five, 'The Message' (1982), were the first rap records to have mainstream chart success and led to greater interest in the musical style. Run DMC, *Raising Hell* (London, 1986) was the first rap album to crossover to the pop charts and brought rap into wider public consciousness. In 1983, the mega-hit film *Flashdance* featured two scenes of Rock Steady Crew members displaying their skills and led to a spate of hip hop films over the next few years, beginning with *Beat Street*. Further indications of hip hop moving into the mainstream were the use of break dancers at the closing of the 1984 summer Olympics, and the institution of a Grammy award for rap (1988). The genre was soon taken up by white youth, white artists (The Beastie Boys) and the major record labels, in a familiar process of the appropriation of black musical styles.

As with other maturing musical metagenres, a number of identifiable subgenres emerged, moving beyond the 'old school' rap of the 1970s. The political 'hardcore rap' of Public Enemy maintained the tradition of socially engaged rap, firmly established by The Message; the group's influential 1988 album *It Takes a Nation of Millions (To Hold Us Back)*, was a critical and commercial success, and is widely considered part of a rap **canon** (see Price, 2006: Appendix). In the 1990s, the blander commercial rap of performers such as M.C. Hammer, Kris Kross and Vanilla Ice, and the increased popularity of rap among white listeners, raised traditional issues of authenticity and the white appropriation. In the 1990s, gangsta rap, with its accompanying controversy and censorship, was instrumental in the music industry (including radio and the music press) increasingly adopting the term 'hip hop', rather than 'rap' to market the music.

By the late 1990s, rap and hip hop became bracketed together as part of mainstream American culture. A *Time* magazine cover story, featuring Lauryn Hill (from The Fugees), proclaimed the arrival of the 'Hip Hop

Nation', referring to 'the music revolution that has changed America' (*Time*, 8 February, 1999: 40–57). The Fugees album *The Score*, Sony/Columbia, 1996, was a huge international success, with sales of seven million by 1997. In adding elements of R&B, soul and ragga rock to the genre, it foreshadowed the contemporary orientation of rap. By 1998, hip hop was the top selling music format in the US market, and its influence pervaded fashion, language and street style. The *Time* story noted that the two terms, rap and hip hop, were now 'nearly, but not completely, interchangeable' (ibid.). This conflation was cemented through the next few years. The record sales, product endorsements, associated fashion merchandizing and public celebrity of artists such as Beyonce (and her former group Destinys Child), Nelly, Dr Dre and Eminem have made hip hop part of contemporary mainstream popular music culture.

During the past decade in the United States, hip hop genres have become increasingly diverse and are often identified by geographical location: notably West Coast, East Coast, Detroit and Southern (Atlanta based) Hip Hop. Many performers, record labels and producers have developed cult followings, such as Dr. Dre, Jay-Z's Roc-A-Fella Records, The Neptunes and Timberland. Contemporary subgenres include Club Hip Hop/Pop Rap, Death Rap/Horrorcore, Gangster rap/G-funk, Rap Rock and Freestyle. Commercially successful artists include Eminem, Jay-Z, 50 cent, Nelly, Nas, Ja Rule, Kanye West and Outkast. Current trends and emergent performers (e.g. Tyler the Creator) can be followed in the dedicated hip hop magazines, especially *XXL* and *The Source.*

The metagenre also became globalized. As Mitchell argued in a major edited study, *Global Noise*: 'Hip-hop and rap cannot be viewed simply as the expression of African–American culture; it has become a vehicle for global youth affiliations and a tool for reworking local identity all over the world' (2001: introduction). The growth of rap in particular national contexts has been the focus of several recent studies, emphasizing the hybridization with local musical styles (e.g., Condry on Japan; the essays in Basu and Lemelle, 2006).

There is a considerable 'populist' literature on rap/hip hop, including compendiums of key performers (Shapiro, 2004), general guides and histories, along with a number of dedicated music/style magazines. In academic studies, frequently overlapping major concerns and themes have been the politics of rap/hip hop; its commodification by the culture industries, along with its incorporation into the wider/white culture (George, 1999); its relationship to ethnicity (Rose, 1994); the role of place and space in its development (Foreman, 2002) and the innovative production and performance techniques associated with the genre (Schloss, 2004). An excellent comprehensive edited reader is Forman and Neal

(2004); this includes many of the above topics, situated historically, with contributions from journalism and academia.

See: **gangsta rap**

Further reading:

Basu, D. and Lemelle, S. eds (2006) *The Vinyl Ain't Final: Hop Hop and the Globalisation of Culture*, London: Pluto Press.

Chang, J. (2005) *Can't Stop Won't Stop. A History of the Hip-Hop Generation*, New York: Ebury Press/Random House.

Condry, I. (2006) *Hip-Hop Japan. Rap and the Paths of Cultural Globalization*, Durham, NC: Duke University Press.

Cross, B. (1993) *It's Not About a Salary: Rap, Race and Resistance in Los Angeles*, New York: Verso.

Forman, M. (2002) *The Hood Comes First: Race, Space, and Place in Rap and Hip-Hop*, Middletown, CT: Wesleyan University Press.

Forman, M. and Neal, M. (eds) (2004) *That's The Joint! The Hip-Hop Studies Reader*, New York: Routledge.

George, N. (1999) *Hip Hop America*, New York: Penguin Books.

Light, A. (1999) *The Vibe History of Hip Hop*, New York: Three Rivers Press.

Mitchell, T. ed. (2001) *Global Noise: Rap and Hip Hop Outside the USA*, Middletown, CT: Wesleyan University Press.

Potter, R. (1995) *Spectacular Vernaculars: Hip-Hop and the Politics of Postmodernism*, Albany, NY: SUNY Press.

Price, E.G. (2006) *Hip Hop Culture*, Santa Barbara, CA: ABC-CLIO. Price includes good biographical sketches of main performers, appendices listing influential hip-hop singles and albums, a timeline, and an extensive listing of resources, including 'organizations, associations and programs'.

Rose, T. (1994) *Black Noise*, Hanover, NH: Wesleyan University Press.

Schloss, J.G. (2004) *Making Beats: The Art of Sample-Based Hip-Hop*, Middletown, CT: Wesleyan University Press.

Shapiro, P. (2004) *The Rough Guide to Hip-Hop*, 2nd edition, London: Rough Guides Ltd.

Magazines: *The Source*; *VIBE*; *XXL*; *Wax Poetics* (dedicated to the art of 'beat-digging')

Listening: see Shapiro (2004) above, and the contemporary hip hop music press

Viewing: *Freestlye: The Art of Rhyme*, Director Kevin Fitzgerald, 2000; documentary on the world of improvised rap; *Hip Hop: Beyond Beats and Rhymes*, Director Byron Hurt, 2006; documentary examining representations of gender roles in hip hop culture

HISTORY; HISTORIOGRAPHY

The history of popular music has been subject to internal critiques and debates in a similar manner to other forms of historical writing. At issue are the boundaries of the field, including its tendency to privilege Anglo-American developments; the treatment of various genres, within it; and the emphases that should be accorded to the context within which popular music is produced. Indeed, it is more correct to talk of *histories*, rather than *history*, in order to stress the contested and contingent nature of historical explanation. As a field of study within popular music studies, the history of popular music has recently enjoyed greater attention. Indications include a dedicated journal (*Popular Music History*), a comprehensive reader (Bracket, 2009) and new editions of various standard textbooks (e.g. Garofalo, 2011; Friedlander, 2006).

There are a number of sites where histories of popular music are presented. These include film and television **biopics** and **documentaries**; **heritage** sites; the **music press** and audio collections representative of particular styles and periods of music (see **box set**; **reissues**). These are important, especially in terms of creating public/popular memories about the musical past, and as such have been given separate entries in this volume. They can be regarded as complimenting and, at times, extending print-based histories, now often also available in digital form, which continue to be the main site for popular music histories. Accordingly, books and journal articles are the focus of this discussion. As examples here, I have primarily used the history of rock'n'roll and rock (for the historiography of genres such as the blues, country and jazz, see their entries).

The history of popular music, especially in relation to the emergence of rock'n'roll and its subsequent generic development and mutation, has usually been presented in a fairly standard form, based around a chronological sequence of genres (see Friedlander, 1996; Garofalo, 1997; Starr and Waterman, 2003). This sees it as essentially a Western tradition, and privileges rock'n'roll and the genres it mutated into. This tradition has been critiqued as 'rockist' (e.g. by Negus, 1996; on this point, see **popular music**). The various histories display a tendency to emphasize performers, genres and texts, with rather less attention to the role of technology and economics. An example of this approach is the weight usually attached to the role of creative individuals in establishing rock'n'roll in the 1950s: Elvis Presley, Little Richard, Bill Haley, Buddy Holly and Chuck Berry are seen to have virtually created the genre and revitalized popular music in the process. At one level, the impact of these performers is undisputed, even though they were adapting existing styles and forms, they were clearly innovative (Gillet, 1983). But as Curtis observes, '*all* popular performers come along at the right time' and 'to explain the success of a given act, you need to make the social and cultural context of that success as specific as possible' (Curtis, 1987: 5). Accordingly, other writers have paid greater attention to the social, economic and demographic situation in the United States and the United Kingdom in the early 1950s, producing rather different accounts.

Framing principles other than chronology used to outline and 'explain' the history of popular music include **gender, technology** and its industrial organization, especially the role of **independent** labels. Histories can also be situated around a particular musical genre or general style, or focus on a particular period and its broader culture, such as 'Swinging London' and the 'invention of cool' in the 1960s. There is a group of histories of popular music whose authors adopt a more idiosyncratic approach, often drawing on insider status. Napier-Bell, for example, presents an historical account of the British music industry, tinged with cynicism reflecting his experiences in it (notably as manager for the Kinks in the 1960s). He attributes a key role to the use/abuse of drugs, as his title indicates: *Black Vinyl, White Powder* (2002).

Revisionist histories

In a sense, all historical writing is 'revisionist', as each generation of historians take a different perspective on the past, informed by their contemporary location (see MacMillan, 2009). More specifically, however, revisionist history is characterized by asking different, sometimes awkward questions of orthodox 'standard' accounts; and the use of a wider range of primary sources, especially popular material, including oral history. In relation to popular music, in addition to these characteristics, revisionist accounts tend to focus on previously neglected periods, styles and performers, often drawing new connections between these. Two recent books are prominent examples of this broad approach, with their titles indicating the revisionist intentions of the authors: 'An alternative history' (Wald, 2009); and, rather less obviously, 'The nineteenth century popular music revolution' (Scott).

Wald's history of twentieth century popular music in the United States has a catchy and intriguing title ('How The Beatles Destroyed Rock'N'Roll'), but one that is rather misleading, as The Beatles only bookend the book: Wald begins with a personal reflection on the impact of their early recordings, and ends with a discussion of the band's historical relationship with previous popular music. However, the broader relevance of the Beatles to his argument is that they represented both a break from previously dominant musical traditions and continuity with them. For Wald, rock'n'roll is not so much a historical genre but rather a process, whereby black dance styles repeatedly transformed pop music and were remade by it in turn.

In his introduction, Wald provides a useful discussion of the historiography of popular music and his own approach. As he observes, history is a reflection of at least two periods: when the events happened and when one is writing, and also of the writer's personal experience (ibid.: 7). A third dimension can be added to this: the previous literature and the manner in which dominant narratives have emerged from it. Wald challenges standard historical accounts and their privileging of a canon of performers and recordings. He wants to step outside of the assumptions of genre-based histories:

> the divisions of eighty years of evolving styles into discrete categories like ragtime, jazz, swing, R&B, and rock. Not because those categories are necessarily inaccurate or objectionable, but because when I step outside them I hear the music differently and understand things about it that I previously missed.
>
> (*Ibid.: 6*)

His intent is to look at some familiar ground with fresh eyes and consider 'an alternative way of telling the story' (ibid.: 9).

If all you do is (now) listen to the records, says Wald, you will probably get it wrong. He uses archival sources and a variety of contemporary publications, including newspapers and trade publications such as *Billboard*, to reconstruct the everyday experience of music for musicians and listeners. His account throws up numerous nuggets of information and fascinating examples, often rescuing music and dance styles and their performers from previous obscurity. It is hard to argue with his point 'that in order to understand the music of any period, you have to be aware of the major artists of the time' (ibid.: 2), but the obvious question is how to define 'major'. A key distinction here is the one drawn between popularity and influence. The most important example of Wald's general argument is Paul Whiteman, who played a central role in popularizing jazz in the 1930s. Whiteman, says Wald, is relatively neglected in popular music histories, in favour of performers seen as more 'ground breaking' and innovative.

Wald makes some provocative general claims about the emphases and partial accounts evident in earlier histories of American popular music, but does not document these. For example, there is no reference to

'standard' accounts, such as that provided by Ennis (1992). He acknowl-
edges the work of earlier rock historians and critics, who began writing
in the late 1960s, and, quite correctly, identifies their role in valorizing
some performers as pioneers and others as imitators. In part, this process
reflected the male dominance of 'rock criticism' and the associated hierarchies of taste involved. I am not convinced, however, by his separation of
'criticism' and 'history', given that cultural validation and judgements (of
recordings, genres, performers and their audiences) are the starting point
for most histories.

Wald covers a broad range of American popular music, including ragtime, swing, the foxtrot and various styles of jazz. Throughout, there are
fascinating discussions of the impact of sound recording on musical life;
the early centrality and subsequent waning of live performance; the considerable overlap (compared to their later general separation) of highbrow
and lowbrow tastes; ragtime as 'the first popular music genre'; the moral
panic surrounding some early dance styles; the value of musical originality
compared to the performance of 'standards; the emergence and different
meanings attached to 'jazz'; and the role of Prohibition, restricting work
for musicians with smaller venues closing. The most informative and revelatory sections are those documenting the significance of **dance** in the
history of popular music. Although the impact of the phonograph was a
significant if a rather mixed blessing, recordings were not that important
for the first half of the twentieth century, with dance music frequently to
the fore. Dancers went to dance, not simply listen to the band.

The phrase 'popular music revolution' usually brings to mind the jazz
age of the 1920s, the 1950s advent of rock and roll, or, most recently, the
impact of the internet and digital music. However, in *Sounds of the
Metropolis*, Derek Scott makes a persuasive case for a nineteenth century
popular music revolution, sited in four cities: London, New York, Paris
and Vienna. In each, original and influential new forms of popular music
emerged to challenge classical tradition: London was the birthplace of
music hall, New York of minstrelsy, Vienna of popular dance music for
couples and Paris of cabaret. Each of these is accorded a chapter in part 2
of the book. In part 1, Scott examines the manner in which this revolution 'was driven by social changes and the incorporation of music into a
system of capitalist enterprise' (2008: 3–4). The main theme here is the
resulting polarization between art and entertainment, between 'commercial' styles of music, and music as 'serious' art, a schism that has continued
into the twentieth century. Scott observes:

> Indeed, one might argue that popular music had become a different
> musical language, and one that might be spoken in different dialects

and with different accents. New art worlds were being created, with the establishment of new musical conventions, new techniques, new organizations, and new networks of distribution.

(2008: 4)

He documents how perceptions changed completely about the perceived nature and value of popular music, and the subsequent legacies of the emergent styles. For instance, blackface minstrelsy in New York added 'a percussive character, a new type of syncopation, and a three-chord model – features inherited by a range of twentieth century styles from blues to punk' (Scott, 2008: 7). In addition to his extensive use of primary sources, some not previously utilized, Scott draws on Gramsci's concept of hegemony and Becker's art worlds to consider the struggle over intellectual and moral leadership in relation to cultural status and the legitimation of musical styles, their performers and their audiences.

The historical sweep of Scott and Wald's studies, tracing the antecedents of post-1950s 'rock' and 'pop' music back to the nineteenth century, provide a useful corrective to 'populist' views of the history popular music as dating from the advent of rock'n'roll.

Further reading:

Historiography (and popular music):

Hamm, C. (1995) *Putting Popular Music in Its Place*, Cambridge, UK: CUP.

Macmillan, M. (2009) *The Uses and Abuses of History*, London: Profile Books.

Moore, A. (2006) "What story should a history of popular music tell?" *Popular Music History*, 1, 3: 329–38.

Popular Music History Journal, 2004–present.

Sansom, J. (2009) "Music History", in J.P.E. Harper-Scott and J. Sansom (eds) *An Introduction to Music Studies*, Cambridge, UK: CUP.

Weisethaunet, H. (2007). Historiography and Complexities: Why is music 'national'? *Popular Music History*, 2, 2: 169–89.

Anthologies; Journals; Readers:

Brackett, D. ed. (2009) *The Pop, Rock, and Soul Reader. Histories and Debates*, 2nd edition, New York: Oxford University Press.

Cateforis, T. ed. (2007) *The Rock History Reader*, New York: Routledge. (See also his insightful discussion of the process of producing the Reader: Cateforis, T. (2009) "Sources and Storytelling: Teaching the History of rock through its Primary Documents", *Journal of Popular Music Studies*, 21, 1: 20–58.)

General Histories:

Ennis, P. (1992). *The Seventh Stream: The Emergence of Rock'n'Roll in American Popular Music*, Hanover: Wesleyan University Press.

Friedlander, P. (2006) *Rock And Roll. A Social History*, 2nd edition, Boulder, CO: Westview Press.

Garofalo, R. (2011) *Rockin' Out. Popular Music in the USA*, 5th edition, Neeham Heights, MA: Allyn & Bacon.

Revisionist Studies:

Bourke, C. (2010) *Blue Smoke: The Lost Dawn of New Zealand Popular Music 1918– 1964*. Auckland: Auckland University Press.

Scott, D. (2008). *Sounds of the Metropolis: The 19th Century Popular Music Revolution in London, New York, Paris and Vienna*. Oxford: Oxford University Press.

Wald, E. (2009). *How The Beatles Destroyed Rock 'N' Roll. An Alternative History of American Popular Music*. Oxford: Oxford University Press.

HOMOLOGY

In general terms, a reproduction or repetition of structure, applied to popular music homology refers to the 'fit' between lifestyle/values and music preferences. The concept was central to the consideration of the place of music in youth subculture, by the subcultural analysts of the 1970s. Their answer to the question 'what specifically does a subcultural style signify to the members of the subculture themselves?' was to identify an homology between the 'focal concerns, activities, group structure and the collective self-image' of the subculture, and the cultural artefacts and practices adopted by the members of the subculture. The latter were seen as 'objects in which they could see their central values held and reflected' (Hall and Jefferson, 1976: 56). The case of skinhead subculture was often used to demonstrate such a homology. The skins' style of heavy 'bovver' boots, braces and drastically cropped hair communicated and asserted their values of 'hardness, masculinity and working-classness. The symbolic objects – dress, appearance, language, ritual occasions, styles of interaction, music – were made to form a unity with the group's relations, situation, experience' (ibid.).

The most extensive and theoretically sophisticated applications of the concept of homology to the preferred music of specific subcultures are Willis's study of bike boys (rockers) and hippies, *Profane Culture* (1978), and Hebdige's various case studies in his hugely influential study *Subculture: The Meaning of Style* (1979). Willis argued that there existed a 'fit' between certain styles and fashions, cultural values, and group identity; for example, between the intense activism, physical prowess, love of machines and taboo on introspection, of motorbike boys, and their preference for 1950s rock'n'roll. For Hebdige, the punks best illustrated the principle:

> The subculture was nothing if not consistent. There was a homological relation between the trashy cut-up clothes and spiky hair, the

pogo and the amphetamines, the spitting, the vomiting, the format of the fanzines, the insurrectionary poses and the 'soulless', frantically driven music. The punks wore clothes which were the satorial equivalent of swear words, and they swore as they dressed – with calculated effect, lacing obscenities into record notes and publicity releases, interviews and love songs.

(1979: 114)

Later writers on subcultures challenged the 'Birmingham position'. Writing at the end of the 1980s, Middleton concludes that subcultural analysis had drawn the connection between music and subculture much too tightly, 'flawed above all by the uncompromising drive to homology' (1990: 161). However, homology still has value as an analytical concept, particularly when used in conjunction with approaches to subculture derived from urban studies. Analyses of the cultural style and values provided in hardcore subcultures such as 'straightedge', and the cultural practices of rap, provide contemporary examples.

See: **scenes**; **subculture**

Further reading: see **subculture**

HOUSE

House is a central style within the broad metagenre of **electronic dance music**. The various accounts of the origins of house music centre on its foundations in New York's underground dance scene in the 1970s. House was a direct descendant of disco and an important element of the dance club scene by the mid-1980s. House music got its name from the late night parties held in warehouses, originally in New York, but then more prominently in Chicago, where DJs mixed the music in elaborate and lengthy sets in which segments of many songs were interspersed with one another. House music was based on the rhythms of disco, but with the emphasis less on lyrics and more on atmosphere and beat.

A number of identifiable variants of house developed (see the useful chart in Woodstra, 2001: 630). Two influential subgenres were Chicago House and Acid House. In Chicago House, DJs combining German techno pioneers Kraftwerk with soul, drum machines. Influential pioneers included Frankie Knuckles at the Warehouse club (where Knuckles played

181

from 1977 until 1983), and Francis Grosso at Sanctuary, a converted church: 'Grosso was the first DJ to segue records together into one, uninterrupted groove, emphasising the hypnotic quality of the music's rhythm track and keeping the dancers locked on the floor' (Kempster, 1996: 11). Acid house saw musicians using Roland 303 and similar drum machines/synthesizers to produce dance music characterized by eclecticism and a splintering off into sub-styles (see Prendergast, 2003; Sicko, 1999). Acid house was part of UK indie music in the 1980s (see **Madchester**) and the **rave** scene.

Straw concludes that 'The most significant event in the history of dance music since 1980 has been the rise of house music'. House was a musical style developed largely outside of rock and pop music; it laid the basis for the massive dance explosion of the 1990s; it gave dance a new rhythmic foundation; and it changed the nature of DJ work (Straw, 2001: 171).

A dimension of house music that has attracted considerable academic interest is the manner in which house music clubs represented 'temporary autonomous zones', largely free of outside surveillance, in which 'the public spectacle is abandoned' and displaced by a new 'tactile-audio space (Rietveld, 1998: 204–5).

See: **EDM**

Further reading: (see also the general histories of dance music in **EDM**)

Prendergast, M.J. (2003) *The Ambient Century: From Mahler to Moby – The Evolution of Sound in the Electronic Age*, London: Bloomsbury.

Reynolds, S. (1998) *Generation Ecstasy: Into the World of Techno and Rave Culture*, Boston: Little, Brown & Company; Chapter 3.

Rietveld, H. (1998) *This is our house: House Music, Cultural Spaces and Technologies*, London: Ashgate.

IDENTITY

Identity is the cultural descriptions of individuals (self and others), groups and sociopolitical entities which we identify with. 'Identity is cultural since the resources that form the material for identity formation - language and cultural practices - are social in character' (Barker, 2002: 225). This emphasizes that identity, rather than being fixed and static, is a process of *becoming*, which is developed out of points of similarity and difference, involving both self-description and social ascription. Popular music is an aspect of attempts to define identity at the levels of self, the local community and national identity.

Self-identity can be expressed through the use of music consumption to indicate membership of constituencies based around class, gender and ethnicity. At times, this is more loosely organized around particular scenes and sounds, as with rave culture and contemporary dance music. Self-identity can also be based on activities such as fandom and practices such as record collecting. These identifications are not fixed and constraining; they produce differentially constructed *identities*, which can draw on an amalgam of factors and are subject to change. Self-identity also involves situating self in relation to competing discourses. For example, adherence to a musical genre can be used to distance oneself from the parent culture/community/social authority.

Popular music plays a prominent role in the creation of community identity in the links between music and locality, especially in local scenes and subcultures. These have remained significant, with the Internet helping to consolidate links between physically removed scenes (Kruse, 2010). At the national level, identity is a part of cultural policies (e.g. quotas) aimed at promoting locally produced music, and the association of particular genres and national settings (e.g. salsa and the Caribbean). National identity can be regarded as a social construct as much as a quality associated with a physical space. While such identities may be constructed or imagined, they are mobilized for particular interests, and emerge partly in relation to different 'others'. Popular music can be a part of this, as evident in Nazi Germany in the 1930s (see Negus, 1996), and in various national cultural movements (see **politics**).

See: **scenes**; **subcultures**

Further reading:

Kruse, H. (2010) "Local Identity and Independent Music Scenes, Online and Off", *Popular Music and Society*, 35, 5: 625–39.

Zuberi, N. (2001) *Sounds English. Transnational Popular Music*, Urbana: University of Illinois Press.

IDEOLOGY

Ideology can be understood,

> in terms of ideas, meanings and practices which, while they purport to be universal truths, are better understood as maps of cultural

significance. Above all, ideology is not separate from the practical activities of life but is a material phenomenon rooted in day-to-day conditions. Ideologies provide people with rules of practical conduct and moral behaviour.

(*Barker, 2002: 225*)

Various world views constitute ideologies, or, to put it another way, all social groups have ideologies. 'Ideology cannot be seen as a simple tool of domination but should be regarded as discourses which have specific *consequences* for relations of power at all levels of social relationships' (ibid.).

An example of ideology in popular music is provided in discussions of the emergence of rock in the 1960s, and the subsequent valorization of that period as 'classic rock'. This was a version of classic Romanticism, an ideology with its origins in art and aesthetics (Gracyk, 2001).

See: **classic rock**

INDEPENDENT RECORD LABELS; INDIE MUSIC

The term 'indie' has been used for a particular form of industrial organization, the independent record label, and, usually associated with such labels, a musical aesthetic or genre. In terms of aesthetics and musical style, indie music remains characterized by a combination of a strong lyrical focus with a marked strain of Romanticism present in these. Both senses of indie are linked to a set of dominant musical values, with authenticity at their core. Indie is often associated with particular local music scenes.

The term had its antecedents in the earlier use of 'alternative' to denote less commercially driven styles of music, and its performers, even where these were commercially successful. Independent recording labels were present from the earliest days of the recording industry (see Kennedy and McNutt, 1999), even if not always consciously referred to as such. The concept of indie and the music it applied to became more widely used in 1980s Britain as an outgrowth of the punk ethos. Using the term in a pure sense, the independent music charts in Great Britain, which began in 1980, considered music independent if it relied on an independent distribution system.

Indie as industrial

As Hesmondhalgh points out, indie is the first genre 'to [take] its name from the form of industrial organization behind it' (1999: 35). The independent, or indie, labels are small sound recording companies which are independent of the **majors**, at least in terms of the artist acquisition, recording and promotion. This distinction, however, is blurred by the often complex relationships between minor labels and major labels in terms of finance, control, and, in particular, distribution. Historically, many indies have relied on majors for the distribution side of their activities and entered into formal agreements for this (e.g. New Zealand label Flying Nun and Mushroom in Australia).

Indie labels are frequently considered to be more flexible and innovative in their roster of artists. It has been argued that independent record companies in the 1950s did not have the corporate hierarchy of the majors and so had greater flexibility in picking up on and promoting new trends and talent, and a greater ability to adjust record production. In companies such as Sun, the owner, record producer, sound technician and promoter often were the same person (as with Sam Philips at Sun). 'The 1950s decade was the golden era for small independents, which embraced blues, gospel, modern jazz, country, R&B, and rock'n'roll' (Kennedy and McNutt, 1999: xvii). From 1948 to 1954, about one thousand new record labels were formed.

The independent sector continued to be an important part of the music industry, often acting as developers of talent for the majors. To maintain their market control, the larger companies have historically adopted several strategies in relation to the independents: buying out their artists' contracts (RCA and Elvis from Sun), or persuading artists to move labels; entering into marketing and other business arrangements with them, or simply buying them out. Several independents acquired a significant market share, as with **Motown** in the 1960s; these became mid-range companies, situated between the Majors and the independents and were subject to absorption by their larger rivals (see **market cycles**). At times, as in the 1950s, independent labels have been associated with the emergence of new styles of music: Stiff and British punk; Sub Pop and grunge; Def Jam and rap; Creation and Britpop; and Word and Christian music. While there are a huge number of independent labels, and they produce two-thirds of the titles released, their market share remains small, usually around 15 to 20 per cent.

The move to be independent of large organizations represents a significant facet of indie ideology, with indie label musicians who moved on from indie labels to major labels often accused by their fans, and in the music press, of 'selling out'. However, the actual operation of the independents and the precise nature of their relationship with the majors is debated. In his case study of Wax Trax! Records, a Chicago-based industrial dance label, Lee argued that market expansion and the necessary links with Majors for distribution force such indies to increasingly adopt the business practices of the majors, in the process moving away from their traditional cultural goals of artistry and creativity. The result is a 'hybrid label – a privately-held company that deals with a major for important production elements or that receives some of its operating funds from a major' (Lee, 1995: 196). The interaction between the majors and independents in such arrangements has remained a dynamic process. The examples of Creation and the career of Oasis and Rough Trade (Hesmondhalgh, 1997) in the United Kingdom during the 1990s illustrated a continued blurring of the boundaries between the independents and the majors.

In the light of the contemporary music industry, where many indies are in fact part of larger networks of labels, Novara and Henry provide a more flexible and qualified definition, with the indie record company 'characterized by some degree of separation from the business practices and creative control of the large corporations operating major labels' (2009: 816).

Indie as an aesthetic

'At some point during the late 1980s to early 1990s', argues Dale, 'indie ceased to be an abbreviation of the word independent, and thus ceased to denote a significant distinction from the major labels'. (Dale, 2008: 173). Indie music became used to describe a broad musical style, often equated with alternative music. At times, this has been so broadly applied as to be meaningless, as illustrated by the *Guinness Who's Who of Indie and New Wave* (Larkin, 1995), where indie music is defined as 'music after the Sex Pistols played by creative on the edge musicians with lots of nice guitars that sound a bit like the Byrds, Velvet Underground and MC5'. Not only does this cover a considerable range of musical styles, but the volume includes 'electro synth' bands like Depeche Mode, 'basic rock bands' like the Del Lords, and the Dead Kennedies, along with a large number of other punk performers. Attitude is perceived as key in such accounts; as Bannister puts it indie has 'a strong in investment in difference, concerned with "what not to do"' (2006: 58). The crossover of indie bands from smaller labels into the mainstream music industry, as occurred with U2, REM, and Nirvana, led to considerable debate among their fans.

More recently, and more precisely, Fonarow identifies two main strains in indie ideology: a musical interpretation of Puritanism, with the 'experience of "true" of "authentic" music' standing in for experience with the divine; and Romanticism (Fonarow, 2006: 28–9). From

Puritanism, Fonarow sees indie as having inherited a 'distrust of authority, a preference for non-corporate, independently owned commercial operations, [...] a promotion of high moral standards regarding issues of sexuality and conduct, and emphasis on education, and an underlying theme of austerity and abstinence'(ibid.: 28). Romanticism provides indie music with a

> characteristic cultivation of emotion, passion, and the spirit, its interest in artistic movements of the past, its preference for the natural, its acclaim for the exceptional man in the guise of the musical genius, its respect for local identities and the working class, and its distaste for middle-class society while being itself middle class.
>
> (*Ibid.: 29*)

These characteristics are also strongly present in the current indie press, in magazines such as *Under the Radar* and on websites such as Pitchfork. These values are cast as diametrically opposed to a stereotyped mainstream. Indie ideology views the music as raw and immediate, while mainstream music is regarded as processed and mediated by 'overproduction'; indie bands can reproduce their music in concert and even improve upon it, while mainstream bands are seen as requiring extensive electronic effects to reproduce their music live. Rather in contradiction to its dominant ethos, most indie performers are white, male and middle class (Bannister, 2006).

Indie remains a constantly shifting set of aesthetic goals and performance practices, situated around the idea based in an ideology of authenticity that privileges artistic expression above commercial concerns.

See also: **alternative**; **authenticity**

Further reading:

Bannister, M. (2006) *White Boys, White Noise. Masculinity and 1980s Indie Guitar Rock*, Aldershot: Ashgate.

Dale, P. (2008) "It was easy, it was cheap, so what? Reconsidering the DIY principle of punk and indie music", *Popular Music History*, 3, 2: 171–93.

Fonarow, W. (2006) *Empire of Dirt: The Aesthetics and Rituals of British Indie Music*, Middletown, CT: Wesleyan University Press.

Hesmondhalgh, D. (1999) "Indie: The Institutional Politics and Aesthetics of a Popular Music Genre", *Cultural Studies*, 13, 1: 34–61.

Kennedy, R. and McNutt, R. (1999) *Little Labels – Big Sound: Small Record Companies and the Rise of American Music*, Bloomington: Indiana University Press. This study provides an excellent history of the 'little labels', from 1920 to 1970.

Novara, V. and Henry, S. (2009) "A Guide to Essential American Indie Rock, 1980-2005", *Notes*, June: 816–32.

Ogg, A. (2010) *Independence Days: The Story of UK Independent Record Labels*, London: Cherry Red Books.

Strachan, R. (2007). "Micro-independent record labels in the UK: Discourse, DIY cultural production and the music industry". *European Journal of Cultural Studies*, 10, 2: 245–65.

Taylor, N. (2010) *Document and Eyewitness. An Intimate History of Rough Trade*, London: Orion. (71 of those involved with the UK indie label, established in 1976, tell their stories.)

Listening: Factory Records Communications 1978–92, Box Set, complied by Jon Savage, Factory, 2009

See: **alternative**; **authenticity**

INTERNET

The Internet has added a major new dimension to the marketing, accessing and consumption of popular music, while creating new problems for the enforcement of copyright. The accompanying debates are central to current popular music studies and are also significant in relation to wider issues surrounding the emergence of a networked society (Castells, 2000).

Created originally for military use, the Internet is a computer-linked global communications technology, with dramatically increasing numbers of people accessing it since the late 1990s. The World Wide Web (WWW), a major part of the Internet, is the graphical network that contains websites dedicated to one topic, person or company. These homepages contain hyperlinks, which allow users to jump to other locations on the Internet. The web soon included sites for online retail music shops, for downloading music as digital files; for record companies and performers; online music journals; online concerts and interviews; web radio and bulletin boards. These represented new ways of inter-linking the audience/consumers of popular music, the performers and the music industry (Jones, 2000).

The major record companies were initially slow to recognize the potential of the Internet, but soon moved to create sites to showcase their activities and their artists. Discussions of the significance of such electronic commerce emphasize the business and economic aspects: the benefits to firms and consumers; the barriers and difficulties associated with doing business via the Net; the demographics of Net users; and the opportunities for companies on the Net. There are also significant cultural issues associated with popular music on the Net, which link up with on-going debates in the political economy of popular music, notably the relative importance (power) of the music industry and the consumers of popular music, and the impact of new technology. The Net has created greater consumer sovereignty and choice by bypassing the traditional intermediaries operating in the music industry (primarily the record companies, but also music retail). It has also changed the nature of fandom, facilitating cyber-based taste communities (see, for example, Baym, 2007). The electronic retrieval possibilities of new web technologies led to considerable controversy over the nature of intellectual property rights and the regulation of these (see **MP3**).

There are several core issues in these developments and debates. At an immediate level has been the question of the impact of downloading on 'legitimate' recording sales. From the industry point of view, and some observers, downloading was clearly hurting the industry (Hull *et al.*, 2011). Others were not so convinced, and there have been some interesting comparisons with similar earlier episodes, notably tape copying. Second, market control was central to the debate around Napster and its successors: were artists and the recording companies being disempowered, and consumers (end-users) being empowered by the increasing availability of online music? (McLeod, 2005). A related aspect is the nature of the engagement of consumers with music through online practices, and the formats and artists downloaded. Any new medium or technological form changes the way in which we experience music, with implications for how we relate to and consume music. In the case of the Net, an interesting question is what happens to traditional notions of the 'distance' between consumer and product, and its technological mediation? (Styvén, 2007).

Music has continued to shift online, with legal downloading taking an increasing market share (Hull *et al.*, 2010), made even more attractive by the development of the **iPod** and its competitors, portable music systems capable of storing huge numbers of songs in digital format.

See: **MP3**; **Peer to Peer (P2P)**; **social network sites**

Further reading:
Baym, N.K. (2007) "The new shape of online community: The example of Swedish independent music fandom", *First Monday*, 12, 8.
Beer, D. (2008). "Making Friends with Jarvis Cocker: Music Culture in the Context of Web 2.0". *Cultural Sociology*, 2, 2: 222–41.

Castells, M. (2000) *The Rise of the Networked Society*, Blackwell: Oxford.

Jennings, D. (2007) *Net, Blogs, and Rock'n'Roll: How Digital Discovery Works and What It Means for Consumers, Creators and Culture*, London: Nicholas Brealey Publications.

Jones, S. (2000) 'Music and the Internet', *Popular Music*, 19, 2: 217–30.

McLeod, K. (2005) 'MP3s Are Killing Home Taping: The Rise of Internet Distribution and Its Challenge to the Major Label Music Monopoly', *Popular Music and Society*, 28, 4 (October): 521–32.

Styvén, M. (2007) "The intangibility of music in the Internet age". *Popular Music and Society*, 30, 1: 53–74.

Tepper, S., and Hargittai, E. (2009) "Pathways to music exploration in a digital age". *Poetics* 37: 227–49.

INTERTEXTUALITY

see **text**

iPOD

Mobile forms of sound reproduction have been important for de-centering the listening process and for being identified with particular lifestyles and social groups. Compact cassette audio tape and cassette tape players, developed in the mid-1960s, appealed because of their small size and associated portability. Initially a low-fidelity medium, a steady improvement of the sound, through modifications to magnetic tape and the introduction of the Dolby noise reduction system, enhanced the appeal of cassettes. The transistor radio (made possible by the invention of the transistor in 1948) and the audio cassette had become associated technologies by the 1970s, with widely popular cheap radio cassette players, and the cassette player incorporated into high-fidelity home stereos.

The Walkman had a major impact when it was introduced during the 1980s, enabling the listener to maintain an individual private experience in public settings. 'Walkman', although a Sony Corporation trade mark, became a popular generic term, for what Bull terms 'personal stereos' (Bull, 2000). As he documents, personal stereos allow their users to re-appropriate place and time, with listeners regaining control of their auditory environments by blocking out undesirable surrounding noise (and people!). They also rearrange user's experience of time, especially while waiting or during travel. Both these factors were part of the appeal of later personal stereos, but with added refinements enabled by the availability of digital music. **MP3** players created practices that were not possible with earlier personal stereos, such as the Walkman and the Discman, which were tied to physical music formats. The first portable MP3 player to be released in the United States was the Rio, from Diamond Multimedia in 1998. Since then many more have appeared on the market, but the most successful and ubiquitous is the Sony iPod from Apple Computer, launched in October 2001.

The iPod has become the sound carrier and fashion accessory of the day, a cross between the Walkman and a hard drive which is used to store files on a computer. The iPod does not play music from physical formats such as cassettes or CDs, but holds it internally as digital data. The iPod is not the only digital music player, but it is the most popular of the brands now on the market.

In terms of use, the advantages of the iPod are presented by its marketers and supporters as threefold. First, it can store a huge quantity of music (how much depends on the capacity of the model), and all you need to carry with you is a small, self-contained device; second, 'you can listen to whatever you want, wherever you are'; and, third, it can be connected up to home stereos or car stereos: 'you can have your entire music collection instantly accessible at home, at friends' houses, when you're driving – even on holiday' (Buckley and Clarke, 2005: 4–5). In addition, using the associated iTunes, the iPod opens up access to a huge range of music:

> You can play tracks downloaded from the Internet without having the hassle of burning a CD. You can instantly compile playlists of selected songs or albums. Or have your player select your music for you, picking tracks randomly from across your whole collection or just from albums of a particular genre.
>
> (*Ibid.*)

The extensive popular and academic discussion surrounding the iPod is reminiscent of that which accompanied the **music video** in the 1980s. The iPod raises questions of marketing and design, mobility and agency, consumerism and the continued validity of the album format and associated notions of a musical **canon**. The control associated with the Walkman is refined by the iPod, as the ability to create customized play lists enables listeners to create their own soundtracks. These can be used to accompany routine activities, with the selections geared to the activity, in terms of both mood generation and required duration. In his quirky take on Descartes, *iPod Therefore I Am*, Dylan Jones (2005) celebrates the ability of his portable device to connect his past musical experiences identity, and thereby to construct a personal musical history. Large parts of the book are made up of song lists, and fictional constructions of meetings with pop and rock stars that influenced his formative tastes – along with those of many of his readers. There are now a number of published/online guides to compile your play lists. These are constructing a new form of musical canon, to a degree superseding the role of the traditional print music press/music critics.

The iPod has collapsed together the musical text, its production and its consumption.

See: **MP3**

Further reading:
Buckley, P. and Clarke, D. (2005) *The Rough Guide to iPods, iTunes & Music Online*, London: The Rough Guides.
Bull, M. (2000) *Sounding Out the City: Personal Stereos and the Management of Everyday Life*, Oxford: Berg.
Bull, M. (2005) "Dead Air! The iPod and the Culture of Mobile Listening", *Leisure Studies*, 24, 4: 345–55.
Jones, D. (2005) *I Pod. Therefore I Am*, London: Phoenix.

JAM BANDS

A label applied to bands whose performances and recordings feature extended improvization – 'jamming'. Associated originally with jazz, especially free and acid jazz, jamming was first evident in rock in the 1960s, especially in the work of the Grateful Dead, and in psychedelic styles more generally (e.g. Cream; Quicksilver Messenger Service). In the late 1960s and through the 1970s, it was central to **progressive** rock, although often in a more constrained fashion. Since the 1990s, the term has been used in the music press to refer to American bands such as Phish and the Dave Matthews Band, and the still active Grateful Dead (in several guises since the death of leader Gerry Garcia in 1995). The commercial and artistic status of these performers was based on their live shows, associated notions of musical authenticity and a dedicated fan base. The fans of jam bands often traded concert tapes (see **bootlegs**; **fans**), reflecting the different musical inflections in bands performance of a standard set list.

Listening: Cream, *Wheels of Fire*, Polydor, 1968; The Greatful Dead, *Live Dead*, WB, 1969; Phish, *A Picture of Nectar*, Elektra, 1991

JAZZ

Jazz is a **metagenre**, embracing a wide range of musical styles, and associated musical and cultural practices. Established at the beginning of the twentieth century, jazz was an American idiom developed from ragtime, blues and the popular music of its day. Shipton, in his overview of the historical development of jazz, identifies the first use of the term in print as occurring in San Francisco in 1913, when it was used to 'describe a dance music full of vigor and "pep"' (Shipton 2001, 1). This association with **dance** indicated that the music formed part of a social and recreational culture, a link that remained an important part of its subsequent development. In tension with this, has been an ongoing emphasis on jazz as an art form (see Lopez, 2002, for an excellent consideration of the creation of a 'jazz art world'). Jazz subsequently became commonly associated with musical styles that emerged from New Orleans in the early twentieth century and were defined through 'a certain rhythmic vitality, often referred to as "swing", in collaboration with a degree of spontaneous improvisation' (Beard and Gloag, 2005: 96; see also the nuanced discussion in Sager, 2002). As the music had African–American origins, jazz has remained framed by issues of **race** and ethnicity: the question of race was bound up in it from the start: 'to a white public it symbolized something "Other", something daring and exotic, while simultaneously, to a black public it was a unifying force, an aspiration' (Shipton, 2001: 1).

The definition of 'jazz', in terms of some sort of natural musical essence, has been problematic. According to Gabbard, 'Jazz is a construct. Nothing can be called jazz simply because of its "nature"' (2002: 1). In this approach, jazz becomes a set of discourses (see **discourse**) mutating around a series of often very different musical practices. As Gabbard notes, 'the term jazz is routinely applied to musics that have as little in common as an improvisation by Marilyn Crispell and a 1923 recording by King Oliver and his Creole Jazz Band' (ibid.).

As various standard histories of the genre demonstrate, the co-existence of multiple styles of jazz at any given time in jazz history was the norm, with increasingly varied and disparate sub-genres, spreading regionally from Southern centers to generate distinct styles in St Louis, Kansas City, Chicago, New York and beyond. Major jazz artists, who at times shifted between these styles, include Benny Goodman, Duke Ellington, Dave Brubeck, Ella Fitzgerald, Count Basie, Sarah Vaughan, Billie Holliday, Louis Armstrong, Miles Davis, John Coltrane, Thelonious Monk, Charlie Parker, and Wynton Marsalis. In attempts to impose some chronological order on this complexity, jazz styles are often considered as either 'premodern' (pre-1940) or the more diverse 'modern' (post-1940). However, as Meeder observes:

> There is always a danger in treating jazz history as a clear, teleological progression of ideas towards an aesthetic ideal. All too frequently, jazz is taught as a clear path from ragtime to New Orleans to swing to bebop, etc. It should be clearly understood that a graphic depiction of jazz history would not be a straight line, but rather a massive and steadily growing pile of parallel lines.
>
> (*2008: xii*)

The latter approach is evident in fuller recent jazz histories (Giddens and DeVeaux, 2009; Shipton, 2001).

The writing on jazz is frequently focussed on individual performers, accentuating the creativity and image of the instrumental soloist as an auteur figure. The American jazz theorist, historian and composer Schuller provides an example for this approach:

> When on June 28, 1928, Louis Armstrong unleashed the spectacular cascading phrases of the introduction to *West End Blues*, he established the general stylistic direction of jazz for several decades to come. Beyond that, this performance also made quite clear that jazz could never again revert to being solely an entertainment or folk music. The clarion call of *West End Blues* served notice that jazz had the potential capacity to compete with the highest order of previously known musical expression.
>
> (*1968: 89*)

Associated with such biographical emphases, was the construction of a jazz **canon** of particular jazz styles and performers; the music press and jazz collectors played a significant role in this.

A significant component of jazz was improvization, in which each performance represents an original and spontaneous creation. Accordingly, at its core, jazz is **live** music, yet 'our understanding of its history comes primarily from recordings, and jazz developed largely in parallel with recording technology' (Meeder, 2008: xiii). This makes for something of a paradox, creating a perspective (on the part of the listener/critic) that may at times be distinct from that experienced at a live performance (a paradox that is also present in genres such as **electronic dance music**).

The tension between conceptions of jazz as art or entertainment were accentuated with the emergence of bebop in the 1940s, usually seen as a reaction to the dominance of the period by the 'swing' style of the big bands. The 'modernist' innovations of musicians such as Charlie Parker, Dizzy Gillespie, Thelonious Monk and others are regarded as a search for artistic status. According to Bernard Gendron,

> Through the idea that jazz is a modernist art form appeared in full force in the revivalist-swing debate, it is bebop that gets credit in the jazz canon for being the first modernist jazz, the first jazz avant-garde, the first form in which art transcends entertainment.
>
> *(2002: 143)*

The evolution of jazz has been punctuated by the renaissance of older styles and the creation of new fusions, most recently hip-bop and acid jazz in the 1990s. A popular dance genre, acid jazz combined elements of jazz, hip-hop, funk and R&B. It has been primarily a singles medium (for a representative compilation, see *Acid Jazz: Collection 1*, Scotti Brothers). At times, jazz has had considerable influence on more 'mainstream' popular music genres, fusing with these to create new forms, such as jazz rock fusion, jazz funk and acid jazz. Jazz was also the first home for many musicians who moved over into other genres in the 1950s (notably **skiffle** in the 1950s), and jazz musicians were prominent in significant house (studio/label) bands in the 1960s (such as the Funk Brothers at Motown). Recent writings on jazz adopt an interdisciplinary perspective, reflecting the essentially hybrid nature of the genre (see **hybridity**). As with other metagenres, jazz is sustained by an ecology of specialized recording labels, magazines, venues, and musicians and audiences.

Given the enormous scope of jazz, I have only provided separate treatment of **jazz rock fusion** (below) selected for its links with, and influence on, 'mainstream' popular music genres, primarily **rock**.

Further reading:

Beard, D. and Gloag, K. (2005) *Musicology: The Key Concepts*, London: Routledge (Jazz entry).

Carr, I., Fairweather, D., and Priestly, B. (2000) *Jazz: The Rough Guide*, 2nd edition, London: Rough Guides Limited.
As the subtitle states, this near 900 page encyclopaedia is "The essential companion to artists and albums"; includes a useful glossary.

Cooke, M. and Horn, D. eds (2002) *The Cambridge Companion to Jazz*, Cambridge: Cambridge University Press.
An excellent set of essays, accompanied by extensive notes, and with a useful chronology of jazz. Topics covered include defining jazz, history, audience, jazz and dance, jazz practices (including improvization), and the global, diasporic spread of jazz.

Gabbard, K. (2002) "The word jazz", in Cooke, M. and Horne, D. (eds) *The Cambridge Companion to Jazz*, pp. 1–8.

Giddens, G., and DeVeaux, S. (2009) *Jazz*, New York: Norton.

Meeder, C. (2008) *Jazz. The Basics*, New York: Routledge.
A succinct introduction, covering 'fundamentals' (improvization, instrumentation, rhythm and melody, 'swing', listening to jazz); the historical evolution of jazz, including sections on major styles (swing, bebop, avant garde, fusion, etc.) and performers (Louis Armstrong, Charlie Parker, Thelonious Monk, Miles Davis, John Coltrane). The Appendix on 'Recommended Recordings' includes significant box sets; the brief bibliography is selective: surprisingly, the Cambridge companion is not included among the 'general studies'.

Sager, D. (2002) "History, myth and legend: the problem of early jazz", in Cooke, M. and Horne, D. (eds) *The Cambridge Companion to Jazz*: Chapter 14.

Schuller, G. (1968) *Early Jazz: Its Roots and Musical Development*, Oxford: Oxford University Press.

Shipton, A. (2001) *A New History of Jazz*, London: Continuum.

Magazines: Downbeat

Viewing: Jazz, Ken Burns, 2001, PBS. A10 part, 19-hour documentary, available as a box set; Lipsitz provides an interesting critique of the series, seeing it as presenting jazz as 'the creation of alienated individuals rather than historical communities': Lipsitz, G. (2007) *Footsteps in the Dark*, Minneapolis: University of Minnesota Press, Chapter 4. *Jazz* strongly featured the opinions of Wynton Marsallis, the primary consultant for the series, who 'infused the documentary with many of his controversial opinions and more than a few factual errors' (Meeder, 2008). Nonetheless, it provides a useful resource, which can be placed alongside other histories, etc. of jazz

Listening: Ken Burns Jazz: The Story of America's Music, (5 CD boxed set; a twenty track sampler is also available: *The Best of Ken Burns Jazz*), Columbia/Legacy and Verve Music Group joint release. Given the huge scope of jazz, I have refrained from including selected albums. See the suggestions in the discographies in the recommended reading (above); also *Downbeat*, January 2010, *Special Collector's edition: Best CDs of the 2000s*

JAZZ ROCK FUSION

The term 'fusion' is variously used to designate the amalgamation of two styles of music, as in the fusion of folk and rock to form **folk rock**, a mix of electric and acoustic instrumentation and sounds. The term is most commonly applied to the music produced by the fusion of jazz and rock: jazz rock; which attempts to fuse elements of both styles.

In the early 1960s, jazz was in something of a commercial and artistic crisis in the United States, and, for some musicians, jazz rock represented a possible new musical avenue to exploit. Their efforts to appropriate rock, 'a resolution of opposites' (Nicholson, 2002: 220–3), raised questions around authenticity and were among the most controversial moments in contemporary jazz history. Jazz rock combines jazz improvization with the instrumentation and rhythm of R&B, employing technology to a greater extent; including at times replacing the piano with the electric piano and the synthesizer. The more 'jazz oriented' versions are usually referred to as fusion, while some commentators prefer the term jazz–rock fusion. In an informative discussion of the evolution of the 'genre' since the 1960s, Nicholson distinguishes between 'jazz–rock', as originally applied to the first wave of experimenters in the late 1960s and early 1970s, and the term 'fusion' that crept into the lexicon around 1973–4 (2002: 221).

The most critical and commercially successful United States exponents included Return to Forever, Blood, Sweat and Tears; and Weather Report; who all had creative peaks in the early 1970s. In the United Kingdom, The Soft Machine were marketed as a 'rock' band, but 'were among the first and most successful groups to combine elements of jazz and rock thoroughly enough to blur the divide and become fusion' (Meeder, 2008: 215). The band Coliseum was a well-known exponent of the style, which was also an element in the work of guitarists such as Jeff Beck. Jazz musicians to work in a jazz rock vein include Stanley Clarke and Return to Forever, Chick Corea, Larry Coryell, John McLaughlin, and, most influential of all, Miles Davis.

Further reading:
Nicholson, S. (1998) *Jazz Rock: A History*, New York: Schirmer.
Nicholson, S. (2002) "Fusions and crossovers", in Cooke, M. and Horn, D. (eds) (2002) *The Cambridge Companion to Jazz*, Cambridge: Cambridge University Press.
Meeder, C. (2008) *Jazz. The Basics*, New York: Routledge; Chapter 19: Fusion.

Listening: Blood, Sweat and Tears, 'Spinning Wheel', *Greatest Hits*, CBS, 1976; Weather Report, *Mysterious Traveller*, Columbia, 1974; Jeff Beck, *Blow By Blow,*

Epic, 1975; Miles Davis, *Bitches Brew* Sony, 1969; The Soft Machine, *Vol. 1 and 2*, Big Beat

KARAOKE

Karaoke can best be considered a performance/singing style, and a social experience. The karoake machine is an electric (and, later, an electronic) apparatus designed especially for amateur 'hidden singers'. Karaoke involves people as singers, co-singers and listeners: 'It combines at the same time musical technologies, personal experiences and collective memories' (Mitsui and Hosokawa, 1998: 3). It was first developed in Japan in the 1970s, where it became something of a social phenomenon over the following decade. Digital technologies, the advent of the CD, and the adding of a visual dimension all enhanced the appeal of karaoke. In the mid- to late 1980s, karaoke became internationalized, with karaoke bars appearing in the Pacific Rim, East Asia, North America and Europe. Reflecting this popularization, academic interest in karaoke grew in the 1990s. The practice was variously condemned as ephemeral and banal, or celebrated as democratic and pleasurable. In a key volume which synthesizes and moves beyond this work, Mitsui and Hosokawa (1998) and their contributors examine what underlies karaoke experiences, 'the cultural meanings produced by the resonance and dissonance between technology, place and behaviour' (introduction).

Further reading:
Mitsui, T. and Hosokawa, S. eds (1998) *Karaoke Around the World: Global Technology, Local Singing*, London: Routledge.

LANGUAGE

The issues here include language choice, dialect and accents in popular music, with these related broadly to the politics of identity, multiculturalism and the global dominance of English. These are evident in the work of a range of musical styles and artists, and also in listener and audience responses to them. The importance of language and lyrical realism is a feature of rap, reggae and the blues (see **lyric analysis**), which also rely on particular oral styles: respectively rapping, toasting, and 'talkin' blues'.

Considerations of which language will gain a wider audience, and the associated concerns of authenticity and musical meaning, have faced artists in countries struggling to maintain local languages (e.g. Wales: see Hill, 2007). Various styles of **world music** have been particularly conscious of the linguistic imperialism exercised by English, although these have frequently turned their exoticism to advantage in the market place, as a marker of authenticity. A similar concern also partly underpins national or regional cultural policies seeking to privilege and preserve linguistic identity, as in Francophone Quebec.

The appropriation of particular dialects, accents and even specific vocabulary is evident in performers' vocal styles, **punk rock** for example. This can involve re-appropriation of derogatory language, a process exemplified by black musicians (and audiences) in the United States using the term nigger (or 'nigga') to signify and affirm ethnic and community solidarity, compared with its historical use by whites. This can be in an ironic mode, as with Sly and the Family Stone's 'Don't Call Me Nigga Whitey' (1969). Re-appropriation can also be gendered, as with the use of 'slut' in **riot grrl**, and women rappers use of 'bitch' and 'ho'.

See: **lyric analysis**

Further reading:
Berger, H. and Carrol, M. eds (2003) *Global Pop, Local Language,* Jackson: University Press.
Hill, S. (2007) *'Blewytirhwng?' The Place of Welsh Pop Music,* Aldershot: Ashgate.

LISTENING

Listening is a physical process situated in social contexts and mediated by technology. Considerations of these aspects of listening have been a small but significant part of popular music studies. Listening to music is an activity which takes place with varying levels of intensity, influenced by the consumption context and the style of the performer: 'the "distracted" environment of many club settings and the hushed concentration typical of singer songwriter concerts might represent two extremes' (Middleton, 1990: 95). More melodious and 'non-abrasive' styles of music form the staple of radio 'easy listening', and the loose genre of 'lounge music', while louder genres (heavy metal; hard rock) have sometimes been seen as dangerous to listeners' hearing. The development of headphones, and portable stereos such as the Walkman, and the **iPod**, enabled different styles of listening, while reconfiguring the social locations and contexts within which it occurred.

Negus identifies two groups of listeners focussed on by Adorno and later theorists: those lost in the crowd, and easily manipulated into the collectivity, and obsessive individuals, alienated and not fully integrated into social life, with both types part of the anxieties of moral guardians (Negus, 1996). Adorno saw the mass culture products of the music industry as requiring very little effort on the part of listeners, arguing that this led to 'de-concentrated listening in which listeners rejected anything unfamiliar, regressing to "child-like" behaviour' (1991: 44–5). One facet of this was what Adorno termed 'quotation listening', where instead of listening to a piece of music and trying to grasp it as a whole, the regressive listener dwelt only on the most obvious aspects of melody. In the process, listeners adopted a 'musical child's language' and responded to different works 'as if the symphony were structurally the same as a ballad'. Adorno referred disparagingly to the category of 'easy listening' as an example of the music industry's deliberately encouraging distracted audience activity, with an emphasis on the most familiar harmonies, rhythms and melodies, and producing a 'soporiphic' effect on social consciousness. Adorno saw this as fulfilling an ideological function in rendering the listening audience passive and making them unable to reflect critically on their world.

This view of passive listening has been challenged, especially by the active audience paradigm prominent in much recent media/cultural studies. Listening to particular musical styles requires distinct cultural capital, including, but not limited to, a knowledge of the sonic codes and conventions of the genre and the previous work of the performer and similar artists. Unfamiliar music requires 'work', musical labour to situate the piece in relation to other, already familiar music. Hennion (2003) has been prominent in developing what he calls a sociology of mediation, and a related history of listening. Undertaking fascinating empirical research into how people listen, he argues that listening technologies have transformed, and in a sense created, the act of listening (see also Tagg and Clarida, 2003).

See: **psychology**

Further reading:
Adorno, T. (1991) *The Culture Industry*, in J. Bernstein (ed.), London: Routledge.
Hennion, A. (2003) "Music and Mediation: Towards a New Sociology of Music", in Clayton, M., Herbert, T. and Middleton, R. (eds) *The Cultural Study of Music: A Critical Introduction*, New York: Routledge, pp. 80–91.

LIVE (MUSIC)

Live music is experienced in venues such as clubs, discos and pubs; and through concerts and music festivals. The pseudo-live performance is through film, stage musicals, radio and as music video. All of these forms mediate the music, creating a diegetic link between performer, text and consumer. Their significance in determining cultural meaning lies in the interrelationship of ritual, pleasure and economics.

Historically, prior to the advent of recorded sound, all music was live and was experienced as such. The term 'live' performance is now usually reserved for those situations where the audience is in physical proximity to the performance, and the experience of the music is contiguous with its actual performance. The status of live recordings is regarded as rather ambivalent, given that many are technologically sonically upgraded prior to their release.

For many critics, fans and musicians, there is a perceived hierarchy of live performances, with a marked tendency to equate the audiences' physical proximity to the actual 'performance' and intimacy with the performer(s) with a more authentic and satisfying musical experience. This view was central to the ideology of rock created during the 1960s. This emphasis on the live as a key signifier of musical authenticity has since been undermined by performers who work primarily, and at times exclusively, in the studio setting. Some genres are now largely studio creations, especially recent styles of techno. At times, performance events have had the capacity to encapsulate and represent key periods and turning points in rock. Their significance is indicated by their use in a cultural shorthand fashion among fans, musicians and writers; for example, 'Woodstock', with an assumed set of connotations: the counter-culture, music festivals, youth and 1960s' idealism.

Currently, live performance has become one of the primary income streams for performers and the music industry; the emergence of Live Nation as a major market force is indicative of this (Hull, *et al.*, 2011: 166–8).

See: **performance**

Further reading:
Auslander, P. (2008) *Liveness: Performance in a Mediated Culture*, New York: Routledge.
Fitzpatrick, R. (2010) "How Live is Live? And does it matter?" *The Word*, 88, June, 70–7.

LOCALITY

see **place**

LYRIC ANALYSIS

In relation to song lyrics, the concept of realism asserts 'a direct relationship between a lyric and the social or emotional condition it describes and represents' (Frith, 1988: 112; see also Middleton, 1990). This is evident in much study of folk song and the analysis of blues lyrics; for example, interpreting American post-war urban blues lyrics as expressing their black singers' personal adjustment to urban ghettoization:

> A more detailed analysis of blues lyrics might make it possible to describe with greater insight the changes in male roles within the Negro community as defined by Negroes at various levels of socio-economic status and mobility within the lower class.
>
> (*Keil, 1966: 74*)

Longhurst (2007: Chapter 4) suggests that realism can also be applied to **ska** in the 1960s, with its concern for Jamaica's 'rude boys', and songs debating whether their activities could be considered a form of social and political protest, or simply anti-social, personally motivated criminality. Later **reggae** music, especially songs by Bob Marley and the Wailers, was also strongly realist, addressing class struggle in Jamaica, and black's international situation in their struggle against the dominance of 'Babylon'. Black under classes in Jamaica, and elsewhere, could readily identify with the issues in such songs.

Much textual analysis of popular music has been concerned with the lyrical component of songs. In a significant historical discussion, 'Why Do Songs Have Words?' Frith shows how through the 1950s and 1960s the sociology of popular music was dominated by the analysis of the words of songs. This was largely because such an approach was grounded in a familiar research methodology – content analysis – and assumed 'that it was possible to read back from lyrics to the social forces that produced them' (Frith, 1988: 106). This approach has continued to be important, although its application has been tempered.

There are numerous examples of attempts to analyse song lyrics as examples of shifts in popular ideologies of sex, romance and relationships.

These frequently emphasize lyrics as mirrors of social, political and personal issues. Given that songwriters are social beings, the words of the songs do express general social attitudes and are worth study. But

> they treat lyrics too simply. The words of all songs are of equal value; their meaning is taken to be transparent; no account is given of their actual performance or their musical setting. Even more problematically, these analysts tend to equate a song's popularity to public agreement with the message.
>
> (*Frith, 1988: 107*)

Songs create identification through their emotional appeal, but this does not necessarily mean that they can be reduced to a simple slogan or message (see Gracyk, 2001, for an instructive discussion of this point).

Lyric analysis also tends to valorize certain forms of popular music, most notably blues, soul, and country, and some varieties of rock and pop: the singer songwriter. These are seen as the authentic expression of popular experiences and needs, whereas mainstream popular music song lyrics are largely seen in terms of **mass culture** arguments, and criticized for their banality and lack of depth. In a left version of this critique, Harker (1980) reads off **Tin Pan Alley** lyrics as straightforward statements of bourgeois hegemony, equating pop's central themes of love and romance with the 'sentimental ideology' of capitalist society. Conversely, Harker argues for 'authentic' lyrics as the expression of 'authentic' relationships, with both reflecting direct experience, unmediated by ideology.

Part of the argument for rock music's superiority over pop and earlier forms of popular music rested on the claim that its major songwriters were poets. Richard Goldstein's *The Poetry of Rock* (1969) and similar anthologies helped popularize this view. Frith (1988: 117) points out that this work emphasized a particular form of rock lyrics – those akin to romantic poetry with lots of covert and obscure allusions. This approach attempts to validate rock in terms of established 'art' forms, elevating the role of the lyrical auteur figure and the ability to work in a recognizably high cultural mode. An extension of this position is the relegation of mainstream commercial rock/pop lyrics to banality and worthlessness. Yet, clearly such lyrics do in some sense matter to their listeners: they are constantly reproduced in both album liner notes for the social commentary of alternative bands and as the words of the latest chart entries in teen-oriented magazines such as *Smash Hits*. This provokes the more critical question posed by Frith (1988: 121), 'how do words and voices work differently for different types of pop and audience?' This necessitates addressing how song lyrics work as ordinary language for variously located listeners and readers.

Further reading:

Frith, S. (2007) "Why Do Songs Have Words?", in *Taking Popular Music Seriously. Selected Essays*, Aldershot: Ashgate. (First published, 1988).

Harker, D. (1980) *One for The Money: Politics and Popular Song*, London: Hutchinson.

Keil, C. (1966) *Urban Blues*, Chicago: University of Chicago Press.

MADCHESTER

A loose label, popularized by the British music press in the late 1980s and early 1990s, Madchester was more of a **scene** than a distinct sound, an example of the role of geography in forging a distinctive orientation to localized alternative music: the club-and-Ecstasy sounds of 'Madchester', led by the Happy Mondays, the Stone Roses and Oldham's Inspiral Carpets. The songs often included clear geographical references to Manchester and reflected localized feelings and experiences; record covers and other promotional imagery incorporated place-related references and a network of alternative record labels (especially Factory Records), venues and an active local press created a supportive network for the bands and their followers. The initial success of the Manchester scene opened the way for many of the **Britpop** bands of the 1990s.

See: **locality**

Further reading:

Oobb, J. (2009) *North Will Rise Again: Manchester Music City, 1976–1996*, London: Aurum.

Listening: The Stone Roses, *The Stone Roses*, Silvertone, 1989

MAJOR (RECORD LABEL)

The international record industry has historically been dominated by a group of large international recording companies commonly referred to as the majors. Middle range record companies have been absorbed by the majors (e.g. Virgin, Motown and Island), while the smaller independent labels are frequently closely linked to the majors through distribution deals. Each major has branches throughout the America and Europe, and, in most cases, in parts of Asia, Africa and Australasia, and each includes a number of record labels: the Philips labels include Polydor, Deutsche Gramophone, Phonogram and Decca; the Sony labels include CBS, Epic and Def Jam. (For an outline of the organization and activities of each of the majors, see Hull *et al.*, 2011).

The majors are part of multinational entertainment conglomerates, which are competing for global dominance of media markets. This involves their attempts to control both hardware and software markets and to distribute a range of related media products – a process labelled 'synergy' – which enables maximization of product tie-ins and marketing campaigns and, consequently, profits.

The majors have been characterized by increased concentration. In the early 2000s, there were six: Thorn/EMI (UK-based); Bertelsmann (Germany); Sony (Japan); Time/Warner (USA); MCA (formerly Japan; recently purchased by Canadian-owned company Seagram) and Philips (Holland). By 2011, further mergers have reduced their number (see Hull *et al.*, 2011, for an overview of the current situation).

The major labels are usually involved in all aspects of the management, production, distribution and sale of recorded music, attempting as far as possible to control these different aspects. They have similar organizational structures, with typical management hierarchies and various divisions: A&R; promotion and sales and marketing (for a detailed discussion, see Hull *et al.*, 2011; for an insightful analysis of the process in the 1980s, which remains relevant and provides an historical 'benchmark' for subsequent developments in the digital age, see Negus, 1992).

The market share exercised by the majors varies from country to country, but in some cases it is more than 90 per cent. There has been considerable debate over the economic and cultural implications of such market dominance, especially the strength of local music industries in relation to marked trends towards the globalization of the culture industries. Some commentators see the natural corollary of such concentrations of ownership as an ability to essentially determine, or at the very least strongly influence, the nature of the demand for particular forms of popular culture. However, more optimistic media analysts, with a preference for human agency, emphasize the individual consumer's freedom to choose, their ability to decide how and where musical texts are to be used and the meanings and messages to be associated with them. The debate in this area is one of emphasis, since clearly both sets of influences/determinations are in operation.

Through the 2000s, the impact of the Internet and digital music has raised serious questions about the continued adequacy of the traditional business model adopted by the majors (for a helpful discussion of their various responses, see Furgason, 2008).

See: **independent**; **Internet**; **music industry**

Further reading:

Furgason, A. (2008) 'Afraid of Technology? Major Label Response to Advancements in Digital Technology', *Popular Music History*, 3, 2: 149–70.

Glasser, R. (2010) *Music Business: The Key Concepts*, London: Routledge.

Hull, G., Hutchinson, T.W. and Glasser, R. (2011) *The Music Business and Recording Industry: Delivering Music in the 21st Century*, 3rd edition, New York: Routledge.

Negus, K. (1992) *Producing Pop: Culture and Conflict in the Popular Music Industry*, London: Edward Arnold.

MANAGERS; MANAGEMENT

In industrial organizations which are part of the **culture industries**, those working in management act as important cultural intermediaries. Although not directly integrated into the music industry, managers play an active role in shaping particular artists and styles of music. Indeed, such personal managers often have the reputation of being 'starmakers and svengalis', manipulating their artists' music and image. In the 1950s and 1960s, several UK managers (e.g. Larry Parnes) were dominating father figures for their artists (Rogan, 1988). Managers more usually operate as representatives and advisers, handling the myriad details of daily business decisions, including arranging media interviews and promotional appearances, dealing with correspondence, maintaining record company relations and organizing tours and concerts (see Passman, 2009, for a detailed account, including the legal aspects). Ideally, managers contribute to the formation of career strategies, resolve conflict and ambiguity, communicate effectively with the different parties involved, control the allocation of resources wisely, shield artists from criticism, and generally provide leadership and advice to artists. In the process, they can be influential in determining the prevailing climate of the music industry.

A personal manager is compensated on a commission basis, typically based on the gross earnings of the artist, with management contracts usually for 2–3 years. More commercially successful artists will have a management team, including a personal manager, legal and accounting advisers to handle contractual and financial arrangements.

See: **cultural intermediaries**

Further reading:
Passman, D.S. (2009) *All You Need to Know About the Music Business*, 7th edition, New York: Free Press.
Rogan, J. (1988) *Starmakers and Svengalis*, London: MacDonald & Co.

MARKET CYCLES

An influential attempt to explain both the emergence of **rock'n'roll** in the 1950s, and subsequent shifts in popular music, is the market cycles explanation developed initially by Peterson and Berger (1975). This suggests that original musical ideas and styles, generated more or less spontaneously, are taken up by the record industry, which then popularizes them and adheres to them as the standard form. Meanwhile, new creative trends emerge which have to break through the new orthodoxy.

Thus develops a cycle of innovation and consolidation, a cycle reflected in the shifting pattern of economic concentration and market control in the music industry. Monopolistic conglomerates are formed during periods of market stability and inhibit the growth of independent record labels, which are usually the source of new ideas. Yet, under conditions of oligopoly, there is also a growing unsatisfied demand from those who are not satisfied with the prevailing product available. Bursts of musical innovation – rock'n'roll, the San Francisco sound, punk – are often associated with youth subcultures, who help draw attention to them. Small record labels emerge to pioneer the new sound and style, followed by re-concentration and market stagnation once more as the majors regain control. The main evidence used by Peterson and Berger is the relative chart shares (in the Top 20) of the competing labels and the relative chart performance of established artists and new and emerging artists.

This approach was subsequently adopted and applied to later periods by other researchers (see Ross, 2005, for an excellent review of this literature, which did not always confirm the thesis).

While the market cycles thesis offers an economic rationale for the bewildering historical shifts in popular music tastes, there have been a number of criticisms of it. There are methodological difficulties posed by its (initial) reliance on commercially successful singles, with the underlying assumption that the diversity of rock music is to be found in the hit parade. This overlooks the predominance of album sales over singles since the early 1970s, and the generally accepted tendency to accord greater aesthetic weight to the longer format. Further, it sees market diversity as a direct function of the number of individual hit records in any one year. To confirm this argument, it would be necessary to undertake a critical stylistic analysis of the actual recordings that were hits on the basis of their musical features rather than the companies that released them. It could also be argued that the products of the independents are by no means always characterized by innovation. Indeed, frequently they themselves copied styles already popularized by their major competitors. Finally, as Peterson and Berger themselves acknowledge, the distinction between majors and independents has not been clear-cut since about 1970, while the two tiers of the industry have historically been linked through the majors' control of distribution.

See: **independent label**; **major**

Further reading:

Peterson, R. and Berger, D.G. (1975) 'Cycles in Symbolic Production: The Case of Popular Music', *American Sociological Review,* 40; (also in Frith and Goodwin (eds) *On Record*).

Ross, P. (2005) 'Cycles in Symbolic Production Research: Foundations, Applications and Future Directions', *Popular Music and Society*, 28, 4: 473–88.

MARKETING

Marketing has come to play a crucial role in the circulation of cultural commodities. It is a complex practice, involving several related activities: research, product planning and design, packaging, publicity and promotion, pricing policy and sales and distribution, and is closely tied to merchandising and retailing. Central to the process is product positioning and imbuing cultural products with social significance to make them attractive to consumers. (For a historically situated discussion of this, see Ryan, 1992.) In popular music, this has centred on the marketing of genre styles and stars, these having come to function in a similar manner to brand names, 'serving to order demand and stabilize sales patterns' (ibid.:185). Fashion is a crucial dimension: the commodity is designed to attract the attention and interest of shoppers: 'commodity aesthetics' necessitate the construction of a desirable appearance around the commodity to stimulate the desire to purchase and possess. In the marketing process, cultural products become a contested terrain of signification.

By the 1990s, the cant term for music within the industry was 'product'. This relates to popular music being an increasingly commodified product: merchandise to be packaged and sold. The music can be reproduced in various formats – vinyl, cassette audio tape, CD, DAT, music video (MV) and digital downloads – and variations within these: the dance mix, the cassette single, the limited collector's edition and so on. These can then be disseminated in a variety of ways – through radio airplay, discos and dance clubs, television MV shows and MTV-style channels and live concert performances. Accompanying these can be advertising, reviews of the record or performance, and interviews with the performer(s) in the various publications of the music press. In addition, there is the assorted paraphernalia available to the fan, especially the posters and the t-shirts. Further, there is the use of popular music within film soundtracks and television advertising. The range of these products enables a multimedia approach to the marketing of the music, and a maximization of sales potential, as exposure in each of the various forms strengthens the appeal of the others.

The marketing of popular music includes the use of genre labels as signifiers, radio formatting practices and standardized production processes (e.g. Stock, Aitken and Waterman and dance pop in the 1980s). Above all, it involves utilizing star images, linking stars and their music with the needs/demands/emotions/desires of audiences.

In terms of the everyday operation of the music industry, marketing has been examined in several studies, with particular attention paid to industry personnel responsible for advertising and sales, and the promotional role of radio, MV and the music press. There is less critical examination of aspects such as packaging (e.g. record covers, performers' dress codes) and the retailing of popular music.

See: **retail**

Further reading:

Hull, G., Hutchinson, T.W. and Glasser, R. (2011) *The Music Business and Recording Industry: Delivering Music in the 21st Century*, 3rd edition. *Chapter 11: The Marketing Function*, New York: Routledge.

Passman, D.S. (2009) *All You Need to Know About the Music Business*, 7th edition, New York: Free Press.

Ryan, B. (1992) *Making Capital From Culture*, Berlin: Walter de Gruyter.

MASS CULTURE; FRANKFURT SCHOOL

A group of German intellectuals, the Frankfurt School developed a revolutionary philosophical variant of Western Marxism, which became known as 'critical theory'. Initially based at the Institute of Social Research in Frankfurt, the school moved to the United States during the 1930s. Its principal figures included Adorno, Marcuse, Horkheimer, Fromm and Benjamin.

In general, the Frankfurt theorists criticized mass culture arguing that under the capitalist system of production culture had become simply another object, the 'culture industry', devoid of critical thought and any oppositional political possibilities. This general view was applied more specifically to popular music by Adorno, especially in his attacks on Tin Pan Alley and jazz. When Adorno published his initial critique 'On Popular Music' in 1941, the music of the big bands filled the airwaves and charts, operating within the Tin Pan Alley system of songwriting that had been dominant since the early 1900s, with the majority of songs composed in the 32-bar AABA format.

Adorno's writings on popular music were only a minor part of his attempt to develop a general **aesthetics** of music; he was not opposed to popular music as such, but rather to its ruthless exploitation by the **culture/music industries**. His examination of the development of music drew on the concepts of diachronic, the analysis of change and, synchronic, the analysis of static states. At the heart of his critique of popular music was the standardization associated with the capitalist system of commodity production.

In his 1941 essay and his subsequent writings on popular music, Adorno continued to equate popular music with Tin Pan Alley and jazz-oriented variations of it, ignoring the rise of rock and roll in the early 1950s. This undermined his critique and resulted in his views generally being strongly rejected by more contemporary analysts (see, for example, Frith, 1981: 43–8; Tagg and Clarida).

Adorno's views on popular music, while contentious, remain widely referenced in popular music studies (Miklitisch, 2006). For instance, Gendron forcefully recapitulates the failings of Adorno's theory, particularly his exaggeration of the presence of industrial standardization in popular music, but also suggests that 'Adorno's analysis of popular music is not altogether implausible', and merits reconsideration (Gendron, 1986). To support this argument, he examines the standardization of the vocal group style **doo-wop**, rooted in the black gospel quartet tradition, which had a major chart impact between 1955–59.

See: **cultural industries**

Further reading:

Adorno, T. with the assistance of Simpson, G. (1941) 'On Popular Music', in Frith, S. and Goodwin, A. (eds) *On Record: Rock, Pop, and The Written Word*, New York: Pantheon Books.

Adorno, T. (1991) *The Culture Industry: Selected Essays on Mass Culture*, edited by Bernstein J., London: Routledge.

Gendron, B. (1986) 'Theodor Adorno Meets the Cadillacs', in Modleski, T. (ed.) *Studies in Entertainment*, Bloomington, IN: Indiana University Press, pp. 18–36.

Miklitsch, R. (2006) *Roll Over Adorno. Critical Theory, Popular Culture, Audiovisual Media*, New York: State University of New York Press.

MARXISM

A social theory based on the nineteenth-century views of Karl Marx and Friedrich Engels, who saw human history as a process rooted in people's material needs and changing modes of production (historical materialism), which 'in the last analysis' determine the nature of class structure. Class struggle and the emergence of socialism were central to this classic Marxist analysis. A very influential critique of capitalism, and imperialism as its highest form, Marxism has informed the subsequent development of social theory, mutating into a range of Marxist perspectives on society. The major variants of Marxism differ in terms of their relative emphasis on base (the classical Marxist term for economic structures – the forces of production, relations of production and mode of production) and superstructure (the family, schools, the church, etc.), the role of social class as a determinant and the nature and operation of ideology. Marxism has been a major theory informing media and cultural studies, especially through **political economy**.

The validity of Marxist approaches, especially in their classical variants (see **mass culture**), has been the subject of extended debate within popular music studies. While few writers on popular music would necessarily consider themselves 'Marxist', its perspectives and concepts have informed (i) discussions of the music industry, at both the national and global level of operation (e.g. Chapple and Garofalo, 1977); (ii) the examination of the constitution of popular music audiences and subcultures (e.g. Moore, 2010) and (iii) studies of the constitution of individual subjectivities and social structures, through the intersection of popular music with class, ethnicity and gender (e.g. Lipsitz, 1994).

Further reading:

Chapple, S. and Garofalo, R. (1977) *Rock'n'Roll is Here To Pay*, Chicago, IL: Neslon-Hall.

Lipsitz, G. (1994) *Dangerous Crossroads: Popular Music, Postmodernism, and the Politics of Place*, London: Verso.

Moore, R. (2010) *Sells Like Teen Spirit*, New York: New York University Press.

MASCULINITY

see **gender**

MEMORABILIA

Memorabilia can be defined as cultural artefacts not to be forgotten – that is, memorable – and accordingly regarded as worthy of preservation and collection. By the late 1980s, rock and pop memorabilia has become a rapidly growing field of collecting. The first such auction, held in London in 1981, included John Lennon's upright Steinway piano. As major auction houses included such items, this field of collecting gained credibility and respectability, and prices began to rise. In 1988, a John Entwistle (The Who's bass player) guitar, used on the group's BBC *Top of the Pops* appearances in the early 1970s, fetched £15,000. Later, tapes of very early Rolling Stones and Beatles 'performances', and instruments such as the guitar used by Jimi Hendrix at Woodstock, realized then record prices.

The majority of early interest was in items related to the Beatles and Elvis Presley, but other artists soon attracted interest, especially those from the 1950s and the 1960s, while the death of a prominent artist lends great appeal to collectability (as with Michael Jackson memorabilia in 2009–10). There are a large range of collectable items: various records, including promotional copies and gold discs; musical instruments; autographs; tour programmes; posters; tour jackets and concert tickets and t-shirts, plus novelty toys and a whole range of ephemera marketed around major artists like the Beatles. Leading auction houses in London and New York (Phillips, Sothebys) continue to conduct high-profile regular sales. In addition to interest from private collectors, the emergence of 'rock museums' such as the Rock and Roll Hall of Fame and the Experience Music Project and the international Hard Rock Café have stimulated the market. A number of books, many well-illustrated, have documented the increased visibility of music memorabilia and the scope of collecting it (for instance, Dogget and Hodgson, 2003).

See: **collecting**

Further reading:
Dogget, P. and Hodgson, S. (2003) *Christie's Rock and Pop Memorabilia*, New York: Billboard Books.

MERSEYBEAT

Historically, the Merseybeat (or Liverpool sound) emerged with the Beatles *et al.* in the 1960s. While its performers were mainly part of British beat music, Mersybeat was marketed as such, especially as part of the British invasion' of the American market. The musical characteristics and general coherence of Merseybeat are debated. Cohen conceptualized the sound, both historically and contemporary, as a complex amalgam of factors; these incorporated a variety of regional, national and international influences, but were all particular to Liverpool, and reflected a range of social, economic and political factors peculiar to the city. Cohen relied on the way in which Liverpool musicians situated themselves and their music, especially in relation to other scenes/sounds. Later accounts have traced the evolution of popular and academic discourses around 'Merseybeat', and considered their validity and the assumptions underpinning them (Inglis, 2009). The case of Merseybeat has been used to interrogate the utility of the concepts of **scene** and **sound**.

See: **British Invasion; beat music**

Further reading:
Cohen, S. (1998) 'Sounding Out the City: Music and the Sensuous Production of Place', in Leyshon, A., Matless, D. and Revill, G. (eds) *The Place of Music*, New York: The Guilford Press, pp. 269–90.
Inglis, I. (2009) 'Historical Approaches to Merseybeat: Delivery, Affinity and Diversity', *Popular Music History*, 4, 1: 39–55.

MOD

A youth subculture, which originated in London around 1963. Mod was basically a working-class movement with a highly stylized form of dress, the fashions of which changed frequently, and an interest in rhythm and blues (R&B) music. Originally called 'modernists' (a bebop jazz phrase), mods were influenced by the urban fashions of young American blacks. Mods wore their hair short and well-cut in a series of changing styles. Mod transport was on highly decorated motor scooters, and their clothes were casual with a parka when out riding, or expensive suits with a specific length of sidevent and the latest Italian shoes. Living for weekend partying, the mods took pep pills, particularly 'purple hearts' (amphetamines). Several class-based strains of mod appeared, each with distinctive styles: an art school, high camp version; mainstream mods; scooter boys and the hard mods, who developed into skinheads. The mod lifestyle parodied and subverted the respectable conventions of their class backgrounds and the relatively unskilled office jobs many of them held.

The Who and The Small Faces were favourite mod groups, along with Tamla Motown artists and ska and blue beat in the late 1970s. The Who's rock opera *Quadrophenia* (MCA, 1973; film, director Franc Roddam, 1979) celebrates mod, as did the stutter vocal of the group's classic single, 'My Generation' (1965). Mods clashed with the rockers in a series of holiday weekends in the mid-1960s, giving rise to a media-fuelled moral panic.

There have been periodic revivals of the subcultural style, notably in the late 1970s when the British **two tone** groups used a combination of mod dress with ska and blue beat rhythms. Various performers, notably Paul Weller, have continued to personify the style, helping maintain interest in it.

Further reading:
Barnes, R. (1979) *Mods*, London: Eel Pie Publishing.

MORAL PANIC

Moral panic is a sociological concept applied to community over-reaction to new media forms and (often associated) deviant subcultural groups. The popular media are seen to amplify and exaggerate episodes or phenomena out of proportion to their actual scale and significance, thereby contributing to the construction of a moral panic. Historically, concern over the impact of popular culture has emerged periodically with the advent of each new mass medium: silent cinema and the talkies, dime novels and comics, television and video. The moral panics around these were episodes in cultural politics, in part representing struggles to maintain dominant norms and values. Popular culture was seen by its critics as diametrically opposed to high culture and something to be regulated, particularly in the interests of the susceptible young.

The concept of moral panic was utilized in the British sociology of deviance and new criminology studies of the 1970s, most notably in Stanley Cohen's classic study (1980) of the clashes between mods and rockers at several seaside resorts in the mid-1960s. The writing on deviance and moral panic drew on labelling theory, which saw deviance not as an intrinsic quality of specific social acts, but rather as socially defined. Becker, for example, argued that societies and social groups 'create deviance by making those rules whose infraction comprises deviance, and by applying them to particular people, and labeling them as outsiders' (Becker, 1963: 9). The mass media are a major source for the labelling process, as they transmit and legitimate such labels (e.g. Cohen's 'folk devils') and contribute to the operation of social control. Labelling theory is evident in popular music studies of various **audiences** and their perceived 'anti-social' behaviour.

Following Cohen's study, moral panic was used in relation to various later youth subcultures (e.g. punk), their associated musical preferences (e.g. heavy metal) and to some consumption practices (e.g. raves). The concept has also been applied to earlier panics around genres; indeed, popular music was seen to have had its own series of moral panics, with particular genres and youth subcultures attracting controversy and opposition, both upon their emergence and sporadically since: for example, jazz in the 1920s; the teds and rock'n'roll in the 1950s; the mods and rockers of the 1960s; punk in the 1970s; goths, heavy metal and rap in the 1980s; British rave culture in the 1990s and death metal in the 2000s (Shuker, 2008: Chapter 13; Cloonan and Garofalo, 2003).

In such moral panics, criticism has centred variously on the influence of such genres on youthful values, attitudes and behaviour through the music's (perceived) sexuality and sexism, nihilism and violence, obscenity, black magic or anti-Christian nature. The political edge of popular music has been partly the result of this hostile reaction often accorded to the music and its associated causes and followers, helping to politicize the musicians and their fans.

Further reading:

Becker, H. (1997) 'The Culture of a Deviant Group: The "Jazz" Musician', in Gelder, K. and Thornton, S. (eds) *The Subcultures Reader*, London: Routledge.

Cloonan, M. and Garofalo, R. eds (2003) *Policing Pop*, Philadelphia, PA: Temple University Press.

Cohen, S. (1980) *Folk Devils and Moral Panics*, Oxford: Robertson.

MOTOWN; MOTOWN SOUND

Motown was the commercially highly successful recording company founded in Detroit in 1959 by Berry Gordy. Motown recordings – what became termed the 'Motown sound' – was identified by 'instantly hummable melodies, pulsing basslines, punchy tambourines and handclaps, rousing horns and violins, and vocals that evoked a gospel flavor with the call-and-response lines between the lead and back up singers' (*All Music Guide to Soul*: 845). Motown represented a blander, more commercial version of soul music, with 'vocals stripped of ghetto inflections' (McEwen, 1992), as Gordy deliberately targeted the white **crossover** market. Songwriters/producers Holland, Dozier, Holland; Smokey Robinson and Norman Whitefield 'combined evocative relationship based lyrics with gospel elements, while avoiding the raw sounds of black R&B which white audiences were reluctant to embrace' (Fitzgerald, 1995). However, while Motown releases did share general similarities, its stars gradually developed strong identities of their own. Leading Motown artists included The Miracles (with lead singer Smokey Robinson going on to a successful solo career), The Four Tops, The Temptations, Marvin Gaye and Stevie Wonder.

In what is regarded as one of the best studies of the company, George (1985) views it as a team effort of performers, songwriters, producers and session players, with Gordy overseeing and coordinating. Motown was sold to MCA in 1988 (for US$61 million), although Gordy retained the lucrative publishing rights to Motown's back catalogue.

The nature and significance of Motown have continued to be a focus of populist writing, and academic inquiry, with several substantial studies (Early, 2004; George, 1985; Smith, 1999). As her subtitle suggests, Smith insightfully relates the company and Gordy to the Civil Rights movement, challenging the popular view that Motown was 'apolitical' by stressing its distinct grassroots political role in Detroit's black community, the example it provided to black entrepreneurship and the political force of songs by Stevie Wonder

See: **soul**

Further reading:

Early, G. (2004) *One Nation Under a Groove: Motown and American Culture*, 2nd editon Ann Arbour, MI: University of Michigan Press.
Fitzgerald, J. (1995) 'Motown Crossover Hits, 1963-66 and the Creative Process', *Popular Music*, 14, 1: 1–11.
George, N. (1985) *Where Did Our Love Go?* New York: St Martin's Press.

Hirshey, G. (1985) *Nowhere to Run: The Story of Soul Music*, New York: Penguin.
Smith, S. (1999) *Dancing in the Street. Motown and the Cultural Politics of Detroit*, Cambridge, MA: Harvard University Press.

Listening: The Four Tops, 'I Can't Help Myself (Sugar Pie, Honey Bunch)', 1965, on *The Greatest Hits*, Motown, 1967; The Temptations, *Anthology*, Motown, 1973; Marvin Gaye, *Super Hits*, Motown, 1973; Stevie Wonder, *Looking Back*, Motown, 1977

Viewing: *Standing in the Shadows of Motown*, Paul Justman, 2002; *Dancing in the Street*, episode 4: 'R-E-S-P-E-C-T'

MP3

A digital encoding format which became an international standard in 1991, MP3 is the standard encoding for the transfer (P2P) and playback of music on computer hard drives and on portable digital audio players (see **iPod**). The MP3 was designed for ease of use, universal compatibility and freedom of movement: it is a 'container technology' for recorded sound, whose shape and function are, by design, oriented towards free circulation (Sterne, 2006). MP3 files are small enough to make it practical to transfer (download) high-quality music files over the Internet and store them: CD-quality tracks downloadable in minutes, with audio quality dependent on the size of the file. Hardly surprisingly, MP3 rapidly became very popular as a way in which to distribute and access music. By the end of the 1990s, it was widely claimed that 'MP3' had become the word most searched for on Web search engines.

Beginning around 1999–2000, the mainstream music industry showed increasing alarm at the impact on their market share of services such as Napster and practices such as the downloading of MP3s and P2P (person to person) file sharing. In 1999, Napster, the first large P2P file-sharing network, began to allow individuals to share MP3 files copied ('ripped') from compact disks, granting them access to all other Napster users and the MP3 files they chose to share. As such practices became increasingly evident, the copyright violation and consequent loss of revenue, led several artists (notably the band Metallica) and record labels to sue Napster for breach of copyright. The issues involved were complex and the litigation process was a lengthy and very public one (Garofalo, 2003, provides a helpful outline and analysis). Napster was forced to close down, but was relaunched as a legitimate service in late 2003 (Napster 2.0).

For consumers, MP3 enables access to a greater variety of music, most of it free, and they can selectively compile their own collections of songs by combining various tracks to create customized playlists without having to purchase entire albums. For artists, MP3 means they can distribute their music to a global audience without the mediation of the established music industry. For Internet music publishing and the production of recordings, MP3 opened up opportunities for smaller innovative companies.

At the same time, MP3 challenged the recording company's control over distribution, and, since the format had no built in way to prevent users from obtaining and distributing music illegally, could represent considerable lost revenue. The majors, through trade organizations such as the Recording Industry Association of America (RIAA), joined together to create the Secure Digital Music Initiative (see www.sdmi.org), in an attempt to reassert control over music distribution, and also began legally targeting Internet Service Providers (ISPs) and individual consumers who download and share music without permission/payment. National administrations have introduced legislation attempting to modify copyright in regard to on-line music distribution, as with the 1998 US Digital Millennium Copyright Act (see Strasser, 2010: 54–55).

An alternative industry strategy also emerged, when in 2000, record companies began establishing copyright deals with Internet music producers. In 2003, the entry of Apple into the music market place, with its iTunes service, met with considerable success, encouraging the development of further such services, most notably eMusic, which only sells music from independent labels. The battle over P2P file sharing has continued, with the music industry targeting new, post-Napster services and individual consumers whom they perceived as infringing copyright. National administrations continue to be involved in such attempts at regulation. In New Zealand, for example, in May 2011 the government passed The Copyright (Infringing File Sharing) Amendment Act, giving more power to a Copyright Tribunal, enabling them to require ISPs to send warning notices if illegal downloading occurs. After three warning letters, a copyright holder can take a claim to the tribunal, which can then impose a maximum fine of (NZ) $15,000 to the current account holder. The act has already provoked considerable hostility and opposition, not least as unsuspecting parents whose children download would be targeted ('Internet law may catch parents unaware', *Dominion Post*, April 15, 2011: A4, is typical of news coverage); questions also remain around the cost of sending such letters (and who will fund them), and it remains to be seen if the legislation is workable. This local debate has mirrored the wider international discourse around downloading practices.

See: **Internet; peer to peer**

Further reading:
Fairchild, C. (2008) *Pop Idols and Pirates*, Aldershot: Ashgate. Chapter 3: 'Power and Property: CDs, MP3s, and Soundscan'.
Garofalo, R. (2003) 'I Want My MP3: Who Owns Internet Music?' in Cloonan, M. and Garofalo, R. (eds) *Policing Pop*, Philadelphia, PA: Temple University Press, pp. 30–45.
Jones, S. and Lenhart, A. (2004) 'Music Downloading and Listening: Finding from the Pew Internet and American Life Project', *Popular Music*, 27, 2: 221–40.
Kinnally, W. Lacayo, A., McClung, S. and Sapolsky, B. (2008) 'Getting Up on the Download: College Students' Motivations for Acquiring Music Via the Web', *New Media Society*, 10, 6: 893–913.
McLeod, K. (2005) 'MP3s Are Killing Home Taping: The Rise of Internet Distribution and Its Challenge to the Major Label Music Monopoly', *Popular Music and Society*, 28, 4(October): 521–32.
Sterne, (2006) 'The Mp3 as Cultural Artefact', *New Media Society*, 8, 5: 825–42.

MTV

The American cable television channel, 'MTV: Music Television', founded in 1981, became almost synonymous with MV as a cultural form. Originally owned by the Warner Amex Satellite Company, but subsequently sold to Viacom International. Currently, VIACOM is the world's third largest media conglomerate, and MTV remains an important site of popular music culture.

MTV became enormously popular during the later 1980s and was widely credited with boosting a flagging music industry, through capturing a considerable share of the advertising directed at the youth and young adult 'yuppie' market, and solving the perennial problem of cable television – how to generate enough revenue for new programming – by having the record companies largely pay for content by financing the video clips. MTV's success spawned a host of imitators in the United States, and a number of national franchises and imitations around the globe, including MTV Europe (1988) and MTV Asia (1991).

By the late 1980s and through the 1990s, the influence of MTV on the United States' music industry – and, therefore, by association, globally – was enormous. Getting a MV on regular MTV play became necessary to ensure chart success, while MTV had become the most effective way to 'break' a new artist, and to take an emerging artist into star status.

However, the format had lost its freshness and was becoming cliché, and the US channel initiated a programme overhaul, designed to lessen its reliance on videos. New shows introduced included *Unplugged*, featuring live acoustic performances, which became established as a vehicle for marketing associated recordings, including chart-topping album releases by Eric Clapton and Mariah Carey.

MTV's format and programming practices have remained very consistent across time (see Burnett, 1990; Banks, 1996; MTV website). While MVs are the staple of such channels' programming, they also screen concerts, interviews and rock-oriented news/gossip items, acting as a visual radio channel. MTV's playlists are compiled from national sales data, video airplay and the channel's own research and requests, building circularity and subjectivity into the process. In the most thorough early study of the operation of MTV, Banks (1996: Chapter. 9) looked at the gatekeeper role of the American MTV channel, the operation of its Acquisitions Committee and the standards, both stated and unstated, which they apply. He concluded that major companies willingly edit videos on a regular basis to conform to MTV's standards, even coercing artists into making changes to song lyrics, while smaller independent companies cannot usually get their videos on MTV. The various MTV channel's contemporary programming continues to reflect this mix.

There is, rather surprisingly given its ubiquity and continued popularity, an absence of current academic research into MTV. Roedy, the Chairman and CEO of MTV International provides an informative entertaining insider's account of the growth of the company, with an emphasis on how 'we took the original American MTV concept of delivering music with a creative cutting edge and adapted it to the customs and desires of almost every culture on every continent' (p. 5).

Further reading:
Banks, J. (1996) *Monopoly Television: MTV's Quest to Control the Music*, Boulder, CO: Westview Press.
Roedy, B. (2011) *What Makes Business Rock: Building the World's Largest Global Networks*, New York: Wiley.

MUSIC INDUSTRY

There is a tendency, especially in general discourse, to equate the 'music industry' with the sound recording companies, who develop and market artists and their 'records' in various formats, including digital. This sector has historically been at the heart of the music industry and certainly remains a very significant part of it (see **majors**; **independents**).

In a broader sense, however, the music industry embraces a range of other institutions and associated markets, encompassing a range of economic activities or revenue streams. The most important of these are music publishing; music retail; the music press; music hardware, including musical instruments, sound recording and reproduction technology; tours and concerts and associated merchandizing (posters, t-shirts, etc.) and royalties and rights and their collection/licensing agencies. These facets are increasingly under the ownership/control of the same parent company, enabling the maximum exploitation of a particular product or performer (for an extensive discussion of the music industry, structured around the concepts of revenue streams and copyright, see Hull *et al.*, 2011).

Academic studies have focussed on the relationships between major and independent recording companies, the global and the local and its form of industrial organization. Populist studies of the music industry have stressed its negative aspects and its recent decline (Knopper, 2009).

The historical development of the music industry is closely tied to the commodification of music (Frith, 1992, 2006). The industry has been characterized by a tendency towards both oligopoly and extreme volatility and is engaged in a constant struggle to control an uncertain market place (historical changes in the industry can be followed in Barfe, 2004). It does this through two main strategies: its marketing practices, using genres and stars to package and promote sound as a commodity (for the processes involved in the 1990s, and earlier, see Negus, 1999) and through the regulation of copyright.

Several organizations represent the interests of the music industry, most notably the internationally active International Federation of the Phonographic Industries (IFPI).

In the present digital age, the music industry's traditional business model has been undermined by major shifts in the manner in which music is produced, distributed and consumed (aspects of this are considered elsewhere: see **Internet**).

Further reading:

Barfe, L. (2004) *Where Have all the Good Times Gone? The Rise and Fall of the Record Industry*, London: Atlantic Books.

Frith, S. (1992) 'The Industrialization of Popular Music', in Lull, J. (ed.) *Popular Music and Communication*, Sage. (Reproduced, though edited down, in Bennett, *et al.* (eds) 2006, *The Popular Music Studies Reader*, London: Routledge (Chapter 24).

Hull, G., Hutchinson, T.W. and Glasser, R. (2011) *The Music Business and Recording Industry: Delivering Music in the 21st Century*, 3rd edition, New York: Routledge.

Knopper, S. (2009) *Appetite for Self-Destruction. The Spectacular Crash of the Record Industry in the Digital Age*, London: Simon & Schuster.

Negus, K. (1999) *Music Genres and Corporate Cultures*, London: Routledge.

The music press is essential to keeping up with current changes in the industry: *Billboard*, *Variety*, and *Music Week*. Business magazine *Forbes* has included some useful material.

Web sites: The RIAA: www.riaa.com; The British Phonographic Industry: www.bpi.co.uk; The IFPI: www.ifpi.org; The IFPI promotes the interests of the international recording industry worldwide. Its members include over 1,400 major and independent companies in more than 70 countries; it also has affiliated industry national groups in 48 countries.

MUSIC PRESS; MUSIC CRITICISM/JOURNALISM; ROCK CRITICS; MUSIC MAGAZINES

The music press includes a wide range of publications. General magazines and newspapers frequently include coverage of popular music, with regular review columns. There have been several critical analyses of the manner in which these publications construct popular music and influence the reception of genres and performers. Inglis, for example, shows how the British press coverage of The Beatles in the 1960s,

> played a crucial role in shaping the early popularity of the Beatles, and also helped to establish a journalistic approach through which popular music became a legitimate and lucrative topic for newspapers in the UK.
>
> (*Inglis, 2010: 549*)

More specifically, the music press refers to specialized publications: lifestyle magazines with major music coverage, music trade papers and weekly and monthly consumer magazines devoted to popular music or particular genres within it. In addition to these are privately published **fanzines** (as these are usually peripheral to the market economy of commercial publishing they are considered separately). There is also a variety of book-length writing on popular music. Although categories frequently overlap, we can distinguish between (i) popular (auto) biographies, histories and genre studies; (ii) various forms of consumer guides, including encyclopedias and dictionaries, discographies and chart listings and com-pilations and (iii) bibliographies of records or other musical texts, usually organized by artist, genre or historical period. The last represent an important aspect of popular music history, which they constitute as well as record and are important texts for fans. There are also more esoteric publications, such as rock quiz books, genealogical tables plotting the ori-gin and shifting membership of groups and 'almanacs' dealing with the trivia and microscopic detail of stars' private lives. These publications vary greatly in the quality of their writing, accuracy and scholarship.

Popular **music criticism/journalism** includes the proliferation of 'quickie' publications aiming to cash in on the latest pop sensation. Reading like press releases and emphasizing the pictorial aspect rather than any extended critical commentary, these are often little more than pseudo-publicity. They reinforce the public preoccupation with stars, feeding fans' desire for consumable images and information about their preferred performers. In these respects, they complement those popular music magazines aimed at the teenage market. Work of a more serious intent is present in a conventional academic mode, and also in what might be termed 'vernacular scholarship', with the boundaries between the two often blurred in popular music studies. The latter is undertaken by 'independent scholars', professional journalists (including rock critics) and fans; I regard it as scholarship, as it is thoughtful and critically analyti-cal of its subjects.

A major part of the historical development of music criticism was in jazz and the blues, where critics established some of the norms which later shaped the field more generally. Subsequently, other genres established their own body of work and associated key publications. Documentation and analysis of these has been particularly evident in regard to 'rock criti-cism', initially associated with the early periods of magazines such as *Rolling Stone* and *Creem* in the United States, and *NME* in the United Kingdom, and the writing of critics such as Greil Marcus, Lester Bangs, Robert Christgau and Dave Marsh in the United States, and Jon Savage, Dave Rimmer, Nik Cohen, Barney Hoskyns and Charles Shaar Murray in the United Kingdom (for a thorough overview of the historical devel-opment, approaches and impact of rock criticism, see Lindbergh *et al.*, 2000). America's most lauded rock critic', Bangs, who died in 1982, was the critic as rock star. An early champion of the proto punk of 1960s gar-age, he is the subject of a biography (DeRogatis, 1982), and his character makes a cameo appearance in the film *Almost Famous*.

Indicative of the commercial and ideological significance of this work is its subsequent appearance in book form, as sustained, in-depth studies of genres and performers (e.g. Savage, 1991, on the Sex Pistols and **punk**

rock); as collected reviews and essays (e.g. Christgau, 1990) anthologies (e.g. Heylin, 1992; Hoskyns, 2003) and its archiving in the Rock's Back Pages website.

While there is obvious overlap – and market competition – among the various types of **music magazines**, they do have distinctive qualities. The music trade papers keep industry personnel informed about mergers, takeovers and staff changes in the record and media industries, and changes in copyright and regulatory legislation and policies; advise retailers about marketing campaigns, complementing and reinforcing their sales promotions and provide regular chart lists based on extensive sales and radio play data (the main publications are *Billboard*, *Music Business International*, and *Music Week*). Musicians' magazines (e.g. *Guitar Player*) inform their readers about new music technologies and techniques, thereby making an important contribution towards musicianship and musical appropriation.

The various consumer or fan-oriented music magazines play a major part in the process of selling music as an economic commodity, while at the same time investing it with cultural significance. Popular music magazines do not simply deal with music, through both their features and advertising they are also purveyors of style and taste. At the same time, these magazines continue to maintain their more traditional function of contributing to the construction of audiences as consumers.

The majority of popular music magazines focus on performers and their music, and the relationship of consumers and **fans** to these. These magazines fall into a number of fairly clearly identifiable categories based on their differing musical **aesthetics** or emphases, their sociocultural functions and their target audiences. For example, 'teen glossies' emphasize vicarious identification with performers whose music and image are aimed at the youth market (e.g. *Smash Hits*); *Melody Maker* and *New Musical Express* (the 'inkies') have historically emphasized a tradition of critical rock journalism, with their reviewers acting as the **gatekeepers** for that tradition; and the 'style bibles' (*The Face*) emphasize popular music as part of visual pop culture, especially fashion. Several relatively new magazines offer a combination of the inkies' focus on an extensive and critical coverage of the music scene and related popular culture, packaged in a glossier product with obvious debts to the style bibles (*MOJO*).

Music press reviews form an important adjunct to the record company's marketing of their products, providing the record companies (and artists) with critical feedback on their releases. In the process, they also become promotional devices, providing supportive quotes for advertising and forming part of press kits sent to radio stations and other press outlets. Both the press and critics also play an important ideological function, distancing consumers from the fact that they are essentially purchasing an economic commodity, by stressing the product's cultural significance. This is reinforced by the important point that the music press and critics are not, at least directly, vertically integrated into the music industry (i.e. not owned by the record companies). A sense of distance is thereby maintained, while at the same time the need of the industry to constantly sell new images, styles and product is met.

Popular music magazines have only recently received much attention in popular music studies. Early accounts of the development of popular music made considerable use of the music press as a source, while largely ignoring its role in the process of marketing and cultural legitimation, while the music press was absent from otherwise far-ranging anthologies (e.g. Frith and Goodwin, 1990), studies of the music business and even encyclopedias of popular music (e.g. Clarke, 1990; Gammond, 1991). The only book-length study of the music press, of its most influential publication, *Rolling Stone* magazine (Draper, 1990), emphasizes biographical expose rather than extended cultural analysis.

More recently, several authors have paid greater attention to the general role of music magazines, along with case studies of particular publications; placing an emphasis on the manner in which their critical discourse constructs notions of authenticity, musical merit and historical value. For example, Atton (2009) compares how a fanzine, *The Sound Projector*, and the avant garde oriented *The Wire* situate their reviews within a shared paradigm of alternative music reviewing; Brennan (2006) explores the relationship between *Rolling Stone* and *Down Beat* and *Jazz*, especially the motivations for jazz publications to begin covering rock music in the late 1060s; in relation to rock and jazz criticism; and Elafros explores the policies and practices through which alternative-oriented magazine *Rockrgrl* (US 1995–2005) 'simultaneously challenges and reinforces many tropes of mainstream rock criticism'.

See: **biography**; **discography**; **fanzines**

Further reading:
Music press:
Brennan, M. (2006) 'This Rough Guide to Critics: Musicians Discuss the Role of the Music Press', *Popular Music*, 25, 2: 221–34.
Draper, R. (1990) *Rolling Stone Magazine: The Uncensored History*, New York: Doubleday.
Feigenbaum, A. (2005) 'Some Guy Designed This Room I'm Standing In: Making Gender in Press Coverage of Ani DiFranco', *Popular Music*, 24: 37–56.

Jones, S. ed. (2002) *Pop Music and the Press*, Philadelphia, PA: Temple University Press.

Leonard, M. and Strachan, R. (2003) 'Music Press', 'Journalistic Practices', Entries in Shepherd, J., Horn, D., Laing, D., Oliver, P. and Wicke, P. (eds) *The Encyclopedia of Popular Music of the World, Volume 1: The Industry, Contexts and Musical Practices*, London: Cassell.

Rock criticism:

Bangs, L. (1990) *Psychotic Reactions & Carburetor Dung*, Marcus, G. (ed.), London: Minerva.

Christgau, R. (1990) *Christgau's Record Guide: The '80s*, London: Vermilion.

Da Capo Best Music Writing: an annual book series, published since 2001.

DeRogatis, J. (1982) *Let it Blurt: The Life and Times of Lester Bangs, America's Greatest Rock Critic*, New York: Broadway Books.

Gorman, P. (2001) *In Their Own Write: Adventures in the Music Press*, London: Sanctuary Publishing Limited.

Hoskyns, B. ed. (2003) *The Sound and the Fury. A rock's Back Pages Reader. 40 Years of Classic Rock Journalism*, London: Bloomsbury.

Lindbergh, U., Guomundsson, G., Michelson, M. and Weisethaunet, H. (2000) *Amusers, Bruisers and Cool-Headed Cruisers: The Fields of Anglo-Saxon and Nordic Rock Criticism*, Arhus: Nordic Institute.

McLeod, K. (2001) '*1/2: A Critique of Rock Criticism in North America'*, *Popular Music*, 20, 1: 29–46.

Rock's back pages: www.rocksbackpages.com. An archive of reviews, interviews, and features on artists; some selected articles are full text; full access is through subscription.

Willis, E. (1981) *Beginning to See the Light: Pieces of a Decade*, New York: Knopf.

Music magazines:

Atton, C. (2009) 'Writing About Listening: Alternative Discourses in Rock Journalism', *Popular Music*, 28, 1: 53–67.

Brennan, M. (2006) 'Down Beats and Rolling Stones: The American Jazz Press Decides to Cover Rock in 1967', *Popular Music History*, 1, 3: 263–84.

Elafros, A. (2010) '"No Beauty Tips or Guilt Trips": Rockrgrl, Rock, and Representation.' *Popular Music and Society*, 33, 4: 487–99.

Inglis, I. (2010) '"I read the news today, oh boy": The British Press and The Beatles.' *Popular Music and Society*, 33, 4: 549–62.

Strausbaugh, J. (2001) *Rock Til You Drop: The Decline from Rebellion to Nostalgia*, New York: Verso (chapter on *Rolling Stone* magazine).

MUSIC VIDEO

Music video (MV) is a hybrid cultural form, encompassing elements of both television and radio. There are several distinct yet overlapping meanings of the term: individual MV programmes within general broadcast

television channel schedules (dealt with separately); the long-form MV cassette and its successor, the DVD, available for hire or purchase; and **MTV** and similar cable/satellite music channels. Each of these has individual MV clips, or MV presentation style, as central components. However, their place in each case is different, as are their associated patterns of consumption.

The long-form MV cassette, available for hire or purchase

These historically began with compilations of MV clips, but these have now largely been superseded by the availability of MVs on sites such as YouTube. The more prominent contemporary examples are television music tour and concert DVDs, documentaries and compilations of television music programmes (see the ubiquitous adverts and reviews in the music press). In their formatting and aesthetics, these are heavily influenced by MV style. Although they constitute a significant and increasing market (see industry data), there remains a dearth of research on these DVDs, their production and marketing, their purchasers and the uses they make of such recordings.

The MV clip

Individual MV clips follow the conventions of the traditional 45 single: they are approximately 2–3 minutes long, and function, in the industry's own terms, as 'promotional devices', encouraging record sales and chart action. Through the 1980s, the analysis of MV clips was one of the major growth areas in both television studies and the study of popular music. The associated literature emphasizes their visual aspect, their perceived violence and sexuality/sexism, and their significance as a central postmodern cultural artefact. Situating themselves in film studies rather than music studies, these analyses accordingly focus on MVs as discrete, self-contained, essentially visual texts. They frequently largely ignored considerations such as MVs' industrial and commercial dimensions, their placement in the flow of television programming and the links between MVs and rock stardom. For a fuller understanding of MVs, it is necessary to consider their production process and their commercial function for the music industry, the institutional practices of channels such as MTV, and their reception as polysemic texts, open to varying audience interpretations. MV is both an industrial/commercial product and a cultural form.

See: **television**; **MTV**

Further reading:
The major studies of music video, which can be usefully read chronologically, are:
Kaplan, E.A. (1987) *Rocking Around the Clock. Music Television, Postmodernism, and Consumer Culture*, New York: Methuen.
Goodwin, A. (1993) *Dancing in the Distraction Factory Music Television and Popular Culture*, Oxford: University of Minnesota Press.
Vernallis, C. (2005) *Experiencing Music Video: Aesthetics and Cultural Context*, Columbia, OH: Columbia University Press.
A still useful compilation, is Frith, S. Goodwin, A. and Grossberg, L. (1993) *Sound and Vision: The Music Video Reader*, London: Routledge.
Now hard to find, but a useful early history of the form, and its main creators, is Shore, M. (1985) *The Rolling Stone Book of Rock Video*, London: Sidgwick and Jackson.

MUSICALS; POPULAR/ROCK MUSICALS

Stage musicals are a historically well established and popular cultural form. Two types are considered here: the classic Hollywood musicals, and later, so called, 'rock musicals'.

The classic Hollywood musical was a hybrid film genre, descended from European operetta and Amercian vaudeville and the music hall. While *The Jazz Singer* (Alan Crosland, 1927) was the first feature film with sound, the first 'all-talking, all-singing, all dancing' musical was *The Broadway Melody* (Harry Beaumont, 1929), which was important also for establishing the tradition of the backstage musical. The musical soon became regarded as a quintessentially American or Hollywood genre, associated primarily with the Warner and MGM studios, and RKO's pairing of Fred Astaire and Ginger Rogers. A major source of Hollywood's musicals was New York's Broadway stage productions.

Early 'classic' musicals had simple even naive plots, promoting 'a gospel of happiness' (Hayward, 2000) and were mainly perceived as vehicles for song and **dance**. The routines and performance of these became increasingly complex, culminating in the highly stylized films of Busby Berkeley. *The Wizard of Oz* (Victor Fleming, 1939) introduced a new musical formula, combining youth and music. Other new forms of the musical were introduced during the 1940s, including composer biographies and biographical musicals of 'show biz' stars. The vitality and audience appeal of the musical continued into the 1950s, with contemporary urban musicals such as *An American in Paris* (Vincent Minnelli, 1951), which portrayed the vitality of the Paris music scene, with a cast including musical stars Frank Sinatra and Bing Crosby.

'The period 1930–1960, despite some severe dips, marked the great era of the Hollywood musical' (Hayward, 1996: 239). Although the 1960s did see several blockbuster musicals, notably *The Sound of Music* (Robert Wise, 1965), the heyday of the classic musical had passed, with fewer Broadway hits now making it to the screen. The 1960s saw a move towards greater realism in the musical, exemplified by *West Side Story* (Robert Wise and Jerome Robbins, 1961), an updated version of Romeo and Juliet. In the late 1960s and through the 1970s, the classic Hollywood musical was primarily kept alive by the films of Barbara Streisand (e.g. *Funny Girl*, William Wyler, 1968). Subgenres such as the performer biography still appeared (e.g. *Lady Sings the Blues*, Sydney Furie, 1972; see **biopic**), along with the occasional backstage musical (*Fame*, Alan Parker, 1980). The classical musical's place was taken by a plethora of new forms associated with the popular musical genres spawned by the advent of rock'n'roll (see below).

The classic musicals were a narcissistic and exhibitionist genre, extremely self-referential: 'the general strategy of the genre is to provide the spectator with a utopia through the form of entertainment. The entertainment is the utopia' (Hayward: 241), which is constituted and characterized by energy, abundance, intensity, community and transparency. Pleasure, especially the visual enjoyment of the dance, is derived from both female and male forms. Ideologically, the genre is selling marriage, gender fixity, communal stability and the merits of capitalism. Classic musicals are situated around a series of binary oppositions, most notably the duality of male and female, which it ultimately resolves, and work versus entertainment. These codes and conventions were questioned by the popular musicals of the 1950s and beyond.

Further reading:
Everett, W. and P. Laird eds (2008) *The Cambridge Companion to the Musical*, Cambridge, UK: CUP.
Hayward, S. (2000) *Key Concepts in Cinema Studies*, London: Routledge.

Popular/rock musicals

In the late 1960s, following the success of *Hair* (1967), the term 'rock musical' became employed by many New York critics to identify any stage show with even the slightest hint of popular styles (Warfield, 2008: 235; he identifies a number of common features of what is an extremely loose category). Although the first musical to include songs in a rock'n'-roll styles was *Bye Bye Birdy* (1960). *Hair* (1967) is widely regarded as the first rock musical. It was followed by a succession of imitators; among the most successful were *Your Own Thing* (1968) and *Salvation* (1969). The early 1970s, argues Warfield, was a high watermark for the rock musical, with the considerable success of *Godspell* (David Greene, 1973), and *Jesus Christ Superstar* (1970) and *Grease* (1972). The last abandoned the usual Broadway marketing model, following a successful release of a double album.

Beginning in the 1970s, an ever-increasing number of Broadway shows had rock-influenced scores, for example *Chess* (1988), 'yet very few of them – and no commercially successful shows for nearly two decades – was ever promoted as "rock musicals"' (ibid.: 242).

In the United Kingdom, *The Rocky Horror Show*, and its subsequent film version *The Rocky Horror Picture Show* (Jim Sharman, 1975), exemplify the cult status rock musicals can attain. Written by Richard O'Brien, *Rocky Horror* was first produced as an experimental work for the Theatre Upstairs, upstairs at the Royal Court Theatre, London, on 16 June 1973. Tim Curry, who had starred in *Hair*, played the part of Frank'n'Furter, 'a sweet transvestite from Transsexual in Transylvania', a modern-day rock-oriented Franken-stein, hard at work on his creation, a boy called Rocky. O'Brien himself played Riff Raff, the devoted servant. The London critics enthused and the fans queued. After a short initial run, the show continued in larger theatres. Opening at the King's Road Theatre in Chelsea on 31 October 1973, *The Rocky Horror Show* ran for seven years. The show won critical praise, awards and a cult audience, many of whom went again and again. The long-running show also proved highly successful when staged in Los Angeles and other centres. *Rocky Horror* was about the fantasy-fun side of popular music, demanding that its audience let go the restraints of everyday reality and have a good time. O'Brien had blended aspects of late-night science fiction and horror movies on **television**, Dr Strange comics and **rock** history for inspiration. He had spent a year playing in *Hair* and wanted his own **rock opera** to reflect not spirituality, but the sexuality of rock, and developed the songs and dialogue accordingly. Weinstock (2007) traces the transformation of *The Rocky Horror Picture Show* from an 'oddball [stage] musical' to a 'celebrated cinematic experience', concentrating on the latter and with extensive textual analysis.

Later successful rock musicals included *Buddy: The Buddy Holly Story* (1989); *Smokey Joe's Café* a revue of songs by Leiber and Stoller (see **songwriters**) and *Blood Brothers* (London, 1983, 1988 revival; New York, 1993); *Mama Mia* and *Rent* (1996).

Warfield concludes that the imprecision of the designation 'rock musical, "confirms the desire of producers to exploit the popularity of rock, while simultaneously suppressing its rebellious spirit and most extreme sounds"' (247). Despite the commercial and critical success of a number of 'rock musicals', they remain an oddly neglected topic within popular music studies.

Further reading:

Warfield, S. (2008) 'From *Hair* to *Rent*: Is "Rock" a Four-Letter Word on Broadway?' in W. Everett and P. Laird (eds) *The Cambridge Companion to the Musical*, Cambridge, UK: CUP.

Wienstock, J. (2007) *The Rocky Horror Picture Show*, London: Wallflower Press.

MUSICIANS; MAKING MUSIC

The term 'musician' is not as straightforward as it seems. Finnegan, in her now classic study of music making in Milton Keynes, found it difficult to distinguish 'amateur' from 'professional' musicians:

> local bands sometimes contained many players in full-time (non-musical) jobs and others whose only regular occupation was their music; yet in giving performances, practicing, sharing out the fees and identification with the group, the members were treated exactly alike (except for the inconvenience of those in jobs that had to plead illness or take time off work if they traveled to distant bookings).
>
> (*Finnegan, 1989: 13*)

Furthermore, the local musicians tended to use 'professional' in an evaluative rather than an economic sense, to refer to a player's standard of performance, musical knowledge and qualifications, and regular appearances with musicians themselves regarded as professional. Later studies (e.g. Shute, 2005) also demonstrate this more expansive use of the term.

The term 'musician' has been associated with singing or playing an instrument, but the development of sampling technology, computer-based composition and DJ/mixer culture undermined such easy equations. Further, the distinctions historically made between the performer, the songwriter and producer have been blurred since the 1950s. Currently, while the three roles can be distinct, the term musician frequently embraces all three activities.

While they are credited as the authors of their recordings, the ability of musicians to 'make music' is, to varying extents, dependent on the input of other industry personnel, including session musicians, songwriters, record producers, sound engineers and mixers, along with those who regulate access to the infrastructure of the industry (such as venue owners, promoters).

See: **session musicians**; **songwriters**; **producers**

Making Music

As most biographies demonstrate, the career trajectory of popular musicians involves skill and hard work, not to mention a certain amount of luck. Detailed ethnographic accounts of rock musicians, for example, suggest that most bands and performers are 'precariously balanced between fame and obscurity, security and insecurity, commerce and creativity' (Cohen, 1991: 4). It is a Darwinian struggle: there are thousands of unsigned artists, and even if a band or performer was signed to a major label, they have only a small chance of breaking even. This historical situation has now been at least modified, if not superseded, by the opportunities offered by the Internet and digital music and the increased importance of live performance.

Our detailed knowledge of how performers actually create their music and attempt to create an audience for their efforts was initially sparse. Writing in 1990, Cohen's summary of the available literature observed that there had been a lack of ethnographic or participant observer study of the process of making music:

> What is particularly lacking in the literature (on rock) is ethno-graphic data and micro sociological detail. Two other important features have been omitted: the grassroots of the industry – the countless, as yet unknown bands struggling for success at a local level – and the actual process of music making by rock bands.
>
> (*Cohen, 1991: 6*)

In addition to Cohen's *Rock Culture in Liverpool*, there are now a hand-ful of 'classic' accounts, along with a large body of biographical profiles of varying usefulness. In addition, there are several compendiums of reflec-tions from musicians; in-depth studies of the making of particular record-ings; further accounts of musicians involved in local musical scenes and several insightful discussions of musical **creativity** and **authorship**. Popular biographies also provide some insights into the way musicians work (rehearsal, recording and touring).

See: **cover versions**; **cover bands**; **tribute bands**; **session musicians**

Further reading:

On the development of musicianship, within the context of local scenes, the classic rock studies are:

Cohen, S. (1991) *Rock Culture in Liverpool: Popular Music in the Making*, Oxford: Clarendon Press.

Finnegan, R. (1989) *The Hidden Musicians: Music Making in an English Town*, Cambridge: CUP.

Shank, B. (1994) *Dissonant Identities. The Rock'n'Roll Scene in Austin, Texas*, Hanover: Wesleyan University Press.

More contemporary studies include:

Azerrad, M. (2001) *Our Band Could Be Your Life. Scenes from the American Indie Underground 1981-1991,* Boston: Little, Brown and Company.

Fonarow, W. (2006) *Empire of Dirt. The Aesthetics and Rituals of British Indie Music*, Middletown, CT: Wesleyan University Press.

Pollock, B. (2002) *Working Musicians. Defining Moments from the Road, the Studio, and the Stage, New York: Harper Collins*.

Shute, G. (2005) *Making Music in New Zealand*, Auckland: Random House.

The changes brought about by new technologies, and the shifting nature and status of the 'musician', are well demonstrated in:

Brewster, B. and Broughton, F. (1999) *Last Night a DJ Saved My Life. The History of the Disc Jockey*, New York: Grove Press.

Schloss, J.G. (2004) *Making Beats. The Art of Sample-Based Hip-Hop*, Middletown, CT: Wesleyan University Press.

Zak III, A.J. (2001) *The Poetics of Rock. Cutting Tracks, Making Records*, Berkeley, CA: University of California Press.

MUSICOLOGY; POPULAR MUSICOLOGY

Musicology developed historically with Western art music, and privileges the text by placing the emphasis firmly on its formal properties. Musicologists investigate genres such as the blues, jazz and, more recently, pop and rock, as music, using conventional concepts derived from the study of more traditional/classical forms of music: harmony, melody, beat and rhythm, along with vocal style and the lyrics. A major early debate in popular music studies was around the value of such an approach to musical texts. Indeed there was an argument as to whether popular music, especially rock and pop genres, even merits such a 'serious' analysis. This was clearly evident in the 1980s, in the bemused reaction of the mainstream British press to the emergence of 'popular music studies', reflecting conservative notions of high culture set against the mass society critiques of popular music.

To illustrate the issues, the discussion here concentrates on rock and pop; musicological approaches to other metagenres are considered within their respective entries. Academic musicologists at first largely ignored rock and pop music. A notable early exception was Mellers sympathetic study of the Beatles, *Twilight of the Gods* (1974); his example was followed by the pioneering work of, among others, Shepherd, Tagg and McLary. Most musicologists, however, were reluctant to engage with a form of music accorded low-cultural value in comparison with 'serious' music. At the same time, many sociologists writing on popular music were wary of musicology. This was due to its tendency to be distant from the mechanics of much actual composition of rock, its 'vague pretentiousness' and 'chronic failure to address what is really at stake in the tunes' (McLary and Walser, 1990: 277; see also Frith, 1983). As Frith noted, both rock musicians and rock commentators generally lack formal musical training: 'They lack the vocabulary and techniques of musical analysis, and even the descriptive words that critics and fans do use – harmony, melody, riff, beat – are only loosely understood and applied' (1983: 13).

Frith saw rock critics as essentially preoccupied with sociology rather than sound, and identified what has been too ready a willingness to dismiss musicology as having little relevance to the study of popular styles. The arguments here were well rehearsed through the 1980s: traditional musicology neglects the social context, emphasizes the transcription of music (the score) and elevates harmonic and rhythmic structure to pride of place as an evaluative criterion. Popular music, on the other hand, emphasizes interpretation through performance and is received primarily in terms of the body and emotions rather than as pure text. Many rock musicians observed that classical music operated according to a different set of musical criteria, which has little validity for their own efforts. Indeed, it can be argued that much popular music is largely a music of the body and emotions, and its influence cannot easily be reduced to a simple consideration of its formal musical qualities.

In the early 1990s, there were signs that the largely negative attitude towards applying musicology to popular music was changing. Several musicologists engaged with popular music genres and texts (e.g. Moore, 1993; Tagg and Clarida, 2003), while popular music scholars generally began to accord musicology more weight in their analyses. This work varies in the degree to which such analysis simply takes as given the concepts and tools of traditional (e.g. more classical music oriented) musicology or modifies these in relation to popular music.

Much of this work recognized that the traditional conception of musicology remains inadequate when applied to popular music in any straightforward manner (equating the two forms). For example, a concentration on technical textual aspects alone – the score – fails to deal with how the effects on listeners celebrate are constructed, what McLary and Walser (1990: 287) term 'the dimensions of music that are most compelling and yet most threatening to rationality'. This takes into consideration the role of pleasure, the relationship of the body, feelings and emotions and sexuality in constructing responses to genres such as dance, rock and the blues. In the light of such trends, musicologist Nicholas Cook referred to a need for 'the reconciliation of today's broadened agenda with the traditional discipline's practices of close textual reading. In other words we need to find ways of talking about music and about its social or ideological meaning at the same time, without changing the subject' (Cook).

The past decade has produced a substantial body of what can be termed 'popular musicology' (Hawkins, 2002). This has engaged further with the more affective domains of the relationship between the text and its listeners, and into the generic and historical locations of texts and performers. There are several substantive edited volumes containing extensive discussion and examples (Scott, 2009; Moore, 2007).

We are more 'musical' than is usually credited. Radio listening – switching stations in search of something recognizable or engaging – and selecting and downloading which music to play on one's personal stereo involves an ability to distinguish between different types of music. This is to utilize a more extended definition of 'musical', where what is crucial is the link between musical structures and people's use of them. As Hawkins observes, 'the task of interpreting pop is an interdisciplinary task that deals with the relationship between music and social mediation. It is one that includes taking into account the consideration of the sounds in their relationship to us as individuals' (2002: 3).

Further readings:

Beard, D. and Gloag, D. (2005) *Musicology: The Key Concepts*, Abingdon, NY: Routledge.

Cook, N. "What is musicology?": www.rma.ac.uk/articles

Covach, J. and Boone, G.M. eds (1997) *Understanding Rock. Essays in Musical Analysis, New York and Oxford University Press*.

Hawkins, S. (2002) *Settling the Pop Score: Pop Texts and Identity Politics*, Aldershot: Ashgate.

Middleton, R. ed. (2000) *Reading Pop: Approaches to Textual Analysis in Popular Music*, Oxford: OUP.

Moore, A.F. ed. (2003) *Analyzing Popular Music*, Cambridge: CUP.

Moore, A. ed. (2007) *Critical Essays in Popular Musicology*, Farnham: Ashgate.

Scott, D. ed. (2009) *The Ashgate Research Companion to Popular Musicology*, Farnham: Ashgate.

Tagg, P. and Clarida, B. (2003) *Ten Little Title Tunes: Towards a Musicology of the Mass Media*, New York: The Mass Media Musicologists' Press.

MUZAK

Muzak is the term applied, rather negatively, to 'functional' or 'background' music. Muzak accounts for the greatest proportion of the music we are exposed to in our daily lives, though we are rarely consciously aware of it. It is used in a deliberate attempt to influence, or manipulate, the buying patterns of supermarket shoppers, the eating habits of restaurant patrons and so on. Muzak is also used as background music in places such as airport lounges, doctors' waiting rooms and lifts (hence the perjorative term 'elevator music'), to 'soothe' the mood of people in such public spaces, and similarly in workplaces to enhance worker satisfaction and output.

Functional music soon became economically very significant: Muzak Corporation, the largest of the programmed music companies, grossed over US$50 million in 1990, when it had 96 franchises supplying 'programmed music' to 135,000 businesses in 16 countries. Such companies have been paying enormous sums to acquire **copyrights** to songs, rearrange them and profile and track the behaviour of various **consumer** groups.

Muzak has been critiqued on **aesthetic** or musical grounds, as a form of banal, 'wallpaper' music; or as an example of bureaucratic rationalism, linked to post-Fordist industrial practices perpetuating the alienation of workers. Jones and Schumacher 'examine the practices and discourses of functional music, how they have evolved historically, their role in the regulation of work and consumption, and their reproduction of particular kinds of economic, spatial, and symbolic power relations' (1992: 157).

See: **listening**

Further reading:
Jones, S. and Schumacher, T. (1992) 'Muzak: On Functional music and Power', *Critical Studies in Mass Communication*, 9: 156–69.

MYSPACE

see **social network sites**

NEW AGE

A marketing label as much as a truly distinguishable musical **genre**. 'More of a mood than a style, new age was soothing instrumental music of the 1980s, based on the softer kinds of classical, jazz and folk' (Hardy and Laing, 1990). New age is characterized by having precious little vocal accompaniment and making considerable use of **ambient** (natural) sounds, synthesizers and **samplers**. 'New Age music is commonly marked by minute variations and an abundance of repeats. This music is all middle; it starts and stops, it is turned on and off, but one does not get a distinct sense of beginnings and endings' (Hall, 1994: 14). It is almost exclusively recorded music, produced and consumed via **cassette audio tape** and **CD**. The Wyndham Hill label was prominent in popularizing the genre, which has its own specialist radio programmes, and is a genre sales category in many **retail** outlets.

New age is sometimes scorned as 'yuppie muzak' (Gammond, 1991), in part because of its appeal amongst relatively well-off and liberally educated listeners. Hall claims new age to be a postmodernist musical style, 'due to its eclectic, constantly shifting character and confusion of boundaries; its spirit of playfulness, taste for irony, and textual looting; its aggressive multiculturalism; and its anti-intellectualism yet devotion to learning' (see Hall, 1994: 17–18, for an elaboration of these claims). Other observers regard the genre as musically a heavily conservative one, leaning towards the formulaic, and oriented towards private introspection.

Further reading:
Hall, D. (1994) 'New Age Music: A Voice of Liminality in Postmodern Popular Culture', *Popular Music and Society*, 18, 2: 13–21.

Listening: Mike Oldfield, *Tubular Bells*, Virgin, 1973

NEW COUNTRY

Country emerged in the United States as a major market force in popular music in the 1990s, and classic stereotypes associated with the genre (especially its maudlin themes and limited appeal) no longer held up. *Billboard* placed Garth Brooks as Top Country Album Artist *and* Top Pop Album Artist for the years 1990, 1991, and 1993. In 1993, all six of his albums were included among the most popular for the year, with two (*No Fences* and *Ropin' the Wind*) having sold about 10 million copies each. Brooks adopted an arena rock aesthetic, using theatre smoke, fireworks and sophisticated lighting shows. His crossover success opened the way on the pop charts for other country artists, with Billy Ray Cyrus, Dwight Yoakum, Mary Chapin Carpenter and Reba McIntyre among the best selling artists of the early mid-1990s. Along with Brooks and others, these artists are often referred to as 'new country'. At the same time, country radio became the second most listened to music format in the United States, second only to adult contemporary, and video channel CMT gained a significant market share.

The subsequent success of the Dixie Chicks, Shania Twain and Faith Hill continued this aggressive resurgence of country music, and were indicative of new themes and approaches in the genre. Shania Twain's 'country' career illustrates several aspects of contemporary 'mainstream' popular music: notably the importance of crossover potential, the significant role of producers and the construction of stardom through a range of media, including the music press and music video. Her success came in the context of the resurgence and new market for country music in the 1990s, and has been attributed to a combination of her songwriting, her striking and attractive looks, her music videos and the role of producer and song co-writer (and husband) Robert 'Mutt' Lange in her recordings (Shuker, 2008: 85–8).

Twain's self-titled debut album (1993, on Mercury Nashville), featured only one of her own compositions, her producers opting instead for songs from established songwriters, a common practice in Nashville. The debut was respectable, without making a major impact, and she made *Billboard's* 1993 list of promising new artists. The accompanying music video for 'What Made You Say That', her own composition, broke with country tradition, celebrating her 'sex appeal', and received considerable play on MTV in North America and Europe. Twain's second album, *The Woman in Me* (1995), was produced by her husband "Mutt" Lange, (they married in 1993) who also partially financed it. Featuring a number of the songs turned down for the first album, *The Woman in Me* took a year and a half and more than half a million dollars to complete, a recording effort far beyond the usual Nashville practice, where budgets of one-tenth of that amount were standard (Hager 1998: 54). It sold 12 million copies by the end of 1998. In producing the album, Lange drew on the 'rock' style which he had used for very successful records with Def Leppard, AC/DC and Bryan Adams. The album was a combination of 'Irresistible songs, sassy lyrics, all backed by Lange's onion-skin production, which reveals more of each song with each play' (Q magazine, review, November 1999). Her third album, *Come on Over* (1998) was also a major commercial success, and the first single from it, 'You're Still the One', topped both the *Billboard* country and pop charts. Her songs, mainly co-written with Lange, reinvigorate traditional county formats and also reasserted personal political concerns, with 'Black Eyes, Blue Tears' alerting listeners to domestic violence.

See: **country**

Further reading:
Escott, C. (2003) *The Story of Country Music*, London: BBC.
Hager, B. (1998) *On Her Way. The Life and Music of Shania Twain*, New York: Berkley Boulivard.

Listening: Garth Brooks, *No Fences*, Capitol/EMI, 1989; Rosanna Cash, *Retrospective 1979–1989*, CBS, 1989; Dixie Chicks, *Wide Open Spaces*, Monument, 1998; Faith Hill, *There You'll Be*, Warner Bros Records, 2001; Shania Twain, *Come On Over*, Mercury Records, 1998

Viewing: *Lost Highway*, (USA, UK joint production), BBC, 2003: episode 3: 'Beyond Nashville'.

NEW ROMANTICS

A rather general label or movement, applied to British synthesizer-based bands of the mid-1980s, who did well in the US market partly because of extensive exposure on **MTV**. The term was also applied to a club scene, and often used interchangeably with New Pop or syth. pop. The new romantics adopted extravagant dress, make-up and period clothes (e.g. Adam and the Ants). Other leading performers were Soft Cell, Duran Duran, Culture Club, Howard Jones and the Human League.

See: **MTV**; **glam rock**

Listening: Duran Duran, *Notorious*, Capitol, 1986; *At Worst … The Best of Boy George and Culture Club*, Virgin, 1993

NEW WAVE

The origins of the term lie with its application to avant garde French film-makers of the 1950s to signal a radical break with dominant

conventions. Musically new wave performers were innovative and progressive, but not necessarily threatening (cf. punk). New wave was usually
more melodic and more accessible, in some cases with a greater emphasis
on song lyrics. In part, new wave provided a convenient marketing label
for record label A&R people, journalists, and DJs to distinguish music
they did not want identified as punk, owing to punk's negative marketing
connotations, especially in the United States.

New wave embraced a wide range of styles. In the United Kingdom,
The Police (with reggae associations), XTC, Elvis Costello and the
Attractions, and Graham Parker and the Rumour. In the United States,
Devo, the Cars, the B-52s, Talking Heads, Blondie (over laid with disco),
Tom Petty and the Heartbreakers (with rock'n'roll antecedents), and
Jonathan Richman and the Modern Lovers. The term is also sometimes
used to refer to new strains of British heavy metal in the 1980s.

See: **punk**

Listening: Talking Heads, *More Songs about Buildings and Food*, Sire, 1978; Blondie,
The Best Of Blondie, Chrysalis, 1981; Elvis Costello and the Attractions, *The Best
of Elvis Costello and the Attractions*, CBS, 1985

NWOBHM (NEW WAVE OF BRITISH HEAVY METAL)

The advent of the New Wave of British Heavy Metal, often referred to as
simply NWOBHM, can be viewed as a watershed for the metal genre in
the late 1970s, marking a point of transition between the earlier hard
rock-oriented styles of Black Sabbath *et al.*, and the later splintering of
metal into a series of subgenres (speed metal, glam metal, nu-metal and
extreme metal).

First used by journalist Geoff Barton in a May 1975 *Sounds* article, as
Waksman observes, 'the phrase itself was a hybrid that appropriated the
capacity of the "New Wave" to embody the cutting edge and applied it
to a genre seen to be anything but the state of the art at the moment'
(Waksman, 2009: 173; and see the entry on **New Wave**). As founding
editor of *Kerrang!*, Barton helped document and popularize the development of the NWOBHM, through its peak period 1979–83. *Kerrang!* was
the first mainstream music press magazine devoted to heavy metal; the
first issue in June 1981 featured Australian hard rock/metal band AC/DC

guitarist Angus Young on the cover), 'Accelerating the flashy ethos in heavy metal songwriting, the force of multiple guitars became a uniquely central element, encouraging more complex musical development'. NWOBHM bands 'modulated their three chords with tempo changes, guitar solos, and shifts in mood and energy' (Christe, 2004: 35).

The genre was consolidated in 1980 with the release of landmark albums by Iron Maiden (self-titled), Saxon (*Wheels of Steel*), Def Leppard (*On Through the Night*) and Motorhead (*Ace of Spades*). In August 1980 Sounds helped promote Monsters of Rock, 'the first exclusively heavy metal festival' (Christe, 37), with Judas Priest, Saxon and so on. Held on the estate of Castle Donnington, the event was attended by 60,000 fans.

The most successful bands were Judas Priest, Iron Maiden, Motorhead, Def Leppard and Saxon (see the bands entries in Berelian, Popoff and Macmillan: in further reading). In addition to doing well in the UK charts, and building a considerable fan base at home these British bands capitalized on the growth of the American market for metal in the early 1980s.

Macmillan (2001) sees 1986 as an approximate end date for the genre but it remained evident, not least with band reunion tours, documentaries and anniversary releases of key recordings (British Steel, 2010). Festivals such as Monsters of Rock have become annual metal mainstays. The British rock press, especially *Classic Rock* magazine, has consistently featured NWOBHM bands (see Classic Rock).

The emergence of **Speed/Thrash** metal in the United States in 1983 was influenced by the NWOBHM, most notably in the early recordings of Metallica, but along with the other speed bands they took metal in a new direction

Further reading:

Berelian, E. (2005) *The Rough Guide to Heavy Metal*, London: Rough Trade Publications.

Christe, I. (2004) *Sound of the Beast: The Complete Headbanging History of Heavy Metal*, New York: Harper Entertainment. Chapter 3.

Macmillan, M. (2001) *The New Wave of British Heavy Metal Encyclopedia*, Berlin: Iron Pages.

Popoff, M. (1997) *A Collector's Guide to Heavy Metal*, Burlington, Ontario: Collectors Guide Publishing.

Waksman, S. (2009) *This Ain't the Summer of Love*, Chapter 5.

Listening: Judas Priest, *British Steel*, CBS, 1980; Iron Maiden, *The Number of the Beast*, EMI, 1982; Motorhead, *No Sleep 'Til Hammersmith*, Castle Communications, 1981 (live); Saxon, *Wheels of Steel /Strong Arm of the Law*, EMI, 1997 (double CD rerelease, originally issued in 1980)

Viewing: *Classic Albums: Iron Maiden, The Number of the Beast*, Eagle Rock Entertainment, 2001; *Classic Albums: Judas Priest, British Steel*, Eagle Rock Entertainment, 2001

NORTHERN SOUL

Northern soul is a regional cult in the UK Midlands, based around ballroom/club culture and all-night dancing to 1960s Motown and independent label (e.g. Cameo, Parkway and Verve) soul records chosen for their 'danceability' (e.g. The Exciters). Northern soul became prominent in the early 1970s, with the Wigan Casino, a First World War dance hall, being declared by American *Billboard* to be the world's best discotheque. The subculture has maintained itself, with fanzines, continued all-nighters and record compilations. While rarity and exclusivity of records and commodity exchange are integral to the Northern Soul scene, dance is at its heart (Wall, 2006).

Hollows and Milestone's case study of Northern Soul demonstrated how Northern Soul produces a sense of identity and belonging based on the consumption of 'music as music', organized around a club scene. Here the records have value both as commodities and as bearers of musical meaning; the exchange, buying and selling of records is an important part of the Northern Soul scene. Indeed, the use of 'white Labels' represents a unique form of fetishization of black musical culture by white consumers (Hollows and Milestone, 1998).

The example of Northern Soul challenged orthodox subcultural theory, and its preoccupation with music as symbol and the homology between musical style and subcultural values, illustrating how 'contemporary youth cultures are characterized by far more complex stratifications than that suggested by the simple dichotomy of "monolithic mainstream" − "resistant subculture"' (Wienzierl and Muggleton, 2003: 7).

See: **soul**

Further reading:
Garratt, S. (1998) Adventures *in Wonderland: A Decade of Club Culture*, London: Headline, Chapter 5.
Hollows, J. and Milestone, K. (1998) 'Welcome to Dreamsville: A History and Geography of Northern Soul', in Leyshon, A., Matless, D. and Revill, G. (eds) *The Place of Music*, New York: The Guilford Press, pp. 83–103.

Wall, T. (2006) 'Out on the Floor: The Politics of Dancing on the Northern Soul Scene', *Popular Music*, 25, 3(October): 431–46.

Listening: *Once Upon a Time in Wigan*, Kent, 2004. A compilation soundtrack to the successful play of the same name; *Soul Boy*, Soundtrack, Universal, 2010

NU-METAL

Nu-metal, sometimes referred to as 'rap metal', moved into the vacuum created by the demise of glam metal in the 1990s, and became one of the most commercially successful genres of the decade.

Lyrically, nu-metal shared the thematic concerns of **grunge**, dealing with angst, inner turmoil and emotional hardship. It also drew on rap, with several bands incorporating hip-hop breaks and using DJs (Deftones). The music is characterized by 'a churning and brutal rhythmic attack, and there are few guitar solos' (Berelian, 2005: 259). Several bands with their roots in the California punk scene added radical political commentary to their music, notably Rage Against The Machine (*The Battle for Los Angeles*, Epic, 1999).

Rage Against The Machine and Faith No More pioneered the style, which reached its peak with Slipknot, 'whose emergence and rapid domination of the metal scene in the new millennium signified the peak of the genre's popularity' (Berelian, 2005: 334–6). Other prominent nu-metal bands to form in the late 1990s were Linkin Park (in 1998), Limp Bizkit (1994) and Korn (1993). By the end of the decade, nu-metal had effectively become part of the mainstream of heavy metal, with its bands sharing concert/festival stages with a range of metal performers.

Further reading:

Berelian, E. (2005) *The Rough Guide to Heavy Metal*, London: Rough Trade Publications.

Christe, I. (2004) *Sound of the Beast: The Complete Headbanging History of Heavy Metal*, New York: Harper Entertainment, Chapter XIV.

Popoff, M. (1997) *A Collector's Guide to Heavy Metal*, Collectors Guide Publishing.

Listening: Linkin Park, *Meteora*, Warners, 2003; Limp Bizkit, *Significant Other*, Interscope, 1997; Faith No More, *The Real Thing*, London, 1989; Slipknot, *Iowa*, Roadrunner, 2001; Korn, self-titled, Immortal/Epic, 1994

OLD-TIME (HILLBILLY) COUNTRY

Country music prior to 1939 was referred to as 'old-time' music, or, in a more negative, pejorative sense, as 'hillbilly'. It was a style rich in oral tradition, based around traditional stringed instruments, such as the fiddle. Old-time country became closely linked to the maintenance of a specific cultural heritage: a celebrated and romanticized view of America's past, centred on notions of authenticity.

The genre was based in the rural areas of the southern United States and had its musical origins in styles of folk music, primarily British ballads, reaching as far back as the seventeenth century.

It existed within a clear time frame: from the late 1800s through the early 1920s, when it was recorded and more widely disseminated. The early British folk influence and instrumentation were added to in the late 1800s and into the early 1900s, with the influence of the blues and vaudeville, and the addition of instruments such as the dobro and the washboard. In the 1920s, this eclectic rural-based music was the template for the development of country music. Later histories of country music have identified this early period, roughly 1923 to 1939, as 'traditional' country.

In the mid-1920s, New York-based OKey Records sent Ralph Peer, an A&R (Artist and Repertoire), to Georgia and Tennessee, to seek out music and musicians with commercial potential. His major 'find' was The Carter Family; in Bristol, Tennessee, between 1927 and 1941, he recorded more than 300 songs by the trio. These have become canonized as 'The Bristol Sessions' and are generally regarded as the origins of country music (Zwonitzer, 2004). The Carter family drew on a range of sources for their songs; one of their best known, their theme song 'Keep On The Sunny Side', was a gospel song from 1899: Collectively, their recordings 'made a compelling statement, almost a lament for paradise lost' (Escott, 2003: 22), exemplified in the classic 'Will The Circle Be Unbroken'. Country music moved into a wider market and audience with the success of the Carter Family, a move consolidated by Jimmy Rodgers, the biggest country star of his day. Rodgers recorded some 110 songs between 1927 and his death in 1933. He had strong roots in traditional 'old-time' country, but recast it in more modern style, as good time music for both the rural community and an urbanizing society.

Pecknold (2007) outlines the commercialization of old-time country in the 1920s and 1930s, and its reshaping into 'country', with a more organized music industry, and the development of a wider audience for the music. Radio played a crucial role in this process of popularizing traditional country, with specialized shows and the revenue these attracted from advertising. A key moment was the first broadcast of the Grand Ole Opry, in November 1925, on WSM in Nashville. The show went on to become the premier institution of traditional country music, with performers establishing their reputations and an audience through their appearances.

The genre has continued to be maintained through the work of Nashville-based performers and the tradition of the Grand Ole Opry. The hit feature film *O Brother, Where Art Thou?* (2000), featured 'old-time' country music songs written between the 1880s and 1935, and 'reclaimed the countriness in country' (Escott, 2003: 173). The soundtrack was also a commercial success, and the response to the film and its music showed the continued appeal of the genre. The basis for this was a mix of nostalgia for a simpler period of life and the authenticity of traditional instruments and vocal styles. 'Old-time' country was in sharp contrast to the pop/rock aesthetic of new country through the 1990s, *see*: **bluegrass** (which old-time country had a marked influence on).

Further reading:

Escott, C. (2003) *The Story of Country Music*. Chapter 2: The Bristol Sessions, London: BBC.

Pecknold, D. (2007) *The Selling Sound: The Rise of the Country Music Industry*, Durham, NC: Duke University Press.

Zwonitzer, M. with Hirschberg, C. (2004) *Will You Miss Me When I'm Gone? The Carter Family & Their Legacy in American Music*, New York: Simon & Schuster Paperbacks.

Listening: This period of country music has been very well served by reissue labels, aiming in part at a dedicated collector market. For fuller coverage of performers and their recordings, see the *All Music Guide to Country*; Jimmy Rogers: Rounder Record has released an eight CD retrospective; some of his best work is on *Riding High 1929-1930* (Rounder, 1991). There are also a number of single CD compilations; The Carter Family: There is a 'complete recordings' series of their Victor recordings, by Rounder; *Anchored in Love – Their Complete Victor, 1927* (Rounder, 1993), is regarded as the best of these, and includes excellent notes by Charles Wolfe

Viewing: *O Brother, Where Art Thou?* (2000); *Lost Highway*, UK, USA; BBC, 2003, episode 1

PAYOLA

A term used for the offering of financial, sexual or other inducements in return for promotion. In 1955, the US House of Representatives Legislative Oversight Committee, which had been investigating the rigging of quiz shows, began looking at pay-to-play practices in rock music radio. Payola, as the practice was then known, had long been commonplace, but was not illegal. 'Song plugging', as the practice was originally termed, had been central to music industry marketing since the heyday of Tin Pan Alley in the 1920s. By the 1950s, DJs and radio station programmers frequently supplemented their incomes with 'consultant fees' and musical credits on records, enabling them to receive a share of songwriting royalties.

During the committee hearings, Dick Clark admitted to having a personal interest in around a quarter of the records he promoted on his influential show. He divested himself of his music business holdings and was eventually cleared by the committee. A clean-cut figure, Clark survived the scandal because he represented the acceptable face of rock'n'roll. Pioneer DJ Alan Freed was not so fortunate; persecuted and eventually charged with commercial bribery in 1960, his health and career were ruined.

Payola did not target all music radio, but was part of a conservative battle to neutralize the impact of rock'n'roll and return to 'good music'. The campaign against payola was underpinned by economic self-interest. The American Society of Composers, Authors and Publishers (ASCAP) supported it by attacking rivals BMI (Broadcast Music, Inc.), whose writers were responsible for most rock'n'roll. The majors supported it as part of a belated attempt to halt the expansion of the independents. Hill goes so far as to conclude that one way to see the payola hearings was as an attempt – ultimately successful – 'to force a greater degree of organization and hierarchical responsibility onto the record industry so that the flow of music product could be more easily regulated' (1992: 41). The involvement of conservative government officials, and a number of established music figures (including Frank Sinatra), was largely based on an often intense dislike of rock'n'roll, a prejudice with only loosely concealed racist overtones, given the prominence of black musicians in the genre.

See: **censorship**; **charts**; **DJ**; **radio**

Further reading:
Hill, T. (1992) "The Enemy Within: Censorship in Rock Music in the 1950s", in A. DeCurtis (ed.) *Rock and Roll Culture*, Durham, NC: Duke University Press, pp. 39–71.

PEER TO PEER (P2P); FILE SHARING

David (2010: 2) defines file sharing as 'the circulation of compressed digital computer files over the Internet using an array of location and exchange software'. In his comprehensive and nuanced study of the phenomenon, he provides a historical and contemporary account of the issues in the fields of law, technology and culture, associated with the ongoing conflict over file sharing, emphasizing 'the contradictions and conflicts within established economic relations, and the possible alternatives that are prefigured in the present' (ibid.: 164). The last include the promise of sharing the world's culture, 'making mediated reproduction truly universal' (ibid.: 168). By encouraging a de-commodification of informational goods, peer-to-peer file sharing took network technology in a radical new direction.

See: **social network**; **MP3**; **Internet**

Further reading: (see also the suggestions with **MP3**)
David, M. (2010) *Peer to Peer and the Criminalization of Sharing*, Los Angeles, CA: SAGE.

PERFORMANCE

Musical performances take place in a range of informal and formal settings and social situations and are closely related to considerations of different valuations of authorship and authenticity (depending on the genre/performers involved; see **live music**). Investigating the processes involved in how performance communicates musical meaning to its constituent audiences in such different contexts has been a significant part of popular music scholarship, especially in relation to genres such as **rock** (Pattie, 2007), **EDM** and **jazz**.

At times, performance events ('gigs', concerts, festivals) have had the capacity to encapsulate and represent key periods and turning points in popular music; examples include the first performance of the modernist composer Stravinsky's Rites of Spring (1919), The Beatles first appearance on the Ed Sullivan Show (1964), Dylan 'going electric' at the Newport folk festival (1965). Their significance is indicated by their use in a cultural shorthand fashion among fans, musicians and writers; for example 'Woodstock', with an assumed set of connotations: the counter-culture, music festivals, youth and 1960s idealism. These are commonly celebrated in the musical press, documentaries, and documented and analysed in several books. Paytress (2005), for example, uses the term 'gig' for a single concert (going back to Benny Goodman at Carnegie Hall in 1938), an extended stay at a venue (Frank Sinatra at The Sands, in 1966; The Beatles at the Cavern Club and in Hamburg, 1961–63) or a tour (Lollapalooza, 1992). The book lacks analysis as to why most of these events are historically significant ('changed the world'), but does include hundreds of pictures and dozens of anecdotes from those involved. The academic essays included in the study by Inglis (2006) cover similar ground, although with greater attention (in some cases at least) to the question of the significance of such performances.

See: **authenticity**; **concerts**; **live**

Further reading:
Cook, N. (2003) "Music as Performance", in Clayton M., Herbert T., and Middleton R. (eds) *The Cultural Study of Music*, New York: Routledge.
Inglis, I. ed. (2006) *Performance and Popular Music: History, Place and Time*, Burlington, VT: Ashgate.
Pattie, D. (2007) *Rock Music in Performance*, Hampshire: Palgave Macmillan.
Paytress, M. (2005) *I Was There: Gigs That Changed The World*, London: Cassell.

Listening: The status of live recording of concerts is regarded as rather ambivalent, given that many are technologically sonically 'tweaked' prior to their release, but the following are examples of live recordings often considered iconic examples of particular performers and genres; The Who, *Live at Leeds* (rock); Motorhead, *No Sleep 'Til Hammersmith* (heavy metal); Keith Jarrett, *The Koln Concert* (jazz)

PIRACY

Piracy is usually simply regarded as a form of theft, and the music industry has generally favoured this definition (Strasser, 2010). However, there has been considerable debate around the various practices associated with music piracy, and whether these are indeed a form of theft. It is probably circumspect, therefore, to always signal this ambivalence by using the term in quote marks: 'piracy'.

The same technologies that have made commercially recorded popular music a global commodity have also made it one of the most vulnerable to 'piracy'. There are a number of practices involved here, and it is important to distinguish between, first, the multiple copying and subsequent on-selling for profit of copyrighted recordings in various formats; and, second, copying by individuals on a 'one off' basis, primarily but not exclusively for personal use. This includes cassette audio home taping; downloading recordings from the Internet, as MP3s, via services such as Napster; and practices including file sharing. A third form of 'piracy' is the unauthorized recording of concerts: bootlegs, usually for personal use or trading among fans; due to their particular cultural nature, these have been considered separately.

See: **bootlegs**; **copyright**; **MP3**; **P2P**

Further reading:

Fairchild, C. (2008) *Pop Idols and Pirates*, Burlington, VT: Ashgate.

Social Science Research Council. (2011) *Media Piracy in Emerging Economies*, SSRC, UK. Available at http://piracy.ssrc.org

PIRATE RADIO

Broadcasts made by unlicensed broadcasters as alternatives to licensed, commercial radio programming.

The best-known and most discussed example of pirate radio is the British pirate stations, operating from ships in the English Channel in the 1960s, who challenged the BBC's lack of attention to pop/rock music.

British pirate radio in its heyday, 1964–8, was an historical moment encapsulating the intersection of rock as cultural politics and personal memory with market economics and government intervention. Given that the BBC's popular music policy was woefully inadequate in the early 1960s, the pirates did cater for a largely disenfranchised audience; they also pioneered some innovative programming and boosted the careers of leading DJs of the time, notably Kenny Everett and John Peel. Twenty-one different pirates operated during this period, representing a wide range of radio stations in terms of scale, motives and operating practices. Chapman (1992) argues that the myth of the pirates is that they were about providing pop music to the disenfranchised youthful listeners, representing a somewhat anarchic challenge to radio convention and commerce; indeed, this is the narrative of the recent feature film *Rock the Boat*. The reality was rather more commercial: as their programming indicated, they were never predominantly about popular music and were heavily oriented toward advertising. All the pirates were commercial operations: 'though work-place and legal judicial circumstances were not typical, in all other respects these were entrepreneurial small businesses aspiring to become entrepre-neurial big businesses' (Chapman, 1992: 167). This was particularly evi-dent in the case of Radio London, set up with an estimated investment of £1.5 million, whose 'overriding institutional goals were to maximize profit and bring legal commercial radio to Great Britain' (ibid.: 80). In this respect, the station succeeded, with the BBC's Radio One, established in 1967 as the pirates were being closed down, borrowing heavily from the practices of pirate radio and hiring pirate DJs.

In contrast to the UK pirates, US pirate radio stations operate on shoestring budgets, broadcast irregularly, rarely attempt to turn a profit, do not solicit advertising and keep a very low profile. The Federal Communications Commission has an attitude of 'selective enforcement', meaning that it acts on complaints and interference, but does not seek out pirate broadcasters.

Further reading:
Chapman, R. (1992) *Selling the Sixties: The Pirates and Pop Music Radio*, London: Routledge.

Viewing: *Rock The Boat* (Feature film, 2010)

PLACE; LOCALITY

Place, often conflated with locality, has become a central concept in con-temporary popular music studies, picking up on well-established trends in cultural geography, and drawing on social anthropological methodology. Cultural geographers have been doing research on music since the late 1960s, seeking to establish the nexus between the social, cultural, eco-nomic and political in musical analysis. The breadth of this work was evi-dent in Carney's (2003) edited collection presenting 'A Geography of American Music from Country to Classic and Blues to Bop' (subtitle). Hamm (1995) helped shape the field and is now regarded as something of a canonical text.

The geographical analysis of popular music emphasizes the dynamics and consequences of the geographical distribution of recorded popular music around the world, especially in urban settings; and how particular musical sounds have become associated with particular locations. In the

1990s, the work of Cohen was important for suggesting that place and locality could be most usefully used in popular music studies in an anthropological sense:

> to discuss networks of social relationships, practices and processes extending across particular places; to imply a methodological orientation concerned with the particular rather than the general, the concrete rather then the abstract. It could also emphasise interconnections and interdependencies between, for example, space and time, the contextual and the conceptual, the individual and the collective, the self and other.
>
> (*Cohen 1995: 65*)

There has since developed a body of work in popular music studies drawing on this agenda, including Cohen's own studies of Liverpool (2007), using place and locality in a number of overlapping ways:

1. To consider global processes of cultural homogenization and commodification, and the intersection of these with the local. The study of the global geographical distribution of recorded popular music is concerned with the nature, status and operation of **cultural imperialism**, and the relationship between local music and the international music industry. Here locality becomes a marker of political experience, juxtaposed against imported repertoire ('the other') to ideologically valorize and support local music.
2. The way in which music has frequently been used to express conceptions of homeland or national, regional or community **identity**.
3. Locality as a social experience, linked to songwriters using it as a theme, as with Bruce Springsteen and New Jersey, an approach regarded as a means of authenticating their music.
4. The notion of localized scenes/sounds. Histories of popular music will often refer to particular geographic locales, usually cities or regions, as being identified at a specific historical juncture with a sound; e.g. Chicago blues. Somewhat contiguous with this usage, is the application of the concept of scene; for example, Athens, Georgia, in the late 1980s. This implies a range of activities, loosely centred around and aligned to a particular style of music and its associated performers. Aside from exploring the characteristics of scenes, a central interest in popular music studies has been the question of *why* they develop at a specific location at a particular time, and interrogating the underpinning assumption that sound and location are in some way connected (see **scenes**; **sounds**).

5.   As an important aspect of urban studies (Krims, 2007; *Popular Music History*, 2010).

In addition to single authored studies, there are a number of useful edited readers containing a range of case studies/general discussion; situated historically, these can be read as constituting a series of benchmarks in the evolution of approaches to the field (Leyshon, Mattress, and Revill, 1998; Stokes, 1994; Whiteley, Bennett, and Hawkins, 2004; see also *Popular Music History*, 2010).

Further reading:

Carney, G. ed. (2003) *The Sounds of People and Places. A Geography of American Music from Country to Classical and Blues to Bop*, 4th edn, Lanham: Rowman & Littlefield Publishers, Inc.

Cohen, S. (1995) "Localizing Sound", in Straw, W. *et al.* (eds) *Popular Music: Style and Identity*, Montreal: Centre for research on Canadian Cultural Industries and Institutions.

Cohen, S. (2007) *Decline, Renewal and the City in Popular Music Culture: Beyond the Beatles*, Aldershot: Ashgate.

Hamm, C. (1995) *Putting Popular Music in Its Place*, Cambridge: Cambridge University Press.

Krims, A. (2007) *Music and Urban Geography*, New York: Routledge.

Leyshon, A., Matless, D. and Revill, G. eds (1998) *The Place of Music*, New York: The Guilford Press.

Popular Music History 4, 2, 2010. Special Issue: music, characterization and urban space.

Stokes, M. ed. (1994) *Ethnicity, Identity and Music: The Musical Construction of Place*, Oxford: Berg.

Whiteley, S., Bennett, A., and Hawkins, S. eds (2004) *Music, Space and Place: Popular Music and Cultural Identity*, Burlington, VT: Ashgate.

POLICY

Policy in relation to popular music is formulated and implemented at the levels of the international community, the nation state, regions and local government. It includes regulation and stimulation of aspects of the production and consumption of music. At an international level, there are agreements on market access and copyright provisions. At the State level, policies include the regulation/deregulation of broadcasting; the use of tax breaks and content quotas; support for local copyright regulation and censorship. The local level involves venue-related regulations and the policing of public space (for a fuller discussion and examples, see Shuker, 2008: Chapter 12).

State attitudes and policies towards popular culture are a significant factor in determining the formulation of such policies, and the construction of meaning in popular music. At the level of attitudes, State cultural policies are indicative of the various views held about the very concept of culture itself, debates over government economic intervention in the market place versus the operation of the 'free market', the operation of cultural imperialism, and the role of the State in fostering national cultural identity.

There is a tradition of work on cultural policy at both the central and local State level. An example of a study of local policy is Kenney's history of the evolution of Chicago jazz, which details how a mix of council regulations, licensing law, moral watchdog organizations and police practices influenced the particular genre form taken by jazz in that city (Kenney, 1993). In a similar project, Chevigney (1991) shows how successive New York City Councils applied a network of zoning, fire, building and licensing regulations to discipline the venues and styles of jazz within the city. In a fascinating study of the regulation of music venues in Sydney, Australia, Homan (2003) demonstrated the complex relationship between city zoning, licensing, and noise regulations in Sydney and the venues for rock and dance, and the styles of music associated with them. These factors are significant in shaping local music scenes.

At the national level, State cultural policies were historically largely based on the idealist tradition of culture as a realm separate from, and often in opposition to, that of material production and economic activity. This meant that government intervention in its various forms – subsidy, licensing arrangements, protectionism through quotas, and so on – was justified to support the values of high culture against damage by market-driven commercial forces. A key part of this view is the concept of the individual creative artist. This ideology has been used by elites in government, administration, intellectual institutions, and broadcasting to justify and represent sectional interests as general interests, thereby functioning as a form of cultural hegemony. In the case of popular music, government attitudes have generally, but not exclusively, tended to reflect a traditional conservative view of 'culture', a high culture tradition, which is used to justify non-intervention in the 'commercial' sphere. Yet, this non-intervention exists in tension with frequent governmental concern to regulate a medium which, at times, has been associated with threats to the social order: **moral panics** over the activities of youth subcultures, the sexuality and sexism of rock, and obscenity. There have been a number of cases where the State has played a significant role in relation to popular music through economically and culturally motivated regulation and intervention. This has usually been to defend national cultural production against the inflow of foreign media products, using trade tariffs, industry incentives and so on.

The past two decades have seen increased Governmental (State) interest internationally in the economic possibilities inherent in the social and economic value of the Arts and Creative Industries, and popular music has been a significant part of this discourse (Wallis and Malm, 1992, documenting the situation at that time; this can be compared with the contributions in Gebesmair and Smudits, 2001; and Cloonan, 2007). This 'turn to policy' in part reflects a concern at the dominance of international music repertoire, along with desire to gain a larger share in this market.

Further reading:

Chevigny, P. (1991) *Gigs: Jazz and the Cabaret Laws in New York City*, New York: Routledge.

Cloonan, M. (2007) *Popular Music and the State in the UK: Culture, Trade, or Industry?* Aldershot: Ashgate.

Gebesmair, A. and Smudits, A. eds (2001) *Global Repertoires. Popular Music Within and Beyond the Transnational Music Industry*, Burlington, VT: Asgate.

Homan, S. (2003) *The Mayor's a Square: Live Music and Law and Order in Sydney*, Newtown, NSW: LCP.

Kenney, W. (1993) *Chicago Jazz: A Cultural History, 1904–1930*, New York: OUP.

Wallis, R. and Malm, K. (eds) (1992) *Media Policy and Music Activity*, London: Routledge.

POLITICAL ECONOMY

Political economy was used in the eighteenth century to describe what became known as 'economics' in the late nineteenth century. The field developed in response to the emergence of mercantile capitalism as the dominant economic force, the expansion of markets and the growth of the state. These changes raised questions of the relationship of the individual to the social order. The theoretical bases of political economy embraced the concepts of social class, the value and division of labour, and moral dimensions such as the nature and operation of self-interest. Political economy became associated with particular variants of economics and was often used as a code word for Marxism. Early (classic) Marxist political economy tended to devalue the significance of culture, seeing it primarily as the reflection of the economic base. In relation to the mass media, this view was given its fullest expression in the work of the **Frankfurt School**, especially Adorno. Later variants of political economy aspired to develop an integrated field that encompassed politics, economics and international relations. Contemporary political economy is interested in the relationship between economic organization and political, social and cultural life. Such an approach frequently labels itself 'critical political economy' to distinguish and distance itself from what it considers the 'cruder' formulations of classical (Marxist) political economy. All variants of political economy require analysis of the way politics shapes the economy and of the way in which the economy shapes politics. Accordingly, current political economy has explored issues such as the place of the economy within the larger social system, the importance of market institutions for individual autonomy, private enterprise and capitalism as a system of economic development, poverty and inequality in market economies, global patterns of wealth and inequality, and the limits of the market and the role of government.

The application of political economy to the study of the media has as its starting point the fact that the producers of mass media are industrial institutions, essentially driven by the logic of capitalism: the pursuit of maximum profit. That these culture industries are owned and controlled by a relatively small number of people and show a marked tendency towards increased concentration is regarded as a situation involving considerable ideological power: the media as 'consciousness industries'. At issue is the control of the media and whose interests it operates in, and the relationship between diversity and innovation in the market. In popular music studies, political economy is a central feature of analyses of the operation of the music industry, especially its recording companies; studies of music and cultural imperialism/globalization; MTV; and central and local state policy towards popular music (see the separate entries on each of these).

Political economy continues to inform popular music studies, but in a more complex fashion than was present in the economic determinism of earlier studies. Contemporary approaches involve examining popular music by asking of the music industry, and governmental institutions: Who produces the popular music text? For what audience, and in what physical contexts? In whose interests? What is privileged, and what is excluded? Such interrogation necessitates examining popular music media institutions in terms of their production practices, financial bases, technology, legislative frameworks, and their construction of audiences. For example, drawing on political economy as an explanatory framework for her analysis Gaines (1992) examines intellectual property law and the contradictions in legal attempts to accommodate late capitalism. Her study attempts to explain how external changes in material production are reflected within internal structures of law and culture. She rejects Marxian political economy, with its emphasis on determining the role of the economic base, and proposes a more complex view of 'political, social, economic, legal and cultural forms as connected yet disconnected' (p. 16) Gaines utilizes a dichotomy of 'circulation-restriction' of cultural commodities to show how the corporate power of monopoly capitalism over signs, images, and meanings is in contest with the doctrine of free enterprise within law. Negus, in a detailed account of the music industry focussed on the process of discovery and development of recording artists, which he uses 'as an organising principle to provide a more general account of the recording industry and the production of pop music' (1992: vi). In so doing, he consciously avoids what he sees as the two dominant approaches to the analysis of popular music: political economy analysts in the tradition of the Frankfurt School, who reduce the music industry to the organizational conventions and commercial logic of capitalism; and, second, subcultural and postmodernist accounts which stress the activities of audiences in their consumption of popular music. Negus is at pains to emphasize 'the cultural worlds being lived and constantly remade, highlighting the webs of relationships and multiple dialogues along and around which the musical and visual identities of pop artists are composed and communicated' (1992: vii).

See: **majors**; **Marxism**

Further reading:

Gaines, J. (1992) *Contested Culture: Image, Voice and the Law*, London: British Film Institute.
Negus, K. (1992) *Producing Pop: Culture and Conflict in the Popular Music Industry*, London: Edward Arnold.

POLITICS

In the general sense of the word, politics permeates popular music studies. Practically, every aspect of the production, distribution and consumption of popular music involves theoretical debates about the dynamics of economic, cultural, and political power and influence, and the reproduction of social structures and individual subjectivities. In a more specific sense, politics is reflected in direct State intervention in the cultural sphere, such as through policy in relation to censorship and the regulation of broadcasting.

There has been considerable discussion of the role of popular music in creating social change, and its mobilization within social movements. A central problem in social theory has been to explain how cultures change and to identify the forms of social activity at work in processes of social transformation. A key part of social change is changes in the cognitive identity (world view; values) of the individuals involved. Popular music has played a prominent role in articulating this process, at both the individual and collective group level. At various historical points, popular music has translated political radicalism into a more accessible idiom, identifying social problems, alienation and oppression and facilitating the sharing of a collective vision. Performers and songs contribute to forging a relationship between politics, cultural change and popular music. Popular music has frequently acted as a powerful means of raising consciousness and funds for political causes. At the same time, however, there is a tendency for such popular music forms to be co-opted, commodified and watered down or neutralized by the music industry.

Examples of popular music playing an overt political role include the Campaign for Nuclear Disarmament (CND) movement in the United Kingdom in the late 1950s; Civil Rights in the United States in the 1960s; Rock Against Racism (RAR) in the United Kingdom in the late 1970s and early 1980s; and the global phenomenon of Live Aid in 1985. In the United States, presidential campaigns regularly see candidates being supported (or criticized) by prominent musicians, as with Bruce Springsteen's endorsement of John Kerry in 2004 and the Dixie Chick's criticism of George Bush in the same campaign (for a fuller discussion of these, and other such episodes, see Denselow, 1990; Shuker, 2008: Chapter 14; Street, 1986). Furthermore, there is a strong historical tradition of protest song, particularly in folk music, which has been carried on in genres such as reggae, punk and alternative music. Within these, and other genres, many artists have individually used their music to make political statements on a variety of issues, including racism, class, gender politics, sexuality and the environment. There is debate as to the cultural significance and force of such statements.

A further dimension of this question is the tendency of many commentators to assume incorrectly that 'youth' represents some sort of 'natural left' political constituency. Yet popular music is hardly the preserve of the political left and broadly progressive politics. It can, and has been, used to support a broad range of political positions. George Bush's presidential inaugurations included an impressive line-up of **blues** and **soul** artists; white supremacist organizations like the National Front in the United Kingdom and neo-Nazi groups in Germany have used the appeal of punk rock and Oi! to attract new recruits; and US anti-abortion activists have co-opted the iconic political folk classic 'We Shall Overcome' to maintain solidarity at sit-ins outside abortion clinics.

See: **censorship**

Further reading:
Denselow, R. (1990) *When The Music's Over: The Story of Political Pop*, London: Faber & Faber.
Street, J. (1986) *Rebel Rock: The Politics of Popular Music*, Oxford: Blackwell.

Listening: *Live Earth. The Concerts for a Climate in Crisis*, DVD, CD, 2007. (Eight concerts held globally, 7 July 2007); … *Next Stop is Vietnam: The War on Record 1961–2008*, Bear Family, Box Set (13 CDs and a LP size hardback book)

POP; DANCE POP

Pop became used in a generic sense in the 1950s as the umbrella name for commercial, chart-oriented music aimed at a teenage market, especially in the United Kingdom. However, pop has a long musical history, predating the 1950s, and can best be regarded as a **metagenre**, embracing a number of related genres. Ennis (1992) considers that pop music comprised three of the defining 'streams' which eventually overlap and fuse in the evolution of American popular music:

1. Pop as the commercial music of the nation, associated with Tin Pan Alley, musical theatre, the motion picture and the rise of radio.
2. 'Black Pop', the popular music of black Americans, commercially domesticated around 1900, and from 1920 to 1948 known as 'race music' (see R&B).
3. 'Country Pop', which was the popular music of the American white south and Southwest.

Along with jazz, folk and gospel, these collectively were the basis for the emergence in the 1950s of what Ennis, in common with many other commentators, terms 'rock'n'roll'. Pop is seen to have emerged as a somewhat watered down, blander version of this, associated with a more rhythmic style and smoother vocal harmony, characteristic of the period of teen idols in the late 1950s and early 1960s.

Musically, pop is defined by its general accessibility, its commercial orientation, an emphasis on memorable hooks, or choruses, and a lyrical preoccupation with romantic love as a theme. The musical aesthetics of pop are essentially conservative: 'It is about providing popular tunes and cliches in which to express commonplace feelings – love, loss, and jealousy' (Frith, 2001: 96). Along with songwriters, producers are often regarded as the main creative force behind pop artists. Accordingly, as a genre in the market place, pop's defining feature is that 'It is music produced commercially for profit, as a matter of enterprise not art' (Frith, 2001: 94). Over the past half century, it has frequently been collapsed into and equated with 'popular', and includes a range of styles under labels such as 'chart pop' and 'teen pop'. Much of pop is regarded as disposable, for the moment, dance music; the best of it survives as 'golden oldies' and 'classic hits'.

Reflecting the dominance of teen pop since the late 1950s, pop became used in an oppositional, even antagonistic sense, to rock music, situating the two metagenres in a dichotomy linked to notions of art and commerce in popular music. Hill exemplifies this view:

> Pop implies a very different set of values to rock. Pop makes no bones about being mainstream. It accepts and embraces the requirement to be instantly pleasing and to make a pretty picture of itself. Rock on the other hand, has liked to think it was somehow more profound, non-conformist, self-directed and intelligent.
>
> (*Hill, 1986: 8; see also Dettmar, 2006: Introduction*)

There are, however, problems with the designation of the work of particular performers in relation to pop and rock, as many bands combine elements of both across their careers and in their recordings, as did The Beatles.

Subsequently, the term pop was used to characterize chart and teenage audience-oriented music, including **bubblegum**, **dance pop**, **power pop**, **New Romantics**/sythnpop, and performers such as **teen idols**, the **girl groups** of the 1960s, their 1990s equivalents and the ubiquitous **boy bands** of the modern era (see the respective entries on each).

The most significant of these styles has been chart oriented, **dance pop**. As with pop generally, dance pop is often maligned, in part because of its perceived commercial orientation and its main audience of adolescent girls – teenyboppers (although for a positive analysis of such consumption, see Baker, 2002). Commercially, highly successful exponents include Kylie Minogue, Paula Abdul and Bananarama in the 1980s; the Spice Girls and Britney Spears in the 1990s, and, currently, Katie Perry, Miley Cyrus and Justin Beiber. The debate around the Spice Girls, who had enormous international success in the late 1990s, exemplified the discourse around dance pop, especially regarding its commodification and authenticity. The Spice Girls 'girl power' slogan, aimed at preteen and teenage girls, stressed female bonding, a sense of sisterhood, friendship and self control; qualities evident in the individual members of the group, their press interviews and the lyrics to their songs. However, critics pointed to the contradictions between the Spice Girls professed self-expression and their subversion to standard sexualized 'feminine' images, and their incorporation into a male-dominated music industry, thereby sustaining dominant gender ideologies (Shuker, 2008: 82-5; Lemish, 2003).

The success of these pop performers was frequently attributed to the svengali-like influence of producers and professional songwriters (e.g. Stock, Aitken and Waterman and Kylie Minogue), and exposure through MTV and energetic video performances (e.g. Britney Spears, Miley Cyrus/Hannah Montana), as much as or more than musical talent. Today, pop is increasingly identified with the wider culture of celebrity. Current pop performers capitalize on their prior public visibility in film and television, fashion and society, using this to, hopefully, launch a recording career (Paris Hilton, Hillary Duff). Teenage-oriented pop magazines (*Smash Hits* etc.) remain important in publicizing/constructing both performers and their fans. Pop remains a major part of contemporary music culture; in addition to its chart success, it is currently prominent in reality television shows such as '**American Idol**' and its numerous international versions.

Further reading:

Dettmar, K. (2006) *Is Rock Dead?* New York: Routledge.

Ennis, P.H. (1992) *The Seventh Stream: The Emergence of Rock'n'Roll in American popular Music*, Hanover, NH: Wesleyan University Press.

Frith, S. (2001) "Pop Music", in Frith, S, Straw, W. and Street, J. (eds) *The Cambridge Companion to Pop and Rock*, Cambridge: Cambridge University Press, pp. 93–108.

Hill, D. (1986) *Designer Boys and Material Girls: Manufacturing the 80's Pop Dream*, Dorset: Blandford Press.

Lemish, D. (2003) "Spice World: Constructing Femininity the Popular Way", *Popular Music and Society*, 26, 1: 17–29.

POP IDOL

see **American Idol**

POPULAR MUSIC

Historically, the term popular has meant 'of the ordinary people'. It was first linked in a published title to a certain kind of music that conformed to that criterion in William Chapple's *Popular Music of the Olden Times*, published in instalments from 1855. Not until the 1930s and 1940s did the term start to gain wider currency. Popular music defies precise, straightforward definition, but several broad approaches can be identified:

Definitions placing an emphasis on 'popular'

Middleton observes that the question of 'what is popular music' is,

> so riddled with complexities ... that one is tempted to follow the example of the legendary definition of folk song – all songs are folk songs, I never heard horses sing 'em – and suggest that all music is popular music: popular with someone.
>
> (*1990: 3*)

However, the criteria for what counts as popular, and their application to specific musical styles and genres, are open to considerable debate. Classical music clearly has sufficient following to be considered popular, while, conversely, some forms of popular music are quite exclusive (e.g. thrash metal).

Definitions based on the commercial nature of popular music and embracing genres perceived as commercially oriented

Many commentators argue that it is commercialization that is the key to understanding popular music: 'When we speak of popular music we speak of music that is commercially oriented' (Burnett, 1996: 35). At the heart of the majority of various forms of popular music is a fundamental tension between the essential creativity of the act of 'making music' and the commercial nature of the bulk of its production and dissemination (see Frith, 1983: Chapter 1).

This approach is related to the emphasis on the popular, arguing that such appeal can be quantified through charts, radio airplay and so forth. In such definitions, certain genres are identified as 'popular music', while others are excluded. However, this approach can suffer from the same problems as those stressing popularity, since many genres have only limited appeal and/or have had limited commercial exposure. Moreover, popularity varies from country to country, and even from region to region within national markets. It also needs to be noted that this approach is largely concerned with *recorded* popular music.

Identification by general musical and non-musical characteristics

Tagg (1982), in an influential and much-cited discussion, characterizes popular music according to the nature of its distribution (usually mass); how it is stored and distributed (primarily recorded sound rather than oral transmission or musical notation); the existence of its own musical theory and **aesthetics** and the relative anonymity of its composers. The last of these is debatable, and I would want to extend the notion of composers and its associated view of the nature of musical creativity (see **auteurs**; **producers**; **songwriters**). However, musicologists have usefully extended the third aspect of this definition, while sociologists have concentrated on the first two dimensions.

In sum, it seems that a satisfactory definition of popular music must encompass both musical and socioeconomic characteristics. Essentially, all popular music consists of a hybrid of musical traditions, styles and influences and are also an economic product which is invested with ideological significance by many of its consumers.

Further reading:

Kassabian, A. (1999) "Popular", in Horner, B. and Swiss, T. (eds) *Key Terms in Popular Music and Culture*, Oxford: Blackwell, pp. 113–23.

Straw, W. (2004) "The 'pop-rockization' of popular music", in Hesmondhalgh, D. and Negus, K. (eds) *Popular Music Studies*, London: Arnold, pp. 21–64.

Tagg, P. (1982) "Analysing Popular Music", *Popular Music*, 2: 37–67.

POSTMODERNISM

Postmodernism as a general term became used in the 1970s to refer to a variety of developments in intellectual culture, the arts and the fashion industry. Postmodernism seeks to blur, if not totally dissolve, the traditional oppositions and boundaries between the **aesthetic** and the commercial, between art and the market, and between high and low **culture**. The precise nature of postmodernism, however, proves hard to pin down, and there is a marked lack of clarity and consistency in all the varying usages of the term (Mikula, 2008; Roberts, 2008).

In a key early contribution, Jameson (1984) overviews postmodernism as the cultural expression of a new phase of capitalism, characterized by communications technologies facilitating the virtually instantaneous shifting of international capital, the emergence of new centres of capital (e.g. Japan) in a global economy, new **class** formations breaking with the traditional labour/capital division, and a consumer capitalism which markets style, images, and tastes as much as actual products. The commodification of culture was seen to have created a new populism of the mass media, a culture centred around the marketing and consumption of surfaces and appearances, epitomized by the ubiquity of commercial television (Jameson, 1984).

Despite its obvious plausibility as a general explanation of developments in popular culture, postmodernism suffers from a number of difficulties, including its frequent lack of specificity; its over-preoccupation with texts and audiences at the expense of locating these within their economic and productive context, within which cultural products reside; its reduction of history and politics and ignoral of 'traditional' sociological notions of production, class and ideology.

The postmodernist view of popular music generally regards it as exemplifying the collapse of traditional distinctions between art and the commercial, the aesthetic and unaesthetic, and the authentic and unauthentic. This view became especially prominent in discussions of **music video**, with its affinities to advertising, and, during the 1980s, with commentators on **rock** who saw the music, once associated with youthful rebellion and political activism, as now thoroughly commercialized and incorporated into the postmodernist capitalist order (see **commodification**).

Further reading:
Jameson, F. (1984) "Postmodernism, or the Cultural Logic of Late Capitalism", *New Left Review*, 146 (July/August): 53–93.

POWER POP

The term power pop has been applied to a more accessible, radio friendly, hybrid of rock and pop, since the 1970s. The genre has been subject to considerable denigration, being viewed as a lightweight pop style, associated primarily with a teenage audience. In the early 1980s, power pop was a somewhat cynical major record company label to market post-punk styles, further undermining any claim it had to critical authenticity. However, power pop actually has a longer history, being applied to various performers since the 1960s. While the style has its share of pale imitators, power pop has produced some excellent bands and much memorable music, and remains strongly present in contemporary pop and rock music.

Dougan (1995) argues that the musical source point for nearly all power pop is the Beatles, who established its style, a combination of lyrics about young love, distinctive vocal harmonies, strong melodies and catchy guitar riffs (e.g. 'From Me To You'). Other major performers credited with developing the genre in the 1960s included the Who, the Kinks, and the Move, who juxtaposed aggressive melodies and loud, distorted guitars (the 'power'). Leading American power pop bands during the same period were the Byrds, who originally modelled themselves on the Beatles, and several performers whose recordings were often denigrated as bubblegum music (lightweight commercial pop), but which have held up as examples of power pop, such as Tommy James and the Shondells, and Paul Revere and the Raiders. Subsequent British exponents of power pop included the underrated, Beatles influenced, highly melodic Badfinger (e.g. the singles 'No Matter What' and 'Baby Blue'), Nick Lowe, Gary Glitter, Slade, and Sweet, the last three with strong glam/glitter associations. For example, Slade mixed upfront lead vocals, a basic foot stomping beat, anthemic choruses, and loud, distorted guitar chords to produce six number 1 UK singles in the early 1970s (although with little impact in the United States).

In the United States, the label was applied to the Raspberries and Big Star in the early 1970s. Big Star's founders Chris Bell and former Box Top vocalist Alex Chilton were fans of 1960s British beat music, especially the Beatles, and combined to produce effervescent guitar pop. Their two studio albums were well received by the music press, but poor distribution and promotion curtailed the commercial impact of their recordings. Big Star nonetheless became one of the most influential cult bands in the history of popular music, and their repackaged albums and compilations reflect continued interest in them. Other major American power pop performers included Cheap Trick, the Knack (largely for the huge success of their sleazy but hook-filled single 'My Sharonna' (1979), which sold over five million copies), the rockabilly-tinged Dwight Twilly Band ('I'm on Fire' (1975)), and, in the 1980s, the Byrds-influenced REM. All were strongly influenced by the 1960s pioneers of the style, producing clever lyrics, strong harmonies and 'punchy' guitar hooks.

During the 1980s and into the 1990s, many of the new wave and post-punk British and American bands incorporated elements of power pop (e.g. the Replacements, the Stone Roses), as did the bands identified with the New Zealand Flying Nun label sound, notably the Chills. Britpop had major musical debts to it (Oasis), as did 1990s 'alternative rock' bands such as Echobelly, Elastica and Nirvana – Kurt Cobain acknowledged the Beatles and Big Star as major influences.

Listening: The Move, *Great Move! The Best of the Move*, EMI, 1994; The Raspberries, *Raspberries Best*, Capitol, 1975; Big Star, *#1 Record/Radio City*, Stax, 1992; (originally released on Ardent, 1972, 1974); Dwight Twilley, *Sincerely*, DDC, 1976; Slade, *Best of Slade*, Polydor, 2000; Cheap Trick, *In Colour*, Epic, 1977

PRODUCERS

The occupation of producer emerged as a distinct job category and career path in the **popular music industry** during the 1950s, initially as someone who directed and supervised recording sessions. Successful producers (e.g. songwriters Leiber and Stoller at Atlantic; George Martin at EMI) began exerting pressure on their recording companies to receive credits (on recordings) and royalties. By the mid–1960s, the studio producer had become an auteur figure, an artist employing multi-track technology and stereo sound to make recording 'a form of composition in itself, rather than simply as a means of documenting a performance' (Negus, 1992: 87). The main example of this new status was Phil Spector (Shuker, 2008: Chapter 4). In the 1970s and 1980s, the producer's important role as a cultural intermediary was consolidated with the development of new technology: synthesizers, samplers and computer-based sequencing systems. Producers became central figures in genres such as dub and dance music.

The way producers operate, their contribution to the session, and the level of reward they are accorded vary widely, depending on the stature of the musicians they are working with and the type of music being recorded. Producers' approaches to recording vary from the naturalistic, 'try it and see what happens', to a more calculated, entrepreneurial attitude, while their production practices represent an amalgam of established techniques and the possibilities offered by the new technologies; see the examples of contemporary producers Jeff 'Mutt' Lange, Butch Vig, Daniel Lanois and Timberland.

See: **auteurs**; **cultural intermediaries**; **reggae**

Further reading: Autobiographical accounts are a very useful source of 'first hand' accounts; see, for example:

Joe Boyd, J. (2006) *White Bicycles – Making Music in the 1960s*, London: Serpent's Tail.

Lanois, D. (2010) *Soul Mining: A Musical Life*, London: Faber & Faber.

Stock, M. (2004) *The Hit Factory. The Stock Aitken Waterman Story*, London: New Holland Publishers.

Critical studies of the role of the producer, and the changing technologies utilized, are:

Moorefield, V. (2005) *The Producer as Composer. Shaping the Sounds of Popular Music*, Cambridge, MA: The MIT Press.

Thompson, G. (2008) *PLEASE PLEASE ME. Sixties British Pop, Inside Out*, Oxford: Oxford University Press. Chapter 2, and his appendix of individual profiles/biographies, has extensive coverage of leading British producers in the period.

Warner, T. (2003) *Pop Music – Technology and Creativity: Trevor Horn and the Digital Revolution*, Aldershot: Ashgate.

PROGRESSIVE ROCK

A broad musical genre, progressive and art rock are frequently conflated (e.g. Moore, 2001) and incorporated in designations such as 'space rock' and 'Kraut rock'. (For convenience I will use 'progressive' here as a collective descriptor.) Progressive rock was associated with attempts to combine classical, jazz, and rock forms, and many of the performers were classically trained musicians. Progressive rock was initially part of the counter-culture/ underground movement of the mid- to late 1960s, especially in the United Kingdom, where it soon became a marketing category, with a number of commercially successful performers (e.g. Traffic). It acquired its paradigmatic form and flourished with early 1970s groups such as the Nice, Yes and ELP (Emerson, Lake and Palmer); then with Eno (early Roxy Music, etc.), Pink Floyd and Genesis. The genre was prominent primarily in the United Kingdom, where it had a strong art-school connection, and in Europe (Tangerine Dream, Kraftwerk, Can: Kraut rock). In the United States, bands such as Kansas, Styx and Boston fall into the genre. Procol Harum's single, 'A Whiter Shade of Pale' (1967), whose distinctive organ sound was based on Bach's Suite No. 3 in D Major, is much cited as the classic example of art rock.

Progressive rock 'is marked, above all, by its diversity, a diversity suggestive of a constellatory, rather than a linear, account' (Moore, 1993: 101–2). The music is primarily not intended for dancing, so largely avoids the standard rock beat, with timbre and texture more important. Macan (1997) stresses progressive rock musicians' conscious imitation of classical music prototypes, and experiments in longer instrumental forms, borrowed from symphonic forms (as with Yes). Space and science-fictional themes were a feature of song titles and lyrics (e.g. Pink Floyd, 'Set the Controls for the Heart of the Sun' (1968)), with such variants being labelled space rock. In performance, progressive rock forged connections with the broader art scene (Walker, 1987), and made considerable use of theatrical conventions, as in Hawkwind's 'Space Ritual' stage show (1969–). The genre embraced the use of fantastic and obscure imagery, mixing conventions from disparate styles. This is evident in the names of several of the key albums, e.g. King Crimson's Lark's Tongues in Aspic, and the album cover art.

Several progressive rock performers integrated their work with classical music (e.g. Rick Wakeman, Journey to the Centre of the Earth (A&M, 1974)). Conversely, classical composers have adapted progressive rock to symphonic conventions: in 1995 Jaz Coleman arranged The Symphonic Music of Pink Floyd. Recorded with the London Philharmonic Orchestra, the album spent 36 weeks at the top of the Billboard crossover charts in the United States and sold nearly 750,000 copies.

The merits of progressive rock have been much debated. Early critics saw it as emphasizing musical virtuosity over emotional intensity (central to sixties rock's authenticity), and frequently lapsing into pretentiousness and self-indulgence. Punk rock was in part a reaction against the perceived excesses of what punks derogatorily called 'prog rock'. The style's commercial appeal waned in the 1980s, although it emerged in hybrid genres such as progressive metal (Queensryche; Dream Theatre). Progressive rock nonetheless maintained a dedicated fan base, underpinned by **fanzines**. It underwent something of a largely positive academic reassessment in the late 1990s (see further reading), and continued interest has led to a reissuing of recordings of several of its key performers, notably Yes.

See: **alternative rock**

Further reading: *Classic Rock Presents Prog* (monthly magazine)

Holm-Hudson, K. ed. (2002) *Progressive Rock Reconsidered*, New York and London: Routledge.

Kotsopoules, N. ed. (2010) *KrautRock. Cosmic Rock and its Legacy*, London: Black Dog Publishing.

Romano, W. (2010) *Mountains Come Out of the Sky. The Illustrated History of Prog Rock*, Milwaukee, WI: Backbeat Books.

Simonelli, D. (2007) "BBC rock music programming on radio and television and the progressive rock audience, 1967–1973", *Popular Music History*, 2, 1: 95–112.

Listening: King Crimson, *In the Court of the Crimson King*, EG, 1969 (rereleased 1989); Hawkwind, *In Search of Space*, One Way, 1971; Kansas, *The Best of Kansas*, CBS, 1984

PSYCHEDELIC ROCK; ACID ROCK

A musical style usually regarded as a **genre**, which emerged in the mid-1960s, psychedelic rock describes **rock** music inspired by or related to drug-induced experience, with the term used more or less interchangeably with **acid rock** (e.g. Whiteley, 1992; the label 'acid' was the common name for the mind-expanding drug LSD). Various artists recorded songs assumed to refer to drugs. Whiteley provides extensive discussions of several key releases, including the Beatles' 'Tomorrow Never Knows' and 'Strawberry Fields Forever' singles, referring to 'the LSD coding' in these (1992: 66). Musicians used fuzztone, feedback, synthesizers and sheer volume, mimicking the supposedly mind-expanding properties of marijuana and LSD. Much of the music was characterized by experimentation and indulgence, with an emphasis on albums rather than singles (although there were some chart successes, such as Jefferson Airplane's 'Somebody to Love' in 1967). Psychedelic/acid rock was related to fashion, poster and record design, and concert visual effects as well as the music, and was broadly linked with the youth counter-culture and, more specifically, with the hippy subculture.

Psychedelic rock had two main foci in the mid- to late 1960s: the West Coast of the United States and London. In San Francisco around 1967–9, a psychedelic scene emerged, based around the Haight-Ashbury area, and free, open-air gatherings and commercial Fillmore **concerts**. With the success of the Monterey Pop Festival, US record companies realized the commercial potential of the genre. The main performers included Jefferson Airplane, The Grateful Dead, Moby Grape, and Quicksilver Messenger Service (see **counter-culture**). In the United Kingdom, psychedelic rock was linked to the 'swinging 60s' London-based scene, tending to be conflated with progressive rock, and featuring prominently in the charts in the late 1960s. Major artists included Cream, Arthur Brown, and Jimi Hendrix; and psychedelia also influenced the leading groups of the period: the Beatles (with *Sgt. Pepper's Lonely Hearts Club Band*, Capitol, 1967) and The Rolling Stones (*Satanic Majesties*, ABKO, 1967).

As DeRogatis (1996; 2003) has shown in some detail, psychedelic rock strongly influenced the subsequent development of other genres, especially alternative, Britpop, heavy metal and progressive rock; its contemporary influence is clear in some styles of dance music and indie rock. The rock press, especially in the United Kingdom (e.g., *MOJO*) regularly devote extensive coverage to the genre and its performers, who are also staples on **classic rock** radio.

See: **counter-culture**

Further reading:

Borthwick, S. and Moy, R. (2004) *Popular Music Genres: An Introduction*, Edinburgh: Edinburgh University Press, (Chapter 3). A useful overview of the genre, placing it in its musical, social and political context; as they observe, the peak early period of psychedelic rock, 1966–69, 'has been mythologised more than any other era in pop's historiography' (p. 42.)

Bromell, N. (2002) *Tomorrow Never Knows. Rock and Psychedelics in the 1960s*, Chicago, IL: University of Chicago Press.

DeRogatis, J. (1996) *Kaleidoscope Eyes: Psychedelic Rock from the '60s to the '90s*, New Jersey: Citadel Press.

DeRogatis, J. (2003) *Turn On Your Mind. Four Decades of Great Psychedelic Rock*, Milwaukee, WI: Hal Leonard. A greatly expanded and revised edition of his 1996 book.

Whiteley, S. (1992) *The Space Between the Notes: Rock and the Counter-Culture*, London: Routledge.

Listening: Cream, *Disraeli Gears*, Polydor, 1967; Jefferson Airplane, *Surrealistic Pillow*, RCA, 1967; The Grateful Dead, *Anthem of the Sun*, Warner Brothers, 1968; Quicksilver Messenger Service, *Happy Trails*, Capitol, 1969; *Cave of Clear Light*. The Pye and Dawn Records Underground Trip, 1967-1975, Pye, 2010

Viewing: *Seven Ages of Rock*, episode 2, 'White Light, White Heat: Art Rock'

PSYCHOLOGY

The psychology of music is a field that has increasingly received a good deal of attention, with several best-selling studies catching the public imagination through presenting its findings in an accessible manner (Levitin, 2006, 2008; Sacks, 2008). There is a well-established tradition of empirical studies of perception and cognition in listening, and social psychology (and philosophy) has examined the link between emotional response and music (Bicknell, 2000, provides an excellent survey of the work; see also Beard and Gloag, 2005: 148–50).

For example, Levitin (2008) combines neuroscience, social anthropology, musicology and evolutionary biology to examine how music has influenced evolution through six themes in songs: friendship, joy, comfort, knowledge, religion and love. Situating these within the history of popular song, from classical to jazz to rock, he devotes a chapter to each, linking music to behavioural traits and showing how music and neurological development are intertwined. Some of Levitin's scientific claims are unproven, and, indeed, are difficult to substantiate; his account can be usefully read alongside that of Sacks, a neuroscientist. Levitin also demonstrates a reductionist view of evolution, but his informative and entertaining anecdotes illustrate the role songs play in everyday life.

Music and the emotions have been linked since ancient times, although

> the precise nature of 'emotion' remains very controversial. It is both
> a term of everyday discourse and a technical term in psychology
> (*Bicknell, 2000: Preface*)

Bicknell brings together how different intellectual traditions: 'the philosophical history of the aesthetic sublime and modern empirical research into the phenomenon of strong emotional responses to music' (ibid.: vii).

She makes an important distinction between two issues: 'music's capacity to *express* emotion and its power to *induce* or *arouse* emotion' (ibid.: xi).

Further reading:
Bicknell, J. (2009) *Why Music Moves Us*, Basingstoke: Palgrave Macmillan.
Sacks, O. (2008) *Musicophilia: Tales of Music and the Brain*, Picador.
Levitin, D. (2006) *This Is Your Brain On Music. The Science of a Human Obsession*, New York: Dutton/Penguin.
Levitin, D. (2008) *The World in Six Songs. How the Musical Brain Created Human Nature*, New York: Dutton.

PUB ROCK

Initially, a musical style and music press and record marketing label, pub rock is now identified more in terms of the pub as a context for the performance and consumption of popular music. The term originated in England during the early 1970s, when some musicians reacted to the excesses of glam/glitter rock by forming energetic bands that derived their sound from early rock'n'roll and R&B; they played primarily in 'pubs', licensed premises similar to US bars, hence the label. Pub rock was important because it brought music back into small venues, closing the distance between band and audience. The style tended to be a muscular, white male-dominated musical form, and the everyday image of the performers was inseparable from the style of their fans. These characteristics, and the discourse of fans and the music press surrounding them, constructed pub rock as a more authentic musical style.

Pub rock had little commercial impact (until the advent of punk, which it clearly influenced, and provided many of the musicians for) although a number of bands recorded/charted. The term also gained some currency in Australia and New Zealand, due to the significance of the pub (and the pub circuit supported by major breweries and their hotels) as a venue for live music. Major performers included Brinsley Schwarz, Ducks Deluxe, Dr Feelgood, Eddie and the Hot Rods, and the Motors. In the 1990s, Oasis were ironically referred to as 'pub rock', with their songs being often played and easily sung along to on jukeboxes in British pubs.

Further reading:

Bennett, A. (1997) "'Going Down to the Pub!' The Pub Rock Scene as a Resource for the Consumption of Popular Music", *Popular Music*, 16, 1: 97–108.

Listening: Brinsley Schwarz, *Brinsley Schwarz*, Capitol, 1970; Dr Feelgood, *Malpractice*, United Artists, 1975

Viewing: *Oil City Confidential*, Julian Temple, 2010 (on Dr Feelgood)

PUNK

A **youth subculture**, closely associated with **punk rock**, during 1977–80 punk became the most visible youth subculture in the United Kingdom and in most Western metropolitan centres (notably London, Los Angeles and Melbourne). In part punk was a reaction to hippy, counter-culture romanticism and a lack of social status – some commentators saw punks as unemployed youth, celebrating their un-employability. There were several strata:

middle-class, art school-influenced punks, influenced by bohemianism; and working-class, 'hard' punks. Punk style was very 'DIY' (do-it-yourself): old school uniforms, plastic garbage bags, and safety-pins were combined to present a shocking, self-mocking image. Punks adopted the swastika as an element of their style, though removed from its Nazi setting and adopted as shock-provoking accessories. Hairstyles were either close-shaved and dyed in bright colours or (later) Mohican haircuts: spiked up into cockatoo plumes. Punk dances were the robot, the pogo and the pose: 'collages of frozen automata' (Brake, 1985: 78). Hebdige (1979) stresses the homology of these elements in the subculture. Punks tended to align themselves with RAR, but theirs was a cultural rather than a political phenomenon.

While punk cultural style (and punk rock) has frequently been regarded as originating in England, and then being taken up internationally, there is a strong case for its origins being rather in New York's alternative music scene in the 1970s. Punk has maintained itself as a subcultural style, while being subjected to considerable commodification.

See: **subculture**; **scenes**

Further reading:
Brake, M. (1985) *Comparative Youth Culture*, London: Routledge and Kegan Paul.
Hebdige, D. (1979) *Subculture, The Meaning of Style*, London: Methuen.

PUNK ROCK

A musical genre which, while usually associated with the United Kingdom 'punk explosion' of *c.* 1977–80, clearly had its antecedents in the **garage rock** bands of the late 1960s, and early 1970s American bands, most notably The Velvet Underground, Iggy and the Stooges, and the New York Dolls. Punk has continued to be a major influence on popular music, with elements of punk style present in a variety of genres, most notably **alternative rock**, **grunge** and **hardcore**).

Stacy Thompson (2004; 9–79) provides a detailed outline of seven major punk scenes, which can be seen in a roughly linear fashion, although with overlapping chronology:

1. The New York Scene, 1974–6.
2. The English Scene, 1976–8.
3. The California Hardcore Scene, 1978–82.

4. The Washington, D.C., Hardcore Scene; First Wave of Straight Edge, 1979–85.
5. The New York Hardcore Scene (Second Wave of Straight Edge, 1986–9).
6. The Riot Grrrl Scene, 1991–5.
7. The Berkeley/Lookout! Pop-Punk Scene, 1990–5.

This is a viable, but US dominated history, and the UK post-punk bands of the 1980s need to be also considered as a distinct group and period (Reynolds, 2005). Furthermore, punk became an international genre, with punk bands and subcultural scenes in Europe, and countries as far a field as Australia and New Zealand. Here, I briefly consider the first two, 'classic' periods of punk; on its subsequent development and scenes, see **hardcore; riot grrl**.

In the mid- to late 1970s, the United States punk scene, based in New York, was an influential one, although most of its performers had only a limited commercial impact. The bands arguably displayed a higher level of musical sophistication than their later British counterparts; leading performers included the New York Dolls, Richard Hell and the Voidoids, Television, and, in particular, The Ramones. Blondie and Talking Heads also played CBGBs early in their careers, but are overlooked in some accounts of punk as they were subsequently (and very successfully) marketed as **new wave**. While early US punk enjoyed critical rather than commercial success, as Thompson's account shows, it subsequently persisted and mutated, being influential on various alternative performers, particularly hardcore, thrash and grunge. UK punk emerged in the United Kingdom in the mid- to late 1970s, with major performers including the Sex Pistols, the Stranglers, the Clash, the Damned and the Buzzcocks. Marcus (1989) links the Sex Pistols and punk rock to the French avant garde (the Situationist internationale) and Dada cultural movements. Other commentators place it against the Thatcher government's new right economic and social policies (although Thatcher was not elected until May 1979), and the alienation and disenchantment of much British youth, especially, but not exclusively, working-class males (see Borthwick and Moy, 2004: Chapter 5).

There are several good studies of the emergence of punk in the United Kingdom and the United States: Savage (1991), in a comprehensive and highly regarded account, places the Sex Pistols within the context of earlier English traditions; Laing (1985); and Heylin (1993), whose history, later expanded and revised, situated punk within the general narrative of American alternative music. In both national contexts, scene was an integral part of punk, as were the role of **fanzines** and **independent** labels. But there were marked differences between these two initial periods of British and American punk, especially in terms of their ante-cedents and class associations. American punk had more bohemian, non-working-class associations than its English counterparts. Most punk bands were male, and music and the subcultural style of its performers and fans both emphasized masculinity. There were female punks, punk rock musi-cians and several successful bands (The Slits in the United Kingdom), but it can be argued that they did not receive as much attention as their male counterparts. A recent study to reconsider their place in the 'moment' of punk is Reddington (2007). There appears to have been little sustained discussion of the 'whiteness' of early punk, although several biographies of The Clash stress their hybridization of punk and reggae.

Stylistically, early punk music was generally loud, fast and abrasive. The myth endures that it was all three chords and an attitude, but the per-formers actually included some very capable and experienced musicians (in the case of Britain, many were from the **pub rock** scene of the mid-1970s), although 'the issue of skill and competence in punk rock remains ideologically charged' (Laing, 1988: 83). Punk bands relied on live shows to establish an identity and build a reputation, and 'techniques of record-ing and of arrangement were adopted which were intended to signify the "live" commitment of the disc' (ibid.: 74). In short, punk records gener-ally sound 'live', as if the studio had not come between the intentions of the musicians and their listening audience. While popular music typically foregrounds the voice, 'punk voices … seem to want to refuse the perfec-tion of the "amplified" voice' (ibid.: 75). With often shouted, snarled vocals, punk emphasizes the sound (voice plus instruments), rather than lyrical meaning. The ideology of sincerity was central to punk; in inter-views, 'the stated beliefs of musicians, and their congruence with the per-ceived messages of their lyrics, became routine topics' (ibid.: 90). But, as Laing demonstrates, in many cases punk **lyrics** are like collages, a series of often fractured images, with no necessarily correct reading.

Punk's mode of address was 'confidential and declamatory', but with only rare use of the confidential stance; there is also an emphasis on addressing individuals other than 'lovers', and a 'plural specific' address (ibid.: 79). The tempo of punk is usually described using terms such as 'basic' and 'primitive'. As a more minimalist genre, punk rock eschewed the growing use of electronic instruments associated with **progressive rock**, and featured a strict guitar and drums instrumental line-up: 'this was a sound best suited to expressing anger and frustration, focusing chaos, dramatizing the last days as daily life and ramming all emotions into the narrow gap between a blank stare and a sardonic grin' (Marcus,

1992: 595). The lack of importance of virtuosity in instrumental solos reflected punk's frequent association of skill with glibness. Punk's attitude to rhythm was crucial to its sense of difference from other popular genres. It tended to submerge syncopation in its rhythmic patterns – the main reason for the 'undanceability' of much punk rock. 'Buzzsaw drone' was the typical punk guitar sound, combined with monadic bass-playing, both evident on the Sex Pistol's 'Anarchy in the UK' on *Never Mind the Bollocks* (Warner Brothers, 1977). This combination 'provided a feeling of unbroken rhythmic flow, enhanced by the breakneck eight to the bar rhythm of much punk rock' (Laing, 1988: 86), adding to the urgency which the lyrics and declamatory vocals evoked.

The nature, impact and significance of punk rock continue to receive extensive coverage in the popular music press, and from academic commentators, attracted by the visibility of its subcultural style and what has been perceived as the vitality and authenticity of the music. Music magazines such as *MOJO* and *UNCUT* in the United Kingdom regularly include features on punk and have issued special issues on the genre, while substantial encyclopaedias and guides to punk rock (and punk culture) continue to be published (e.g. Spicer, 2006; Cogan, 2008. Both are very useful). Recent academic studies of punk have focussed on questions of its historical and geographical location, relating the emergence and internationalization of the genre to issues of musical syncretism and hybridity (Lentini, 2003; O'Connor, 2002), and its nature and legacy (Sabin, 1999).

Further reading:

Cogan, B. (2008) *The Encyclopedia of Punk*, New York: Sterling.

O'Connor, A. (2002) 'Local-Scenes and Dangerous Crossroads: Punk and Theories of Cultural Hybridity', *Popular Music*, 21, 2: 225–36.

Heylin, C. (1993) *From the Velvets to the Voidoids: A Pre-Punk History for a Post-Punk World*, London: Penguin.

Heylin, C. (2007) *Babylon's Burning. From Punk to Grunge*, New York: Viking/Penguin.
A greatly expanded edition, with greater attention to the United Kingdom, and with the inclusion of punk internationally.

Laing, D. (1988) 'The Grain of Punk: An Analysis of the Lyrics', in McRobbie, A. (ed.) *Zoot Suits and Second Hand Dresses: An Anthology of Fashion and Music*, Boston: Unwin Hyman, pp. 74–101.

Laing, D. (1985) *One Chord Wonders: Power and Meaning in Punk Rock*, Milton Keynes: Open University Press.

Lentini, P. (2003) 'Punk's Origins: Anglo-American Syncretism', *Journal of Intercultural Studies*, 24, 2: 153–74.

Marcus, G. (1989) *Lipstick Traces: A Secret History of the 20th Century*, London: Faber & Faber.

Marcus, G. (1992) 'Anarchy in the UK', in DeCurtis, A. and Henke, J. (eds) *The Rolling Stone Illustrated History of Rock and Roll*, 3rd edn, New York: Random House, pp. 594–608.

McNeil, L. and McCain, G. (1996) *Please Kill Me: The Uncensored Oral History of Punk*, New York: Grove Press.

Reddington, H. (2007) *The Lost Women of Rock Music: Female Musicians of the Punk Era*, Aldershot: Ashgate.

Reynolds, S. (2005) *Rip It Up and Start Again: Post Punk, 1978–1984*, Faber & Faber: London.

Sabin, R. ed. (1999) *Punk Rock: So What? The Cultural Legacy of Punk*, London and New York: Routledge.

Savage, J. (1994) *England's Dreaming: Sex Pistols and Punk Rock*, London: Faber & Faber.

Thompson, S. (2004) *Punk Productions: Unfinished Business*, New York: State of New York Press.

Listening: United Kingdom: The Buzzcocks, 'Orgasm Addict' (1977) on *Singles Going Steady*, EMI, 1980; The Sex Pistols, *Never Mind the Bollocks*, Warner Brothers, 1977; The Clash, *London Calling*, Epic, 1979

Listening: United States: The Velvet Underground, 'White Light, White Heat' (1968) on *Velvet Underground Live*, Polygram, 1974; The Ramones, *Ramones*, Sire, 1976; Richard Hell and the Voidoids, Blank Generation, 1977; Television, *Marquee Moon*, Elektra, 1977

Compilations: England's Dreaming, 25 Tracks Before and After Punk, compiled by Jon Savage, Trikout, US, 2004; *No Thanks! The 70s Punk Rebellion, Rhino/Warner, 2003*. (four CD box set, with excellent 115 pp. booklet)

Viewing: Dancing in the Street, episode 7; *The Seven Ages of Rock*, episode 5; *Sid and Nancy*, Alex Cox, 1986; *The Decline of Western Civilization, Part One*, Penelope Spheeris, 1981; *The Punk Rock Movie*, Don Letts, *1978*; now available as a DVD, with an interview with Johnny Rotten from 1983; EMI, 2006

RACE

see **African–American**; **ethnicity**

RADIO

Until the advent of MTV in the late 1980s, radio was indisputably the most important broadcast medium for determining the form and content of popular music. The organization of radio broadcasting and its music formatting practices have been crucial in shaping the nature of what constituted the main 'public face' of much popular music, particularly rock and pop and their associated sub genres. Radio has also played a central role at particular historical moments in popularizing or marginalizing music genres. The discussion here provides a brief history of radio in relation to popular music, and sketches the current state of 'music radio'.

Radio developed in the 1920s as a domestic medium; it was aimed primarily at women in the home, but also played an important role as general family entertainment, particularly in the early evening. Radio in North America was significant for disseminating music in concert form, and helped bring regionally based forms such as traditional country (hillbilly) and western swing to a wider audience. Historically, the enemy of the record industry during the disputes of the 1930s and 1940s around payment for record airplay, radio subsequently became its most vital promoter. The reshaping of radio in the 1950s was a key influence in the advent of rock'n'roll, with radio airplay becoming central to commercial success, especially through the popular new chart shows. 'Hit radio was "one of America's great cultural inventions", revitalising a medium threatened by television' (Barnes, 1988: 9). The disc jockey (DJ) emerged as a star figure, led by figures such as Bob 'Wolfman Jack' Smith, Dewey Phillips and Alan Freed. Fisher (2007) provides a good historical account of the impact of radio in the United States.

FM radio was developed in the early 1930s, using a frequency modulation (hence FM) system of broadcasting. It did not have the range of AM, and was primarily used by non-commercial and college radio until the late 1960s, when demand for its clearer sound quality and stereo capabilities saw the FM stations become dominant in the commercial market. They contributed to what became a dominant style of music radio in the 1970s and 1980s (radio friendly; high production values and relatively 'easy listening'). Most radio stations now followed formats shaped by consultants, with a decline in the role of programme directors at individual stations, a situation that persisted into the 1990s. Though video became a major marketing tool in the 1980s, radio continued to play a crucial role in determining and reflecting chart success (see Hendy, 2003).

Radio stations are distinguishable by the type of music they play, the style of their DJ's, and their mix of news, contests, commercials and other programme features. We can regard radio broadcasts as a 'flow', with these elements merging. The main types of radio station include college, student, pirate and youth radio (e.g. the US College stations and Australia's Triple J network); State national broadcasters, such as the BBC; community radio and, the dominant group in terms of market share, the commercial radio stations. (Due to its unique nature and historical significance, **pirate radio** has been considered separately.) There is a longstanding contradiction between the interests of record companies, who are targeting radio listeners who buy records, especially those in their teens and early twenties, and private radio's concern to reach the older, more affluent audience desired by advertisers. To some extent, this contradiction has been resolved by niche marketing of contemporary music radio, with a wider range of formats.

Station and programme directors act as gatekeepers, being responsible for ensuring a prescribed and identifiable sound or format, based on what the management of the station believes will generate the largest audience – and ratings – and consequent advertising revenue. The station's music director and the programme director – at smaller stations the same person fills both roles – will regularly sift through new releases, selecting three or four to add to the playlist. The criteria underpinning this process will normally be a combination of the reputation of the artist; a record's previous performance, if already released overseas; whether the song fits the station's format; and, at times, the gut intuition of those making the decision. In the case of the first of these factors, reputation and previous track record, publicity material from the label/artist/distributor plays an important role, jogging memories or sparking interest in a previously unknown artist. This process is examined by Hendy (2003) on UK Radio One's playlist, and by Neill (2005), on New Zealand's commercial networks). Chart performance in either the United States or United Kingdom is especially significant where the record is being released in a 'foreign' market. Radio functions as a gatekeeper, choosing whether or not to play particular genres of popular, significantly influencing the nature of the music itself. This is illustrated in the shifting attitude of radio to heavy metal, which moved from a receiving practically no airplay through the 1970s, to major exposure in the 1980s.

Historically, radio formats were fairly straight forward, and included 'top 40', 'soul' and 'easy listening'. Subsequently, formats were more complex, and by the 1980s included 'adult-oriented rock', classic hits (or golden oldies), contemporary hit radio and urban contemporary (Barnes, 1988). Urban contemporary once meant black radio, but now included artists working within black music genres. In the United States, black listeners constitute the main audience for urban contemporary formats, but the music also appeals to white listeners, particularly in the 12–34 age group. Today, radio in most national contexts includes a range of formats: the dominant ones, reflecting historical developments in addition to current demographics, are indie rock (US College radio), contemporary chart pop, adult contemporary and classic rock.

As channel switching is common in radio, the aim of programmers is to keep the audience from switching stations. Common strategies include playing fewer commercials and running contests which require listeners to be alert for a song or phrase to be broadcast later, but the most effective approach is to ensure that the station does not play a record the listener does not like. While this is strictly impossible, there are ways to maximize the retention of the listening audience. Since established artists have a bigger following than new artists, it makes commercial sense to emphasize their records and avoid playing new artists on high rotation (i.e. many times per day) until they have become hits, an obvious catch-22 situation. The most extreme example of this approach is the format **classic rock**, or classic hits, which only plays well-established hits from the past.

The concern to retain a loyal audience assumes fairly focused radio listening. Paradoxically, while the radio is frequently 'on', it is rarely 'listened' to, instead largely functioning as aural wallpaper, a background to other activities (on this point, and who is listening to the radio, see consumption). Yet high rotation radio airplay remains vital in exposing artists and building a following for their work, while radio exposure is also necessary to underpin activities like touring, helping to promote concerts and the accompanying sales of records. The very ubiquity of radio is a factor here; it can be listened to in a variety of situations, and with widely varying levels of engagement, from the walkman to background accompaniment to activities such as study, domestic chores and reading (For a succinct discussion of the characteristics of radio, see Hendy, 2003).

The advent of web radio and new broadcasting technologies have fostered an explosion of radio stations, even although many have a very localized signal. In the commercial sector, digital technologies have produced new production aesthetics and reshaped the contemporary radio industry.

See: **pirate radio**

Further reading:

Barnes, R. (1988) 'Top 40 Radio', in Frith, S. (ed.) *Facing the Music*, New York: Pantheon Books.

Ennis, P. (1992) *The Seventh Stream*, Hanover: Wesleyan University Press. Chapter 5: 'The DJ Takes Over, 1946-1956'.

Fisher, M. (2007) *Something in the Air: Radio, Rock, and the Revolution that Shaped a Generation*, New York: Random House.

Hendy, D. (2003) *Radio in the Global Age*, London: Polity Press.

Neil, K. and Shanahan, M. (2005) *The Great New Zealand Radio Experiment*, Southbank, Victoria: Thomson/Dunmore Press.

Rothenbuhler, E. (2006) 'Commercial radio as Communication', in Bennett, A., Shank, B., and Toynbee, J. (eds) *The Popular Music Studies Reader*, London: Routledge (first published 1985).

RAGTIME

A piano style developed around the turn of the century, with the first published rag appearing in 1897, ragtime was the dominant popular music of the day. Its popularity lasted through until around 1918 and the advent of jazz, which ragtime strongly influenced. Ragtime was primarily a black music genre with prominent European influences present, and reflected the continued fascination with Black American music on the part of white listeners. The popularity of the style saw an increased involvement of black performers within the music industry.

Ragtime is a composed music although it originated in oral, unwritten traditions; its musical features are a left hand based on chords, which are broken up differently on each beat (commonly in a four-beat phrase); a melodic right hand with complex figuration; and uneven accenting between the two hands (syncopation). Most popular ragtime songs were energetic marches. Its most famous practitioner was Scott Joplin, whose 'Maple Leaf Rag' remains one of the best-known ragtime compositions. Joplin's death in 1917 is usually seen as marking the end of the ragtime era, although the style has enjoyed periodic revivals and continued interest.

Further reading:
Berlin, E.A. (1994) *King of Ragtime. Scott Joplin and His Era*, New York: Oxford University Press.

Listening: Scott Joplin never recorded, the recordings attributed to him are made from piano rolls he cut; his compositions are to be found on a variety of piano music

RAP

see **hip hop**

RASTAFARI

Rastafari, variously considered as a social movement, a religious cult and a youth subculture, came out of the ghettos of Kingston, Jamaica in the

1950s. Rastafarianism preaches the divinity of Haile Selassie of Ethiopia; characterizes white domination as 'Babylon', and advocates a black return to Africa, focused on Ethiopia. Rastafarian males grow their hair in long, plaited dreadlocks while women cover their heads, use no cosmetics and wear long modest dresses. Rastas wear woollen caps coloured green (Ethiopia), red (for blood of their brothers), yellow (the sun) and black (their skin). The use of marijuana (ganga) is given a religious significance. (see Gilroy, 1987 for elaboration). Rasta, at least at the level of cultural style, was widely adopted among 'black' groups internationally; for example, Maori in New Zealand. Rastafari is strongly associated with reggae music, which plays a major role in communicating the ideals of the movement, through its artists acting as role models, and through the themes and lyrics of the music.

Further reading: (see also the references in **reggae**)
Bishton, D. (1986) *Black Heart Man*, London: Chatto & Windus.

RAVE CULTURE; RAVES

Rave culture is the general term applied to youth associated with raves, ecstasy use, and the various dance musics, especially house, from the mid-1980s onward, especially in the United Kingdom. The use of the drug ecstasy provoked a **moral panic** in the United Kingdom, and a number of other countries during the early 1990s, with severe penalties introduced in an attempt to regulate raves (Collins, 1988).

Raves grew out of semi-legal warehouse parties organized by young entrepreneurs in the United Kingdom and United States in the late 1980s. Raves were held outside established dance venues in unconventional places, such as disused warehouses, aircraft hangers and tents in farmer's fields; these gatherings attracted up to 15,000 people in the United Kingdom in the early 1990s.

By the end of the decade, as Luckman observed, following the trajectory of earlier subcultures, 'rave culture can be seen and critiqued as the paradigmatic model of a lapsed subculture, redeemed via commodity co-option, under systems and processes of advanced capitalism' (Luckman, 1998: 45). The commodification of rave culture and the mainstream adoption of rave as a cutting edge youth style continued into the 2000s.

Rave culture attracted a good deal of academic attention, especially from within cultural studies (see Luckman for a summary of the early literature). Generally speaking, two broad explanations were offered for the phenomenon: a hedonistic 'rush culture' of escapism and the pursuit of a transcendental higher consciousness: 'Rave is more than the music plus drugs; it's a matrix of lifestyle, ritualized behaviour, and beliefs. To the participant, it feels like a religion' (Reynolds, 1998: preface).

See: **club cultures**; **EDM**; **subcultures**

Further reading:

Collins, M. (1998) *Altered States: The Story of Ecstasy Culture and Acid House*.

Luckman, S. (1998) 'Rave Cultures and the Academy', *Social Alternatives*, 17, 4: 45–9.

Reynolds, S. (1998) *Energy Flash*, London: Picador.

REALITY TELEVISION

see **television**

RECORD COLLECTING

see **collecting**

REGGAE

Reggae can be considered a metagenre: the collective term for a number of successive forms of Jamaican popular music, including ska, dancehall, dub reggae and rocksteady. Popular in Anglo-American markets since the 1960s, and now internationally evident, reggae has had an influence on popular music vastly disproportionate to its limited commercial success. Reggae is strongly associated with Rastafari, variously considered as a social movement, a religious cult and a subculture (see separate entry).

Reggae initially developed in the 1950s when Jamaican musicians combined indigenous folk music with jazz, African and Caribbean rhythms and New Orleans R&B. The resultant hybrid was ska. In the mid-1960s, influenced by American soul music, ska's hyper rhythms gave way to the slower loping beats of rocksteady. Around the end of the 1960s, these styles of Jamaican popular music came to be known as reggae, which

> embellished the bedrock rhythms of ska and rocksteady with politi-
> cal and social lyrics, often influenced by Rastafarianism, racial pride,
> and the turbulent Jamaican political climate. The rhythms ebbed
> and flowed with the hypnotic, jerky pulse that has become reggae's
> most identifiable trademark
>
> *(Erlewhine, 1995: 938)*

along with the bass and choppy rhythm tracks. The reggae of this period is sometimes referred to as 'roots reggae'; key performers included Toots and the Maytals, The Wailers, Burning Spear and Jimmy Cliff.

While the influence of ska and reggae were evident in some western popular music, for instance the Spencer Davis Group's hit 'Keep on Running', (1967), the genre initially had only a cult follow-ing outside of Jamaica. This changed in the 1970s, with the international success of the feature film *The Harder They Come* (1972), and Island Record's astute marketing of Bob Marley and the Wailers (Stephens, 1998). Marley himself became a revered cult figure, even more so after his death in 1981 (see White, 1989). Reggae was influential on many white and mixed ethnicity bands, working in genres such as New Wave (The Police); punk (The Clash; see Letts, 2007) and two tone (UB 40). Reggae continued to evolve, with toasting (a DJ talkover style) and dub forms in the 1980s, both of which demonstrated the importance of the record producer and the Jamaican sound system to the genre.

In commercial terms, the success of Bob Marley aside, the genre remained a minority taste, although several 1980s and 1990s reggae pop hybrids (Aswad) achieved chart success, as did some rap performers who utilized reggae rhythms (e.g. Shinehead, *Unity*, Elektra, 1988). Reggae has maintained a commercial and artistic presence through into the 2000s, often forming an important constituent of national hybrid styles (such as Fijian reggae) and other popular music genres. Fan and collector interest in reggae's back catalogue and the work of its producers (see **dub**) have boosted reissue labels, such as Trojan. Contemporary dance music draws heavily on reggae as part of its eclectic musical palette, notably in drum'n'bass and dubstep.

I have included separate entries on several important associated genres:

- Dancehall
- Dub
- Ska

Reggae has attracted considerable attention from the popular music press and academic popular music studies. Much of this focuses on the iconic status of Bob Marley and producers such as King Tubby; the internationalization and hybridization of reggae and associated cultural styles and the adoption of these by white youth (e.g. Jones, 1988). Good introductory studies and overviews of the genre are Barrow and Dalton (2001), Katz (2004), and Bradley (2001).

See: **Rastafari**

Further reading:

Barrow, S. and Dalton, P. (2001) *Reggae: The Rough Guide*, 2nd edition, edited by Buckley. J., London: The Rough Guides.

Bradley, L. (2001) *Bass Culture: When Reggae Was King*, London: Penguin Books.

Potash, C. (1997) *Reggae, Rasta, Revolution: Jamaican Music from Ska to Dub*. An anthology of writing on all Jamaican music forms. The book has sections on roots, Marley, reggae, ska, dub, dancehall, calypso, and rocksteady; and includes bibliographies and discographies.

Jones, S. (1988) *Black Culture, White Youth. The Reggae Tradition from JA to UK*, London: Macmillan.

Katz, D. (2004) *Solid Foundation. An Oral History of Reggae*, London: Bloomsbury.

Stephens, M.A. (1998) 'Babylon's "Natural Mystic": The North American Music Industry, the Legend of Bob Marley, and the Incorporation of Transnationalism', *Cultural Studies*, 139–67.

Letts, Don, With David Nobakht (2007) *CULTURE CLASH. Dread Meets Punk Rockers*, London: SAF.

Steffens, R. (2007) *The Reggae Scrapbook*. The author is the leading archivist and collector of reggae memorabilia, and the book is heavily illustrated.

Ward, E. (1992) 'Reggae', in *The Rolling Stone Illustrated History of Rock and Roll*, 3rd edition, New York: Random House (includes discography).

Listening: roots reggae (see also the suggestions on related sub genres): *Tougher than Tough. The Story of Jamaican Music*, four CD box set; researched and compiled by Steve Barrow, Island Records, 1993; Toots and the Maytals, *Funky Kingston*, Island, 1973; Bob Marley and the Wailers, *Legend* Island,1984 ('greatest hits'); Peter Tosh, *Equal Rights*, Columbia, 1977

RETAIL

Music retail includes the sale of sheet music, musical instruments, music-related merchandise, concert tickets, music DVDs, music magazines and books. Primarily, however, the term 'music retail' refers to the sale of sound recordings to the public, which is the aspect dealt with here. Information on this topic is sparse, and there is a history of music retail yet to be written, but a quick sketch is possible.

Sound recordings were first available through shops already selling sheet music and musical instruments. In the early 1900s, chains of department stores began supplying hit songs, along with sheet music. Later, smaller, independent and sole proprietor shops (the so-called 'mom and pop' stores in the United States) emerged. By the 1970s, record retailers included independent shops, often specializing in particular genres; used record stores; chain stores and mail order record clubs. The subsequent significance and market share of each of these has reflected the broader consolidation of the music industry, along with shifts in recording formats and distribution technologies. In addition to the impact of the Internet and on-line shopping, retailers have had to adapt to changes as mundane as the need for different shelf space to accommodate new formats. The introduction of electronic bar coding in the 1990s enabled retail, distribution, and production 'to be arranged as an interconnected logistic package'; this allowed 'music retailers to delineate, construct and monitor the "consumer" of recorded music more intricately than ever before' (Du Gay and Negus, 1994: 396). A similar process later occurred with the tracking of browsers and purchasers preferences in on-line shopping through the Internet.

As with the **culture industries** generally, concentration has been a feature of music retail. By the early 1980s record retailing was horizontally integrated and monopolistic, and the continued conglomeration and homogenization of music retail outlets during the 1990s led to a decline in the small, idiosyncratic record shop run by a music enthusiast. The 1990s saw the emergence of large discount retail chains, including the new megastores, such as Tower; Virgin and HMV (part of EMI). Often horizontally linked into the record industry, the music megastores were organized around a supermarket model in terms of their layout, access and customer service. While they carry recorded music in various formats, they also stock music videos, posters, books and magazines, with inventory tracked using bar coding. Straw referred to the 'abundance and pluralism' of these new record superstores, with their layout showing a 'moralistic concern' for the consumer's comfort, and assuring confidence in the customers' ability to make a choice.(Straw, 1997: 58–9). The mega-stores published newsletters; have appearances by artists; sponsor radio shows; may even put out their own records (samplers) and run loyalty programmes with rewards for purchasers. They have been hit by the recent downturn in sales of recorded music; there have been several closures (e.g. Sam's in North America) and a general 'downsizing' in the megastores scale of operation.

A large proportion of recordings are now sold through general retailers (these include Woolworths in the United Kingdom, Walmart in the United States and The Warehouse in New Zealand and Australia) and the surviving music megastores. This concentration influences the range of music available to consumers and the continued economic viability of remaining smaller retail outlets. The general retailers frequently use music as a loss-leader: reducing their music CD and DVD prices to attract shoppers whom they hope will also purchase other store products with higher profit margins. This situates music as only one component of the general selling of lifestyle consumer goods. In the face of this competition, smaller local music chains have been forced to retrench by consolidating shops and 'downsizing' staff, or have kept operating through niche marketing and their increased use of the Internet.

Indie and second hand

Historically, indie or specialist record shops occupy a distinct space within the music market (Koningh and Griffiths, 2003). In many cases, they contribute significantly to local music scenes by promoting shows, supporting local artists and selling tickets, T-shirts, fanzines and other merchandise not handled by major retailers. Part of the appeal of such shops is the shoppers' relationship with the staff, which frequently involves trusting their musical knowledge and recommendations, along with a reciprocal recognition, often hard won, of the collectors' own expertise. The 1980s was something of a high point for the specialist and used record store. As Hayes notes of the United States:

> While many small (largely regional) labels continued to release music on 7″ and 12″ records throughout the 90s, locating their products was often a difficult task since mainstream retail outlets such as Tower Records and HMV shelved few if any LP releases after deleting previous stock.
>
> (Hayes, 2006: 56)

This limited vinyl enthusiasts to two main sites of acquisition: a small number of independent retailers who continued to stock vinyl releases, usually limited pressings by small labels; and used record stores.

Emma Pettit (2008) has documented how independent (and second hand) record shops continue to form a minor but still culturally significant part of record retail. However, they have increasingly struggled, with the impact of the Internet and its auction websites, increases in rent for traditional central city areas, especially as these become 'gentrified'/renewed, and the ongoing concentration of music retail generally. They have managed to survive, and in some cases even flourish, by using the Internet, by catering to specialist interests and continuing to stock vinyl (see **collecting**).

Further reading:

Du Gay, P. and Negus, K. (1994) 'The Changing Sites of Sound: Music Retailing and the Composition of Consumers', *Media, Culture and Society*, 16, 3: 30–45.

Hayes, D. (2006) 'Take Those Old Records off the Shelf', *Popular Music and Society*, 29, 1: 51–68.

Koningh and Griffiths, (2003) *Tighten Up! The History of Reggae in the UK*, London: Sanctuary.

Pettit, E. (2008) *Old Rare New: The Independent Record Shop*, London: Black Dog.

Straw, W. (1997) 'Organized Disorder: The Changing Space of the Record Shop', in Steve Redhead (ed.) *The Club Cultures Reader*. Oxford: Blackwell, pp. 57–65.

RHYTHM & BLUES (R&B)

R&B was one of the most important precursors of rock'n'roll, and a crucial bridge between blues and soul. George accords R&B a socio-economic as well as a musical meaning, linking it to a black community sense of identity 'forged by common political, economic and social conditions' (1989: introduction).

The earliest R&B artists emerged from the American big band and swing jazz era (in the 1930s and 1940s), playing dance music that was louder, used more electric instrumentation, especially the new bass guitar, and accentuated riffs, boogies and vocals. The first popular style of R&B was jump blues, which blended a horn dominated line-up with swing rhythms from jazz, and general chord structures and riffs from blues. Several different styles evolved: vocal 'shouters' (e.g. Big Joe Turner); instrumentalists with strong jazz connections, especially saxophonists, and smoother, urbane vocal styles. Associated with independent labels, notably Speciality, jump blues was popular in cities with growing black communities, especially LA. Louis Jordan was the most prominent performer, enjoying considerable **crossover** success through the 1940s and early 1950s. Regional styles emerged, notably piano based New Orleans R&B.

In the early 1950s, 'race' music as it had been termed in the industry since the 1920s (see **classic blues**), was renamed R&B by *Billboard* magazine. While popular on its own charts, and black radio stations, it received little airplay on white radio stations. Indeed, R&B records were sometimes banned because of their explicit sexual content, as occurred with Hank Ballard's 'Work With Me Annie', Billy Ward's 'Sixty Minute Man', and the Penguin's 'Baby Let Me Bang Your Box'. Jerry Wexler, an A&R man at Atlantic, helped shape jump blues into more commercial styles, which pointed the way for rock'n'roll. Around the same time, New Orleans R&B also crossed over, with the success of Fats Domino ('Ain't That a Shame', 1955). R&B elements were merged into the various styles of rock, notably **Blues Rock**/British R&B of the 1960s (The Rolling Stones; The Pretty Things; Them) and subsequently into disco, funk and rap. Indeed, so broad has been the presence of R&B, that the term is sometimes used as a general name for the corpus of black music.

A major point of contention has been the manner in which R&B was appropriated by white musicians and record companies, for a white audience.

Further reading: (see the general histories listed under rock, below)

REISSUES

see **back catalogue**

RIOT GRRRL

In the early 1990s, originating in Washington DC, and Olympia, Washington, Riot Grrrl quickly became the focus of considerable media attention. Through fanzines and sympathetic role models among female musicians, riot grrrls asserted the need to break down the masculine camaraderie of the alternative and hardcore music scenes, which marginalized girls and young women. They drew on feminism and punk DIY ideology to question conventional ideas of femininity; and rejected rock ideas of cool and mystique, challenging the view that enhanced technical virtuosity is necessary to create music. Some writers referred to them as 'punk feminists', as riot grrrls aimed to create a cultural space for young women in which they could express themselves without being subject to male scrutiny and domination. They played with conflicting images and stereotyped conventions; for example, their appropriation of 'girl' and their assertive use of the term 'slut'. Musically, the performers linked to the riot grrrl movement sounded very like traditional hardcore and late 1970s punk bands, but their emphasis was on the process rather than the product. Performers/supporters included L7, Bikini Kill and Kim Gordon (Sonic Youth).

Further reading:

Leonard, M. (1997) 'Rebel Girl, You are the Queen of My World: Feminism, "Subculture" and Grrrl Power', in Whiteley, S. (ed.) *Sexing the Groove: Popular Music and Gender*, London: Routledge.

Marcus, S. (2010) *Girls to the Front: The True Story of the Riot Grrrl Revolution*, New York: Harper Perennial.

Listening: L7, *Bricks Are Heavy*, Slash/WB, 1992; Bikini Kill, *Pussywhipped*, Kill Rock Stars; originally an EP, 1992; CD 1993

ROCK'N'ROLL; ROCKABILLY; ROCK

These three genres can be usefully considered together as a roughly chronological sequence: beginning with rock'n'roll (also labelled 'rock and roll'), in the early to mid-1950s, and rockabilly, almost contiguous with rock'n'roll, which can be considered a 'bridge' to the emergence of 'rock' in the 1960s. Subsequently, rock has mutated into an enormous range of styles, and, together with these antecedent styles, clearly constitutes a **metagenre**.

Rock'n'roll was the genre of popular music that emerged when black rhythm and blues songs began to get airplay on radio stations aiming at a wider, predominantly white audience, and when white artists began rerecording black R&B songs. R&B, American country music, and 1940s and 1950s boogie-woogie music are all elements of early rock'n'roll.

Some writers conflate the genre with rock, which became the more general label for the various musical styles which followed in the 1960s (see below).

Alan Freed, a Cleveland DJ, is usually given credit for coining the phrase 'rock'n'roll in the early 1950s. However, as Tosches (1984) documents, the style had been evolving well prior to this, and the term 'rock'n'roll', with its sexual connotations, was popularized in the music of the 1920s. In 1922, blues singer Trixie Smith recorded 'My Daddy Rocks Me (With One Steady Roll)' for Black Swan Records, and various lyrical elaborations followed from other artists through the 1930s and 1940s. In April 1954, Bill Haley and the Comets made 'Rock Around the Clock'. The record was a hit in America, then worldwide; eventually selling 15 million copies. Along with the success of the film which featured the song on its soundtrack, the record represented a critical symbol in the popularization of the new musical form. Subsequent major performers included Chuck Berry, Little Richard, and, in particular, Elvis Presley.

Aside from simply documenting its key performers and recordings, there have been three focal points of debate in the literature on rock'n'-roll: the reasons for its emergence; the moral panic around it and the issue of its appropriation by white performers and the music industry. Explanations as to why rock'n'roll emerged in the mid-1950s include situating it against the significance of the emergent post-war baby boom (see **demography**); the importance of individual creative figures in popularizing the genre (especially Elvis Presley) and a 'production of culture' approach, situating rock'n'roll in relation to changes in the organization of broadcasting, and the music industry, especially the role of independent labels.

The new music provoked considerable criticism, with many older musicians contemptuous of rock'n'roll. British jazzman Steve Race, writing in *Melody Maker*, claimed:

> Viewed as a social phenomenon, the current craze for rock 'n' roll material is one of the most terrifying things ever to have happened to popular music ... Musically speaking, of course, the whole thing is laughable ... It is a monstrous threat, both to the moral acceptance and the artistic emancipation of jazz. Let us oppose it to the end.
>
> (*Rogers, 1982: 18*)

Other criticism focused on the moral threat, rather than the new teenage music's perceived aesthetic limitations, with rock'n'roll seen as hostile and aggressive, epitomized by Elvis Presley's sensual moves (see **moral panic**).

Rock'n'roll is a significant part of the debate on the role of race, and the issue, once again, of white **appropriation** of a black musical style.

Further reading:

General histories of popular music, (especially those concentrating on 'rock', broadly defined, and developments post-1945) include rock'n'roll as a key part of their narrative: for example: Garofalo, 2011, Chapters 4 and 5; Gillet, 1983, Chapter 2; Starr and Waterman, 2003, Chapter 8. More musicological treatments of the genre can be found in Charleton, 1994; Everett, 2009; Moore, 2001 (for bibliographic details, see **rock**: further reading).

Bordowitz, H. (2004) *Turning Points in Rock'n'Roll*, New York: Citadel Press.

Bradley, D. (1992) *Understanding Rock'n'Roll: Popular Music in Britain 1955–1964*, Buckingham: Open University Press.

Ennis, P.H. (1992) *The Seventh Stream: The Emergence of Rock'n'Roll in American Popular Music*, Hanover, London: Wesleyan University Press.

Listening: *We're Gonna Rock, We're Gonna Roll*, Proper Records, London, 2005. A four CD box set, tracing the origins of rock'n'roll and its emergence in the 1950s; includes an excellent 68pp. booklet on the 118 recordings and their performers; Elvis Presley, 'Heartbreak Hotel' (1956) and 'Hound Dog' (1956), on *Elvis Rock'n'On*, double album compilation, RCA; There are numerous compilations of the recordings of Chuck Berry, Little Richard, Bill Haley and the Comets, *et al.* A recent CD series from Decca, marking what was considered the 50th anniversary of rock'n'roll (1955–2005) is well-packaged and includes good booklets

Rockabilly

An early fusion of **black** and **country** music in the American South, rockabilly pre-dated (just) and overlapped with **rock'n'roll**, with its peak in the mid-1950s. Blues inspired and bluegrass based; rockabilly was described by exponent Carl Perkins as 'blues with a country beat'. Primarily a male form; key figures included Perkins, Gene Vincent, Eddie Cochran and Elvis Presley (the Sun sessions). Guralnick (1989) claims the form started and ended with Elvis.

Rockabilly tended to be a rigid and strictly defined form, with imitation at its core (at least in the 1950s):

> Its rhythm was nervously uptempo, accented on the offbeat, and propelled by a distinctively slapping bass. The sound was always clean, never cluttered, with a kind of thinness and manic energy that

was filled by the solid lead of Scotty Moore's guitar or Jerry Lee's piano. The sound was further bolstered by generous use of echo ...

(Guralnick, 1989: 68)

Rockabilly was subsequently carried on by late 1950s and 1960s performers such as Roy Orbison and the Everley Brothers, and was an influence on the work of many rock'n'roll performers, including the early Beatles.

Its subsequent period revivals illustrate how genres continue to maintain a presence well after their initial emergence and peak. In his major study of rockabilly, Morrison traces its revival in England in the mid-1970s and continued into the mid-1980s. This 'received its momentum from the interplay of several factors' and 'a combination of the energies of four diverse groups of people' (1996: Preface). The first included dealers, collectors, reissue labels (such as Ace and Charley in England) and 'new labels devoted exclusively or extensively to rockabilly', such as Rollin' Rock in California, which started in 1971. Second, 'scholars, reporters, and certain serious fans' gathered and spread knowledge, fostering the revival through their involvement with specialist radio shows and fanzines, notably *New Kommotion* from England. Third, the audience 'sustained the revival by consuming the records, frequenting the discos that featured rockabilly, attending the live shows, and living a rockabilly lifestyle.' Fourth, the musicians of the revival, who revitalized the original 1950s styles of rockabilly giving it fresh life. The appeal of rockabilly was the vitality of the music, while interest in it was also 'about connecting to a mental scenery, to a mythical place, where people are imbued with both white and black music traditions, feeling things deeply, and having a down-to-earth life' (Morrison, 1996: Preface).In the 1980s bands like The Blasters and Jason and the Scorchers played a style of rock fusing elements of rockabilly, country and punk.

Further reading:

Escott, C. with Hawkins, M. (1991) *Good Rockin' Tonight: Sun Records and the Birth of Rock'n'Roll*, New York: St Martin's Press.

Guralnick, P. (1992)'Rockabilly', in DeCurtis, A. and Henke, J. (eds) *The Rolling Stone Illustrated History of Rock and Roll*, 3rd edition, New York: Random House (includes a discography).

Morrison, C. (1996) *Go Cat Go! Rockabilly Music and Its Makers*, Urbana: University of Illinois Press.

Listening: *The Legendary Story of Sun Records* (2CD), Union Square Records, 2002; The Blasters, 'Marie Marie' (c.1981); from *The Blasters Collection*, Slash/WB, 1990; *Rock This Town: Rockabilly Hits*, Volumes 1 & 2, Rhino, 1991; Elvis Presley, *The Complete Sun Sessions*, RCA, 1987

Rock

Rock is the broad label for the huge range of styles that have evolved since the early 1960s. The term 'rock' was first used in the music press in the early 1960s, and continued to be used rather interchangeably with 'rock'n'roll' throughout the decade. A semantic shift was confirmed by the influential *Crawdaddy* magazine, in March 1967 changing its cover subtitle, from 'The magazine of rock'n'roll' to 'The magazine of rock'. Several early introductory surveys used the generic term 'rock' throughout (e.g. Carl Belz, *The Story of Rock*, Oxford University Press: Oxford, 1969; on the problem of naming', see Dettmar, 2006).

Aside from simply documenting its key performers and recordings, there have been several focal points in the literature on rock: the reasons for why it emerged in the 1960s, and the subsequent valourizing of that period; the relationship between rock music, the counter-culture, and politics and ideology (rock as, in some sense, revolutionary); the constitution of rock styles and their audiences in terms of race, gender and class and the globalization of rock. The musicology of rock is comprehensively considered in Covach and Boone (1997), Everett (2009), and Moore (2001). I have referred to these topics in related entries; for an insightful discussion of the constitution of 'standard' narratives and ideologies of rock, in relation to romanticism and modernism, see Keightley, (2002).

In the mid-1960s, rock was already splintering into a number of distinct genres, identified as such by the music press, the music industry and fans (for instance, psychedelic rock and hybrids such as country rock). This process of fragmentation has continued since the 1970s. Rock genres have been linked to region (Southern Rock) and nation (Oz Rock: Australia); subcultural styles (punk and punk rock); a combination of industry organization and ideology (alternative and indie); musical style and instrumentation (hard rock; soft rock; acoustic rock) and considerations of marketing and radio formats (Classic Rock; New Wave). A number of more significant rock genres are given separate treatment in this guide:

- Classic rock
- Garage rock
- Glam rock
- Goth rock
- Hard rock
- New wave
- Progressive rock

- Psychedelic rock
- Punk rock
- Pub rock
- Surf rock

See also the entries on hybrid styles: **blues rock, folk rock** and **country rock**, and related genres: **alternative, indie, EMO**.

It is worth noting (once again) that musicians are not always comfortable with these labels, and frequently resist attempts to categorize and 'pigeon hole' their work in terms of a specific genre or style.

Listening: See the reviews in magazines such as *Rolling Stone, UNCUT* and *Classic Rock.* Contemporary bands considered 'rock' include The Killers, The Strokes, Velvet Revolver and Queens of the Stone Age

Further reading:
Histories:

Garofalo, R. (2011) *Rockin' Out: Popular Music in the USA*, Upper Saddle River, NJ: Pearson/Prentice Hall.

Gillet, C. (1983) *The Sound of the City: The Rise of Rock and Roll*, Revised edition, London: Souvenir Press.

Marcus, G. (1991) *Mystery Train*, 4th edition, New York: Penguin (first published 1977).

Miller, J. (1999) *Flowers in the Dustbin: The Rise of Rock and Roll, 1947–1997*, New York: Simon & Schuster.

Palmer, R. (1995) *Rock & Roll: An Unruly History*, New York: Harmony Books. This is a companion to the PBS/BBC 10–part television series, Dancing in the Street.

Musicology:

Covach, J. and Boone, G.M. eds (1997) *Understanding Rock. Essays in Musical Analysis*, New York: Oxford University Press.

Everett, W. (2009) *The Foundations of Rock: From 'Blue Suede Shoes' to 'Suite: Judy Blue Eyes'*, Oxford: Oxford University Press.

Moore, A. (2001) *Rock: The Primary Text – Developing a Musicology of Rock*, 2nd edition, Buckingham: Open University Press.

General:

All Music Guide to Rock (1995, and there are several later editions), M. Erlewine, V. Bogdanov, and C. Woodstra (eds), San Francisco, CA: Miller Freeman. A comprehensive guide to performers and styles; this can now be updated on their website: www.allmusic.com

Dettmar, K. (2006) *Is Rock Dead?* New York: Routledge.

Keightley, K. (2002) 'Reconsidering Rock', in Frith, S., Straw, W. and Street, J. (eds) *The Cambridge Companion to Rock and Pop*, Chapter 5.

Discographies: Most general histories of rock include extensive discographies; see also Strong, M. (2006) *The Essential Rock Discography*, Edinburgh: Canongate. Lists every track recorded by more than 1,200 artists. Discographies of performers and genres of rock are a feature of the collecting press, especially the magazine *Record Collector* (UK)

Viewing: *Dancing in the Street*, PBS/BBC, 1995; *The Seven Ages of Rock*. A UK–US joint production, which adopts a British-centric view (it gets through the first episode without mentioning Elvis or Chuck Berry, treating 1965 as 'Year Zero for Rock')

ROCK OPERA

Concept albums first emerged in the 1960s as rock music aspired to the status of art, and some were accordingly termed 'rock operas'. Pete Townshend of the Who is usually credited as pioneering the concept, with the double album *Tommy*, MCA, 1969, although Townshend was partly inspired by the Pretty Things *P.F. Sorrow*, (Edsel, 1968) which had appeared the previous year. Subsequent examples included Frank Zappa and the Mothers of Invention, *We're Only In It For the Money*, (Verve, 1967); the Kinks' *Arthur, or Decline of the British Empire*, (Reprise, 1969), initially planned as a TV musical, and one of several concept albums penned by Ray Davies, the leader of the group; the Who's *Quadrophenia* (MCA, 1973); and the Eagles' *Desperado* (Asylum, 1973), which equated rock'n'roll musicians with Old West outlaws. The Beatles' *Sgt. Pepper's Lonely Hearts Club Band*. (1967) is often considered a concept album, for its musical cohesion rather than any thematic unity. Some late 1960s and 1970s stage musicals and their film versions can be considered rock operas; for example 'Hair' and 'the Rocky Horror Show' (see **musicals**).

As the above examples suggest, the form may well have had its classic period, and contemporary examples appear scarce. More recently, Green Day's album *American Idiot* (2004) was described by the band's lead singer as a 'punk rock opera'. These and similar efforts have enjoyed commercial success, and at times been critically well-received, but there is debate around the utility of the album format for such conceptual projects.

ROCKERS

Rockers were a prominent youth subculture in the United Kingdom in the 1960s, (they were also known as bikers, or greasers, especially in the

United States). The **rockers** wore black leather jackets, jeans and boots; had greased hair and rode motorbikes. Largely low-paid, unskilled manual workers, they were a male-oriented subculture; female followers rarely rode. Willis saw a homology between the rocker's masculinity, rejection of middle-class lifestyle, the motor bike and the preference for rock'n'roll. Key values: freedom. Music was 1950s rock'n'roll: Elvis, Gene Vincent and Eddie Cochran. The rockers clashed violently with the mods in 1963–4 at southern English holiday resorts, producing a moral panic. They have never entirely vanished as an identifiable subculture. Contemporary bikers show a preference for Heavy Metal.

See: **subculture**

Further reading:
Willis, P. (1978) *Profane Culture*, London: Routledge.

ROCK CRITICS

see **music press**

'ROCK SUICIDES'

see **effects**

ROOTS; ROOTS MUSIC

The term 'roots' is variously used to refer to (1) an artist's sociological and geographical origins, and the relationship between these and their music; (2) the audience/environment in which the artist's career is rooted and (3) more generally, for artists who are considered the originators of musical styles/genres of 'major roots musicians' in rockabilly, C&W and blues (as in Guralnick, 1989). Roots is often a genre specific term, being most frequently used in relation to styles such as folk, the blues and various world music genres. It is also often a constituent of populist notions of authenticity. Musically, roots is based on the notion that the sounds and the style of the music should continue to resemble its original source. Acceptance of this can lead to a questioning of 'traditional' artists adopting new musical technologies.

Further reading:
Guralnick, P. (1989) *Feel Like Going Home*, London: Omnibus Press.
Several music magazines include a 'Best Roots Albums' in their yearly retrospectives; e.g. *Q*, January 2008: 78.

Listening: Chuck Prophet, *Soap and Water*, Cooking Vinyl, 2007

SALSA

Salsa is Spanish for 'sauce' or 'spice' and has been used in relation to music since the 1920s in a similar fashion to 'funky'. For many musicians and commentators, salsa is a euphemism for Cuban music. It is appropriate to consider salsa as a hybrid genre, related to the Caribbean diaspora (Lipsitz, 2007); it is sometimes marketed as part of the metagenre of **world music**, despite its continued popularity in mainland United States.

The word salsa was used for many years by Cuban musicians before the genre became popularized in New York in the late 1960s, and salsa provided a neutral marketing label to bypass the US economic blockade of Cuba following the Castro-led revolution of 1959. Concord Picante, the salsa label of the Concord jazz company, helped popularize the genre in the 1980s. Historically significant salsa musicians include Celia Cruz, the Queen of Salsa and mambo bandleader Tito Punte. Reuben Blades, the most prominent contemporary salsa performer, has helped popularize the genre since the 1980s.

The staple musical elements present in salsa – the son and the clave – are derived from essentially Cuban styles. However, this direct link between salsa and Cuba is problematic, given that salsa is produced mainly by Cubans and Puerto Ricans living in New York and Puerto Rico. Furthermore, a number of other features have been detected in the music, including Puerto Rican 'folkloric' forms such as the bomba, big-band jazz, soul, call-and-response patterns from work songs and even funk and rock elements (Negus, 1996: 117).

The association between salsa and working-class Puerto Ricans has been argued using content analysis of song lyrics (e.g. Padilla, 1990). This assumes an intrinsic connection between social context, the production and reception of the music and song lyrics. Claims for salsa's expression of a pan-Latin consciousness are similarly based. Negus shows how the case of Reuben Blades illustrates the difficulties with any such straightforward correspondences, arguing instead for a more complex process of mediation of the music. Blades, who was born in Panama, educated at Harvard, and lives in New York, writes and performs socially committed songs, which began to reach a wider audience following his signing to Elektra in 1984.

See: **world music**

Further reading: (Coverage of the genre can also be found in the Rough Guides to World Music)

Lipsitz, G. (2007) *Footsteps in the Dark*, Minneapolis, MN: University of Minnesota Press. Chapter 9.

Padilla, F. (1990) 'Salsa: Puerto Rican and Latin American Music', *Journal of Popular Culture*, 24: 87–104.

Waxer, L. ed. (2002) *Situating Salsa*, New York: Routledge.

Listening: Reuben Blades, *Nothing but the Truth*, Elektra, 1988; Reuben Blades, *Buscando America*, Elektra, 1994; Celia Cruz, *Celia and Johny*, Voya, 1975

SAMPLING

The practice of using computer technology to take selected extracts from previously recorded works and using them as parts of a new work, usually as a background sound to accompany new vocals. Sampling has been the subject of considerable controversy, with debate around issues of author-ship and creativity, the nature of musicianship, the authenticity of the recordings it produces and the legality of the practice. Sampling can be viewed as part of popular music's historic tendency to constantly 'eat itself', while also exemplifying its postmodern tendencies:

> The willful acts of disintegration necessary in sampling are, like cub-ism, designed to find a way ahead by taking the whole business to pieces, reducing it to its constituent components. It's also an attempt to look to a past tradition and to try and move forward by placing that tradition in a new context.
>
> (*Beadle, 1993: 24*)

Digital sampling allows sounds to be recorded, manipulated and subsequently played back from a keyboard or other musical device (see Theberge, 1999). Introduced in the late 1970s and subsequently widely used, digital sampling illustrates the debates surrounding musical technologies. Its use is seen variously as restricting the employment of session musicians, and as enabling the production of new sounds, for example, the use of previously recorded music in the creation of rhythm tracks for use in rap and dance remixes. The increasing emphasis on new such technologies is significantly changing the emphases within the process of producing popular music: 'As pop becomes more and more a producer's and programmer's medium, so it increasingly is a sphere of composition, as opposed to performance' (Goodwin, 1998: 130).

The process of 'digging in the crates' for rare vinyl records, to provide the raw material for sample-based hip hop, illustrates the point that sampling is very much a social practice:

> digging serves a number of other purposes for the production community. These may include such functions as manifesting ties to hip hop deejaying tradition, 'paying dues', educating producers about various forms of music, and serving as a form of socialization between producers.
>
> (*Schloss, 2004: 79*)

See: **copyright**, **rap**, **technology**

Further reading:
Beadle, J. (1993) *Will Pop Eat Itself? Pop Music in the Soundbite Era*, London: Faber & Faber (includes a useful discography).
Goodwin, A. (1998) in *Mapping the Beat*.
Hesmondhalgh, D. (2000) 'International Times: Fusions, Exoticism, and Antiracism in Electronic Dance Music', in Born and Hesmondhalgh, *Western Music and Its Others*.
Schloss, J.G. (2004) *Making Beats: The Art of Sample-Based Hip Hop*, Middleton, CT: Wesleyan University Press.

Listening: The controversies surrounding the following early example of recordings featuring extensive sampling established the parameters for the arguments that followed: The Jams, *Shag Times*, KLF, 1988; De La Soul, *3 Feet High and Rising*, Tommy Boy, 1989; Jive Bunny and the Mixmasters, *Jive Bunny the Album*, Telestar, 1989

SCENES

As indicated elsewhere (see **place**), there is considerable exploration of the role and effectiveness of music as a means of defining identity. Situated within this, the concept of scene has become a central trope in popular music studies, a key part of the 'spatial turn' evident in urban and cultural studies generally. To an extent, scene, as an analytical concept of greater explanatory power, is now regarded by some writers as having displaced the earlier use of **subcultures**. The rhetoric of the music press commonly identifies artists with scenes, while fans and musicians both uphold the notion of a correspondence between local sounds and scenes.

Scene can be understood as 'a specific kind of urban cultural context and practice of spatial coding' (Stahl, 2004: 76). A basic reference point for later discussion was an essay by Straw (1992), in which he argued for greater attention to scene in popular music studies, defined as the formal and informal arrangement of industries, institutions, audiences and infra-structures. Also influential were Cohen's study of 'rock culture' in Liverpool, and Shank's study of the rock'n'roll scene in Austin, Texas (1994). Researchers subsequently engaged with, refined and applied the concept of scene to a wide range of settings and locales; much of this work, along with theoretical discussion of the concept of scene(s) can be found in Cohen (1999), Olsson (1998) and Stahl (2004), and several very useful edited collections (Whiteley *et al.*, 2004; Bennett and Kahn-Harris, 2004; Hodkinson and Deicke, 2007). The journal *Popular Music and Society* in 2010 devoted an issue to the topic.

A particular focus, in part arising from the earlier fascination with sub-cultures, has been on alternative music scenes. (The term 'underground' is also used for non-commercialized alternative scenes, as the performers in them are hidden from and inaccessible to people who are not 'hooked into' the scene.) Alternative music scenes fall into two basic categories. They are either college (US tertiary institutions) or university towns, or large cities that are somehow 'alternative', usually to even larger urban centres nearby (e.g. Minneapolis and Chicago). Most important North American college towns had local music scenes self-consciously perceived as such in the 1980s, with these linked as part of an American indie underground (see **indie**).

The most prominent were Athens, Georgia (source of the B52's, Love Tractor, Pylon and REM); Minneapolis (source of the Replacements, Hüsker Dü, Soul Asylum and Prince) and Seattle. Sometimes a small college town and nearby large city have contributed to a shared scene; for example, Boston and Amherst, MA (sources of Dinosaur Jr., the Pixies,

Throwing Muses and the Lemonheads), with bands moving back and forth between the two centres. Alternative scenes worldwide appear to conform to this basic pattern. While alternative music is often linked to particular local scenes, the question is why then and there? Such scenes have generally developed out of a combination of airplay on the local college radio stations, access to local live venues, advertisements and reviews in local fanzines and free papers and, especially, the existence of local independent record companies.

The specific configuration and dynamics of particular alternative scenes have been examined in numerous ethnographically oriented studies. Examples include Bennett (2000) on urban dance music (including house, techno and jungle) in Newcastle upon Tyne, England; Fairchild (1995) on punk/**hardcore** in Washington DC and Stahl (2004) on Montreal.

The relationship of the local to the global is a key part of the dynamic of local music scenes, alternative or otherwise. For many participants in alternative local scenes, the perceived dualities associated with indie and major record labels are central to their commitment to the local. However, by the mid-1990s, the 'local' had become increasingly allied with other localities, tied together by social networks, publications, trade groups and regional and national institutions. This globalizing of the local is a process encouraged and fostered economically by the major record companies, who place particular local sounds within larger structures, reaching a larger market in the process; for example, the marketing of the Seattle Sound in the 1990s (see **grunge**). Similarly, local sounds/scenes and their followers are ideologically linked through internationally distributed fanzines, music press publications and the Internet.

Further reading:

Cohen, S. (1999) 'Scenes', in Horner, B. and Swiss, T. (eds) *Key Terms in Popular Music and Culture*, Oxford: Blackwell, pp. 239–50.

Hodkinson, P. and Deicke, W. eds (2007) *Scenes, Subcultures and Tribes*, New York: Routledge.

Olson, M.J.V. (1998) '"Everybody Loves Our Town": Scenes, Spatiality, Migrancy', in Swiss, T., Sloop, J. and Herman, A. (eds) *Mapping the Beat: Popular Music and Contemporary Theory*, Malden, MA: Blackwell, pp. 269–90.

Shank, B. (1994) *Dissonant Identities: The Rock'n'Roll Scene in Austin, Texas*, Hanover: Wesleyan University Press.

Stahl, G. (2004) '"It's Like Canada Reduced": Setting the Scene in Montreal', in Bennett, A. and Kahn-Harris, K. (eds) *After Subcultures*, London: Ashgate.

Whiteley, S., Bennett, A. and Hawkins, S. eds (2004) *Music, Space and Place. Popular Music and Cultural Identity*, Aldershot, Burlington: Ashgate.

SEMIOTICS

see **structuralism**

SESSION MUSICIANS; HOUSE BANDS

Generally anonymous, session musicians are the pieceworkers of the music industry, yet their role is more important than is usually recognized. The label is a generic one, referring 'to a range of practices, all of which involve the participation of a musician in a recording session featuring an artist or band with which the session musician does not regularly perform' (Bowman, 2003: 104). The emergence of session musicians as musical labour was historically tied to greater professionalism and spiralling costs of recording session. During the 1960s, music centres such as Nashville, New York and London, developed highly competitive session musician scenes, with a select group of players able to make a lucrative living playing sessions. The role could be a demanding one: To be a session musician, one was generally expected to be able to sight-read musical notation quickly and accurately, to be able to transpose a part from one key to another instantly, to be able to play in a wide range of styles and emulate the licks, techniques and stylistic nuances of other notable instrumentalists, and, in some genres, to be able to continuously develop appropriate and catchy grooves, riffs and lines for recording after recording (ibid.: 105). Session musicians remain widely used in country and pop recordings.

Some session musicians attain critical recognition for their contributions. Reggae performers Sly Dunbar and Robbie Shakespeare established themselves as 'the' rhythm section, and keyboard player Billy Preston is credited, along with the group (the only time they shared authorship), for the Beatles single *Get Back*. The efforts of a few session musicians attain near legendary status, as with Jeff Beck and Jimmy Page's guitar solos on a variety of records in the 1960s, but usually only when they later become successful in their own right, creating interest in this aspect of their back catalogue.

House bands are the backing musicians used by particular record labels at a majority of their recording sessions, usually drawn from leading session musicians in an area. Their emergence was also linked to increased musical specialization and studio costs, as well as studio recording convenience. The practice began with jazz in Chicago in the 1920s, and was revived by rock music in the 1960s. Several house bands, such as Booker

T and the MGs, at Stax in Memphis, received considerable credit for their creative input. Others, equally talented, tended to remain more in the background, as with The Funk Brothers at Motown in Detroit.

Further reading:
Bowman, R. (2003) 'Session Musicians', in Shepherd *et al.* (eds) *The Continuum Encyclopedia of Popular Music*, volume 2, London: Continuum.

SEXUALITY

Sexuality refers to the expression of sexual identity, through sexual activity, or the projection of sexual desire and attraction; this occurs primarily in relation to other people, but can also be related to material/cultural artefacts. Sexuality and desire are central human emotions, or drives, which have been an essential part of the appeal of the culture/entertainment industries, including popular music, and the social processes whereby performers and their texts operate in the public arena. Popular music is also a significant area of culture in which sexual politics are struggled over. (For a comparison of how these concepts and process operate in film, see Hayward, 2000.)

Sexuality is central to discussions of how male and, more frequently, female performers are conceived of – socially constructed – as sex objects or symbols of desire. Here certain forms of subjectivity/identity are projected as 'normal', as with traditionally white, male sexuality. The operation of this process is a major focus in studies of music video and stars/ stardom, and in relation to particular genres. It involves considerations of the nature of spectatorship and the (gendered) gaze, utilizing conventions primarily developed in film studies.

Sexual ambiguity is central to many forms of popular music, which has frequently subverted the dominant sexuality constructed around male–female binaries. Discussion of this has concentrated on exploring the relationship between sexual orientation, public personas and a performer's music. Some performers openly represent or subvert and 'play with' a range of sexualities. Others constitute themselves, at times very self-consciously, as objects of heterosexual desire or as icons for different ('deviant'?) sexualities and their constituencies. Some genres/performers are linked to particular sexualities/ communities; for example, **disco** generally celebrates the pleasure of the body and physicality, and was initially linked to the gay community and specific club scenes; **heavy metal** has traditionally been associated with overt masculinity, as have some forms of rock (e.g. hard rock).

There is a historical tradition of popular music genres' song lyrics dealing with heterosexual love, desire, longing and lust; sexual orientations and sexual practices; and, at times, openly supporting or expressing solidarity with particular sexualities and criticizing non-heterosexuality and presenting homophobic or misogynist views (see **gangsta rap**). There is considerable argument over whether these texts are 'read' by their listeners, audiences and fans in any straightforward manner, or whether the artists intended or preferred readings, embedded in the text, are acknowledged, let alone assimilated into individual and social values and meanings (see Geyrhalter, 1996; Hawkins, 2002).

See: **gender**; **lyric analysis**

Further reading:

Evans, L. (1994) *Women, Sex and Rock'n'Roll: In Their Own Words*, London: Pandora/HarperCollins.

Frith, S. and McRobbie, A. (1990) 'Rock and Sexuality', in Frith, S. and Goodwin, A. (eds) *On Record: Rock, Pop, and the Written Word*, New York: Pantheon Books, pp. 371–89 (first published in 1978).

Geyrhalter, T. (1996) 'Effeminacy, Camp and Sexual Subversion in Rock: The Cure and Suede', *Popular Music*, 15, 2: 217–24.

Hawkins, S. (2002) *Settling the Pop Score: Pop Texts and Identity Politics*, Aldershot: Ashgate.

Whiteley, S. (2000) *Women and Popular Music: Sexuality, Identify and Subjectivity*, London: Routledge.

Listening: The following is a short list of historical examples, which were contentious in their day: Billy Ward and the Dominos, 'Sixty Minute Man', 1951; Little Richard, 'Tutti Frutti', 1956; The Kinks, 'Lola', 1970; Lou Reed, 'Walk on the Wild Side', 1973; Donna Summer, 'Love to Love You Baby', Casablance, 1975; Frankie Goes to Hollywood, 'Relax', 1984; Suede, 'Animal Nitrate', on *Suede*, 1993; Liz Phair, 'Flower' and 'Fuck and Run', on *Exile in Guyville*, Matador, 1993; Nellie, 'Tip Drill', 2005 (the video was also contentious)

See also: **gangsta rap**

SKA; TWO TONE

In the 1950s, Jamaican musicians combined indigenous folk music with jazz, African and Caribbean rhythms and New Orleans R&B. The resultant hybrid was ska.

In the early 1960s, ska was exported to the United Kingdom, with some chart success: the Skatalites; Millie Small. There was a ska revival in the United Kingdom in the late 1970s, primarily associated with Coventry and the Two Tone record label. Bands with both black and white members worked with elements of reggae, ska, dub and rock, in bands including UB40, the Specials, Madness, Selector and Bad Manners. Their record lyrics were politically and socially conscious, often containing British working-class themes and criticizing the 'establishment'.

See: **reggae**

Further reading:
Barrow, S. and Dalton, P. (2001; second edition) *Reggae: The Rough Guide*, in Buckley. J. (ed.), London: The Rough Guides.

Listening: Madness, *Complete Madness*, Stiff, 1982; The English Beat, *I Just Can't Stop It*, IRS, 1980; The Specials, 'Ghost Town' (1981 UK no. 1); on the album *The Specials. The Singles Collection*, Chrysalis, 1991

SKIFFLE

A musical genre which emerged in Britain in the mid-1950s, skiffle was arguably more significant as a catalyst than as a musical style. Cohen (2006) discusses it as a form of folk music, but it was more of a hybrid, drawing on blues and jazz, with several prominent jazz musicians picking up the style (Chris Barber). Skiffle appealed as a 'do it yourself' style of music, and thousands of groups sprang up. It had a simple rhythm section (homemade string bass and washboard), augmented by banjo and guitars. The most successful performer was Lonnie Donegan, who took his first name from bluesman Lonnie Johnson. Donegan drew on American blues and folk, especially the work of Woody Guthrie and Leadbelly, with his cover of the 'Rock Hardin' Line'.

By the early 1960s, skiffle had developed into beat and instrumental groups (the Shadows) using electric instrumentation. Skiffle was influential as a training ground for beat musicians; for example, John Lennon's Quarrymen.

Further reading: (see **rock'n'roll**)
Cohen, R. (2006) *Folk Music: The Basics*, London: Routledge.

Listening: *The UK Skiffle Boom 1954–57*, Southbound, 2011 (a four-disc set, with a booklet); Lonnie Donegan, *The EP Collection*, see for Miles, 1992; re-masters of his work up to 1962, this includes a substantial biography

Viewing: *Dancing in the Street*, episode 3

SKINHEADS

A youth subculture, first appearing in Britain in the late 1960s, skinheads were a working-class reaction to the hippy counter-culture and their own social marginalization. They made a virtue of working classness: hair cropped to the scalp, working shirts and short jeans supported by braces, heavy boots (cherry red, Dr Martens; accordingly, skinheads were some-times referred to as 'bootboys') was the standard uniform. Often associated with football hooliganism, skinheads became increasingly racist and were involved in attacks against immigrants, especially Asians. While they were targets for neo-Nazi recruitment by the National Front, skinheads were largely apolitical. By the late 1960s, they had become highly visible and a clear example of 'folk devils'. English skinheads espoused traditional con-servative values: defence of their local territory, hard work and extreme patriotism; essentially they attempted to 'magically recover the traditional working-class community' (Clarke, 1976). Skinheads became an interna-tional phenomenon, present in North America, Europe (especially Germany, where they were linked to Nazi revivalism) and Australia and New Zealand, though these were groups essentially derivative of their British counterparts.

Originally skinheads musical preferences embraced black music genres: ska, bluebeat and reggae, in contradiction to their racism; and subse-quently Oi! Oi! first appeared in 1981, as a manifestation of British punk rock; it was characterized by a loud, driving guitar sound, basic, abrasive, nihilistic and often racist lyrics. Oi! groups adopted skinhead dress style and played at National Front meetings. The most prominent performers were the 4 Skins, though they attained only limited commercial success. Sham 69, though not normally considered an Oi band, also developed a strong skinhead-National Front following. Skinheads have remained visi-ble, at least at the level of their style, which has often been incorporated into hardcore and post–punk/indie subcultures.

See: **hardcore**; **moral panic**; **subcultures**

Further reading:

Clarke, J. (1976) 'The Skinheads and the Magical Recovery of Community', in Hall and Jefferson (eds) *Resistance Through Rituals*.

Listening: The 4 Skins, *The Good, The Bad, and The 4 Skins, Secret*, 1982; Sham 69, *The First, The Best, and The Last*, Polydor, 1980

Viewing: *Romper Stomper*, Australia, 1992

SOCIAL NETWORK SITES

A development that directly paralleled file-sharing has been the growth of social network sites, Napster and Myspace both beginning in June 1999. Myspace enables its users to host their own profiles within its formatting protocols, and the member can then post a variety of personal information which can be accessed and viewed (with possible restrictions imposed at the member's discretion) by other users of the network. Other similar social network services followed, with Myspace's main competitors Facebook and Bebo the most successful. Social networking erodes the distinction between client and server, although access still requires logging on through the network's website, and promotes the idea of democratic media: 'Where peer-to-peer file-sharing encourages a de-commodification of informational goods, social network sites promote the democratisation of information' (David, 2000: 38; see also Buckley, 2006).

Facebook, Myspace and Bebo all require users to log on to the company's website in order to access their own and others portfolios; this enables the services to stream advertising within the common pages that all users can see. Advertising based media companies soon recognized the potential to move beyond traditional mass media, especially to reach younger consumers, and began acquiring social network sites. This advertising potential led Fox Interactive Media, a subsidiary of News Corporation (Rupert Murdoch), to buy Myspace in July 2006.

In July 2010, Facebook announced that more than 500 million people now used it, and that a user on average posted photos, links to websites, videos and news stories, or created other content about 30 times each month ('Third of net users now on Facebook' *Dominion Post* (reproducing content from *The Times*), 23 July 2010: B1). Mark Zuckerberg, one of its founders, was *Time* magazine's Man of the Year for 2010. The phenomenon even led to a Hollywood feature film, *Social Network*, on the development of Myspace and the personalities and arguments around who took the credit (and the financial rewards) for this. The commercial and critical success of the film was a further indication of the impact of social networking on digital global culture.

In relation to popular music, social network sites provide an opportunity for performers to promote their music and activities, including new recordings, but also concerts and touring. Fans can get involved in this process, as well as 'meet' those interested in similar styles of music, to exchange information and debate opinions. There have been a number of well-documented studies and success stories of bands use of social networks; these include both established performers (Radiohead and Madonna), bands seeking primarily to better exploit their back catalogues while alerting fans to their current activities (Simply Red and The Charlatans), and new bands, such as the Arctic Monkeys and Enter Shakira (see David, 2010: Chapter 9; also those performer's websites and their social networking pages).

Further reading:
David, M. (2010) *Peer to Peer and the Criminalization of Sharing*, Los Angeles, CA: Sage.

SONG COLLECTING

'The term "song collecting" is used for an anthology of songs from various sources, and "song collector" for a person who collects and edits such songs for publication'. (Oliver, 2001: 43). Prior to the development of recording equipment in the early twentieth century, the songs of traditional performers and folk singers could be collected only through direct notation from live performance 'in the field', as was undertaken by the English collector Cecil Sharp in the Appalachian Mountains (in the southern United States). Others relied on the compilation of material from published and manuscript sources (such as broadsides, ballad sheets and chapbooks), as did Francis James Child. Later, with the advent of portable recording machines, collectors such as John Lomax and his son, Alan, maintained the tradition of field recording in the United States (*Lomax the Songhunter*, documentary 2004). Such work was supported and encouraged nationally by the Archive of Folk Music of the Library of Congress and the American Folklore Society in the United States, and by the National Folk Association in the United Kingdom. These were complimented at the regional and local level by groups committed to the collecting of folk songs. Song collecting was not confined to Britain and the United States, with prominent collectors in Canada (Ernest Gagnon), Australia and Europe.

The broad goal of song collecting was cultural preservation, especially of what were seen as dying traditions of rural music, along with public and school-based education about these. Alongside this sat a valourization of community cultural identity, with the various country and folk musics connoting authenticity. Early publications such as Child's *English and Scottish Ballads* (1857–9) reached a wide readership and defined the field for subsequent collectors. The emphases and practices of these early song collectors have been strongly criticized for their cultural conservatism: largely for separating out 'ballads' from other forms of folk and popular song, but also in some cases the editing out of sexual content or connotations.

See: **folk music**

Further reading:
Harker, D. (1985) *Fakesong: The Manufacture of British 'Folksong', 1700 to the Present Day*, Milton Keynes: Open University Press.
Oliver, P. (2001) 'Song Collecting', in Shepherd, J. *et al.* *The Continuum Encyclopedia of Popular Music*, volume 1, London: Continuum.

Viewing: *Lomax the Songcatcher*, Rogier Kappers, 2004

SONGWRITERS; SONGWRITING; SINGER SONGWRITERS

In comparison with the writing on other roles in the music industry, and the nature of the creative process in popular music, the role of the songwriter has not received much sociological or musicological attention. The limited amount of published work has concentrated on song composition, the process of songwriting and the contributions of leading songwriters, especially those associated with the Brill Building in New York (see below). London in the 1960s had its own group of successful pop and rock songwriters (see Thompson, for a detailed discussion of their work and influence).

Some songwriters have been accorded auteur status, especially when they have later successfully recorded their own material (e.g. Carol King; Jackson Browne; Joni Mitchell), or are performing as singer songwriters (see below).

There are numerous examples of songwriters exercising considerable influence over artists/styles. In the 1950s, Leiber and Stoller got an unprecedented deal with Atlantic to write and produce their own songs; the resulting collaborations with performers such as the Drifters and Ben E. King produced sweet soul, a very self-conscious marriage of R&B and classical instruments, notably the violin. In the 1960s, Holland, Dozier, Holland contributed to the development of the Motown sound. In the 1970s, Chin and Chapman composed over 50 British top ten hits in association with producers Mickie Most and Phil Wainman, 'using competent bar bands (Mud, Sweet) on to whom they could graft a style and image' (Hatch and Millward, 1987: 141), to produce highly commercial power pop, glitter rock and dance music.

In the late 1950s and early 1960s, a factory model of songwriting, combined with a strong aesthetic sense, was evident in the work of a group of songwriters (and music publishers) in New York's Brill Building: 'the best of Tin Pan Alley's melodic and lyrical hall marks were incorporated into R&B to raise the music to new levels of sophistication' (Erlewine, 1995: 883). The group included a number of outstanding songwriting teams: the more pop-oriented Goffin and King; Mann and Weil and Barry and Greenwich; the R&B-oriented Pomus and Sherman, and Leiber and Stoller. Several also produced, most notably Phil Spector, Bert Berns and Leiber and Stoller, who wrote and produced most of the Coasters hits. One factor which distinguished the group was their youth: mainly in their late teens or early twenties, with several married couples working together, the Brill Building songwriters were well able to relate to and interpret teenage dreams and concerns, especially the search for identity and romance. These provided the themes for many of the songs they wrote, especially those performed by the **teen idols** and **girl groups** of the period. Pomus and Sherman, and Leiber and Stoller, wrote some of Elvis Presley's best material. Collectively, the Brill Building songwriters were responsible for a large number of chart successes, and had an enduring influence (Leiber and Stoller, 2009; Shaw, 1992). The role of such songwriters, however, was weakened with the British invasion and the emergence of a tradition of self-contained groups or performers writing their own songs (most notably The Beatles), which weakened the songwriting market.

The term **singer songwriter** has been given to artists who both write and perform their material, and who are able to perform solo, usually on acoustic guitar or piano. An emphasis on lyrics has resulted in the work of such performers often being referred to as song poets, accorded auteur status, and made the subject of intensive lyric analysis. The folk music revival in the 1960s saw several singer songwriters come to prominence: Joan Baez, Phil Ochs and, especially, Bob Dylan. Singer songwriters were a particularly strong 'movement' in the 1970s, including Neil Young, James Taylor, Joni Mitchell, Jackson Browne and Joan Armatrading. In the 1980s, the appellation singer songwriter was applied to, among others, Bruce Springsteen, Prince and Elvis Costello; and in the 1990s to Tori Amos, Suzanne Vega, Tanita Tikaram, Tracy Chapman and Toni Childs. More recently, alt. country performers such as Ryan Adams and Lucinda Williams; and pop artists such as Taylor Swift, who compose the bulk of their recorded material, are lauded in the music press for their efforts.

This female predominance led some observers to equate the 'form' with women performers, due to its emphasis on lyrics and performance rather than the indulgences associated with male-dominated styles of rock music. The application of the term to solo performers is problematic, in that most of those mentioned usually perform with 'backing' bands, and at times regard themselves as an integral part of these. Nonetheless, the concept of singer songwriter continues to have strong connotations of greater authenticity and 'true' auteurship.

Further reading:

Flanaghan, B. (1987) *Written in My Soul: Rock's Great Songwriters Talk about Creating their Music*, Chicago, IL: Contemporary Books.

Hoskyns, B. (2006) *Hotel California: Singer-Songwriters and Cocaine Cowboys in the LA Canyons, 1967–1976*, London: Harper Perennial.

Leiber, J. and Stoller, M. with David Ritz (2009) *Hound Dog: The Leiber and Stoller Autobiography*, New York: Simon & Schuster.

Shaw, G. (1992) 'Brill Building Pop', in DeCurtis, A. and Henke, J. (eds) *The Rolling Stone Illustrated History of Rock and Roll*, 3rd edn, New York: Random House, pp. 143–52 (includes a discography).

Thompson, G. (2005) *Please Please Me. Sixties British Pop*, Chapter 5: The Write Stuff. Songwriting and the Articulation of Change.

Zollo, P. (1997) *Songwriters on Songwriting*, New York: Da Capo Press.

Listening: Carol King, *Tapestry*, Ode, 1971 (songwriter turned recording artist; one of the bestselling albums of the period); Neil Young, *Harvest Moon*, WB, 1992; Tracy Chapman, *Matters of the Heart*, Elektra, 1992; Alanis Morissette, *Jagged Little Pill*, WEA, 1996

Viewing: *Walk On By. A History of Popular Song*; *Dancing in the Street*, episode 2 (includes an interview with Leiber and Stoller)

SOUL

Originally a secular version of gospel, soul was the major black musical form of the 1960s and 1970s and remained evident in various hybrid styles since (e.g. contemporary neo-soul and soul jazz). Soul had originally been used by jazz musicians and listeners to signify music with a greater sense of authenticity and sincerity. As it developed in the 1960s, soul was a merger of gospel style singing and funk rhythms. Funk was originally used in the 1950s to describe a form of modern jazz which concentrated on 'swing' and became used in the 1960s in R&B and soul music; especially for the recordings of 'Soul Brother Number One', James Brown.

Guralnick defines soul as 'the far less controlled, gospel based, emotion-baring kind of music that grew up in the wake of the success of Ray Charles from about 1954 on and came to its full flowering, along with Motown, in the early 1960s' (1991: 2). The genre was often ballad in form, with love as a major theme. Most soul music was vocally led, with either soloists, or groups featuring a lead vocalist with backing harmonies (e.g. The Impressions, with Curtis Mayfield). Major soul singers in the 1950s included Sam Cook and Jackie Wilson; in the 1960s James Brown, Bobby Bland, Aretha Franklin, Otis Redding and Percy Sledge.

Soul became closely identified with several independent record labels: Atlantic, Stax/Volt and Motown, each with its own 'stable' of performers, producers/songwriters and house bands, with and an identifiable sound. These labels were frequently associated with particular geographic locations and music scenes: for example, Motown in Detroit; 'Philly soul' (Philadelphia) and Southern Soul. Commercial mainstream soul was best exemplified in the recordings of Motown. Soul was politically significant through the 1960s, paralleling the Civil Rights movement, while the music and associated dress styles influenced both black youth and white subcultures such as **mod**.

Soul had ceased to an identifiable genre by the late 1970s, gradually being absorbed into various hybrid forms of black music and **dance music** more generally. Its major performers and their records still enjoy a considerable following, indicated by the sales of soul compilation albums, and the international success of the film *The Commitments* (1991) and its soundtrack of soul covers.

As a metagenre, soul has been the subject of a number of comprehensive studies, and extensive attempts to map its many variants (AMG). There are insightful biographies and autobiographies of many of its major artists, for example, Guralnick's comprehensive analysis of Sam Cooke, arguably the greatest soul singer. Bowman (1997) is an excellent study of Stax Records.

See: **Motown**; **northern soul**

Further reading:

Bogdanov, V. Bush, C. Woodstra, S. eds (2003) *All Music Guide to Soul*, San Francisco, CA: Miller Freeman.

Borthwick, S. and Moy, R. (2004) 'Soul; from gospel to groove', *Popular Music Genres: An Introduction*, Edinburgh: Edinburgh University Press.

Bowman, R. (1997) *Soulsville, USA: The Story of Stax Records*, London: Books With Attitude.

Guralnick, P. (1991) *Sweet Soul Music*, London: Penguin.

Guralnick, P. (2009) *Dream Boogie: The Triumph of Sam Cooke*, New York: Little Brown.

Hirshey, G. (1985) *Nowhere to Run: The Story of Soul Music*, New York: Penguin.

Potter, R. (2001) 'Soul into Hip-Hop', in Frith, S. *et al. Cambridge Companion to Pop and Rock*.

Listening: *60s classic soul*; James Brown, *Live at the Apollo*, Polydor, 1963; Aretha Franklin, *30 Greatest Hits*, Atlantic, 1986; Otis Redding, *The Very Best of Otis Redding*, Rhino, 1993; Percy Sledge, 'When a Man Loves a Woman', 1966 single, the first southern soul record to cross over and top both the R&B and pop charts; available on various compilations

SOUND; SOUND PRODUCTION; SOUND RECORDING; SOUND REPRODUCTION

The history of sound recording and its contemporary practice are the focus of a number of researchers in popular music studies and related fields such as the history of technology, and the following can be only a brief introduction to this large body of work (see the suggested readings).

In physical, scientific terms, sound is the sensation caused in the ear by the vibration of the surrounding air, or what is or may be heard, with musical sound produced by continuous and regular vibrations. In popular music studies, primary interest has been on changes in the nature of sound reproduction and recording, especially the manner in which new technologies have influenced the nature and product.

New technologies of **sound production** are democratizing, opening up performance opportunities to players and creating new social spaces for listening to music. However, these opportunities and spaces are selectively available, and exploited by particular social groups. There are a number of excellent studies of these developments and their implications, including the impact of nineteenth-century brass band instruments

(Herbert, 1998); the microphone in the 1930s (Chanan, 1995: Chapter 7); the electric guitar in the early 1950s; the MOOG synthesizer in the 1970s and MIDI since the 1980s.

Further reading:

Chanan, M. (1995) *Repeated Takes: A Short History of Recording and its Effects on Music*, London: Verso.

Day, T. (2000) *A Century of Recorded Music: Listening to Musical History*, New Haven, CT: Yale University Press.

Kealy, E. (1979) 'From Craft to Art: The Case of Sound Mixers and Popular Music', in Frith, S. and Goodwin, A. (eds) *On Record*, pp. 207–20.

Zak III, A. (2001) *The Poetics of Rock*, Berkeley, CA: University of California Press.

Sound recording is the process of transferring 'live' musical performance onto a physical product (the recording). The history of sound recording is one of technical advances leading to changes in the nature of the process, and the tasks and status of the associated labour forms. Such changes are not narrowly technical, as different recording technologies and their associated working practices (e.g. multitracking, overdubbing and tape delay) enable and sustain different aesthetics (for a detailed history, see Cunningham, 1996; for a concise overview, see Chanan, 1995). Major sound studios have historically been linked to particular production aesthetics and personnel; Coogan and Clarke (2003) profile some of these fascinating 'Temples of Sound', as they term them.

In the recording studio, the work of the sound mixer, or sound engineer, 'represents the point where music and modern technology meet' (Kealy, 1979). Initially designated as 'technicians', sound mixers have converted a craft into an art, with consequent higher status and rewards. Zak refers to them as 'both craftsmen and shamans' (2001: 165), who are now responsible for much of what we hear on a recording, acting as a kind of translator for the other members of the recording team (including the musicians). Through the 1980s and into the 2000s new recording technologies have continued to open up creative possibilities and underpinned the emergence of new genres, notably the variants of techno and hip hop.

Particular recordings demonstrate advances in sound recording, at times accompanied by greatly increased use of studio time. For example, Les Paul and Mary Ford, 'How High Is the Moon', which occupied the number one position on the *Billboard* chart for 9 weeks in Spring 1951, launched the concept of sound-on-sound recording, coupled with Paul's discovery of tape delay (Cunningham, 1996: 25). Approaching the history of popular music from this perspective creates quite a different picture of artistic high points and auteur figures, in comparison with the conventional chronologies (ibid.).

See: **producers**

Further reading:

Coogan, J. and Clarke, W. (2003) *Temples of Sound: Inside the Great Recording Studios*, San Francisco, CA: Chronicle Books.

Cunningham, M. (1996) *Good Vibrations: A History of Record Production*, Chessington: Castle Communications.

Sound reproduction as part of home entertainment had its origins in the late nineteenth century (see **gramophone culture**), with an ongoing history of gradual improvements in fidelity, realism and portability (see Millard, 2005; Shuker, 2008: Chapter 3). In addition to home stereo systems, and their predecessors, there are more mobile forms of sound reproduction, important to particular lifestyles. These include the transistor radio; the Jamaican sound system, imported to the United Kingdom during the 1950s; and the walkman, which had a major impact when it was introduced during the 1980s. More recently, iPods and mobile phones (which now also play music and screen videos, and use ringtones to alert their owners to incoming calls) have become necessary fashion accessories, especially for younger consumers.

A further example of a socially situated playing/listening technology is the 'Sound System', a term given to large, heavily amplified mobile discos and their surrounding **reggae** culture. These initially emerged in Jamaica, from the 1950s onwards, and were subsequently transplanted to Britain with the influx of Caribbean immigrants.

> The basic description of a sound system as a large mobile hi-fi or disco does little justice to the specificities of the form. The sound that they generate has its own characteristics, particularly an emphasis on the reproduction of bass frequencies, its own aesthetics and a unique mode of consumption.
>
> (*Gilroy, in Gelder and Thornton, 1997: 342*)

See: **iPod**

Further reading:

Millard, A.J. (2005) *America on Record: A History of Recorded Sound*, 2nd edition, Cambridge, MA: Cambridge University Press.

Read, O. and Welch, W.L. (1976) *From Tin Foil to Stereo: The Evolution of the Phonograph*, Indianapolis, IN: Howard Sams.

Steffen, D. (2005) *From Edison to Marconi: The First Thirty Years of Recorded Music*, Jefferson, NC: McFarland.

SOUNDTRACKS

There are three main types of music soundtrack: in feature film and documentary; in television and in electronic/video games. Mainstream narrative cinema has used two types of musical soundtrack to compliment the film itself: (i) theme music, usually composed specifically for the film (*Star Wars*, *Jaws* and *Lord of the Rings*); (ii) a soundtrack consisting of selected popular music, usually contemporary with the temporal and physical setting of the film, or representative of the period evoked (*The Big Chill*, *Singles* and *American Graffiti*). Occasionally, there may be two 'soundtracks' released, and the two approaches are sometimes combined (*Dead Man Walking*, 1996).

Rock Around the Clock (1956) and many of the films featuring Elvis Presley demonstrated the market appeal of popular musical soundtracks, as indeed had many Hollywood **musicals** before them. Mainstream narrative cinema has increasingly used popular music soundtracks to great effect, with accompanying success for both film and record. The film to really demonstrate the commercial possibilities of such successful marketing tie-ins was *Saturday Night Fever* (1977). Such soundtracks feature popular music composed specifically for the film, or previously recorded work which is thematically or temporally related to the film. This enables multimedia marketing, with accompanying commercial success for both film and record. Prince's soundtrack for the film *Batman* (1989) provided another early template for this approach: the album was part of a carefully orchestrated marketing campaign, which successfully created interest in the film and helped break Prince to a wider audience, primarily through exposure (of the promotional video clip).

Further reading:
Wojcik, P.R. and Knight, A. eds (2001) *Soundtrack Availability: Essays on Film and Popular Music*, Durham, NC: Duke University Press.

SPEED/THRASH METAL

Initially largely a US phenomenon, speed/thrash developed out of hardcore and punk, and became a journalistic convenience for guitar-based non-mainstream metal, usually played faster and louder. Popoff (1997), and Christe (2004: 137), two of metal's most insightful reviewers, argue for a clear distinction between 'thrash' and 'speed', and prefer the latter term. Other commentators use speed and/or thrash more generally, in a loose fashion for the same bands.

Although speed was centred on the United States, international versions of it followed and became identified as such, for instance, the 'German Speed Metal' of Kreator, Sodom and Celtic Frost (Swiss–German). I focus here on Metallica, the most important of the thrash bands, who have generated the bulk of academic (and populist) writing on the genre.

Metallica's debut album, *Kill 'Em All* (1983) was immensely influential on thrash, but the style really became consolidated with the work of Metallica and three other bands in the mid-1980s: Anthrax, Megadeth and Slayer (see the suggested listening below). These subsequently became commonly grouped together as 'the big four' of thrash metal. The **crossover** success of Metallica in the 1990s, notably with The Black Album which sold 6 million copies, brought the style to mainstream attention (McIver, 2004; on the making of the album, and the role of producer Bob Rock in reshaping the band's sound, see the Classic Rock documentary). Metallica's success was based on a particularly intense relationship with their fans, who strongly identified with the song lyrics.

There is some excellent journalistic writing on thrash metal, notably in several studies by McIver, but rather less academic treatment of the genre. Much of this concentrates on Metallica; the most successful and best known of the thrash bands. In the early 1990s, Breen saw Metallica and Anthrax as generating a new form of 'the true rock experience', which ran in direct contradiction to the 'the established expectation of pleasure and fun often associated with rock music' (Breen, 1991: 191). This new form was apocalyptic in its visions of negation, and constructed through the live concert as much as its recorded forms. As a sociologist, Kotarba was 'drawn to the dynamics by which Metallica serves as a primary cultural resource for many of its audience members. This cultural resource provides viable meanings for life, its problems and its possibilities' (1994: 142). Kotarba, a Metallica fan since 1988, considered the band to be reflecting the state of rock in the 1990s and postmodern culture more generally. This claim was based on metal's broadening of its fan base, to no longer simply reference teenage males; its lyrics being open to a variety of interpretations ('an open horizon of meaning'); the 'integration of and ambiguity towards good and evil in the postmodern world'; and the manner in which its music could be framed as children's culture, exemplified by the highly successful single and video for 'Enter Sandman' (ibid.: 154–8). The status of Metallica was indicated by an edited volume of essays by philosophers, discussing aspects of the work of the band. Editor Irwin argued that Metallica, the 'thinking man's' metal band, is 'the greatest American rock band of all time', a claim based largely on the significance of James Hetfield's lyrics (Irwin, 2007: 1–2).

Thrash metal remains an established part of the metal scene, with Metallica still active.

Further reading: (see also the general entry: **Heavy Metal**)

Breen, M. (1991) 'A Stairway to Heaven or a Highway to Hell? Heavy Metal Rock Music in the 1990s', *Cultural Studies*, 5, 2: 191–203.

Irwin, W. ed. (2007) *Metallica and Philosophy: A Crash Course in Brain Surgery*, Malden, MA: Blackwell.

Kotarba, J. (1994) 'The Postmodernization of Rock and Roll Music: The Case of Metallica', in Epstein (ed.) *Adolescents and Their Music*, New York: Garland.

McIver, J. (2004) *Justice for All: The Truth About Metallica*, London: Omnibus Press.

Pillsbury, G. (2006) *Damage Incorporated: Metallica and the Production of Musical Identity*, New York: Routledge.

Popoff, M. (1997) *A Collector's Guide to Heavy Metal*, Burlington, Ontario: Collectors Guide Publishing.

Viewing: Metallica, *The Black Album*, Classic Album series, Eagle Rock, 2001

Listening: Metallica, *Master of Puppets*, 1986; Metallica, *And Justice for All*, Elektra, 1988; Anthrax, *Spread The Disease*, 1985; Megadeth, *Killing Is My Business ... And Business Is Good*, 1985; Destruction, *The Antichrist*, Nuclear Blast, 2000; Slayer, *Reign in Blood*, 1986

STARS; STARDOM; CELEBRITY

Stars are individuals who, as a consequence of their public performances or appearances in the mass media, become widely recognized and acquire symbolic status. Stars are seen as possessing a unique, distinctive talent in the cultural forms within which they work. Initially associated with the Hollywood film star system, stardom is now widely evident in sports, television and popular music.

The important question is how stars function within the music industry, within textual narratives, and, in particular, at the level of individual fantasy and desire. What needs to be explained is the nature of emotional investment in pleasurable images: 'stars are popular because they are regarded with some form of active esteem and invested with cultural value. They resonate within particular lifestyles and cultures' (O'Sullivan, 1994: 207), and represent a form of escapism from everyday life and the mundane.

Stardom in popular music, as in other forms of popular culture, is as much about illusion and appeal to the fantasies of the audience, as it is about talent and creativity. Stars function as mythic constructs, playing a key role in their fans ability to construct meaning out of everyday life. Such stars must also be seen as economic entities, a unique commodity form which is both a labour process and product, effectively brands who mobilize audiences and promote the products of the music industry. Accordingly, audience identification with particular stars is a significant marketing device; for example, Madonna is as much as an economic entity as a purely cultural phenomenon, as over the course of her career with Time-Warner she generated more than US$500 million in world-wide music sales. Madonna represents a bankable image, carefully constructed in an era of media globalization (Schwichtenberg, 1993; O'Brien, 2010). Several popular music stars have continued to generate enormous income after their death, which freezes their appeal in time while enabling continued marketing of both their **back catalogue** and previously unreleased material, as has occurred with Jimi Hendrix, Bob Marley and Kurt Cobain (Nirvana).

Yet the enormous fascination with stars' personal lives suggests a phenomenon which cannot be simply explained in terms of political economy. Fans both create and maintain the star through a ritual of adoration, transcending their own lives in the process (see **fans**). Stars appeal because they embody and refine the values invested in specific social types: Kylie Minogue in the 1980s as 'the girl next door', and Bruce Springsteen, whose image is founded on authenticity. Contemporary 'established' stars are frequently at pains to exercise considerable control over their artistic lives, perhaps because this has often been hard won; all have an ability to retain an audience across time, either through reinventing their persona and image, or through exploring new avenues in their music; many have produced a substantial body of work, often multimedia in form; while seeking, to varying degrees, new ways of reinterpreting or reaffirming popular music styles and traditions. In these respects, such stars are frequently considered to be **autuers**.

While there is a large body of theoretically oriented work on film stars (see Dyer's canonical study; also Hayward, 2000), the study of stardom in popular music is largely limited to personal biographies of widely varying analytical value. The most extensively considered popular music stars are Elvis Presley, Bob Dylan and the Beatles (as a group, and as individuals). Bruce Springsteen and Madonna are the popular music stars of the past 20 years who have generated the greatest amount of academic (and popular) analysis and discussion. In summary, the discourse surrounding them shows how stardom has become a construct with a number of dimensions: the economic, the cultural and the aesthetic or creative – the relationship between stardom and auteurship. In addition to the wealth of populist writing, some of it well-worth investigating (see **biography**), there have been a number of academic biographies of popular music stars; several of these have taken a different approach to their subject, moving past the usual life story narrative (e.g. the study of Bob Dylan by Marshall). A number of brief but more considered star profiles are included in Frith, Street and Straw (2001).

The recently established and related field of **celebrity** studies is adding another dimension to the study of stars and stardom, involving a redefinition of the public/private boundary, where the emphasis is on the private life rather than the career (Holmes and Redmond, 2006). An example is Cashmore's analysis of 'black' singer and celebrity Beyonce, as embodying 'a narrative, a living description of a culture in which race is a remnant of history and limitless consumer choice has become a substitute for equality' (Cashmore, 2010: 135).

See: **fans**

Further reading:

Cashmore, E. (2010) 'Buying Beyonce', *Celebrity Studies*, 1, 2: 135–50.

Dyer, R. (1986) *Heavenly Bodies: Film Stars and Society*, London: Routledge.

Holmes and Redmond, (2006) *Framing Celebrity: New Directions in Celebrity Culture*, London: Routledge.

Marshall, L. (2007) *Bob Dylan: The Never Ending Star*, Polity.

Schwichtenberg, C. ed. (1993) *The Madonna Connection: Representational Politics, Subcultural Identities, and Cultural Theory*, St Leonards, NSW: Allen & Unwin.

STRUCTURALISM; SEMIOTICS; POST-STRUCTURALISM

An intellectual enterprise characterized by attention to the systems, relations and forms – the structures – that make meaning possible in any cultural activity or artifact. Structuralism is an analytical or *theoretical* enterprise, dedicated to the systematic elaboration of the rules and constraints that work, like the rules of a language, to make the generation of meanings possible in the first place.

(*O'Sullivan, 1994: 302*)

Structuralists' attempts to establish such 'rules of meaning' led to several distinct approaches during the 1970s: semiotics; deconstruction (overwhelmingly a mode of literary analysis, derived from the work of Derrida) and post-structuralism.

'Structuralist' views of popular culture and media forms concentrate on how meaning is generated in media texts, examining how the 'structure' of the text (visual, verbal or auditory) produces particular ideological meanings. Such study is primarily through **semiotics**, the study of signs, which has been applied widely in the study of communications, providing a method for the analysis of both verbal and non-verbal messages. Semiotics distinguishes between signifier, signified and sign. The signifier can be a word, an image or a physical object; the signified is the mental concept associated with the signifier; the sign is the association of signifier and signified. Signs may be organized into linked codes, as with dress fashions. Social convention may influence the precise nature and strength of the relationship between signifier and signified. Barthes argued that signs can form myths, in that a sign may represent a whole range of cultural values. In addition to associating an image or an object with a concept (dennotation), signs also carry connotations, engendering emotions.

In popular music studies, semiology has been used in analyses of **song lyrics**, **music videos**, **record covers**, **youth subcultures** and photographs (on the last, see Longhurst's instructive decoding of a press photograph of Courtney Love and Sinead O'Connor at the 1993 MTV Awards, to show how such images/texts contain different levels of meaning; Longhurst, 2007: 153–5). Traditional musicological approaches can be loosely regarded as a structuralist form of cultural analysis, since they privilege the text by placing the emphasis firmly on its formal properties. Musicologists tackle popular music as music, using conventional tools derived from the study of more traditional/classical forms of music: harmony, melody, beat, rhythm and the lyric. However, this preoccupation with the text in and of itself has been critiqued for its lack of consideration of music as a social phenomenon. In traditional musicology, the music itself becomes a disembodied presence, lacking any social referents. The concept of musical codes is a structuralist approach to investigating how meaning is conveyed in musical texts, and has also been used to inform discussions of competence, the differing ability of listeners to decode or interpret musical texts (see Middleton, 1990; Tagg and Clarida, 2003).

Post-structuralism,

> is hard in practice to separate from structuralism. It is more alert to psychoanalytic theories and the role of pleasure in producing and regulating meanings than was the highly rationalist early structuralism. Post-structuralism is also more concerned with the external

structures (social process, class, gender, and ethnic divisions, historical changes) that make meaning possible.

(*O'Sullivan, 1994: 304*)

These emphases shifted the focus from the text to the reader/viewer/
listener. Within popular music studies, post-structuralist ideas have
informed discussions on the nature and significance of **class**, **gender** and
ethnicity in relation to changes in the production and consumption of
music.

STYLE

see **fashion; genre; subculture(s)**

SUBCULTURE(S)

As the contributors to a major edited reader demonstrate, while there is no
consensus about the definition of a subculture, they can be broadly considered to be social groups organized around shared interests and practices
(Gelder and Thornton, 1997: part 2). Subcultures often distinguish themselves against others; factions of the larger social group, they usually set
themselves in opposition to their parent culture, at least at a cultural level.

In the mid-1970s, rather than being part of a coherent youth culture,
it seemed to many observers that youth consisted of a 'mainstream'
majority, and minority subcultures whose distinctiveness was shaped
largely by the social class and ethnic background of their members (cf.
the **counter-culture** of the 1960s, and the view of youth as a generational unit). Sociological interest concentrated on the various youth
subcultures, whose members were seen to rely on leisure and style as a
means of winning their own cultural space, and thus represented cultural oppositional politics at the symbolic level.

Music is one of a complex of elements making up subcultural style. Its
role in terms of pleasure and cultural capital is similar to that played out
among more mainstream youth, but in an accentuated form. The relationship between popular music and youth subcultures was comprehensively explored in a number of influential studies during the 1970s and

early 1980s (Hall and Jefferson, 1976; Hebdige, 1979; Willis, 1978). Collectively, these argued what became a frequently asserted thesis: that youth subcultures appropriate and adopted musical forms and styles as a basis for their identity, and, in so doing, assert a counter-cultural politics. This perspective was primarily associated with writers linked to the influential Birmingham (UK) Centre for Contemporary Cultural Studies. Starting from the premise that style in subculture is 'pregnant with significance', Hebdige illustrated this through a comprehensive analysis of various spectacular subcultural styles: Beats and Hipsters in the 1950s, Teddy Boys in the 1950s and 1970s, Mods in the early 1960s, Skinheads in the late 1960s, Rastas in the 1970s, Glam Rockers in the early to mid-1970s, and, most visible of all, Punks in the mid-1970s. In his analysis, subcultures rely on leisure and style as a means of making their values visible in a society saturated by the codes and symbols of the dominant culture. The significance of subcultures for their participants is that they offer a solution, albeit at a 'magical' level, to structural dislocations through the establishment of an 'achieved identity' – the selection of certain elements of style outside of those associated with the ascribed identity offered by work, home or school. The expressive elements of this style offer 'a meaningful way of life during leisure', removed from the instrumental world of work:

> Subcultures are therefore expressive forms but what they express is, in the last instance, a fundamental tension between those in power and those condemned to subordinate positions and second class lives. This tension is figuratively expressed in the form of subcultural style.
>
> (*Hebdige, 1979: 132*)

The majority of youth were seen to pass through life without any significant involvement in such subcultures. Associated aspects of subcultural fashion and musical tastes may be adopted, but for 'respectable' youth these are essentially divorced from subcultural lifestyles and values. Members of youth subcultures, on the other hand, adopt symbolic elements to construct an identity outside the restraints of class and education, an identity which places them squarely outside of conservative mainstream society. Membership of a subculture was seen to necessarily involve membership of a class culture and could be either an extension of, or in opposition to, the parent class culture (as with the skinheads). Writers such as Hebdige were at pains not to overly privilege this class dimension, and to accord due analytical weight to gender and ethnic factors (see also Muggleton, 2000).

The BCCCS writers' sociocultural analyses represented an original and imaginative contribution to the sociology of youth cultures, but were critiqued for their overemphasis on the symbolic 'resistance' of subcultures, which was imbued with an unwarranted political significance; the romanticizing of working-class subcultures; the neglect of ordinary or conformist youth; and a masculine emphasis, with little attention paid to the subcultural experiences of girls. And while music was regarded as a central aspect of subcultural style, its homological relation to other dimensions of style was not always easy to pin down. At times, stylistic attributes were too quickly attributed to a specifically subcultural affiliation, rather than recognizing their wider adoption.

Writing at the end of the 1980s, Middleton concludes that subcultural analysis had drawn the connection between music and subculture much too tightly, 'flawed above all by the uncompromising drive to homology' (Middleton, 1990: 161).

While this convergence between music and cultural group values is evident in some contemporary youth subcultures, most notably **emo**, **heavy metal** and **grunge**, subsequent theoretical discussions and case studies suggest that the degree of homology between subcultures and music has been overstated. Indeed the very value of the concept 'subcultures', and particularly its conflation with oppositional cultural politics, became seriously questioned. For many youthful consumers during the 1980s and 1990s, the old ideological divides applied to popular music had little relevance, with their tastes determined by a more complex pattern of considerations than any 'politically correct' dichotomizing of genres. This is most evident in the constituencies for alternative and dance music.

Recent research in popular music has retained elements of the subcultural approach, but moved towards a more sophisticated understanding of the activities of music audiences, drawing heavily on the concept of scenes (Muggleton and Weinzierl, 2003).

See: **homology**; **scenes**

Further reading:

Bennett, A. and Kahn-Harris, K. eds (2004) *After Subcultures*, London: Ashgate.
Gelder, K. and Thornton, S. eds (1997) *The Subcultures Reader*, London: Routledge.
Hall, S. and Jefferson, T. eds (1976) *Resistance Through Rituals: Youth Subcultures in Post-War Britain*, London: Hutchinson.
Muggleton, D. (2000) *Inside Subculture: The Postmodern Meaning of Style*, Oxford: Berg.
Muggleton, D. and Weinzierl, R. eds (2003) *The Post-subcultures Reader*, Oxford: Berg.

Stahl, G. (2003) 'Tastefully Renovating Subcultural Theory: Making Space for a New Model', in Muggleton, D. and Weinzierl, R. (eds) *The Post-subcultures Reader*, Oxford: Berg, pp. 27–40.

Willis, P. (1978) *Profane Culture*, London: Routledge.

SUBJECTIVITY

see **identity**

SURF MUSIC; SURF ROCK

An initially short-lived but influential musical phenomenon, surf music began as part of a regional scene in Southern California, associated with the emerging surfing subculture (along with hot rod cars and drag racing). With the success of performers such as Jan and Dean and the Beach Boys, surf music became a marketing label in the early 1960s. The majority of surf music recordings were issued between 1961 and 1965. Their chart success was largely confined to Southern California but their influence was more widespread. Subsequently, the genre contributed to alternative music styles favoured by the surfing culture, and, post-2000, the emergent skate and snow boarding X-games scene.

Surf music was the most guitar-oriented style of early 1960s rock music and had enormous influence on subsequent electric guitar playing styles. Reflecting this emphasis, there was a strong surf instrumental vein, with the Surfaris ('Wipe Out', 1963), the Chantays ('Pipeline', 1963) and the Ventures all making the national charts. However, the 'King' of the Surf Guitar was Dick Dale, whose reverb guitar sound evoked the waves and 'runs' of surfing, a teenage subculture which initially developed in California and Hawaii in the late 1950s. The surf board was the crucial component of this subcultural style, which also included dress (board shorts, or 'baggies', Hawaiian shirts and wet suits) and surf music. Its core values were leisure as a form of conspicuous consumption, and individualism, primarily expressed through the skill and enjoyment of surfing.

Dale developed a technique based on the tremolo playing used in Middle Eastern plucked instruments such as the bouzouki, sustaining notes by plucking strings up and down, calculated to evoke 'the feeling of white water caving around your head in a tube ride' (White 1994: 137).

A surf music craze was sparked by Dale and the Del-Tones' 1961 single 'Let's Go Trippin', with hundreds of surf bands emerging. While surf was a male-dominated genre, there were several girl surf groups, most notably the Honeys (the Revill Sisters).

The most commercially successful surf performers were vocal duo Jan and Dean and the Beach Boys, who became the leading and most enduring of the 1960s surf bands. Creatively led by Brian Wilson, the Beach Boys were heavily influenced by the 1950s vocal group style and harmonies of the Four Freshmen and Chuck Berry's rock'n'roll; their early hit 'Surfin USA' is based on Berry's 'Sweet Little Sixteen'. In a series of songs, the Beach Boys distilled the essence of the California dream: good time music, with references to sun, sand, surfing, hot rods and (obliquely) sex. The band's early singles deliberately set out to provide theme songs for the surfing subculture, including 'Surfin' Safari (1962) and 'Surfin USA' (1963). Wilson became a disciple of Phil Spector's 'Wall of Sound'; increasingly obsessed with studio technology, he led the Beach Boys to largely abandon surfing themes and broaden their scope after 1963.

'Classic' 1960s surf music continues to maintain a cult status, associated with specialist labels (e.g. Surfdog, Surf's Up and Sundazed), reissues of classic surf albums, and compilations (most notably Rhino's *Cowabunga!* boxed set, 1996), dedicated discographies (Blair, 2007) and strong interest from record collectors.

Surf music experienced a revival in the 1980s, through into the 1990s, as it became an element of more contemporary genres, most notably grunge. During the late 1990s, there was a further resurgence of interest in surf music, especially its instrumental side, with new surf bands emerging, including The Space Cossacks, Merman and the Boardwalkers, and Satan's Pilgrims. Twenty-first-century 'surf music' has moved well beyond the 1960s instrumental-oriented style. The new surf bands, primarily from Southern California and Australia, typically play variants of thrash metal (e.g. Sprung Monkey from San Diego, California and Frenzal Rhomb from Australia). They appeal to fans with an investment in surfing as a cultural pursuit or as a competitive international sport (the X-games and extreme sports). The connections between surf music and surfing are also evident in the recordings of singer songwriters who are also active surfers, such as Pico (from Australia) and Jack Johnson (USA).

Surf music provided the soundtrack for the beach movies of the 1960s, and for documentaries celebrating surfing and the associated lifestyle (e.g. *The Endless Summer*, 1964). Beattie (2003) documents how changes in surf music since the 1960s can be seen in the soundtracks of surf documentaries. These soundtracks have moved from drawing on the instrumental, 'jangly guitar' sound of the 1960s, through the surf and progressive rock soundtrack for films such as *Crystal Voyager* (1972), with Pink Floyd's 'Echoes' accompanying the last 18 minutes of the film. Recent surf videos are structured around music popular within the surfing subculture, most notably forms of hardcore and thrash, and are an important part of the heavily televised global circuit of surfing competitions and extreme games. Videographers sometimes tour with bands such as Pennywise and Sprung Monkey, screening their surfing videos while the band plays. Concert DVDs by surf bands will include surf footage, as with Powderfinger's *These Days*, which includes extracts from surf filmmaker Jack McCoy's *Blue Horizon*.

Further reading:

Beattie, K. (2003) 'Radical Delirium: Surf Film and Video and the Documentary Mode', in Gilbert, K. and Skinner, J. (eds) *Some Like It Hot: The Culture of the Australian Beach*, Germany: Meyer and Meyer, pp. 129–53.

Blair, J. (2007) *Illustrated Discography of Surf Music, 1961–1965*. Revised and expanded 4th edition. Self-published; available through www.johnblair.us

Miller, J. (1992) 'The Beach Boys', in DeCurtis, A. and Henke, J. (eds) *The Rolling Stone Illustrated History of Rock and Roll*, Revised edn, London: Plexus.

White, T. (1995) *The Nearest Faraway Place: Brian Wilson, The Beach Boys and the Southern California Experience*, New York: Macmillan.

Listening: The Beach Boys, *Best of*. Capitol/EMI, USA, 2005; *Cowabunga: The Surf Box* (4 CD boxed set). Rhino Records/WEA, USA 1966; Dick Dale and His Del-Tones, *King of The Surf Guitar*. Rhino, USA, 1989; Jack Johnson, *In Between Dreams*. Universal, USA, 2005; Jan and Dean, *Surf City*. BGO Records, USA, 2004; The Surfaris, *Wipe Out! The Best of the Surfaris*. Varese Sarabande, USA, 1994

Viewing: *Crystal Voyager*, director George Greenhalgh, USA, 1972; *Dancing in the Street*, PBS/BBC, episode 2. Includes the Beach Boys and Dick Dale; *The Endless Summer*, director Bruce Brown, USA, 1966. Features music by the Sandalls; Powderfinger, *These Days*, director Gregory Jordan, Universal, Sydney 2003 Concert (includes extracts from surf filmmaker Jack McCoy's *Blue Horizon*)

SYNCRETISM

Syncretism indicates a reconciliation, a blending or fusion of pre-existing elements. This involves the creation of a new style by combining rhythms, timbres, vocal styles and so on from earlier forms; rock'n'roll in the 1950s was the result of blending R&B (itself derived from blues, boogie and gospel), and southern country and bluegrass. In a sense, all contemporary popular music is the result of syncretism, with the coexistence of various genres fuelling the emergence of new styles; for example, the combination of pop, rock and rap genres with various styles of world beat/music in the 1990s.

See: **appropriation** (and the suggested reading therein)

TASTE; CULTURAL CAPITAL; TASTE CULTURES

Taste refers to our cultural preferences and is usually used in the sense of 'good taste'. Particular activities, practices and cultural texts have acquired a higher status than others (see **culture**). Those who consume these are viewed as having 'good taste', being regarded as culturally and aesthetically discerning. Related to this are notions of a **canon** of cultural texts, underpinned by ideology and aesthetics. However, there are problems posed by the subjectivity of the discourse surrounding taste, and the shifting historical nature of what constitutes taste. Furthermore, texts connoting 'good taste' are usually validated by those who are considered to have such taste, a process of self-confirmation. In short, what constitutes taste is socially constructed.

Cultural capital

In its contemporary formulations, taste is frequently conflated with the concept of **cultural capital**. Originating in the work of Pierre Bourdieu, cultural capital 'describes the unequal distribution of cultural practices, values and competencies characteristic of capitalist societies', with classes defined not only by their economic capital, but also by their differential access to cultural capital and symbolic power (O'Sullivan, 1994: 73). In simple concrete **consumption** terms, in relation to the media, this means the preference of individuals and social groups for particular **texts** – for example, European movies or Hollywood action movies – and the role such tastes play as both means of self-identification and as social indicators to others.

The designation of popular music is as much sociological as musical, a view reinforced by the varied reception of specific music texts. Bourdieu (1984, 2010) showed how 'taste' is both conceived and maintained in social groups efforts to differentiate and distance themselves from others, and underpinning varying social status positions. Music has traditionally been a crucial dimension of this process. The musical tastes and styles followed or adopted by particular groups of consumers are affected by a number of social factors, including class, gender, ethnicity and age.

Consumption is not simply a matter of 'personal' preference, but is, in part, socially constructed. Linked to this process, is the manner in which musical tastes serve as a form of symbolic or cultural capital.

Musical cultural capital is demonstrated through a process whereby the individual, in acquiring a taste for particular artists, both discovers the 'history' and assimilates a selective tradition. He or she is then able to knowledgeably discuss artists, records, styles, trends, recording companies, literature, etc. This process occurs with music which is popular among the individual's peer group or subculture. In both cases, it serves a similar function, distancing its adherents from other musical styles. In the case of allegiance to non-mainstream genres/performers, cultural capital serves to assert an oppositional stance; this is the pattern with many youth subcultures, which appropriate and innovate musical styles and forms as a basis (subcultural capital) for their identity. There is a historical tendency to dichotomize cultural capital in popular music by distinguishing between listeners oriented towards a commercial mainstream and a marginalized minority preferring more independent or alternative music. (For an early example, see Riesman, 1950; this can be compared with later studies of subcultures; see that entry.) The availability of online music services such as iTunes and last fm, which generate recommendations, and 'taste neighbours' on the basis of what the registered user likes/plays most, has added a new dimension to the construction of taste (www.last.fm/about). While such sites function as industry tools, and a platform for sales, they also can operate as community building mechanisms.

See: **class**, **subcultures**

Further reading:

Bourdieu, P. (2010) *Distinction: A Social Critique of the Judgement of Taste*, London: Routledge. First published, 1984.
Riesman, D. (1950) 'Listening to Popular Music', in Frith, S. and Goodwin, S. (eds) (1990) *On Record*, New York: Pantheon Books.

Taste cultures

American sociologist Herbert Gans developed the concept of taste cultures in the 1960s, to refer to the differentiation of cultural consumption among social groups, and the manner in which such patterns were shaped. A taste culture is a group of people making similar choices, with these being related to similar backgrounds: class and education are the key determinants of membership in taste cultures. This has much in common with the notion of lifestyles: distinctive configurations of cultural identity and sets of social practices which are associated with particular consumption groups, taste cultures and subcultures. There is debate over the degree of individual autonomy/choice involved in the construction of lifestyles, and the extent to which they allow for a genuine plurality of expression, including resistance. In an anthropological sense, both taste cultures and lifestyles refer to particular forms of symbolic consumption, along with the rhetorics and discourses in play in the production or regulation of modern cultural life.

These concepts, and the associated debates, have informed popular music studies of **audiences** and **consumption**. Much of this work takes musical taste/cultural capital as central to identity formation, situating this in relation to gender, and adolescent peer group identity.

TECHNO

Techno emerged as an identifiable genre in the 1980s, partly associated with new, computer-generated, sound/composition technologies available to musicians. Techno is often conflated with house and ambient music, or used contiguously with the whole corpus of EDM (**electronic dance music)**. Techno became closely associated with a particular social setting, being the staple music at large-scale parties (raves); with the associated use of the drug ecstasy, these generated considerable controversy in the early mid-1990s in the United Kingdom (see **rave culture**).

The defining musical characteristics of techno are, in most cases, a slavish devotion to the beat and the use of rhythm as a hypnotic tool (usually 115–160 bpm); these are primarily, and often entirely, created by electronic means; a lack of vocals and a significant use of samples. There are a number of variants, or subgenres within techno, often linked with particular record labels/regional scenes. The 'proto-techno' of the original Detroit (US) creators of techno (notably Derrick May), shows a mixture of influences, especially influential German electronic band Kraftwerk's 'assembly line technopop', and the funk of George Clinton and Parliament. From this basis came 'Detroit techno', a stripped-down, aggressive funk sound, played mostly on analogue instruments and characterized by a severe, pounding rhythm, and 'hardcore techno', speed metal tunes played on Detroit techno instrumentation. Subsequent variants included the more accessible and commercial 'techno-rave'; 'breakbeat', a style using sped-up hip hop beat samples and 'tribal', with rhythm patterns and sounds drawing on Native American and world music. Some techno performers have moved progressively with and through a number of these styles; for example, The Shamen's initial recordings combined psychedelic rock with hardcore **rap** rhythms, while their later work made greater use of samples, drum machines and heavily amplified guitar sounds.

See: **EDM** (and the suggested reading there)

Listening: Kraftwerk, *TransEurope Express*, Klink Klang, 1977. Remastered and rereleased on CD by EMI in 2009; The Shamen, *Boss Drum*, Epic, 1992; Leftfield, *Leftism*, Hard Hands/Columbia, 1995; Underworld, 'Born Slippy', on *Trainspotting: Original Soundtrack*, EMI, 1996; Rhythim is Rhythim, (Derrick May), 'Strings of Life', Transmat, 1987

TECHNOLOGY

In sociological usage, technology embraces all forms of productive technique, including handcraft, but the more popular use of technology is synonymous with machinery. Both understandings of the term are evident in considerations of the relationship between popular music and technology. However, as Theberge observes, 'technology' is not to be thought of simply in terms of 'machines', but rather in terms of practice, the uses to which sound recording and playback devices, recording formats, and radio, computers and the Internet are put: 'in a more general sense, the organization of production and consumption' (1999: 216–17).

The history of music is in part one of a shift from oral performance to notation, then to music being recorded and stored, and disseminated utilizing various mediums of sound (and visual) transmission. These are hardly discrete stages, but they do offer an organizing logic for the overview here. Any new medium of communication or technological form changes the way in which we experience music, and this has implications for how we relate to and consume music. Technological changes in recording equipment pose both constraints and opportunities in terms of the organization of production, and the development of new forms of musical instruments allowed the emergence of 'new' sounds. New recording formats and modes of transmission and dissemination alter the process of musical production and consumption, and raise questions about authorship and the legal status of music as property. The creation of music and technological innovation have historically been closely related, but discussions of this relationship have been conscious to avoid overbalancing into technological determinism: the notion that the form(s) of technology are the principal factor producing cultural/social change.

These topics have been the subject of intensive study, and their importance has warranted separate treatment; they are simply indicated here (for further, more specific reading, see their respective entries):

- **Sound production**: the influence of new instrumentation, for example, the electric microphone, the guitar and the synthesizer.
- **Sound recording**: the role of the recording studio; the importance of amplification and the changing status of formats.
- **Sound reproduction**: the phonograph and its descendants.
- Sound dissemination: the historical impact and contemporary importance of **radio**, and the **Internet** and **MP3**.
- The combination of sound and visuals: **film**, **television** and **MTV**, **music video**.
- The deployment of new technologies in the area of music **retail**.

It is also important to acknowledge that prior to recorded sound, print was central to the transmission of music. Even before the invention of the printing press, handwritten songs were circulated. The printing press facilitated the circulation of broadside ballads from the early sixteenth century, and sheet music, which peaked at the end of the nineteenth century (see **Tin Pan Alley**).

Technology is an inherent part of some definitions of popular music, with attempts to maintain a distinction between a 'folk mode' predicated on live performance, and a mass culture form associated with recording. Innovations such as music video and electronic technologies of composition have generated a certain amount of 'techno-phobia' (Pinch and Bijsterveld, 2003). Negus makes an intriguing comparison between contemporary antipathy to such developments and the hostile reception initially accorded the piano (Negus, 1992: 31).

The discourse surrounding music and technology embrace divergent views about creativity and musicianship, artistic freedom and property rights (copyright). New technologies are variously seen as democratizing or consolidating established music industry hierarchies; rationalizing or disruptive of and distribution processes; confirming or challenging legal definitions of music as property and inhibiting or enabling of new creativities and sites of authorship (Thornton, 1995: 31).

Further reading:

Eisenberg, E. (1988) *The Recording Angel: Music, Records and Culture From Aristotle to Zappa*, London: Pan Books.

Katz, M. (2004) *Capturing Sound: How Technology has Changed Music*, Berkeley, CA: University of California Press.

Pinch, T.J. and Bijsterveld, K. (2003) '"Should One Applaud?" Breaches and Boundaries in the Reception of New Technology in Music', *Technology and Culture*, 44, 3: 536–59.

Théberge, P. (1997) *Any Sound You Can Imagine: Making Music/Consuming Technology*, Hanover, NH: Wesleyan University Press.

Théberge, P. (1999) 'Technology', in Horner, B. and Swiss, T. (eds) *Key Terms in Popular Music and Culture*, Oxford: Blackwell, pp. 209–24.

TEDDY BOYS

Originally a British phenomenon, **Teddy boys**, or 'teds', first appeared in the mid-1950s. Mainly from unskilled backgrounds, the teds had been left out of youth's new affluence. Their style included hair worn in elaborate quiffs (the DA, etc.), dressed with grease, long, pseudo-Edwardian drape jackets (hence the name), thick crepe-soled shoes ('brothel creepers') and thin string ties: 'the "Teddy boy" appropriation of an upper-class style of dress "covers" the gap between largely manual, unskilled near-lumpen real careers and life chances, and the "all-dressed-up-and-nowhere-to-go" experience of Saturday evening' (Hall and Jefferson, 1976: 48). The teds music preferences were early rock'n'roll and rockabilly. There were international imitative versions of the teds in the 1950s, for instance in New Zealand and Australian, where they were termed 'bodgies'.

The Teddy boys' activities centred around rock'n'roll music, coffee bars and cafes with jukeboxes and pubs. They were involved in riots in cinemas and dance halls during the advent of rock'n'roll, and in the 1958 UK race riots: 'the ted was uncompromisingly proletarian and xenophobic' (Hebdige, 1979: 51). There have been periodic ted revivals, notably in the 1980s, although the 'modern' teds dress and manner carried rather different connotations, being more reactionary and closer to their working-class machismo parent culture.

See: **rock'n'roll**; **subculture** (and the references there)

TEENAGERS; TEENYBOPPERS; TEEN IDOLS

A teenager is a person in their teens (13–19 years of age), and a teeny-bopper is a teenage girl who follows the latest fashions in clothes, hairstyles and pop music. The term 'teenager', has a long history, emerging out of the concept of 'adolescent', which dates back to American social psychology in the early 1900s. Historically, the activities of youth, a collective label for both, have been the subject of periodic conservative concern (**moral panic**).

First used in the late 1950s, teenybopper soon acquired strongly derogatory connotations, being applied to girl fans and their preferred artists and musical styles: teen idols and 'teen pop'. Teen idols represented a blander, less rebellious version of rock'n'roll, and the music of Paul Anka, Booby Vee, Bobby Vinton and Tommy Sands prospered in the charts in the early 1960s. Successful female singers, who followed the same 'clean cut' personal styles, included Leslie Gore and Connie Francis. The teen idols projected a mixture of sexual appeal and innocent youth to a receptive teenage market.

Academic analysis has concentrated on the social construction of teenagers as an identifiable social group, their musical preferences and their (declining) significance as a market (see **demographics**). Profiles of popular music consumption show a clear pattern of age- and gender-based genre preferences. Teenagers are traditionally a major audience for, and consumers of, popular music, especially pop, dance music, bubblegum and power pop. (Other genres will frequently include variants and performers aimed at the teenage market: e.g. the 'lite' heavy metal of Bon Jovi in the 1980s; the 'soft' rap of Kriss Kross in the 1990s.) That girls enjoy commercial pop music more than boys reflects the segmented nature of the market, with certain performers having a clear appeal for younger listeners, particularly girls, and being marketed as such; for example, Kylie Minogue, Duran Duran and Bananarama in the 1980s; the Back Street Boys and the Spice Girls in the 1990s; Miley Cyrus and Justin Bieber more recently. There is a major genre of music magazines aimed at the teenybopper/younger market (e.g. *Smash Hits*). The majority of their readers are girls, who buy them partly for their pin-up posters, reflecting their frequent obsession with particular stars and what has been termed teenybopper bedroom culture.

See: **boy bands**; **girl groups**; **pop**

Further reading:

Baker, S. (2002) 'Bardot, Britney, Bodies and Breasts: Pre-teen Girls' Negotiations of the Corporeal in Relation to Pop Stars and their Music', *Perfect Beat*, 6, 1: 3–17.

Savage, J. (2007) *Teenage: The Creation of Youth Culture*, London: Chatto & Windus.

Listening: *The Very Best of Connie Francis*, Polydor, 1963; *Bobby Vee*, Legendary Masters Series, EMI, 1990

TEJANO (TEX-MEX)

Tejano, also referred to as conjunto ('group' in Spanish), is a genre comprising folk and popular music which has its origins with the Mexicans who settled in Central and South Texas in the nineteenth century. It blended traditional Mexican music, including corridos, while incorporating European styles, such as the polka. The central instrument is the accordion, and much of the genre is dance music. The later addition of electric guitars and drums, saw the music develop into a hybrid genre associated with Chicano, Mexican and Texan musicians, blending rock, country, R&B, blues, traditional Spanish and Mexican music. Although the genre had a much longer history, it came to wider attention with the chart success of Richie Valens in the late 1950s ('La Bamba'). Tex-Mex emerged as a marketing label for it in the 1980s, primarily with the commercial success of Los Lobos, along with Freddy Fender, Doug Sahm and Flaco Jimenez.

The style, which is sometimes identified as a form of world music in spite of its location, has also been a part of the assertion of cultural identity by the considerable Latino/Spanish population living in the United States.

Further reading:
Miguel, S. (2002) *Tejano Proud: Tex-Mex Music in the Twentieth Century*, College Station, TX: Texas A&M University Press.
Reyes, D. and Waldman, T. (1998) *Land of a Thousand Dances: Chicano Rock'n'Roll from Southern California*, Albuquerque, NM: University of New Mexico Press.

Listening: Los Lobos, *How Will the Wolf Survive*, Slash, 1984; Sir Douglas Quintet, *Mendocino*, Acadia/Evangeline, 2002 (original release 1969; now with bonus tracks); Texas Tornados, *Texas Tornados*, Reprise, 1990 (won a Grammy)

TELEVISION; REALITY TELEVISION

Television has been an important mode of distribution, promotion and formation for the music industry. The discussion here is of free-to-air, broadcast television and the popular music programmes which form part of its schedules (see also **MTV**). These programmes include light entertainment series based around musical performers, music documentaries and the presentation of musical acts as part of television variety and chat/interview shows. It is also worth noting that popular music plot themes, music segments and signature tunes are also an important part of many television genres, especially those aimed at children (e.g. *Sesame Street*) and adolescents (*The Simpsons* and *The X Files*), but also 'adult' dramas such as *The Sopranos* and *Ashes to Ashes* (at times, with the accompanying release of **soundtrack** albums).

A contradictory relationship has traditionally existed between television and popular music.

> Television is traditionally a medium of family entertainment, collapsing class, gender, ethnic, and generational differences in order to construct a homogeneous audience held together by the ideology of the nuclear family. In contrast, many forms of popular music, especially rock'n'roll and its various mutations, have historically presented themselves as being about 'difference', emphasizing individual tastes and preferences. The rock tradition viewed television as 'always after the event – young viewers might have learned to move and dress directly from the TV screen, but the assumption was that it was a window on the real youth world that was somewhere out there.
>
> (*Frith, 1988: 212*)

The introduction of public broadcast television in the United States and the United Kingdom in the early 1950s coincided with the emergence of rock'n'roll. Television helped popularize the new music, and established several of its performers, most notably Elvis Presley, as youth icons. For some fans, especially those outside of the United States and the United Kingdom, television provided their only access to 'live' performance. Television was quick to seize the commercial opportunities offered by the emergent youth culture market of the 1950s. This led to a proliferation of television popular music shows. The better-known of these on US television included *American Bandstand*, one of the longest running shows in television history (1952–), and *Your Hit Parade* (1950–59). Britain had *Juke Box Jury* and *Top of the Pops*, both starting in the late 1950s, and *The Old Grey Whistle Test* (launched by the BBC in 1971, and aimed at more album-oriented older youth). In 1963, *Ready Steady Go!* (RSG) began showcasing new talent, who usually performed live, compared to the *Top of the Pops* studio lip-synchs with backing from a house orchestra. In addition to the music, such shows have acted as influential presenters of new dances, image and clothing styles, as with *Soul Train*'s coverage of black culture in the 1960s in the United States. Several of these shows later became marketed as sell-through videos or DVDs (*The Best of the Old Grey Whistle Test*, BBC DVD, 2001), consolidating their role as valuable documents of historically significant performers and styles.

Television's presentation of rock music prior to the advent of music video (MV) was generally uninspiring (see Shore, 1985, for a full history of the development of music video in relation to television). The 1980s success of MTV boosted televised music videos, reshaping the form and the broadcast programme that relied on music videos for their content. In the United States and Canada, nearly every major city had its own televised music video show, with several nationally syndicated. MV programmes also became an influential stock part of television channel viewing schedules in the United Kingdom and Western Europe, and New Zealand and Australia.

Mainstream television's MV shows were significant primarily because of their importance to advertisers, drawing a young audience whose consuming habits are not yet strongly fixed. A number of studies illustrated the factors at work in the emergence and nature of popular music programmes on commercial television, particularly their place within scheduling practices and the process of selection of the music videos for inclusion on them. Of particular interest are the links between such programmes, advertising and record sales. While it is difficult to prove a direct causal link, as with radio airplay and chart 'action' there is evidence that, in the 1980s and into the 1990s, exposure on such programmes had an influence on record purchases. The nature of such shows, and their tendency to play music videos which are shortened versions of the associated song, exercised considerable influence over the way in which videos are produced and their nature as audiovisual and star texts (see Negus, 1992: 97). Also significant, especially in small nations such as Australia, New Zealand and the Netherlands, is the status of locally produced music videos compared with their imported counterparts, who are competing for space on such programmes, a form of cultural imperialism. The significance of such mainstream free-to-air television shows has steadily waned with the impact of competing sites, most notably YouTube.

'**Reality television**' is used to describe a variety of programming ranging from crime and emergency-style shows, to talk shows, docusoaps and some forms of access-style programming. Emerging in the 1980s in the United States, it established itself as a central part of mainstream, popular television by the mid-1990s. In the 2000s, reality television become a leading programme format, with many successful shows internationally franchised (e.g. *Survivor* and *Big Brother*). A hybrid genre, reality television draws on and reworks generic codes and conventions from a variety of sources, using new technology (camcorders) to convey as sense of immediacy and authenticity to viewers. Reality television has been criticized for being reliant on shock value and pandering to viewer voyeurism and the lowest common denominator; and celebrated as a form of 'democratainment', with its emphasis on viewer participation (Casey *et al.*, 2002).

Popular music has provided a significant vehicle for reality television. Popular series like *The Monkees* in the 1960s (Stahl, 2002) and *S Club 7 in Miami* in the late 1990s (Shuker, 2008: 153–4) reinforced the public profiles and commercial success of their performers. In their use of manufactures groups, they foreshadowed the later *Pop Idol* and *Popstars* series. These musical talent quests have become an international phenomenon, creating new pop stars in a number of countries, although the career of some has been short-lived (e.g. True Bliss in New Zealand). Hear'Say, put together through *Popstars*, topped the UK album and singles charts in 2001, while *Pop Idol* launched the careers of Will Young and Gareth Gates in the United Kingdom, and Ruben Studdard, Kerry Underwood and Kelly Clarkson in the United States (see **American Idol**).

See: **music video**; **MTV**

Further reading:

Casey, B., Casey, N., Calver, B., French, L. and Lewis, J. (2002) *Television Studies: The Key Concepts*, London: Routledge.

Frith, S. (2007) 'Look! Hear! The Uneasy Relationship of Music and Television', in *Taking Popular Music Seriously* (The article was first published in 2002).

Popular Music, 21, 3, 2002: Music and Television (special issue).

Stahl, M. (2002) 'Authentic Boy Bands on TV? Performers and Impresarios in The Monkees and Making the Band', *Popular Music*, 21, 3: 307–29.

TEXT; TEXTUAL ANALYSIS; INTERTEXTUALITY

The term text has traditionally been used to refer to an author's original words, or a prose work – especially one recommended for student reading. More recently, as a cultural studies term, text refers to any media form that is self-contained, television programmes, recordings, films and books. Popular music texts are quite diverse, and include recordings, record sleeve covers and music videos. The most prominent are sound recordings, in various formats, and their packaging (album covers, box sets, etc.). In addition there are several other important forms of popular music texts: musical performances, especially concerts; DJ discourse, music videos, music magazines, posters, T-shirts, tour brochures and fan club merchandize. These texts are frequently interconnected and mutually reinforcing.

Textual analysis is concerned with identifying and analysing the formal qualities of texts, their underpinning structures and constituent characteristic. As such, it has become closely associated with **semiotic** analysis, often linked to psychoanalytical concepts. In the case of popular music, textual analysis takes several forms. The most important is the examination of the musical components of songs, including their lyrics, in their various recorded formats (see **musicology**).

Other forms of popular music texts, such as record covers, concerts, music video, lyric analysis and DJ talk have been examined through various approaches to content and discourse analysis. Album coves, for example, convey meaning through the semiotic resources they draw on and display, via language, typography, images and layout. While texts are usually analysed independently, they can also be considered collectively, as with content analysis of chart share in terms of genres, record labels (majors compared to independents: see **market cycles**) and the proportion of charting artists who are women. A similar approach has been applied to radio and MTV airplay.

Intertextuality is 'a blanket term for the idea that a text communicates its meaning only when it is situated in relation to other texts … often characterized as meaning that "arises" between texts' (Gracyk, 2001: 56). Examples of this process are the dialogue that occurs between cover versions of their songs and their antecedents, and fan discourse around preferred styles and performers. Intertextuality is also implicit in the repackaging of recordings as generic compilations and boxed sets. Gracyk (2001: Chapter 3) provides a number of interesting musical examples, making the point that such 'influences, connections, and allusions that create nuances of meaning that cannot be grasped simply through a general intertextuality' (59).

A point of debate around popular culture is its ideological role in reinforcing/reproducing dominant values through their representation in popular texts. Critics who concentrate on the text itself, often using concepts from semiotic and psychoanalytic analysis, argue that there frequently exists in the text a preferred reading, that is, a dominant message set within the cultural code of established conventions and practices of the producers/transmitters of the text. However, while many consumers may, at least implicitly or subconsciously, accept such preferred readings, it must be kept in mind that it is not necessarily true that the audience as a whole do so. In particular, subordinate groups may reinterpret such textual messages, making 'sense' of them in a different way. This opens up the idea of popular resistance to, and subversion of, dominant cultures. This notion has informed analysis of the nature and reception of popular song lyrics and music videos.

Further reading:

Gracyk, T. (2001) *I Wanna be Me: Rock Music and the Politics of Identity*, Philadelphia, PA: Temple University Press.

Machin, D. (2010) *Analysing Popular Music*, Los Angeles, CA: Sage.

TIN PAN ALLEY

In the late 1800s, songwriters and publishers began congregating in a section of New York which became known as Tin Pan Alley from the 'tinny' sound of the upright pianos used there. Tin Pan Alley dominated mainstream American popular music from around 1900 through to the 1940s, and was the beginning of the popular music industry. Historians of the period emphasize that Pan Alley was not just a style of music, but also a set of values and associated practices (Shepherd, 1982; Whitcomb, 1974).

The division of labour in Tin Pan Alley, with professional songwriters, musicians and star singers, and music publishers, became typical of the music industry. Tin Pan Alley was characterized by its association with sheet music, as composing and publishing were the main sources of revenue for those involved. Songwriters sold their songs to a publisher for a lump sum. The music publisher then made their money through the sale of sheet music, containing just the vocal line and piano accompaniment of a song, and promoted the song through getting it sung by well-known artists in vaudeville shows. Sheet music also met a steadily increasing public demand for piano music, with the production of pianos reaching a peak at the end of the 1890s. Tin Pan Alley had a close association with Broadway musicals, with each providing publicity for the other.

Hamm has identified several important characteristics that characterized Tin Pan Alley-style songs: verses were kept short, with the emphasis on the longer, repeated refrains which followed them; the melodies were built upon simple three-chord forms in major keys; often contained novelty devices and they employed a first-person form of address. The market for Tin Pan Alley songs were white, urban, literate, middle- and upper-class Americans. The songs remained practically unknown to large segments of American society, including most blacks and the millions of poor, white, rural Americans in the South and the lower Midwest. These two groups had their own distinctive types of music, the oral traditions of country and blues. 'Tin Pan Alley did not draw on traditional music, 'observed Hamm', it created traditional music' (Hamm, 1983: 325; see also Shepherd, 1982; Starr and Waterman, 2003). Many Tin Pan Alley songs became 'standards' within popular music repertoire, for example 'After the Ball' (1892), the first 'mega-hit' pop song, selling over 5 million sheet music copies (for an analysis of the song, its composer and impact, see Starr and Waterman, 2003: 31–33). The major Tin Pan Alley songwriters were Irving Berlin, George Gershwin, Cole Porter and Richard Rogers.

Tin Pan Alley catered to popular tastes, incorporating and homogenizing elements of new musical styles as they emerged, especially ragtime, blues and jazz. The overwhelming proportion of its songs focused on romantic love, and helped celebrate and legitimize changes in sexual codes of behaviour in America in the 1920s. Tin Pan Alley songs catered to young women, often from middle-class families, who in the 1920s and 1930s were moving for work in the larger American cities: 'female record purchasers and radio listeners could appreciate the exhilaration of finding "someone" in the newly freed social space of the impersonal city' (Horowitz, 1993: 39).

In the early 1950s, the transition from Tin Pan Alley to rock'n'roll reflected important demographic, social and cultural shifts in American society (Ennis, 1992).

See also: **musicals**; **songwriters**

Further reading:

Ennis, P.H. (1992) *The Seventh Stream: The Emergence of RocknRoll in American Popular Music*, Hanover: Wesleyan University Press.

Hamm, C. (1983) *Yesterdays: Popular Song in America*, New York: W.W. Norton.

Horowitz, D. (1993) 'The Perils of Commodity Fetishism: Tin Pan Alley's Portrait of the Romantic Marketplace, 1920–1942', *Popular Music and Society*, 17, 1: 37–53.

Shepherd, J. (1982) *Tin Pan Alley*, London: Routledge & Kegan Paul.

Starr, L. and Waterman, C. (2003) *American Popular Music*, New York: Oxford University Press, Chapters 3 and 4.

TOUR; TOURING

A tour is a scheduled, consecutive series of concerts in different centres; tours can be of short duration, with a small number of concerts over a period of several weeks, or can be world affairs, lasting for up to 2 years. For the band or performer who has risen beyond the purely local, further commercial success is closely linked to touring, which is necessary to promote a new release and build up an audience. Tour schedules are frequently extremely gruelling, resembling 'package' vacation tours, with performers playing different cities each night and much of the intervening time consumed by travel. In genres such as rock and heavy metal, tour books, band biographies and many classic songs document 'life on the road', with its often attendant excesses, and exhilaration at audience enthusiasm coupled with fatigue.

Tours expose performers and their music to potential fans and purchasers, building an image and a following. Tours were important historically for helping 'break' English rock bands in the United States at various times, and this remains more generally true for the present national and international touring scenes. At the top end of the scale, are the global tours of the top international acts, which are massive exercises in logistics and marketing, and also hugely profitable: for example, The Rolling Stones' Voodoo Lounge Tour of 1994–5, the Kiss Tour of 1996–7. The US$20.1 million worth of tickets sold by 1980s rock band Bon Jovi, on their 2009–10 international tour, made them the top concert attraction for that period, indicating the continued importance of the live income stream to musicians (see **live**). On the other hand, tours by indie bands in North America in the 1980s relied on a nexus of local promoters, venues and fan support, including places to stay, a situation that has continued as part of the indie/alternative ethic (see **indie**).

While most tours by popular musicians are commercial affairs, there have been significant tours supporting political causes. The Amnesty International tour of North America in 1988, in support of the human rights organization, is estimated to have added some 20,000 new members to the organization in the United States alone. Another variant is the package tour, where a group of artists are placed on the same bill. This was a popular style of tour during the 1960s, when it was important for internationally popularizing British beat performers, and has resurfaced with the successful Lollapalooza tours of 1991 onwards, which put together a number of alternative acts.

See: **documentaries**; **live**; **performance**

Further reading:
The monotony of touring is captured in Bruce Thomas, *The Big Wheel*, 1990, a 'novel' about a band tour of America. Thomas was bass player with Elvis Costello and the Attractions.

TRIBUTE BANDS

The extreme example of **cover bands** are those groups who not only directly model their repertoire on established bands, but actually copy their appearance, presenting themselves as simulacra of the originals:

tribute bands. In the process, many such bands are very convincing representations of the original performers, and have also demonstrated a high level of musical competence. Now widely referred to as tribute bands, these have become big business; for example, Björn Again, the Australian Abba tribute band, who take their name from a member of the highly successful original Swedish group. Supporters of the tribute bands argue that the imitators are bringing the music to a new, younger audience, opening it up to a generation who never saw the originals and thereby encouraging them to seek out their material. In some cases, tribute performers are filling a gap created by the inactivity or demise of the original artists, as occurred with metal tribute bands in the early 1990s. Their detractors point to the difficulties in policing performing rights and regard it as at best unfortunate that the original artist, if still performing, are forced to share audiences with their imitators.

Tribute bands are an international phenomenon: Beatles tribute bands exist in Christchurch (New Zealand), Sydney, London and Tokyo; Madonna acts perform in Thailand, Japan, Germany and North America. As a largely imitative culture, with little room or audience desire for tributes that include 'twists' upon the original performers, tribute bands raise a number of interesting questions: the bases of their appeal; their popularity with music venue booking agents; the types of acts chosen for imitation; the composition of their audience; their international nature and music industry and musicians attitudes towards them (Homan considers these in the introduction to his edited volume, which includes a useful range of case studies).

Further reading:

Homan, S. ed. (2006) *Access All Eras: Tribute Bands and Global Pop*, Milton Keynes: Open University Press.

Viewing: *Tribute*, 2004 (Richard Fox; Kris Curry). A documentary that traces the fortunes of Kiss, Queen, Judas Priest, and Monkees tribute bands in the United States

TRIP-HOP

Trip-hop began to circulate as a term in the British music press during the mid-1990s, for a 'movement' led by Massive Attack, Portishead and Tricky. Trip-hop was dance music which was 'a dark, seductive combination of hip-hop beats, atmospheric reverb-laden guitars and samples, soul hooks, deep bass grooves and ethereal melodies' (Erlewine, 1995: 506). The style had actually been around for several years, in several mutating guises, all forms of slowed down hip hop.

See: **EDM** (and the further reading there)

Listening: Massive Attack, *Blue Lines*, Virgin, 1991; Portishead, *Dummy*, Polygram, 1994

TWO TONE

see **ska**

VIDEO GAMES

In the past 20 years, video games, also referred to as 'electronic games', have become a pervasive part of popular media culture. They can now be played on several platforms: online, as with Xbox Live 360; on personal computers and on the most recent mobile phones. In addition to the games themselves, and their associated music magazines and websites, video games have 'crossed over' to feature films. They are no longer simply a male-dominated leisure form, and have a wider and older range of consumers. Video games are a significant part of the revenue of media corporations, including the music industry (Hull *et al.*, 2011). In 2008, the global gaming industry was worth US$30 billion a year, and growing.

Several composers specialize in writing music for video games. The most successful is Tommy Tallarico, whose work has appeared in over 300 video games, including the best selling *Prince of Persia*, *Mortal Combat*, *Advent Rising* and *Tony Hawk Pro Skate*. In 2005, Tallarico hosted a multimedia show Video Games Live, in which an orchestra and choir performed music from popular video games, while a large screen showed excerpts from the games. The world premiere, at the Hollywood Bowl with the Los Angeles Philharmonic, attracted an audience of 11,000 and the show went on to tour internationally.

In addition to licencing earlier songs for use in games soundtracks, an increasing number of 'rock' musicians are writing for video games, and the British Academy of Film and Television Arts now has an awards category for video game soundtracks.

An emerging trend is the popularity of the *Guitar Hero Rock Band* interactive Xbox games as a way for fans (and aspiring musicians) to play along with popular songs, in effect, a form of home **karaoke**. The most successful of these has been *The Beatles Rockband* (2009). Made in consultation with the surviving Beatles, this includes dozens of the group's original songs, to play on *Rockband*-style guitar, bass, and drums or just sing along to.

Academic studies of the composition and role of music in such video games, and the social experience of playing them, are beginning to be published (see further reading) and the topic is one that is going to generate further interest.

Further reading:

Collins, K. ed. (2008) *From Pac-Man to Pop Music. Interactive Audio in Games and New Media*, Basingstoke: Ashgate. The essays cover a range of topics, including issues of aesthetics, economics, technology, and music making. The book includes a good introductory overview and an extensive bibliography. An excellent starting point.

George, D.R. (2010) 'Conceptualizing the Cognitive and Functional Benefits of Playing Beatles Rock Band from an Ecological Bio-Psychological Perspective', *Journal of Popular Music Studies*, 22, 4: 466–81.

Audiovisual: *The Beatles Rockband* (2009), Xbox 360. Game play is easy to grasp following the tutorial included. Songs are ranked in 'level of difficulty'; you can start with their first songs played at The Cavern club in Liverpool and work your way through to recoding Abbey Road, or just choose any song to play and sing

VOICE

'Popular music is overwhelmingly a "voice music". The pleasures of singing, of hearing singers, is central to it', and 'there is a strong tendency for vocals to act as a unifying focus within the song' (Middleton, 1990: 261, 264). Discussions of the role of the voice within popular music have focused on the relationship between lyrics, melodic types and the singing styles (and vocal timbres: tone quality as it relates to the characteristic differences among singing voices) characteristic of various genres and performers. A key semiological notion is the 'grain' of the voice (very broadly its feeling), as opposed to the direct meaning of lyrics, and the way in which particular styles of voice convey certain sets of emotions, often irrespective of the words they are singing.

A number of authors have discussed how the voice is used in popular music, particularly with regard to genres such as folk, blues and rock. Prominent here have been attempts to distinguish between 'black' and 'white' voices, which tend to see the 'black' voice as demonstrative and communicating through a variety of vocal techniques, and the 'white' voice as more restrained and restricted. A second distinction is between 'trained' and 'untrained' voices, with the former found in a range of older popular music (e.g. old-time country) rather than more contemporary forms. The 'untrained' voice is important in signifying **authenticity**, as in early styles of heavy metal and hard rock, where the 'straining' quality of high voices is indicating great effort, naturalness and a lack of artifice. A third approach has been to associate specific genres with vocal styles, which are linked in turn to gender. An example of this is the view of 'cock rock' as male (see **hard rock**) and teen **pop** as female. Shepherd notes that the hard, rasping vocal sound typical of hard rock is 'produced overwhelmingly in the throat and mouth, with a minimum of recourse to the resonating chambers of the chest and head'; he contrasts with the 'typical vocal sound of woman-as-nurturer: soft and warm, based on much more relaxed use of the vocal chords and using the resonating chambers of the chest', present in much pop music (1991: 167).

Moore argues that such distinctions are problematic because of their essentialist assumptions: 'they emphasise only one aspect of vocal production, and attempt to read meaning into the voice's presence on the basis of that single aspect', ignoring that a multitude of factors characterizes a vocal style (1993: 42). He suggests and elaborates four such factors: the register and range which any particular voice achieves; its degree of resonance; the singer's 'heard attitude' to pitch and the singer's heard attitude to rhythm. Moore usefully illustrates these through a discussion of the vocal styles of Bill Haley, Little Richard, Fats Domino and Elvis Presley.

The manner in which singers sing, rather than what they sing, is frequently central to their appeal to listeners. Compare, for instance, the vocal styles of Elvis Presley, Björk, Margot Timmins (the Cowboy Junkies), Johnny Rotten (Sex Pistols), Robert Johnson, Frank Sinatra and Mick Jagger.

See: **musicology**

Further reading:
Middleton, R. (2000) 'Rock Singing', in Potter (below): Chapter 3.
Moore, A. (1993) *Rock: The Primary Text*, Buckingham: Open University Press.
Potter, J. ed. (2000) *The Cambridge Companion to Singing*, Cambridge: Cambridge University Press.

WORLD MUSIC

While it can be considered a metagenre, world music is really more of a marketing category. World music became prominent in the late 1980s, as a label applied to popular music originating outside the Anglo-American nexus. The term was launched in 1987 as a new category of popular music by 11 independent British, European and American record labels specializing in music from Third World countries, who were seeking to better market their catalogues. In the United States, the term world beat was sometimes initially used, along with **roots** music for American forms. It is useful to distinguish between world music primarily situated within the Western music industry, and styles of 'world music' which are the subject of **ethnomusicology** (as in the ten-volume *Garland Encyclopedia of World Music*).

World music was encouraged by the interest in, enthusiasm for and borrowings from non-Western national musical styles by Western artists such as David Byrne, Peter Gabriel and Paul Simon, although Simon's use of African forms, notably in *Graceland* (1986) has proved contentious (see **appropriation**). The category has been defined in essentially two, related ways. First, world music is seen in a very heterogeneous manner as 'the other': music in opposition to the mainstream, Anglo-American and European genres (Taylor, 1997). Second, in an extended form of the first definition, world music includes music from Europe, America and Australia and New Zealand geographically, but this is largely music from diasporic, oppressed or marginalized minorities (such as Aboriginal music in Australia). Both definitions recognize world music as the result of processes of globalization and the hybridization (and, in some cases, appropriation) of regional and nationally based music (for a helpful discussion of the definition of world music, see Guilbrualt, 2001).

The resultant breadth of world music is seen in the steadily expanding *Rough Guides* to the metagenre: the first was published as a single (albeit large) volume in 1994; this was subsequently expanded to two, regionally based volumes and recently these have been revised and published in three large reference guides. The series construct the category around national **identity**, even though that is clearly tenuous, given the diversity of styles within particular countries. As such, discussions of world music will embrace, among others, Rai music from Algeria, Nigerian juju, Carribean Zouk and Brazilian bossa nova. Hybrid forms like the Anglo-Indian Bhangra, and Franco-American Cajun and Zydeco, along with the globalized 'Celtic', are also included under the broad rubric.

A further aspect is the manner in which world music has becoming self-defined by virtue of musical festival programming (especially the success of WOMAD: World of Music Arts, and Dance, established by Peter Gabriel in 1982); and the role of the music industry in constructing it as a 'genre market' (Negus, 1999; Laing, 2008: 224–31), primarily through record labels specializing in the metagenre, notably Real World. An important role has been played by several music magazines (fRoots and Songlines), along with regular coverage of performers and recordings in more general 'rock' magazines, such as UNCUT.

I have included separate entries on several world music genres, chosen as representative of the processes of syncretism, hybridization and globalization of the meta/marketing genre. For example, bhangra has its origins in traditional Indian music, but later became part of the assertion of cultural identity among a diasporic Asian population in the United Kingdom, taking on elements of EDM in the process and broadening its appeal to a wider audience.

See:

- Bhangra
- Bossa Nova
- Celtic
- Salsa
- Tejano

Perhaps more so than other forms of popular music, world music is open to processes of **hybridization** and musical **acculturation**, factors which in part account for the considerable attention given to it in recent academic literature. An important aspect here is the role of race/ethnicity in categorizations of 'world music' (Haynes, 2010), which, in popular perceptions and in the music press is often equated with 'non-white' or 'black' music. The discourse is rather polarized between celebration and condemnation (Frith, 2000), although as Guilbrault argues,

> world music should not be seen as simply oppositional or emancipator. Neither, however, should world music be viewed as merely the result of cultural imperialism or economic domination. To understand world music fully, we must look at its place within the complex and constantly changing dynamics of a world which is historically, socially and spatially interconnected.
>
> (*Guilbault, 2001: 176*)

Further reading:

Bohlman, P.V. (2002) *World Music: A Very Short Introduction*, Oxford: Oxford University Press.

Frith, S. (2000) 'The Discourse of World Music', in G. Born and D. Hesmondhalgh, D. (eds) *Western Music and its Others: Difference, Representation, and Appropriation in Music*, pp. 302–22. This is also in Frith, 2007.

Guilbrault, J. (2001) 'World Music', in S. Frith, W. Straw and J. Street (eds) *The Cambridge Companion to Pop and Rock*, pp. 176–192.

Haynes, J. (2010) 'In the Blood: The Racializing Tones of Music Categorization', *Cultural Sociology*, 4, 1: 81–100.

Laing, D. (2008) 'World Music and the global music industry: Flows, corporations and networks', *Popular Music History*, 3, 3: 213–31.

Nidel, R. (2005) *World Music. The Basics*, London: Routledge. A survey organized by continent and country (a total of 130). Entries include a statement about the history of the country, a discussion of the major genres and styles, a list and description of instruments, and the most important artists. The entries are very brief, and there is little discussion of the issue of definition; the accompanying discographies are more extensive, and there is a useful glossary. Essentially a mini-version of the *Rough Guide* approach.

The Rough Guide to World Music. Volume 1 Africa & Middle East (2006) 3rd edition, London: Rough Guides Ltd. Compiled and edited by S. Broughton, M. Ellingham, and J. Lusk, with D. Clark.

The Rough Guide to World Music. Volume 2 Europe, Asia & Pacific (2009) 3rd edition, London: Rough Guides Ltd. Compiled and edited by S. Broughton, M. Ellingham, and J. Lusk.

The Rough Guide to World Music. Volume 3 Latin, USA, and Caribbean (forthcoming).

Magazines: *Songlines*. The 50th 'Collector's Edition' issue, March 2008, is particularly useful; it includes '50 Best Top of the World Albums' (see also the related CD., in Listening), and '50 Great Moments in World Music'; *fROOTS*. Subtitled 'Local Music From Out There', and advertised as 'The Essential Worldwide Roots Music Guide'; As with other music press magazines, these include annual best of retrospectives in the first issue of the following year; for example, *SONGLINES*, Issue 57, January/February 2009

Listening: Compilations are the best point of entry to world music; they include those put out with *Songlines* (notably the double CD of selected tracks from the '50 Great Moments in World Music' issue (above); issues from The Sound of the World BBC Radio show; and the numerous Rough Guide series, on particular regions/genres

TIMELINE

The following key events and developments are a selection of milestones in popular music, in terms of music, economics, technology and symbolic importance, or some combination of these. Obviously, there are some 'judgment calls' here, and readers can no doubt construct alternative chronologies. See also the more detailed, specialized chronologies listed with the further reading in many genres.

1877   Thomas Edison patents the 'Phonograph', a sound system based around a tin foil cylinder.

1884   Emile Berliner records 'The Lords Prayer' on a cylinder; now in the BBC Sound Archive, it is believed to be the world's oldest surviving record.

1887   Thomas Edison's first public demonstration of his phonograph, a talking machine, marks the beginning of recorded sound. Emile Berliner invents the flat recording disc.

1892   'After the Ball', the first sheet music mega hit (Tin Pan Alley).

1896   Edison and Columbia introduce the first phonograph (later known as the gramophone) to the home market.

1899   Scott Joplin's 'Maple Leaf Rag' becomes a best seller, and consolidates the Ragtime craze.
        HMV buy the picture of a dog named Nipper, which becomes central to the iconic company logo.

1900   The Gramophone Company produce a catalogue with some 5,000 recordings.

1909   US Copyright Act (amendment) establishes the basis for royalty payments for recorded music, turning the popular song into a marketable commodity.

1912   W.C. Handy publishes 'Memphis Blues', the first blues to appear in print.

1913   The word 'jazz' appears in print for the first time.

1914   American Society of Composers, Authors and Publishers (ASCAP) is formed; enabling songwriters to claim the income due under the Copyright Act.

1917   First recorded jazz, by Original Dixieland Jazz band; in 1919 they create a sensation in London.

Death of Scott Joplin regarded as marking the end of the Ragtime era.

1920   First recording of vocal blues by a black singer, Mamie Smith's 'Crazy Blues'.

1923   The first news-and-music US radio station, Westinghouse's KDKA, begins broadcasting.

Classical music oriented 'The Gramophone' (UK) launched; helps shape 'gramophone culture'.

1924   George Gershwin composes 'Rhapsody in Blue'.

1925   Regular use begins of electrical recording (using microphones).

1926   BBC is created as a public corporation; its Music Department is set up the following year.

The birth of the LP: Edison produces Diamond Discs, capable of playing 20 minutes per side.

1927   The Carter Family first record; these Bristol Sessions are seen as the origins of modern 'country' music.

1929   'The Broadway Melody': the first 'all-talking, all-singing, all-dancing' film musical.

1931   The Gramophone Company and Columbia merge to form EMI; a trend towards consolidation that is to become a feature of the music industry.

1934   Jazz journal *Downbeat* launched in Chicago.

1936   Key recordings of Robert Johnson (Delta blues).

Charles Delaunay's 'Hot Discography' published in English, establishing field of 'discography'.

1939   Broadcast Music Incorporated (BMI) is formed, to represent the blues and country music largely ignored by its competitor, ASCAP.

1942   *Billboard* sets up a 'race' chart: the Harlem Hit Parade.

1947   Formation of Chess Records in Chicago: central to the development of R&B and Chicago blues.

1948   CBS release the first modern long-playing vinyl records; they play at 33 rpm and need a special player.

1949   *Billboard* ends 'race' chart category; replaced by rhythm'n'blues.

1951   Jackie Brenston and Ike Turner release 'Rocket 88': often considered the first rock'n'roll recording.

1952   DJ Alan Freed names his radio show 'Moondog's Rock'n'Roll Party'.

'American Bandstand' first broadcast in the United States.

Harry Smith's 'Anthology of American Folk Music': a major influence on the folk revival.

1953   Bill Haley and the Comets, 'Crazy Man Crazy': the first rock'n'-roll record to make the *Billboard* charts.

1954   Elvis Presley records 'That's All Right Mama' at Sun Studios in Memphis.

1955   Little Richard, 'Tutti Frutti' and Chuck Berry 'Maybelline': key rock'n'roll recordings.

Bill Haley and the Comets 'Rock Around the Clock' is performed in film *The Blackboard Jungle.*

Miles Davis's Quartet, featuring tenor saxophonist John Coltrane, first record.

1956   Fats Domino's 'Blueberry Hill' demonstrates crossover potential of R&B.

Elvis Presley's 'Heartbreak Hotel' is No. 1 for 8 weeks in United States; reaches No. 2 in the United Kingdom.

Lonnie Donegan releases 'Rock Island Line', popularizing skiffle in the United Kingdom.

1957   *American Bandstand* is broadcast nationally in the United States.

1958   First stereo recordings released.

1959   Buddy Holly, Richie Valens and the Big Bopper are killed in an air crash.

Juke Box Jury begins on BBC TV: celebrities vote on whether a single will be a 'hit' or a 'miss'.

Formation of Stax Records; Miles Davis releases 'Kind of Blue'.

1960   US Congressional investigation into payola begins.

Studios begin using multitrack recorders.

1961   The Miracles, 'Shop Around'; first hit for Tamla Motown.

1962   The Beatles release 'Love Me Do'; and later their first LP, 'Please Please Me'.

Bob Dylan releases his first album, Bob Dylan.

Gerry and the Pacemakers 'How Do You Do It?' is No. 1 in the United Kingdom (Merseybeat).

James Brown releases 'Live At The Apollo', the first million selling R&B album.

1963   'Ready Steady Go!' begins broadcasting on Independent Television (ITV).

Introduction of the compact tape cassette.

1964   The Beatles appear on the Ed Sullivan Show.

The Beatles play at New York's Shea Stadium (attendance: 55,600, then a world record).

The pirate stations Radio London and Radio Caroline begin broadcasting in the English Channel.

The first edition of BBC's 'Top of the Pops' is broadcast.

Robert Moog markets his synthesizer.

1965   Otis Redding's 'Otis Blue' album is released.

Bob Dylan is booed (by some of the audience) at the Newport Folk Festival for 'going electric'; releases epic single 'Like A Rolling Stone'.

The Beatles play their last ever tour concert, at Candlestick Park, San Francisco.

The Rolling Stones, '(I Can't Get No) Satisfaction': includes rock's most famous riff.

James Brown, 'Papa's Got a Brand New Bag'.

1966   The Monkees television show (and the group) debut in the United States; in the United Kingdom in 1967.

First Grammy Award for best album cover; won by the Beatles, 'Revolver' (artwork by Klauss Vorman).

1967   The Beatles release 'Sgt. Pepper Lonely Hearts Club Band'.

Monterey International Pop Festival (performers include, among others, Jefferson Airplane, Janis Joplin, Ravi Shankar, Otis Redding and Jimi Hendrix) is attended by 30,000 fans.

Rolling Stone magazine is launched; *Downbeat* extends its coverage to rock music.

BBC's Radio 1 begins broadcasting, replacing the now illegal pirate stations.

The Velvet Underground's debut album (The Velvet underground and Nico) released.

'Hair': widely seen as the first 'rock musical'.

1969   Led Zeppelin release their first album 'Led Zeppelin'.

The Who release their rock opera 'Tommy'.

The Woodstock Festival attracts 400,000 fans; musicians include Jimi Hendrix, The Who, Santana.

The Altamont, California-free festival, organised by the Rolling Stones; Hell's Angels attack and kill a member of the audience.

The Archies, 'Sugar, Sugar', by a manufactured 'bubblegum' group, is the biggest selling single of the year.

1970   Jimi Hendrix and Janis Joplin die; The Beatles disband.

'Soul Train' begins on US television; syndication rights are bought by CBS TV in 1973.

Black Sabbath's albums 'Black Sabbath' and 'Paronoid': seen as birth of Heavy Metal.

1971   'The Old Grey Whistle Test' starts on BBC2, with bands performing live.

The Canadian government implements 'Canadian Content' regulations, which require that radio station playlists contained specified minimum amounts of Canadian music; this provides a model for similar quota policies elsewhere.

Marvin Gaye, 'What's Goin' On'.

King Tubby and Lee Perry create dub, the template for much modern dance music.

1972   Chick Corea forms jazz rock fusion band, 'Return to Forever'.

'Nuggets', compiled by Lenny Kaye, creates new interest in 1960s garage bands, influences punk rock.

David Bowie creates Ziggy Stardust, launches glam rock.

'The Harder They Come' (feature film) brings Jamaican reggae to a wider audience.

1973   Pink Floyd's album 'Dark Side of the Moon' enters US charts, beginning a record breaking stay.

1975   Bruce Springsteen releases album 'Born to Run'; becomes one of the biggest selling albums and establishes 'The Boss' as a rock superstar.

Bob Marley and the Wailers first hit single 'No Woman, No Cry'; Marley becomes the first international reggae star.

1976   The Ramones, release 'Ramones', epitomizing much of New York punk rock.

Sex Pistols release 'Anarchy in the UK'; create controversy; regarded as part of the punk canon.

The launch of the 12-inch single, a format that underpins house, hip hop and techno.

1977   Elvis Presley dies, aged 42.

Kraftwerk release 'Trans Europe Express': influences hip hop and dance culture.

'Saturday Night Fever': The Bee Gees and John Travolta bring disco into the mainstream.

1978   Contemporary Christian Music (later CCM) begins publication; gives its name to the genre.

1979   Introduction of the SONY Walkman.

Bauhaus, 'Bela Lugosi's Dead': credited with establishing goth in the United Kingdom.

1980   John Lennon is murdered in New York.

Monsters of Rock, Castle Donnington (UK): the first exclusively heavy metal festival.

1981   MTV is launched in the United States, later franchised globally; becomes synonymous with music video.

Establishment of IASPM (The International Association for the Study of Popular Music).

Death of Bob Marley.

Kerrang! begins publication: first mainstream music magazine devoted to heavy metal.

1982   Michael Jackson's album 'Thriller'; goes on to become *the* biggest selling album of all time.

Grandmaster Flash and the Furious Five, 'The Message', brings rap to wider mainstream attention.

1983   The first CDs go on sale.

The importance of music video is acknowledged with the first American Video Awards.

The Musical Instrument Digital Interface (MIDI) becomes available, creating new technical possibilities for music making.

New Order, 'Blue Monday': the best selling British 12-inch single; very influential on dance music.

1984   Band Aid release 'Do They Know It's Christmas?'

1985   Live Aid raises £50 million.

Bruce Springsteen releases album 'Born in the USA'.

Parents Music Resource Center (PMRC) gives evidence to Senate committee on the explicit sexual and violent content of records. Record companies introduce 'Parental Advisory' labelling on records to appease PMRC complaints.

1986   Paul Simon's 'Graceland' creates controversy over whether it breaches sanctions imposed on South Africa; helps create interest in 'world music'.

Madonna's 'True Blue' enters the UK album chart at No. 1, the first US artist to do this.

1987   MTV is launched in Europe.

M/A/R/R/S have a No. 1 hit with 'Pump Up the Volume': marks the rise of music made with deejay skills and sampler technology.

1988   CDs now outsell vinyl records.

Dance culture 'Summer of Love' begins in United Kingdom.

1989   Public Enemy release 'It Takes a Nation of Millions to Hold Us Back'; influential on black culture and hip hop.

1990   Robert Johnson, 'The Complete Recordings' (box set).

1991   Nirvana album 'Nevermind': credited with initiating grunge and mainstreaming American indie.

Metallica, 'Metallica' (The Black Album): establishes thrash metal as part of commercial mainstream.

1992   Garth Brooks, 'Ropin' the Wind': the first country album to top the US pop charts.

CDs now outsell cassettes (as well as vinyl records, a steeply declining format).

Ice-T's 'Cop Killer': heightens controversy around gangsta rap.

Montreaux Jazz Festival (founded in 1967) renamed 'Montreaux Jazz and World Music Festival'.

1993   Snoop Doggy Dogg's 'Dogstyle': the first debut album to enter 'Billboard' charts at No. 1.

1994   British government introduces Criminal Justice and Public Order Act which is intended to curb illegal raves (and music that uses 'repetitive beats').

1995   Oasis, 'What's The Story, Morning Glory': the height of Britpop.

Shania Twain's 'The Woman in Me': becomes the biggest selling country album by a female artist.

'No Depression' magazine begins publication (alt. country, America; roots).

1996   Pop group Spice Girls 'Wannabe' is No. 1 in 22 countries.

'Buena Vista Social Club' (feature film and soundtrack); create greater interest in world music.

The Fugees, 'The Score': a huge commercial success, consolidates hip hop in the mainstream.

1997   MP3 is introduced.

1998   'Time' magazine cover story (8 February) proclaims arrival of 'Hip Hop Nation'.

Madonna wins a record six MTV Music Video awards.

'Classic Rock' magazine (UK) begins publication.

Elton John's elegy for Princess Diana, 'Candle in the Wind'; sells 1.5 million copies in its first week.

1999   Napster software is introduced, greatly increasing access to music on the Internet.

US charts dominated by rap/nu-metal acts: Limp Bizkit, Rage Against the Machine.

Myspace launched; leads rapid growth of social networking, online culture.

2000   Napster is used by Metallica for breach of copyright.

Record companies establish copyright deals with Internet music providers.

'O'Brother, Where Art Thou?' (feature film), revives interest in traditional country music.

2001   Hear'Say, a group assembled through 'Popstars' (UK television), become the first band to top the UK album and singles charts simultaneously with their debut releases.

The iPod introduced; becomes the main portable sound carrier.

Apple introduce iTunes.

2002   'American Idol' debuts on US television.

2003   Year of the Blues in the United States.

2005   Live 8: 'End Poverty'; the sequel to 1985s Live Aid; 10 concerts held internationally on 2 July.

Downloads of singles incorporated into the UK singles charts (reflecting rapid increase in downloading).

HMV and Virgin launch online music stores.

2006   Arctic Monkeys, 'Whatever People Say I Am, That's What I'm Not' (Domino) becomes fastest selling UK debut album.

The Beatles, 'Love' (EMI): the soundtrack of a Las Vegas show by Cirque Du Soleil, tops album charts internationally.

Death of Syd Barrett, legendary reclusive founder member of Pink Floyd.

2007   Led Zeppelin reunion: a 'one off' charity concert at London's O2 venue; enormous demand for tickets.

Apple launch iPhone: an iPod/mobile phone hybrid.

Prince's new album 'Planet Earth' free as a cover mount CD with UK's *Mail on Sunday*, a move heavily criticized by his record company HMV, and music retailers.

Radiohead make their latest album 'Rainbows' available through an 'honesty box' system on the band's website, allowing fans to name their own price.

Madonna leaves Warner Music Group, after 25 years with the company, and signs a US$120 million deal with concert promotion firm Live Nation.

2009   Glastonbury Festival (UK) attended by 137,500.

'The Beatles Rockband', Xbox 360 video game released; success demonstrates the importance of gaming industry to music.

Susan Boyle's performance on UK reality TV show 'Britain's Got Talent' is disseminated globally on YouTube, gaining record hits; her debut album 'I Dreamed a Dream' sells 1.2 million copies in first 2 weeks of its release.

Death of Michael Jackson, 'King of Pop', while preparing for a series of 'comeback' concerts.

'Guitar Hero: Metallica' launched.

2010   Facebook announces that more than 500 million people now use the social network site.

SELECTED REFERENCES

The following are general introductory studies, edited readers and reference books on popular music culture that I have used at various points throughout this guide. The individual entries provide guidance to more specific reading. I have also included separately below, a list of popular music academic journal titles. For further references, an invaluable resource is the IASPM online data base: http://iismc.cini.it/

I have only included English language works; it needs to be emphasized that there is a considerable body of popular music scholarship in languages such as Spanish, French, German, Chinese and Japanese. Only a small proportion of this is available in translation; details of some of this work can be accessed through the regional branches of IASPM.

Albertazzii, D. and Cobley, P. eds (2010) *The Media: An Introduction*, Harlow, England: Longman Pearson.
Barker, C. (2002) *Making Sense of Cultural Studies: Central Problems and Critical Debates*, London: Sage Publications.
Beard, D. and Gloag, K. (2005) *Musicology: The Key Concepts*, New York, Routledge.
Bennett, A., Shank, B. and Toynbee, J. eds (2006) *The Popular Music Studies Reader*, London: Routledge.
Billboard (2009) '*The Decade in Music: Special Double Issue*', December 19.
Bloustein, G., Peters, M. and Luckman, S. eds (2008) *Sonic Synergies: Music, Technology, Community, Identity*, Aldershot: Ashgate.
Borthwick, S. and Moy, R. (2004) *Popular Music Genres: An Introduction*, Edinburgh: Edinburgh University Press.
Charlton, K. (1994) *Rock Music Styles: A History*, 2nd edition, Madison, WI: Brown and Benchmark.
Clayton, M., Herbert T. and Middleton, R. eds (2003) *The Cultural Study of Music. A Critical Introduction*, New York: Routledge.
Covach, J. and Boone, G.M. eds (1997) *Understanding Rock. Essays in Musical Analysis*, New York: Oxford University Press.
De Curtis, A. and Henke, J. (1992) *The Rolling Stone Illustrated History of Rock and Roll*, 3rd edition, New York: Random House.
Erlewine, M., Bogdanov, V. and Woodstra, C. eds (1995) *All Music Guide to Rock*, San Francisco, CA: Miller Freeman.

Frith, S. (1978) *The Sociology of Rock*, London: Constable.

Frith, S. (1983) *Sound Effects: Youth, Leisure and the Politics of Rock 'n' Roll*, London.

Frith, S. (1988) *Music for Pleasure: Essays in the Sociology of Pop*, Cambridge: Polity Press.

Frith, S. (1996) *Performing Rites: On the Value of Popular Music*, Cambridge, MA: Harvard University Press.

Frith, S. (2007) *Taking Popular Music Seriously. Selected Essays*, Aldershot: Ashgate.

Frith, S. and Goodwin, A. eds (1990) *On Record: Rock, Pop, and the Written Word*, New York: Pantheon Books.

Garofalo, R. (2011) *Rockin' Out: Popular Music in the USA*, 5th edition, Needham Heights, MA: Allyn & Bacon.

Hatch, D. and Millward, S. (1987) *From Blues to Rock: An Analytical History of Rock Music*, Manchester: Manchester University Press.

Hayward, S. (2000) *Key Concepts in Cinema Studies*, London: Routledge.

Hesmondhalgh, D. and Negus, K. eds (2004) *Popular Music Studies*, London: Arnold.

Horner, B. and Swiss, T. eds (1999) *Key Terms in Popular Music and Culture*, Oxford: Blackwell.

Kotarba, J. and Vannini, P. (2009) *Understanding Society Through Popular Music*, New York: Routledge.

Lewis, J. (2008) *Cultural Studies. The Basics*, Los Angeles, CA: Sage.

Longhurst, B. (2007) *Popular Music and Society*, 2nd edition, Cambridge: Polity Press.

Middleton, R. (1990) *Studying Popular Music*, Milton Keynes: Open University Press.

Mikula, M. (2008) *Key Concepts in Cultural Studies*, Basingstoke: Palgrave Macmillan.

Negus, K. (1996) *Popular Music in Theory*, Cambridge: Polity Press.

Negus, K. (1999) *Music Genres and Corporate Cultures*, London: Routledge.

O'Sullivan, T., Hartley, J., Saunders, D., Montgomery, M. and Fiske, J. (1994) *Key Concepts in Communications*, London: Methuen.

Roberts, K. (2009) *Key Concepts in Sociology*, Basingstoke and New York: Palgrave Macmillan.

Scott, D. ed. (2009) *The Ashgate Research Companion to Popular Musicology*, Farnham: Ashgate.

Shepherd, J., Horn, D., Laing, D., Oliver, P., Wicke, P., Tagg, P. and Wilson, J. eds (1997) *Popular Music Studies: A Select International Bibliography*, London: Mansell.

Shepherd, J., Horn, D., Laing, D., Oliver, P. and Wicke, P. eds (2003a) *The Continuum Encyclopedia of Popular Music, Volume One: Media, Industry and Society*, London: Continuum.

Shepherd, J., Horn, D., Laing, D., Oliver, P. and Wicke, P. eds (2003b) *The Continuum Encyclopedia of Popular Music, Volume Two: Performance and Production*, London: Continuum.

Shuker, R. (2008) *Understanding Popular Music Culture*, London: Routledge.

Starr, L. and Waterman, C. (2003) *American Popular Music*, New York: Oxford University Press.

Swiss, T., Herman, A. and Sloop, J.M. eds (1998) *Mapping the Beat: Popular Music and Contemporary Theory*, Malden, MA: Blackwell.

Tagg, P. and Clarida, B. (2003) *Ten Little Title Tunes: Towards a Musicology of the Mass Media*, New York: The Mass Media Musicologists' Press.

Wall, T. (2003) *Studying Popular Music Culture. Studying the Media*, London: Arnold.

JOURNALS

IASPM@Journal: *The Journal of the International Association for the Study of Popular Music*: www.iaspm.net

MSMI: *Music, Sound, and the Moving Image*: http://msmi.lupjournals.org

Perfect Beat

Popular Music

Popular Music and Society

Popular Musicology Online: www.musicology-online.com

INDEX